THE STILL SMALL VOICE

Note about the cover image

Artist: François Chifflart (1825–1901)
Title: Deutsch: Das Gewissen
           English: The Conscience
Date: 1877
Medium: Charcoal on paper

http://en.wikipedia.org/wiki/File:Chifflart_-_Das_Gewissen_-_1877.jpeg

Date: 1877
Technique: Charcoal on paper, 56.7 x 41.4 cm
Illustration for Victor Hugo's La Conscience
The famous Cain poem, written in 1853 and appearing in the 1859 first edition of *La Légende des Siècles*, is an apt rendering of Victor Hugo's moral preoccupations, in this case, the first recorded biblical murder, when Cain killed his brother Abel. Hugo's short narrative (sixty-eight lines) traces the itinerary of the fleeing Cain who, with his family, seeks asylum from the powerful wrath of Jehovah. The motif of a long voyage, filled with suffering, already exploited by Hugo in the Massepa poem of *Les Orientales* (1829) is here reiterated as a frightening exodus, as Cain, his family, and his descendants seek calm and peace. But for Cain there is none, for he is pursued by the Eye of God. Thus, even when he attempts to bury himself underground, the eye is always there, menacing and judging: *L'oeil était dans la tombe et regardait Cain* (The eye was in the tomb and kept looking at Cain). This poignant and persistent symbol of a bad conscience, hence the title of the poem, is somewhat akin to similar symbolism found in the writings of Edgar Allan Poe (1809-1849). Helmut Hatsfeld in his *Initiation à l'explication de textes français* (Munich: Max Hueber, 1957) speaks of Hugo's success in fusing history and symbolism, making Cain's murder of Abel a very typical Romantic and visionary text.
(John Andrew Frey, A Victor Hugo encyclopedia) http://darkclassics.blogspot.ca/2012/02/francois-nicolas-chifflart-conscience.html

THE STILL SMALL VOICE
Psychoanalytic Reflections on Guilt and Conscience

Donald L. Carveth

KARNAC

First published in 2013 by
Karnac Books Ltd
118 Finchley Road
London NW3 5HT

British Library Cataloguing in Publication Data

A C.I.P. for this book is available from the British Library

ISBN-13: 978-1-78049-168-4

Typeset by V Publishing Solutions Pvt Ltd., Chennai, India

Printed in Great Britain

www.karnacbooks.com

For Eli Sagan

But the LORD was not in the wind:
And after the wind an earthquake;
But the LORD was not in the earthquake:
And after the earthquake a fire;
But the LORD was not in the fire:
And after the fire a still small voice.

—*1 Kings* 19:11–12

CONTENTS

ABOUT THE AUTHOR

Donald Carveth is emeritus professor of sociology and social & political thought and a senior scholar at York University in Toronto. He is a training and supervising analyst in the Canadian Institute of Psychoanalysis and current director of the Toronto Institute of Psychoanalysis. After completing a doctorate (Carveth, 1977, 1984a) comparing and contrasting sociological and psychoanalytic theories of human nature, he undertook clinical psychoanalytic training, graduating from the Toronto Institute of Psychoanalysis in 1985. With Dr. Eva Lester and others he helped found the *Canadian Journal of Psychoanalysis/Revue Canadienne de Psychanalyse* of which he is a past editor-in-chief. He has published some fifty papers in various academic journals. Over the past decade his work has concentrated on issues of guilt, guilt substitutes, and the differentiation of conscience as a fourth component of the structural theory of the mind in addition to the id, ego, and superego. He is in private practice in Toronto. He may be found on the web at: http://www.yorku.ca/dcarveth

ACKNOWLEDGEMENTS

Several years ago, a colleague (Sheppard, 2006) wrote of the psychoanalyst's need for "a trusted fellow traveller" with whom to share some of the unusual burdens of this profession. In marrying a psychoanalyst I obtained both a partner and an "analytic friend". For years both my thinking and my clinical work have been shaped in and through an ongoing dialogue with Jean Hantman who continues to amaze me with her clinical psychoanalytic acumen. In addition to being present on every page, she contributed to Chapter Five and wrote one of the two case studies in Chapter Seven.

For over a decade, Eli Sagan's (1988) classic, *Freud, Women, and Morality: The Psychology of Good and Evil*, sat on my shelf unread. When I finally picked it up, I was stunned. Here were answers to many of the central problems in psychoanalytic theory that had troubled me for years, expounded with both scholarly erudition and rare lucidity. I wrote him a letter which he answered and, though already in my sixties, I found a mentor. Psychoanalysts know something of the role of transference in creativity; this book is the product of my idealising transference to Eli Sagan which has been, in many ways, healing for me.

Without the resumed personal development stimulated by my connection with Eli, I doubt I could have reached out to Salman Akhtar for advice regarding publishing my work. He replied within hours of receiving my request with a title, a table of contents, and suggestions for some additional chapters. With respect to what he called his audacity in responding this way, he wrote: "… but, hey, we are adults, creative and friends." I'm grateful to Salman for his friendship, his generosity, and his help.

After more than four decades teaching sociology and social and political thought at Glendon College of York University in Toronto I decided it was time to retire. One becomes a professor because one loves to read, think, and write, only to find that one's academic duties almost preclude doing so. Though I managed over the years to publish a respectable number of papers in academic journals, with retirement from full-time teaching I lost my excuse for not settling down and publishing a book. But if it interfered with my creativity, my academic career at the same time stimulated it and allowed it to ferment. I got to try out all these ideas on captive audiences over the years, students and then candidates in psychoanalytic training, and their questions, comments, and challenges kept me going, as did my dialogue with colleagues too numerous to mention.

It was my good fortune as a young social scientist to be appointed to a department of sociology oriented more towards history and social theory than towards positivism, in a university committed from the start to multi- and inter-disciplinarity. Thanks to Dennis H. Wrong's (1961) classic critique of "The Oversocialised Conception of Man in Modern Sociology", I was able to write a dissertation comparing and contrasting sociological and psychoanalytic theories of human nature. My colleagues accepted my growing psychoanalytic focus and allowed me to teach courses in "Freud and": Freud and Marx; Freud and G. H. Mead; Freud and Existentialism; etc. Few if any eyebrows rose when in the late Seventies a Victorian style analytic couch was carried down the hall into my office. Analysing in the morning, teaching in the afternoon, and grading papers in the evening may not quite fulfil the Marxian vision of non-alienated labour, but I surely cannot complain.

In addition to including hitherto unpublished material, this book draws upon a range of papers that originally appeared in academic journals: *Psychoanalysis and Contemporary Thought* (1984a, 1984b, 1994);

International Review of Psycho-Analysis (1992); *Psychoanalytic Studies* (2001); *American Imago* (2003); the *Canadian Journal of Psychoanalysis/ Revue Canadienne de Psychanalyse* (2006a, 2007b, 2011b, 2012a); *Modern Psychoanalysis* (2010); *Clio's Psyche* (2011a, 2012b); and *Vocabulary for the Study of Religion* (2013).

Naturally, having acknowledged some of my debts, I need to take responsibility and bear the guilt for the crimes committed in this book.

FOREWORD

In trying to write this foreword in a way that does justice to Don Carveth's ideas, I find myself right at the outset having a problem. My general notion of what a foreword is supposed to say, and what a reader is typically looking for in a foreword, would suggest that I should take approach #1: *"This is an important book. You should read it and here's why ...."* In terms of its importance, I would like to make Dr. Carveth's book required reading for all psychoanalytic therapists (and recommended reading for their patients) who are working every day on issues of guilt and shame, so approach #1 definitely feels to me like the right way to go—a brief pithy appetiser that whets the appetite for the main course.

My problem is that I have already had to discard three previous introductory paragraphs to this foreword because each of them was pulling me (or was a product of my feeling pulled) in a different direction, towards a more complicated and questionable approach #2: *"My friend and colleague Don Carveth has written a very important book. Don asked me to write a foreword after we discovered at a recent psychoanalytic meeting that the central theme of his book—the crucial distinction between the love-based self-actualising activity of conscience and the fear-based self-sabotaging activity of the superego—is an idea that we had both been working on for many years independently, Don from a more psychological/cultural perspective, I from a more psychological/philosophical perspective, neither of us aware of what the other was doing. So I am uniquely qualified to know and fully appreciate just how important Don's idea is, because it is also my idea (Frattaroli, 2013). My other qualification is that I'm one of the very few psychoanalysts other than Don who would be willing to come so far out of the closet of received psychoanalytic wisdom (i.e., what is safe and proper for a psychoanalyst to write, or even think) in order to openly espouse such a radically subversive, transformative idea.*" As much as I feel tempted to take this more self-indulgent and self-congratulatory approach—and I am *very* tempted—I cannot help but feel that it would be the wrong way to go—an unnecessarily elaborate appetiser that competes with and potentially detracts from the main course.

What to do then? Clearly I have a choice to make.

This is an important book. You should read it and here's why:

Short version

You should read this book because it explains why I am so conflicted about how to write this foreword. It explains my conflict, not in terms of Oedipal drives and prohibitions as defined by Freudian theory, but in terms of basic morality—good and evil—as defined or, more properly, as *apperceived* by the conscience we all have in common, the kind of conscience that is synonymous with consciousness.

Consider the difference: in terms of classical Freudian theory my problem would be viewed as an inhibition of my Oedipal desires to demolish Don (father) and appropriate his readers (mother) as my own. The "healthy" solution would be to realise that my inhibition is a product of an overly harsh superego; that these anachronistic childhood Oedipal desires are operating unconsciously to make whatever here-and-now competitiveness I have with Don feel disproportionately dangerous and destructive. Adopting this view does not exactly tell me what I should do, but it can easily be taken to suggest that I really have nothing to feel conflicted about and should feel free to follow my natural inclination. Witness Freud's canonical interpretation of Hamlet: that he was inhibited by a neurotic Oedipal prohibition against killing his father, which prevented him from following his natural *and appropriate* inclination to righteously avenge his father's murder by killing his uncle in cold blood. Nowhere does Freud consider the possibility that Hamlet might have been inhibited by the feeling that it is morally wrong to kill *anyone* in cold blood.

According to Don Carveth, this all too familiar kind of interpretation that attributes current moral conflicts to unconscious wishes and prohibitions from childhood, is no more than a self-serving disingenuous rationalisation for behaving badly and not caring. Because Oedipal prohibitions are based on fear and have nothing to do with morality. They are enforced not by our conscience but by our superego. Where conscience makes judgments in terms of the authentic morality and the loving reciprocity of the Golden Rule, the superego makes judgments in terms of the primal need to avoid the dangers of annihilation, abandonment, rejection (shunning), and physical violation (castration). So the familiar concepts of id, ego, and superego are not enough to explain the central human dilemma of inner conflict and its resolution. Psychoanalytic theory needs to be expanded to include the all-important fourth dimension of conscience. This is Carveth's theory in a nutshell. He sets it forth clearly and succinctly in Chapter One, and each succeeding chapter is an expansively illuminating variation on its theme.

Psychoanalysts are used to thinking—erroneously—that superego and conscience are equivalent terms (one formal, the other informal) for the same inner agency. Carveth takes great pains to explain the error in this way of thinking and to clarify the crucial distinction between superego and conscience. This distinction—between a superego motivated by fear and a conscience motivated by love—is a *seminal* contribution to the psychoanalytic understanding of human nature. The superego, according to Carveth (following Eli Sagan, 1988) is based on identification with the aggressor. It embodies the punitive, rejecting parental and societal attitudes which we internalised in childhood in order to repress our Oedipal desires, so it reflects the mentality of a tyrannical six year old. At the same time, the superego incorporates the persecutory projections of Melanie Klein's paranoid position, so it can also reflect the primitive mentality of a rageful terrorised baby. Conscience, on the other hand, is based on identification with the nurturer. It is the "still small voice" of true moral discernment, reflecting our innate tendency towards loving reciprocity and, with it, our innate recognition of the universal morality of the Golden Rule.

Understood in these terms my problem with how to write this foreword is a genuine moral dilemma: should I ignore my overly harsh superego prohibition and give in to my impulse to treat Don as a cardboard antagonist in my Oedipal drama, taking his big and powerful idea as a threat to my own narcissistic sense of self-importance and seeking to restore that endangered self-importance by stealing from him the attention and admiration of *his* readers? Or should I treat Don as I would want to be treated in the same situation, as a friend and colleague whom I recognise and applaud for a truly extraordinary contribution to human knowledge, a contribution that deserves and will reward the reader's *undivided* attention?

Long version

I first met Don Carveth in 2001, when I joined two online psychoana- lytic discussion groups. These groups had a broad-ranging interdiscipli- nary focus, covering psychoanalysis not only as a therapy and theory of human nature, but as a participant in a larger cultural conversation with other fields of human knowledge as well. The group members included practising psychoanalysts and university scholars most of whom— judging from the messages they posted—seemed to have expertise in two or three areas of interdisciplinary knowledge. Even in this distin- guished company, it was immediately apparent to me that Don Carveth was exceptional. Not only was he both a practising psychoanalyst *and* a university professor, his messages regularly demonstrated expertise in all the areas under discussion: psychoanalysis, literature, cinema, art, philosophy, theology, science, sociology, culture, politics, and interna- tional relations. As the reader will soon discover, this is the same range of human knowledge that is covered—and integrated—in the remark- able book you now hold in your hands.

What was not so immediately apparent to me in 2001 but, as I got to know Don over the years, became my favourite thing about him, is his passionate heart. Not only does Don know a lot; he cares a lot, and his knowledge is informed and energised by his caring. This puts Don on a very short list of psychoanalytic writers—a list which notably does not include Freud but does include Bruno Bettelheim and Erik Erikson— whose understanding of psychoanalysis is informed and enriched by their caring; who have thought long and hard about what it is in psy- choanalysis that matters so deeply to them, and have then had the wis- dom and courage to write openly, based on why it matters to them, about why psychoanalysis should matter to everyone.

Even when we "talk amongst ourselves" in professional conferences and journals, psychoanalysts rarely talk about why psychoanalysis mat- ters. We take for granted that it matters but if pressed to explain why, most of us would privately be at a loss and would publicly offer a formulaic answer that failed to capture what inspires us about psychoanalysis or why anyone else should care about it. I believe this failure reflects a reluctance to examine, or even acknowledge, the way in which psychoanalysis embodies our deepest private personal beliefs, especially the kind of beliefs that Don Carveth explores in this book, that concern values and morality. Following Freud, we prefer to think of psychoanalysis as a value-free scientific enterprise that has nothing to do with morality.

Freud was clearly wrong, however, and this pseudo-scientific attitude has long outlived its usefulness. It constitutes a bad faith denial of what should be obvious to any self-reflective person: that what we do with our lives is intimately and intrinsically related to what we value in life. More specifically, it is a denial of what I suspect all psychoanalysts privately believe and that Don Carveth makes public in this book: we believe that effective psychoanalytic therapy fosters patients' innate tendency towards self-actualisation, a tendency to heal and grow into better, more loving human beings; and as a corollary we believe that psychoanalytic understanding has the power to make the world a better place.

It may be too harsh (too superego-ish) to call our collective denial of these beliefs bad faith. Probably the main reason psychoanalysts do not talk about what we really believe is that our beliefs are mostly unconscious. We literally do not know what we really believe, or have a very incomplete understanding of it. Moreover, our official theory reinforces whatever personal need we might have to remain unconscious of our beliefs. Freud was notoriously oblivious to his own beliefs and notoriously dismissive of any beliefs other than those of nineteenth-century positivist science. That is why he could believe in a universal need for sex and aggression (which he considered scientifically verifiable facts) but not in a universal need for compassion and morality (which he considered "sublimated" epiphenomena that are far from universal). That is why his concept of superego explains conscience as a kind of neurological imprinting of rules and prohibitions from without rather than an innate "knowledge of good and evil" from within. That is why until now, psychoanalysis has not had the language—the concepts—that would allow us to include morality and the capacity for moral discernment in our understanding of ourselves and of human nature.

Don Carveth, with this book, has changed all that. Not only does he introduce important new terms—like conscience, reciprocity, objective guilt, moral judgment (discernment)—into the psychoanalytic lexicon. He shows how many of our familiar, supposedly value-free, concepts—Eros, Thanatos, narcissism, object love, making the unconscious conscious (*wo Es war, da soll Ich werden*: where it was, there shall I become)—have always had a distinctive moral valence. Carveth shows how, privately and unofficially, morality and values have always been part and parcel of the psychoanalytic process, even while the official public theory of psychoanalysis has claimed to be value neutral.

This dramatic discrepancy between what psychoanalysts practise and what we preach is significant. It shows how much our theorising has been inhibited by our superegos. We have not allowed ourselves to think outside the box of what Freud could allow himself to think. We do practise outside this box, but we have had to avoid acknowledging and theorising about the conscience that actually informs our practice. As Carveth points out, this inconsistency has been hiding in plain sight as far back as Freud's 1914 essay "On narcissism". I was especially impressed, in fact stunned, by Don's brief but highly illuminating comment on this essay because, of all Freud's writings, "On narcissism" is unique in its combination of profundity and obfuscation. It marks the midpoint of his psychoanalytic career and in the evolution of his thinking. It was his first concerted effort to free himself from the self-imposed limitations of his dehumanisingly reductionistic libido theory. Unfortunately, it was so confused and confusing an effort that although all psychoanalysts have recognised it as one of Freud's most important essays, no psychoanalyst has ever been able to explain *how* it is important. Its theory is so incoherent that no one, not even Freud himself, was ever able to build on it to develop new theory. So it pretty much blew me away when I realised that Don Carveth, in a passing comment, had been able to capture the central meaning of Freud's essay in a way that also explains why no one has ever understood it:

> In distinguishing and valorising "object love" in which we actually recognise the other as *other*, from "narcissistic love" in which the other merely stands for the self we are, or were, or wish to be, Freud (1914c) incorporates a moral value into a manifestly de-moralising psychoanalysis under the guise of the purely clinical sounding term "narcissism".

In fact, Freud's disguise was even deeper than Don suggests here. Not only did he use the term narcissism in a clinical rather than a moral sense; he further de-moralised and dehumanised the term by equating it with the incoherent concept of "ego libido". So Freud was secretly—unconsciously?—*trying* to write about the moral and relational dimension of psychoanalysis, but he disguised and sabotaged this progressive movement in his thinking by framing it in the regressive, reductionistic, and ultimately Procrustean terms of his libido theory. This is akin to discussing the aesthetics and cultural significance of a da Vinci painting in terms of the chemistry of its paint pigments.

Psychoanalysts are so skilled at emulating Freud in using this kind of theoretical obfuscation to talk *around* the discrepancy between our authentically moral practice and our inauthentically amoral theory that it is generally impossible to tell how much the discrepancy is a product of conscious deception and how much it is a collectively unconscious act of self-deception. So we privately think of ourselves as healers but publicly pretend to be scientists in order to maintain our academic respectability and socio-economic status? Or does our unconscious False Self take over for our completely repressed True Self in order to protect it from condemnation and annihilation by our archaic persecutory superego, as reflected in the hostile contemptuous attitude towards psychoanalysis taken by the cognitive neuroscience establishment.

Interestingly, as Carveth points out, psychoanalysts are not the only group in our culture that suffers from this kind of profound resistance to—based on fear of—being authentic, needing to intellectualise, rationalize, and de-moralise its intrinsically moral and relational commitments. In fact, after reading Carveth, I find myself thinking that this resistance to authenticity pervades modern culture to such a degree that it must represent a fault line in human nature.

> Psychoanalytic therapy has always been grounded in a moral ethic that it practises while refusing to preach. From Freud on, psychoanalysts have sought to "de-moralise" what is an intrinsically moral enterprise. Like the "scientific socialists", the scientific psychoanalysts have sought to disguise their humanistic morality behind a façade of positivism. But the dictum "where id was, there shall ego be", far from representing a value-free, scientific/medical perspective, entails a moral ethic valuing not merely the conscious over the unconscious, but prudence and self-control over impulsive acting-out, sublimation over primitive drive, the binding of *Thanatos* by *Eros* and, most significant, the transcendence of narcissism in favour of object love. In practical terms, psychoanalysis has always subscribed to the Judaeo-Christian ethic of love while trying its best

to disguise the fact. In the political domain humanistic liberalism and socialism have sometimes suffered disadvantage in relation to their loudly moralising reactionary opponents due to their need to focus upon issues in an apparently pragmatic, "de-moralised" way instead of openly avowing their moral vision. In the same way, psychoanalysis has been hampered by its need to find self-deceptive euphemisms such as promoting "mental health" or the overcoming of "pathological narcissism" to describe a pilgrim's progress towards becoming a more responsible and loving rather than irresponsible and hating human being.

This passage, taken from Carveth's concluding summary, illustrates his book's intertwined themes of psychological/moral healing and economic/social reform. These themes reflect the interdisciplinary expansiveness of the author's thinking but, more important, they reflect his passionate moral commitments as a psychoanalyst, as a sociologist, and as a person. The passage reminds me of Martin Buber (1957), another passionately moral writer who saw psychoanalysis's reductionistic denial of morality and of the problem of authentic guilt as symptoms of a much larger problem in modern culture:

The perception of one's fellow man as a whole, as a unity, and as unique—even if his wholeness, unity, and uniqueness are only partly developed, as is usually the case—is opposed in our time by almost everything that is commonly understood as specifically modern. In our time there predominates an analytical, reductive, and deriving look between man and man. This look is analytical, or rather pseudoanalytical, since it treats the whole being as put together and therefore able to be taken apart ... An effort is being made today radically to destroy the mystery between man and man. The personal life, the ever-near mystery, once the source of the stillest enthusiasms, is leveled down. (p. 109)

The fact that Don's writing reminds me of Buber rather than of his own favourite religious thinker, Bonhoeffer, points to an interesting difference in our way of thinking about the conscience/superego distinction. Bonhoeffer was a social activist. Buber was a spiritual teacher. For Buber, and for me, loving reciprocity (an element of the I-Thou) is the central manifestation of "the spirit" in human life, whereas for Don—with a nod to Bonhoeffer's "religionless Christianity"—loving reciprocity is a natural (not supernatural) outgrowth of the nurturing mother-infant bond. These two ideas are by no means mutually exclusive, of course, as evidenced by the ubiquitous Christian images that locate the spirit in the relation of Madonna and Child. For many people, myself included, these images speak to a deeply felt personal experience of an ineffable something that can only be called spirit that is manifest precisely in the loving connection between people, especially so in the connection a parent feels looking into his or her baby's smiling eyes. (As I've recently discovered, this joyous feeling happens quite powerfully with grandchildren too!) I agree with Don that this is a completely natural phenomenon but I cannot help but feel that there is something transcendent in it as well.

Don writes about conscience based on "identification with the nurturer" as the counterpart to a superego that is based on "identification with the aggressor", both identifications being products of a natural reciprocity that is (presumably) genetically programmed into human nature. Simply put, he writes, we tend to respond to love with love and to hate with hate.

> The fundamental principle of reciprocity that governs the psyche, the need to give back what one has been given, manifests not only in our need to repay the love we have received through loving, but also in the *lex talionis* whereby we repay aggression with aggression.

This principle of reciprocity can and has been further extended through the work of Sylvan Tomkins and others (see Nathanson, 1997) who theorise that it is in the nature of human emotion that *any* affective expression in one person will instinctively evoke the same affect (or an unconscious defence against it) in another person. So not only do humans respond to love with love, and hate with hate. We respond to anger with anger, anxiety with anxiety, agitation with agitation, shame with shame, contempt with contempt, depression with depression, surprise with surprise, joy with joy, interest with interest, and excitement with excitement.

The question that then captures my attention is: If all emotions evoke this natural reciprocity, how is it that love is the *only* such emotional reciprocity that provides us with a conscience and an authentically moral sensibility? How do humans *recognise* that love is intrinsically moral in a way that sadness and contempt are not, for example. How do we recognise the moral difference between reciprocal love and narcissistic love? What specifically do we recognise in reciprocal love that moves us to generalise it into a universal moral code like the Golden Rule or the categorical imperative? On the other hand, how do we *know* that the talion law—"Do unto others exactly what they do to you"—although it is a time-honoured and universal practice of reciprocity (the form of both legal justice and revenge), nevertheless does *not* constitute an authentically moral way of treating people? Or to put it in terms of the Kleinian theory that informs Don Carveth's thinking, how do we know that depressive guilt is more authentically moral than persecutory guilt?

I submit that in order for us to be able to recognise and know these things as true, our moral sensibility has to be so deeply innate that it *precedes* and informs our very earliest experiences of loving and hating, so that these earliest experiences simply awaken and give shape to moral pre-sentiments that were already there in us, waiting to be awakened. This puts us in the realm of *a priori* Kantian categories, Platonic forms, and Bionian "thoughts without a thinker", quasi-mystical concepts which go against the grain of Don's secular humanist sensibility. He argues (pp. 15, 71, 76–77) that such concepts are unnecessary; that they add no explanatory value and are no more conducive to moral behaviour than is Eli Sagan's concept of conscience as identification with the nurturer. I am not so sure.

Not that I am eager to invoke Kant or Bion. Trying to make sense of Kant tends to give me a headache and, as for Bion .... Nevertheless I do think that Kant, Bion, Plato, and (by the way) Descartes, were all trying to describe a noumenal or spiritual dimension of human experience and human nature that really does exist and is an essential element of conscience. Without including such a spiritual dimension as an irreducible element in our theory of human nature, I believe it is impossible to account for the experience of moral discernment and free moral choice. But I like to keep my philosophising simple so I call this dimension simply our higher consciousness or our self-reflective, moral consciousness. Following Robert Waelder (1930), I think of it as the level of consciousness that is uniquely human, in contrast to the ordinary in-the-moment animal consciousness—the consciousness of our ego-of-adaptation—that gets us through most of the day most of the time.

To the extent that conscience is an identification with the nurturer, I would say that it belongs to this animal level of consciousness. It is an instinctive automatised response pattern that, like identification with the aggressor, is in principle reducible to a conditioned, highly complex, neurological reflex—a learned Jiminy Cricket program embedded in our brains. The development of a fully human conscience, however—what Genesis calls the "knowledge of good and evil", what turned

Pinocchio into a real boy—requires an awakening in us of the human spirit, the transcendent or meta-level of consciousness that is capable, first, of distinguishing between feelings based on identification with the nurturer and feelings based on identification with the aggressor and, second, of using the distilled awareness of these feelings to assess (discern) what is moral and what is immoral in a course of action towards which our emotions are impelling us.

Don Carveth writes from the perspective of such an awakened spirit and he takes this meta-level of consciousness for granted as *implicit* in his concept of conscience. By distinguishing this awakened morally discerning conscience from the benighted persecutory superego, Don has made a potentially revolutionary contribution to the psychoanalytic understanding of human nature. By equating it with Eli Sagan's concept of identification with the nurturer, however, I think he has mistaken a necessary for a sufficient condition. This is not to deny the vital importance of Sagan's previously unrecognised concept. Sagan has identified and illuminated something essential in the emotional life of human beings and in the formation of our moral conscience that, until now, has been conspicuously and shamefully absent from psychoanalytic theory. As Carveth and Sagan point out, this scotoma-to-the-point-of-blindness in our thinking reflects a (paradoxically) irrational prejudice in favour of the rational mind with its logical thinking and against the instinctive body with its deeper logic of the emotions. I could not agree more.

Sagan argues, as have others, that behind this rationalist prejudice lies a phallocentric prejudice against, and dread of, women. Again I agree. The fear of women/body/instinct/feelings gives rise to an undervaluing of the emotional, the relational, and the social, and an overvaluing of disembodied abstract reasoning. In our culture this means that scientists who study only what can be described in terms of mathematics have much higher status than scholars who study human experience in any form, especially forms that require an understanding of human emotion.

Don Carveth has done us a great service by turning this counterphobic cultural attitude on its head. He views embodied feelings as more reliable, in fact more rational, than disembodied reasoning. For example, it is only because we can *feel* the difference between nurturing love and hostile aggression and between depressive guilt and persecutory guilt, that we can know there is an important distinction to be made between a genuinely moral conscience and an irrationally punitive superego. Freud missed this important distinction entirely because he was too much in his head, reasoning about the body in a completely disembodied way, and in this context he viewed emotions as much more disruptive than informative.

It is curious that my one disagreement with Don—about whether a spiritual dimension is a necessary element of conscience in particular and human nature generally—is based on something we are in complete agreement about: the fundamental importance of feelings as the basis for understanding human beings. Don mistrusts psychological explanations that invoke a spiritual dimension because he views the spirit as disembodied, disconnected from feeling. I feel the need for such explanations because I view the spirit as the *essence* of feeling. I realise that this is distinctly a minority opinion. Certainly most Western thinkers, following Plato, have viewed the spirit or soul as *disembodied* and have equated it with reason rather than with feelings; or, like Freud, they have glorified disembodied reason and put it *in place of* the spirit.

I share Don's mistrust of this kind of disconnected spirituality. He is right to insist that disembodied rationality can never be a reliable guide or motive for moral action. Only feelings can serve this function, and certainly identification with the nurturer is an important source of these feelings. But as important as feelings are, I would argue that feelings by themselves—whether based on identification with the nurturer or identification with the aggressor, or on anything else for that matter—are not quite enough to explain the activity of a fully human conscience. In addition there has to be a feeler of the feelings, a higher consciousness that can recognise and process the moral messages that are the encoded essence of our feelings.

Practically speaking, my disagreement with Don is little more than a philosophical quibble. For me, moral consciousness is an ontologically distinct element, along with moral feelings, in the experience of conscience. For Don moral consciousness is implicit in and pretty much synonymous with the moral feelings that constitute conscience. We are both talking about the same human experience, perhaps the most uniquely human of all experiences, and one that has—shockingly—never before been included in the psychoanalytic account of inner conflict or of human nature. In the end our disagreement boils down to a familiar unanswerable question: if there is no higher consciousness there to hear it (and decode its subtle language of feeling), does the still small voice of conscience really make a sound?

Elio Frattaroli

PREFACE

Although over the years I have published on a range of topics not addressed in this book, what does appear here represents my attempt to put between two covers what I feel are the most important conclusions I have reached about human personality and the human situation through my career as a student of the human sciences and as a practising psychoanalyst.

Since undertaking analytic training in the 1970s, I have felt privileged to have had access to the clinic as a kind of laboratory in which sociological and philosophical, as well as psychoanalytic, ideas could be tested in my dialogue with my patients. In Chapter One I explain why, though I am a non-medical psychoanalyst, I continue to employ the latter term to describe the people who choose to talk to me about their lives.

In ways that I hope will become clear in the course of the book I feel that clinical psychoanalytic work amounts to something more than a therapeutic practice, the application to patients of professionally validated psychological theories and techniques. For me at least, it also entails elements of an ethico-philosophical dialogue, but one less about abstractions of one sort or another than about the very particular and personal issues and agonies that constitute not only my patients' lives, but that come over time to constitute our lives together, insofar as these come to overlap in a series of fifty-minute encounters, often over many years. If I have changed them, they have certainly changed me, and continue to do so.

I became a university teacher to enjoy the dialectic of ideas with my students, both in and out of the classroom, and I have certainly done so. But there is a limit to how far this dialogue can go in a purely academic setting, or even in my office or the cafeteria or the pub after class. I wanted to go further, deeper, into highly personal and emotional territory, ground that can only ethically be trodden in the professionally maintained "frame" of the psychoanalytic encounter.

What lies before you is a summary of the key issues emerging from my dialogues with students and with patients, but also with all those significant others with whom I have shared my life and struggles and who have deeply influenced what I have come to consider important: my teachers; the mentors I have known personally and the many others I have encountered only through their writings; my personal analysts, all four of them; my supervisors; my colleagues; and, naturally, last but not least, those I have loved and who have loved me.

So what are the issues? Love. Hate. Guilt. Self-deception. Suffering. Conscience. Contrition. Reparation. Forgiveness.

Toronto, September 2012

CHAPTER ONE

The moral ambiguity of psychoanalysis

For decades what Freud (1933a) himself regarded as "the preferred field of work for psychoanalysis", namely "The problems which the unconscious sense of guilt has opened up, its connections with morality, education, crime and delinquency ..." (p. 61), has been neglected in favour of a preoccupation with narcissism, shame, self, relatedness and, most recently, the neurological foundations of mind. But recently issues concerning the superego, guilt, and conscience appear to be returning from repression. No doubt this "comeback" amounts to a reflection in psychoanalysis of a shift in the wider culture: the "culture of narcissism" (Lasch, 1979) got us into hot water. What three decades ago Rangell (1980) described in *The Mind of Watergate* as the "syndrome of the compromise of integrity" led eventually to the 2008 crisis of "casino capitalism". It is time we began rethinking the psychoanalytic theory of morality.

As early as my doctoral research (Carveth, 1977) I was struggling with what I saw as the grossly inadequate psychoanalytic position with respect to moral questions. In this connection, I remember being struck by Abram Kardiner's (1977, pp. 107–109) account, in *My Analysis with Freud: Reminiscences*, of one of his first clinical encounters after qualifying as a psychoanalyst and hanging out his shingle. A man presented with a

1

work inhibition that he sought to have cured by analysis. It turned out he was a hit man, a professional killer, who was suddenly and inexplicably having trouble performing his job. After a few sessions in which both patient and analyst recognised the mutual threat they constituted to one another, the man did not return, leaving Kardiner wondering whether or not he had "cured" him.

Kardiner's case raises a range of significant issues that psychoanalysts, with few exceptions, have sought to evade. The patient came with a psychological problem, an inhibition of function. In the traditional view, the psychoanalyst, like the physician, abstains from moral judgement and employs his expertise in the service of relief of the patient's "inhibitions, symptoms and anxiety" (Freud, 1926d). So in a case like this, does the analyst get on with the job and help the patient overcome his neurotic inhibition against killing? If not, why not? If the analyst declines to help in this instance, is he or she now, like the patient, suffering neurotic inhibition? Is the analyst suffering from an unresolved moralistic countertransference? Does he or she require more analysis, especially of his or her superego? Or could it be that the idea of psychoanalysis as a scientific, technical, ethically neutral or "value-free" enterprise amounts to a cover story disguising the fact that, in reality, despite its avowed commitment to honesty and to putting everything into words, psychoanalysis practises an ethic it simply refuses to preach?

Half a century before the invention of psychoanalysis, in *The Concept of Anxiety* (1844), *The Sickness unto Death* (1849), and other works, Søren Kierkegaard advanced a view of emotional disturbance in which issues of morality and guilt are central. As Barrett (1958) explains, for Kierkegaard:

> The condition we call a sickness in certain people is, at its centre, a form of sinfulness. We are in the habit nowadays of labelling morally deficient people as sick, mentally sick, or neurotic. ... But the closer we get to any neurotic the more we are assailed by the sheer human perverseness, the wilfulness, of his attitude. If he is a friend, we can up to a point deal with him as an object who does not function well, but only up to a point; beyond that if a personal relationship exists between us we have to deal with him as a subject, and as such we must find him morally perverse or wilfully disagreeable; and we have to make these moral judgments to his face if the

friendship is to retain its human content, and not disappear into a purely clinical relation. *At the centre of the sickness of the psyche is a sickness of the spirit.* Contemporary psychoanalysis will have eventually to reckon with this Kierkegaardian point of view. (p. 170; my emphasis)

Though Freud himself possessed "the mind of a moralist" (Rieff, 1959)—to Pfister he wrote that "[O]n the whole I have not found much of the 'good' in people" and that "Most of them are in my experience riff-raff" (letter cited by E. Jones, 1961, p. 445), while to Putnam he commented on "the unworthiness of human beings, even of analysts" (letter cited by Jones, 1961, p. 433)—in marked contrast to Kierkegaard, he sought to "de-moralise" therapeutic discourse. The founder of psychoanalysis did not believe that immorality is at the root of neurosis, or that its cure renders people morally improved. "Why", he asks, "should analysed people be altogether better than others? Analysis makes for unity, but not necessarily for goodness" (letter to Putnam cited by Jones, 1961, p. 433). The patient was to be viewed not as a morally troubled soul in need of redemption, but as a victim of an "illness", albeit one caused less by biological factors than by conflicting unconscious psychological forces and mechanisms in need of readjustment through becoming conscious.

In psychiatry de-moralisation has been more consistent than in psychoanalysis; patients have been viewed as victims of illnesses rather than moral agents implicated in their own suffering. The psychoanalytic position on this question has been ambiguous. On one hand, in keeping with Freud's psychic determinism, patients have at times been depicted as pawns of unconscious forces and the compulsion to repeat, though ego psychology (Hartmann, 1939) attempted to resist such reductionism. On the other hand, psychoanalysis reveals the degree to which patients are the unconscious agents of their suffering. Whereas Freud (1916–17) attributed much of the resistance to psychoanalysis to the challenge it constitutes to the notion of free will ("But human megalomania will have suffered its third and most wounding blow from the psychological research of the present time which seeks to prove to the ego that it is not even master in its own house, but must content itself with scanty information of what is going on unconsciously in its mind" (p. 284)), Schafer (1976) drew attention to a complementary truth: that the resistance to psychoanalysis has as much or more to do with its widening, rather than shrinking, the range of human responsibility, its revelation that "People … are far more creators and stand much closer to their gods than they can bear to recognise" (p. 153). Schafer asks:

> What, after all, did Freud show in the *Studies on Hysteria* … but that a neurotic symptom is something a person *does* rather than *has* or has inflicted on him or her? It is a frightening truth that people make their own mental symptoms. It is an unwelcome insight that if neurosis is a disease at all, it is not like any other disease. It is an arrangement or a creation, an expression of many of an individual's most basic categories of understanding and vital interests. … Consequently, the widespread rejection of psychoanalysis may be understood as a species of disclaimed action. It is a way of asserting: "Do not tell us how much we do and how much more we could do. Allow us our illusions of ignorance, passivity, and helplessness. We dare not acknowledge that we *are* masters in our own house". (pp. 153–154)

Despite rejection of free will in favour of strict determinism in psychoanalytic metapsychology, the clinical psychology of psychoanalysis reveals patients as the unconscious agents and creators of their emotional "illnesses", however much they may also be victims of the circumstances to which such "illnesses" are a response. In pointing this out, Schafer was in no way seeking to replace a one-sided determinism with an equally one-sided voluntarism, but simply drawing our attention to the fact that we tend to err in two directions: at times excessively *claiming* responsibility and, at other times, excessively *disclaiming* it. Like Sartre (1943, 1960), he recognised that human beings are both subjects and objects.

While never denying the reality of emotional or psychological disturbance and suffering, nor the validity of psychoanalysis as therapy, the claim that someone is "mentally ill", like the claim that an economy is "sick", could for the psychoanalyst Thomas Szasz (1961) never be more than a metaphor. Where so-called "mental illness" can be shown to have an organic or neurochemical cause, then it is physical not mental illness. The latter term is reserved for conditions psychiatry *wants* to believe are illnesses but cannot prove to be so in any literal sense. It may *look* like "illness" in certain respects, but it is not illness unless its physiological, biological, anatomical, neurological, or neurochemical causes are discovered, in which case it is physical not mental illness. In Szasz's view, and in mine, psychoanalysts are metaphorical "doctors" treating metaphorical "sicknesses" of the soul. If I continue to refer to my analysands as "patients" it is not because I consider them to be suffering from a literal illness, but because the term "patient" shares with the term "passion" the common Latin root *patiens*, from the verb *pati*, meaning "to suffer". Patients are sufferers. Those of us who seek to work with them therapeutically share a commitment, if not a "calling", that transcends the professional or business element and cash nexus conveyed, to my ear at least, by the term "client".

While psychoanalysis has been ambiguous with respect to the question of the causation of emotional disturbance and the degree to which patients are the victims or the agents of their suffering or both, it has, at least manifestly, shared the psychiatric attitude towards treatment, viewing it as a technical rather than a moral enterprise. The goal of psychoanalytic therapy was to render unconscious forces conscious and to thereby enhance the patient's freedom to choose, but the resulting choice, for good or ill, was the patient's business, not the analyst's. In other words, the goal was to make people freer and saner, not necessarily better. (I leave it to the ambitious philosopher to attempt to reconcile the psychoanalytic commitment to expanding patients' freedom with Freudian psychic determinism.) Rieff (1959) describes the psychoanalytic "counter-ideal of health" as follows:

> The chaotic id and the "rigid" superego are the areas of psychic vulnerability; the ego, having flexibility and craft, is Freud's category of resolution. Where conscience, or an ideal, has divided personality against itself in constraints of its own devising, the therapeutic task is to help the ego move from mere defensiveness on to the offensive in an effort to achieve a new integrity. But this integration of self is no harbinger of goodness. It is possible to become more sound of mind and yet less good—in fact, worse. To be a complete man, self-united and controlled, states that counter-ideal of health in the name of which the old constraining ideals of devotion and self-sacrifice are rejected. (pp. 64–65)

One reason for the hostility towards psychoanalysis on the part of certain religious traditions is that they took seriously the, in my view false, claims that psychoanalytic therapy is not about helping people to be good, but only to become more rational and sane, and that "it is possible to become more sound of mind and yet less good—in fact, worse."

Let it be clear that I am in no way arguing that therapists should moralise with their patients or seek to indoctrinate or convert them in one way or another. On this point I am a traditionalist. Except in extreme circumstances where the patient constitutes a danger to himself or others, it is the analyst's responsibility to abstain from acting-out his or her countertransference in such ways, independent of whether such countertransference derives from the analyst's superego, or from what I distinguish as his or her conscience. But what I do claim is that it is not possible for a person to become sane ("of sound mind; not mad" (O.E.D.)) without at the same time becoming morally improved. This is because a person's immorality is always known to and disapproved by conscience, and sometimes also punished by the superego (even where the superego is the instigator of the immorality, a not uncommon situation as I will argue). When it is unconscious, bad conscience cannot promote positive change and reparation. In this circumstance the unconscious superego seizes the opportunity to inflict punishment, generating emotional disturbance, however obscure its manifestations and effects may be.

Although analysts may be reluctant to admit it, no patient is genuinely helped by psychoanalysis who does not in the process become morally improved, for it is necessary to become morally improved in order to overcome neuroses, character and personality disorders, and the suffering they entail. The churches misunderstood psychoanalysis because psychoanalysis misunderstood, or at least misrepresented, itself. The exceptional circumstances mentioned above, where the patient constitutes a danger to himself or others, are circumstances that force the analyst to "come out of the closet" as it were and acknowledge and act upon the moral values that undergird the entire therapeutic enterprise, but that are normally hidden behind a mask of moral neutrality, unless and until the patient forces our hand. The fact that there may be good, pragmatic, clinical reasons for wearing such a mask, at least for a time, should not be allowed to blind us to the fact that it is a mask. In "the scientistic self-misunderstanding of metapsychology", Habermas (1971, Chapter Eleven) discusses Freud's misrecognition of psychoanalysis as a natural science rather than an interpretive, hermeneutic enterprise (I personally believe like other human or social sciences it contains elements of both). A related element of this self-misunderstanding is the failure of psychoanalysis to grasp, or at least acknowledge, the inherently moral dimension of its practice. The Kleinians have come far closer than the Freudians to recognising this, but even they have been reluctant to make it explicit.

Freud (1933a) argued that psychoanalysis has no other *Weltanschauung* than that of science itself and is only interested in "submission to the truth and rejection of illusions" (p. 182). While acknowledging that in practical life the making of *ultimate* value judgements is unavoidable, these are left to the liberty and responsibility of the individual. In this view, psychoanalysis is committed only to a *penultimate* "ethic of honesty" (Rieff, 1959, ch. 9), restricting itself to helping analysands to transcend self-deception. But the idea that psychoanalysis has no ethic other than that of honesty is not honest. At best it is an illusion, hopefully without a future. For, like it or not, "Where id was there ego shall be" (Freud, 1933a, p. 79) is a moral imperative requiring far more than replacing illusion with truth: it enjoins us to transcend impulsive action and, instead, develop ego strength, prudence, discretion, and rational self-mastery. Developing ego where id was "is a work of culture—not unlike the draining of the *Zuider Zee*" (p. 80); sublimation of primitive drive is encouraged. But overcoming our illusions, developing self-control, sublimating our drives—this is still not enough. In addition, we must transcend narcissism in favour of object love, we must bind *Thanatos* with *Eros*, and we must overcome the harsh, primitive superego that is a "pure culture of the death instinct" (Freud, 1923b, p. 52) if we are to avoid self-destruction. In these and other ways the Freudian ethic far exceeds the demand for self-knowledge. While others fail to practise what they preach, psychoanalysts refuse to preach what they practise.

Four decades have now passed since Karl Menninger (1973) asked *Whatever Became of Sin?* In so doing he drew attention to a de-moralising trend in psychiatry and psychoanalysis mirroring that of the wider culture. Increasingly, it seems, we have come to reject Cassius's conviction that "the fault … lies not in our stars, but in ourselves" (*Julius Caesar*, 1.2) in favour of that proto-narcissist Lear's protestation that we are "more sinned against than sinning" (*King Lear*, 3.2). Such de-moralisation, such guilt evasion, is only to be expected in the culture of narcissism. If, as the old saying has it, the superego is soluble in alcohol, then in narcissism it seems it may be liquidated altogether. But this is merely an appearance, for when the anaesthetic wears off the superego takes its sadistic revenge—it may even have cunningly instigated the whole process precisely to be able to do so. As Britton (2003) points out, the narcissistic disorders are grounded in evasion of what Bion (1959, p. 313) called the ego-destructive superego; but in my view they also entail flight from conscience conceived as a fourth structure of the mind distinct from id, ego, and superego. Narcissistic preoccupation with our grandiosity or inferiority, or each in turn in cyclothymic or bipolar oscillation, is characteristic of the paranoid-schizoid position (Klein, 1946) where splitting (idealisation/devaluation) reigns. But self-obsession, of either form, precludes genuine concern for the other. While viewing the self as all-good obviously prevents any admission of wrongdoing, a sweeping judgement of the self as all-bad entails an obvious distortion that removes any realistic focus upon the *particular* sins of which we may be guilty.

Might it have been easier to bear guilt back in the days when the Judaeo-Christian doctrine of the Fall of Man, of our intrinsic moral imperfection, was widely accepted, or when the need for capitalist accumulation made self-restraint a virtue, than in late capitalist consumer societies promoting oral-narcissistic regression and instinctual release rather than repression? Today the idea of moral imperfection as an intrinsic feature of being human—"For all have sinned, and come short of the glory of God" (*Romans* 3:23 *KJV*)—is widely rejected (*viz.*, the letter to the editor cited in Chapter Two from a woman who was not a sinner). It is worth noting that moral imperfection precludes being perfectly bad as much as it precludes being perfectly good. I expect it has always been difficult to consciously bear guilt and not evade it by attacking either the self or others. When our narcissism renders conscious moral suffering (depressive or reparative guilt) intolerable, the superego exacts its pound of flesh either through unconsciously constructed forms of self-torment (persecutory guilt and shame) or by scapegoating others onto whom one's guilt is projected. That is, when reconciliation with conscience is refused, the ego-destructive superego has a field day, however unconsciously. I will argue that the only viable escape from the clutches of the superego is reconciliation with conscience.

Prior to the 1960s, psychoanalysts viewed superego analysis as central to the analytic process, for it was widely agreed that the dynamics of guilt and self-punishment play a crucial role in both psychopathology and cure. Some analysts never lost sight of such fundamental Freudian and Kleinian insights, implicitly agreeing with Rangell's (1974, 1976, 1980, 1997) view that, in addition to the ego-id conflicts resulting in neurosis, there are the ubiquitous ego-superego conflicts that frequently result in what Rangell called the "syndrome of the compromise of integrity" and that I think of as "the psychopathy of everyday life". But I think it is fair to say that many of the newer psychoanalytic theories that came to prominence in the 1970s and 1980s ("coincidentally" with the emergence of the culture of narcissism and the rise of neo-liberalism or market fundamentalism)—the types of object-relational theory and relational psychoanalysis that draw on those parts of Winnicott's (1960a, 1962) multifarious thinking that stress "ego-relatedness" and on Kohut's (1977) "self psychology" that is so congruent with this— tended to downplay intrapsychic conflict among superego, ego, and id in favour of an emphasis upon trauma, deprivation, abuse, and neglect by caretakers, that is, the ways in which we are more injured than injurious.

By the late 1950s, Sandler (1960) had already noticed that in the index- ing of cases at the Hampstead clinic there was a "tendency to veer away from the conceptualisation of material in superego terms"; he was won- dering why "therapists have preferred to sort their clinical material in terms of object relationships, ego activities, and the transference, rather than in terms of the participation of the superego" (p. 129). Two dec- ades later, Arlow (1982) observed that "[S]uperego function has been shunted to one side by the current preoccupation with the persistence of the regressive reactivation of archaic idealisations" (p. 230) and that "[T]he concept superego itself rarely appears as the central topic of a clinical or theoretical contribution" (p. 229). Wurmser (1988) referred to the superego as the "sleeping giant" of contemporary psychoanalysis. While the giant slept, having been anaesthetised in both society at large and the psychoanalytic thinking it encouraged, Thatcher, Reagan, Milton Friedman, Friedrich von Hayek, Ayn Rand, Alan Greenspan, and a host of others laid the foundations for the dismantlement of the welfare state and, with the avid assistance of the "banksters" and fraudsters of Wall Street and "the City", prepared the ground for the economic crisis of 2007–8. In my view narcissistic self-indulgence, however rationalised as libertarianism or individualism, inevitably leads to pain, if not in the short then in the long run.

In referring to the displacement of psychoanalytic focus from intra- psychic conflict to issues of trauma, deprivation, abuse, and neglect by carers, there is no intention to deny the significance of such factors in generating emotional disturbance. But one of the ways in which trauma, deprivation, abuse, and neglect are damaging is that they cause the victim to become a hateful and sadistic agent towards the self and others. Such reactive hate, envy, and destructiveness, however understandable in terms of the conditions that elicit them, lead either to guilt, or if guilt is unbearable, to an unconscious need for punishment that takes the form of the self-sabotaging and self-tormenting behaviours inflicted by Freud's sadistic superego or Fairbairn's (1944) "internal saboteur". Psychoanalysis cannot eradicate past trauma and deprivation, but it can help patients understand how their responses to these events have been destructive and assist them in finding better ways of coping. But the Freudian and Kleinian approaches that focused on such interior conflict, on issues of "crime and punishment", have in some quarters been marginalised over the past four decades. As Horowitz (2005) pointed out, "All patients (and each of us) have had private theories of pathogenesis of neurosis and for the most part these theories have been about trauma at the hands of parents. It is still difficult to demonstrate to patients or students the role of conflict in neurosogenesis" (p. 2).

One of the few major psychoanalytic writers to explicitly move against the de-moralising trend was Erik Erikson (1950, 1968). His formulation of the psychoanalytic theory of development as a process in which successful transcendence of the conflict and crisis at each epigenetic stage results in the development of a particular *virtue* (hope, will, purpose, competency, fidelity, love, caring, wisdom) threatened to undermine the positivistic and medical façade that psychoanalysis had adopted to disguise its ethical existentialism. Burston (2007) points out that Erikson's left-wing critics (Berman, 1975; Roazen, 1976) viewed such talk of virtues as a regressive attempt to reintroduce a pre-psychoanalytic moralism into a discipline that, in their opinion, had transcended it. My view is that, on the contrary, Erikson's work entailed a forthright admission of what psychoanalysis has always intrinsically been despite its ongoing attempts to deny it. In criticising Erikson for making manifest the underlying ethic of psychoanalysis, such critics display their own commitment to a positivistic de-moralising façade for both psychoanalysis and socialism, both of which are grounded in a moral ethic, though so-called "scientific" socialists, with a few brilliant exceptions such as Eagleton (2009, 2010), have been as ashamed as psychoanalysts to admit this.

Back to Kardiner's case: imagine the analyst overcoming his scruples and proceeding to treat the patient. What if through the ministrations of such an (unscrupulous) analyst the hit man's inhibition was cured? Given his "new integrity", would he then be a "complete man, self-united and controlled"? Can a professional killer ever really be a "complete" man, let alone have "integrity"? Can one really become saner without becoming better? Are neuroses, character disorders, and even certain types of psychoses really separate from and unrelated to a person's moral or immoral life? Is an intelligent and successful psychopath really sane? If not, why not? And in what, if any, sense can a psychopath really be "successful"? These are some of the issues addressed in the course of this book.

The evasion of such questions by psychoanalysis not only leaves us unable to account for our uneasiness regarding the idea of curing inhibited killers but also with the problem of moral relativism. For Freud (1923b, 1930a), conscience is a function of the superego which is grounded in aggression towards the Oedipal rivals turned back against the ego, plus the internalisation of cultural values via introjection of the parental superegos, in addition to other socialisation and group pressures (Freud, 1921c). While id aggression turned against the ego forms its core, the superego "represents more than anything the cultural past" (Freud, 1940a, p. 205). Though recognising the superego as to a considerable degree a social derivative, psychoanalysts have shown little concern over the consequence that one's superego will inevitably reflect the values of the milieu in which socialisation occurred—that is, its racism, sexism, etc. Freud and subsequent psychoanalysts have for the most part evaded the problem of the immorality of the *normal* superego. Where superego immorality is addressed at all, it is thought to be due to the internalisation of the antisocial values of a deviant familial or social milieu, or to superego *lacunae* arising from a failure to properly internalise "normal" values. In this way the immorality of normal values and the normal superego have been evaded and the superego preserved as a largely prosocial force opposing the immorality arising from the id.

Psychoanalysis has located the roots of immorality and the antisocial in man in the id, not the superego. Uniquely human forms of destructiveness unknown in animal life have been projected onto the beasts and identified with the animal in man—when in reality animals are seldom beastly, at least not in the ways humans often are. There is no need to deny the existence of antisocial impulses in the id or their acting-out in destructive ways in order to recognise that the destructiveness enacted by id-driven criminals and psychopaths amounts to nothing compared to that accomplished by superego-driven ideologists, "do-gooders" who employ technical rationality and ego function to organise mass murder, nor to be aware of the more subtle forms of "soul murder" (Shengold, 1989) inflicted by the superego in everyday life. This failure to comprehend the uniqueness of human destructiveness and its roots in the superego and ego in addition to the id is perhaps the greatest failure of psychoanalysis as a human science.

Freud was not much concerned to reject the form and content of one superego in favour of another; for instance, to distinguish and devalue a racist or sexist superego as opposed to one less loaded with such cultural garbage. Rieff (1959) writes: "Freud insisted we that we 'keep firmly to the ... separation of the ego from an observing, critical, punishing agency'; in other words that we preserve reason from what he considered the tyranny of moral principles embodied in the superego" (p. 63). Freud (1933a) argues that "Our best hope for the future is that intellect—the scientific spirit, reason—may in process of time establish a dictatorship in the mental life of man. The nature of reason is a guarantee that afterwards it will not fail to give man's emotional impulses and what is determined by them the position they deserve" (p. 170). Do we know of many reasonable dictatorships? A pretty good description of the pathological narcissist or severe psychopath is a personality characterised by ego dominance and a dictatorship of the intellect. Kardiner's hit man probably consulted him because the dictatorship of his intellect was breaking down.

A good deal of the difficulty psychoanalysis has had with moral issues arises from its rationalism. Though Jewish, Freud's philosophic orientation was far more Hellenistic than Hebraic. From Plato he acquired the idea that kings should be philosophers and philosophers kings—for Freud such philosopher-kings being those well-analysed folks who, in keeping with Nietzsche's ethic, have earned the right to master others by first mastering themselves. From Plato, Freud also derives the metaphor of the rider and the horse: ego (Plato's "reason") should constitute the rider dominating both id (Plato's "appetites") and superego ("spirit"). The problem is that today few philosophers defend the Platonic notion of the intellectual apprehension of the form of the good; most agree that whatever other good things reason and science, the intellect and the rational ego, can give us, they cannot provide moral guidance. We cannot in logic deduce an *ought* from an *is*. Science is *descriptive*, not *prescriptive*. If the rational ego establishes dominance over id and superego, from where will the ego-dominated personality derive moral direction? If the answer is from the pleasure and reality principles, we encounter yet again the problem of the intelligent, reality-oriented, enlightened hedonist, prudentially calculating gain over loss, and out for number one. Far from considering such pleasure- and reality-oriented personalities to be paragons of mental health, both traditional and most contemporary psychoanalytic perspectives would diagnose them as suffering from narcissistic personality disorder because of their relative inability to transcend narcissism in favour of object love.

In distinguishing and valorising "object love" in which we actually recognise the other as *other*, from "narcissistic love" in which the other merely stands for the self we are, or were, or wish to be, Freud (1914c) incorporates a moral value into a manifestly de-moralising psychoanalysis under the guise of the purely clinical sounding term "narcissism". We have seen that psychoanalysis has an ambiguous position on the question of freedom and determinism. Here we witness yet another of the key ambiguities characterising psychoanalytic theory. While presenting itself as a positivist, de-moralised, scientific/medical discourse, psychoanalysis is at the same time committed to an ethic of love, which it attempts to disguise by equating the capacity to love as "health" and the inability or unwillingness to love as "pathological narcissism". Heinz Kohut (1979) wanted to substitute the term "self disorder" for "pathological narcissism" because he rejected what he saw as the hidden Judaeo-Christian ethic of love contained in the "health and maturity morality" (p. 12) of the Freudians. He was certainly correct that psychoanalysts were disguising a morality behind a façade of pseudo-objective medical and psychological terminology, but he was no more capable than Freud of presenting a de-moralised psychology: his notion of therapeutic advance from "archaic" to "higher forms and transformations of narcissism" is just another language in which to describe a pilgrim's moral progress, albeit one less demanding of self-dispossession in favour of the other than was Freud's (1914c) for whom: "A strong egoism is a protection against falling ill, but in the last resort we must begin to love in order not to fall ill, and we are bound to fall ill if, in consequence of frustration, we are unable to love" (p. 84).

It is worth noting Freud's need to justify his ethic of love on utilitarian grounds: he does not just say it is better to love than to hate, only that we will "fall ill" if we fail to love, hence it is in our interest to love. Freud insists on clinging to his rationalism and hedonism: the enlightened hedonist chooses love over hate, not because love is intrinsically better than hate, but only because loving will in the long run lead to greater happiness. This way of putting it is consistent with the idea that human beings are fundamentally self-seeking and if they choose the good it is only because it is in their interest to do so, not because of any primary drive towards it. Likewise, for Freud, the infant has no primary drive to form an attachment to the nurturer (still most often the mother), but only learns to value her as a necessary means to the end of drive-discharge, an idea discredited by Bowlby (1969–80) and others who have established attachment as a primary (unlearned) rather than secondary (learned) drive. Observers such as Harold Searles (1975) have pointed out that infants will put their own needs and development on the back burner and entirely devote themselves to attempting to cure their depressed or anxious mothers—not merely out of a need to get her to straighten up and fly right so as to provide the mothering they need (the utilitarian explanation), or a need to make reparation for aggressive feelings and phantasies towards her (the Kleinian explanation), but also out of sheer dumb love and the simple desire to make her happy. But even while asserting our need to transcend narcissism in favour of object love, for Freud the others we love remain "objects" of drive gratification, means to an end not ends in themselves. Yet, despite its need to justify it on utilitarian grounds, the fact remains that psychoanalysis is grounded in an ethic, even though it has usually been ashamed to "speak its name": it is an ethic of life and love (*Eros/Agape/Caritas*) that opposes hate, evil, and death (*Thanatos*).

For Freud (1933a, lecture 31) the superego subsumes "the functions of self-observation, of conscience and of [maintaining] the ideal" (p. 65). Having subsumed both conscience and the ego ideal into the superego, the latter is the only judge and there is no other judge to judge it, no higher court of moral appeal. We can only describe superegos with different content, ones that are racist and sexist and ones that are less so, right-wing and left-wing ones, harsh and critical or more loving and forgiving ones. But to move beyond description and to prefer one type of superego to another is itself a superego judgement, and traditional psychoanalysis, manifestly committed to a de-moralising positivism, has been unwilling to overtly advocate any moral principle that would justify such judgement. While clinically preferring a forgiving superego to a harshly critical one, psychoanalysts have for the most part sought to maintain a façade of moral neutrality, leaving their commitment to an ethic of love and forgiveness largely unspoken. Owing to his positivism Freud no doubt felt he lacked any defensible grounds upon which to justify the psychoanalytic ethic of love and, owing to his personal distaste for both Judaism and Christianity, he no doubt felt embarrassed advocating their ethic. After the breakdown in 1914 of his first dualistic drive theory (sexual *vs.* self-preservative drives), for six years he was forced to endure an instinctual monism of love (though a subordinate dualism remained in which libido was divided between self and other). In 1920, with palpable relief, following his Greek philosophical precursor Empedocles he abandoned such "monotheism" for the twin "deities", *Eros* and *Thanatos*, perpetually struggling for dominance in the human psyche.

Today moral relativism has been relativised and philosophers and social scientists widely recognise a universal moral standard beyond or beneath all cultural variations and constructions: the ethic of reciprocity (do not do to others what you do not want them doing to you) that Kant (1785) elaborated as the categorical imperative—"Act only according to that maxim whereby you can at the same time will that it should become a universal law" (p. 30). Here is the basis of both conscience and the conscientious critique of the superego. Without it, critics of the superego, such as Alexander (1925), Ferenczi (1928) and, more recently, Britton (2003), have been forced to appeal to reason against the superego's moralism. They call for the ego, the seat of rationality in the psyche, to judge the superego. But reason is not up to the task, for while it is capable of judgement in matters of fact, it is incapable of moral judgement. Even the deeper sort of *thinking* envisaged by Bion (1962) is incapable of providing moral direction, unless such "thinking" is defined so broadly as to include what Rousseau (1754) called "pity" or fellow-feeling, in which case one is forced to wonder why it is called thinking instead of feeling. Like Alexander, Ferenczi, and Britton, I believe the ego needs to be empowered to resist the ego-destructive superego; but it cannot hope to replace it as the moral centre of the personality: that is the job of conscience. From conscience we derive the moral guidance and strength to expose the immorality of the superego and, with the help of the ego, to grow up, emancipate ourselves from and overcome it.

Over time Freud came increasingly to emphasise the harshness and punitiveness of the superego; hence his wish to maintain and strengthen the ego which, owing to his rationalism, he believed (incorrectly in my view) capable of providing sufficient guidance. Clinical psychoanalytic critique of the sadistic superego—which Eagleton (2009) associates with "the Satanic or super-egoic image of God" (p. 21)—in favour of one that is more loving and forgiving began soon after Freud (1923b) introduced the concept of the superego (Alexander, 1925; Ferenczi, 1928; Strachey, 1934). According to Strachey's (1934) theory of the therapeutic action of psychoanalysis, superego modification occurs due, among other factors, to the patient's projection of the punitive superego onto the analyst, only to discover the projection is contradicted by the analyst's far more understanding and forgiving stance.

It has not commonly been recognised that Strachey's theory requires the patient to be able to perceive the analyst's real (hopefully loving rather than sadistic) attitudes, a requirement not easily reconciled with the idea of the analyst as a mirror or a surgeon (Freud, 1912e), or even with the requirement that analysts should strive not to reveal their countertransference. I am in no way seeking to justify indiscriminate countertransference confessions, nor implying that encountering the analyst's love is the sole or sufficient basis of the cure, only pointing out that Strachey's theory of the cure depends on patients being able to perceive and encounter enough of the analyst's reality as a person to counteract their distorting superego projections. In any case, the idea that analysts *could* hide their countertransference from the patient is hard to reconcile with Freud's (1905e) belief that "He that has eyes to see and ears to hear may convince himself that no mortal can keep a secret. If his lips are silent, he chatters with his finger-tips; betrayal oozes out of him at every pore" (pp. 76–77). Of course, Freud had the patient in mind, but analysts, no matter how "well analysed", remain human and, hence, "leak". And it is a good thing they do; otherwise there would be nothing to contradict patients' projections. There is no intrinsic contradiction between Gray's (1994) emphasis on the importance of analytic neutrality in order to be able to analyse the analysand's defensive resort to both morally threatening and morally soothing superego images as resistance, and Freud's own formulation of the overall goal of analysis as the therapeutic deconstruction of the superego, a formulation cited by Gray himself (p. 115). Freud (1940a) writes of the superego-driven negative therapeutic reaction: "In warding off this resistance we are obliged to restrict ourselves to making it conscious and attempting to bring about the slow demolition of the hostile super-ego" (p. 180).

Strachey's work implicitly devalues the harsh in favour of the more forgiving superego and offers a theory of superego modification. For Alexander (1925), "The super-ego … is an anachronism in the mind. It has lagged behind the rapid development of civilized conditions, in the sense that its automatic, inflexible mode of function causes the mental system continually to come into conflict with the outer world" (p. 25). The therapeutic task, he writes, "is carried out by limiting the sphere of activity of the automatically-functioning super-ego, and transferring its role to the conscious ego" (p. 25). Two years later, Ferenczi (1928) went further: "Only a complete dissolution of the super-ego can bring about a radical cure" (p. 100). But because, like Freud, most psychoanalysts have identified conscience with the superego, unlike Freud and Ferenczi they have feared its demolition would be tantamount to the promotion of psychopathy. Hence they have called, with Strachey, for its modification and maturation (Britton, 2003; Gray, 1994; Jacobson, 1964; Kernberg, 1976; Schafer, 1960) rather than its replacement by conscience. While few psychoanalysts have gone as far as Ferenczi and defined the goal of psychoanalysis as *elimination of the superego* (viewing conscience, *contra* Freud, as a separate psychic function altogether), most have shared Strachey's implicit devaluation of the harsh superego and his conception of the analytic cure as involving, among other things, substantial superego modification or modulation, a development conceived most often as advance beyond an archaic or pathological superego towards a more mature or healthy one. The use of terms such as "archaic" *vs.* "mature", and "pathological" *vs.* "healthy", obscures once again what is really a moral judgement defining love and forgiveness as superior to hate and retribution.

But while writers such as Alexander, Ferenczi, and Strachey accepted Freud's view of the superego's sadism and therefore sought to either radically modify it or eliminate it altogether as a bad internal persecutory object, Schafer (1960), reacting against Freud's own focus upon its sadism, advanced the idea of a "loving and beloved superego" that he constructed from small hints and suggestions appearing here and there in Freud's writings but that Freud himself had notably not allowed to alter his overall view. Admitting that "Freud was not prepared to pursue to its end the line of thought leading to a loving and beloved superego or to integrate such a conception with his decisive treatment of the criticizing and feared superego" (Schafer, 1960, p. 163), Schafer nevertheless proceeded to do the job for him. Subsequent readers of Schafer's paper, no doubt aided by wish-fulfilment, seem to have thought the paper revealed that Freud himself recognised a more benign in addition to the sadistic superego, when what the paper truly revealed was what Schafer and others *wished* had been Freud's view of the superego, not the superego he actually gave us.

A sociologist might suggest that whereas Freud himself gave us a late nineteenth-century European father-superego, Schafer gave us that of mid-twentieth-century America. If this were so, it would imply social progress: that we were getting a more modulated view of the superego because superegos had become modulated. But is that fact or wish? At the very time Schafer was advancing his view of the superego as more "Pop" than "*Vater*", Kohut was celebrating the passing of "Guilty Man" altogether in our culture. Here we must boldly bring psychoanalytic thinking to bear and distinguish between what is conscious and what is unconscious. Perhaps owing to changes in culture, gender roles, family structure, etc., harsh paternal authority had diminished and, at least on the conscious level, the authoritarian superego along with it. Yet Freud (1930a, pp. 128–129) explained how a severe superego may result from a lenient upbringing, its severity having more to do with the turning of aggression against the ego than with simple internalisation of parental behaviour. It may even be possible that the decline in parental authority has led to an increase in the severity of the unconscious superego. In any case, our clinical experience would suggest little decline in the role of the sadistic, tyrannical unconscious superego in psychopathology. Of course, this is a point that one is only in a position to affirm or deny to the extent that in clinical work one still "listens with the third ear" (Reik, 1948) to the unconscious. Those who report the disappearance of Guilty Man in our culture and the absence of the dynamics of guilt and self-punishment in their clinical practices would appear to attest to the absence of the unconscious in their work.

Schafer's post-Freudian revision of Freud's theory of the superego has been very influential, even among analysts not usually fond of Freudian revisionism, and for several reasons. First, it compensated to some extent for the lack of any concept of a loving and forgiving conscience with which to offset the harshness of the superego. And second, it did so in the absence of any direct critique of the superego as such. Even today there is strong resistance to anything approaching a radical critique of the superego. Psychoanalysts are all in favour of its modification, its modulation, its transformation from a harsh to a more loving authority—but it remains, after all, in phantasy, the parent, and good children that we are, we must *honour* parental authority, even *defer* to it out of respect, and certainly not "act-out" our unresolved Oedipal aggression by seeking to overthrow it. Even Britton (2003), who possesses a clear understanding of the role of the ego-destructive and envious superego in psychopathology, refrains from conceptualising the superego as such as a bad internal object which it generally was for Klein and also for Freud in his clinical as distinct from sociological writings. Britton seeks only to liberate the ego-destructive superego from hostile, alien, internal, bad occupying forces rather than disempower or overthrow it altogether—a U.N. style peace-keeping, not a revolutionary operation, nor anything approximating Pastor Bonhoeffer's (Metaxas, 2010) joining the plot to assassinate the *Führer*.

In calling for the strengthening of the ego and modification of the superego Britton would certainly be joined by mainstream, American psychoanalysis which, likewise, failing to clearly recognise the superego as an intrinsically bad object, seeks only its "maturation", not its disempowerment or displacement in favour of conscience. Like Schafer, Britton preserves the notion of a superego that is not ego-destructive. Whereas Klein and in his clinical writings even Freud were fairly unambivalent about the superego as an internal aggressor or persecutor, much subsequent psychoanalysis has retreated from this understanding, maintaining a much more ambiguous attitude towards it. Significantly, Ferenczi who, like Alexander, clearly recognised its destructiveness and called for its elimination was a political as well as a psychoanalytic radical. But mainstream psychoanalysis is anything but radical. It has been in love with the idea of "compromise-formation" and like contemporary liberalism has been only too eager to compromise, Chamberlain-like, with the uncompromising forces of authoritarian reaction (superego) that would destroy the ethic of compromise (i.e., democratic institutions) altogether. While from a democratic point of view it would be both unrealistic and wrong to call for the elimination of those seeking the destruction of democracy, it seems entirely reasonable to suggest that such opponents should not be compromised with but imprisoned and encouraged to mature, behind bars.

Psychoanalytic critique of the superego has focused almost exclusively upon its destructive manifestations in the life of the individual, in self-punishment, self-sabotage, masochism, depression, and suicide, and not upon the morally objectionable internalised sociocultural ideologies of which the superego is comprised and that are reflected even in its normative, let alone its pathological expressions. While the id has been scapegoated and blamed for human destructiveness, the superego has been viewed as a prosocial rather than an antisocial force, despite our awareness of its destructive clinical manifestations. Even when the superego has been seen as destructive, its destructiveness has been attributed to its "pathology", thus sparing the so-called "normal" superego from critique and preserving it as a largely prosocial force. Very little critique has been directed by psychoanalysts at the racism, sexism, heterosexism, classism, childism, possessive individualism, consumerism, commodity fetishism, and other ideologies of domination and exploitation that constitute the conventional and normative, yet nonetheless immoral and destructive superego. As Theodor Adorno (1966) pointed out in connection with Ferenczi's call for elimination of the superego, "A critique of the super-ego would have to turn into one of the society that produces the super-ego; if psychoanalysts stand mute here, they accommodate the ruling norm" (p. 274). Mainstream psychoanalysis has pretty much stood mute here, accommodating the ruling norm.

The crucial contribution of Eli Sagan's (1988) *Freud, Women and Morality: The Psychology of Good and Evil* is his positing of a conscience, forming in the first year of life through identification with the nurturer, distinct from Freud's superego forming at the end of the Oedipal phase through identification with the aggressor. While Freud enabled us to understand mental conflict between the three structures of the mind— id, ego, and superego—Sagan implicitly adds a fourth. It seems the science that Ernst Kris (1938) defined as "*the* psychology of the innermost mental processes of man in conflict" (p. 140) has been unable to properly address one entire dimension of mental conflict: that between the superego and the conscience. To illustrate this, Sagan employs Mark Twain's (1885) description of the battle raging in the mind of Huck Finn, torn between the demand of his racist superego that he turn his runaway slave companion, Jim, in to the authorities and the conflicting demand of his conscience that he protect the friend he loves. Although, in theory at least, in addition to *intersystemic* conflict between id, ego, and superego we have recognised *intrasystemic* conflict within each, in reality we have devoted little attention to the latter, especially as it occurs within the superego. In order to begin to grasp mental conflict more adequately, especially moral conflict and "moral injury" (Nash, 2012)—such as the PTSD resulting from committing unconscionable acts at the behest of a superego shaped by familial and military authority—it is, I believe, necessary to recognise a conscience, separate from and frequently in conflict with the superego, as well as with id, ego, and external reality.

Our tripartite structural theory needs to be expanded into a four-part structural theory. But in recent years, rather than seeking to elaborate structural theory, prominent psychoanalytic theorists, such as Schafer (1976), Brenner (1994, 1998, 2002), and others, have become concerned with the problem of reification of psychoanalytic concepts, such as id, ego, superego, conscience, and the very notion of "psychic structure" itself, all of which they view as abstractions referring ultimately to the human actions and compromise-formations of which they are comprised. I agree we must seek to avoid what Whitehead (1925) called "the fallacy of misplaced concreteness" or the literalisation of metaphor. I myself have long been a critic of reification of psychoanalytic concepts (Carveth, 1984b); Chapter Nine of the present book contains my critique of the reified concept of *the* psychopath as such, as distinct from a continuum of degrees of psychopathy, and Chapter Ten concerns reification and de-reification in theology. But since all thinking and communicating depends upon metaphor (Lakoff & Johnson, 1980), I believe we must take care not to extend our critique of reification of abstraction to a condemnation of abstraction *per se*. Philosophers do not prescribe but only analyse what scientists do; we must not allow philosophical strictures to impede scientific creativity and communication. I believe it sometimes serves us to work at the molecular rather than the atomic or subatomic levels of analysis. It is true, to take but one example, that "social structure" is an abstraction referring ultimately to human individuals acting and interacting in patterned ways, yet sociologists have found the concept highly productive in social analysis. Like Freud, who followed Plato closely in this respect, I believe it remains useful to distinguish id (the passions), ego (reason), and superego (our identifications with the aggressor and socially internalised values and ideologies). But we need to recognise a fourth psychological structure, the conscience, rooted in our early identifications with the nurturer and their later development into an ethic of care and concern. It is one of the purposes of this book to call attention to the need for psychoanalysis to develop this expanded structural theory of the mind.

If conscience has its roots, as Sagan believes, in the infant's earliest and continuing identifications with the nurturer (usually but not necessarily the mother, for fathers and a range of others may do the primary nurturing), following Melanie Klein we locate the roots of the superego in the infant's earliest and continuing identifications with the aggressor. In this view, Freud's punitive superego, which for him formed at the end of the Oedipal phase, is a later development of this early identification with the aggressor (the bad, persecutory part-object of Kleinian theory). Similarly, the "loving and beloved superego" (Schafer, 1960) is a later development of the infant's early identification with the nurturer (initially the good, gratifying part-object and later the whole good object), that is, the conscience. The loving superego is the conscience in a more developed form, a conscience that continues to develop throughout the lifespan and opposes hate (*Thanatos*) in the name of love (*Eros/Agape/ Caritas*). The reason it is important to recognise and properly rename this loving superego as the conscience is to facilitate the developmental step psychoanalysis has been reluctant to take—namely to see clearly, as Klein and often Freud himself did—the intrinsically pathological and persecutory nature of the superego as such.

These are some of the themes pursued in the course of this work. In the section headed Clinical Realm, Chapter Two describes the nature and varieties of guilt. Chapter Three concerns the distinction between conscience and superego, as well as the whitewashing of the latter and projection of human destructiveness onto a scapegoat, the bestialising of the id in psychoanalytic theory. Chapter Four discusses the function of self-punishment, persecutory or punitive guilt inflicted by the superego, as a means of evading or defending against the advance towards the capacity to bear depressive anxiety, concern, or reparative guilt, manifestations of conscience. In Chapter Five such less recognised manifestations of guilt as the old and new hysterias and psychosomatic conditions are viewed as guilt-substitutes and forms of guilt evasion. Chapter Six is a study of such hysterical guilt evasion in the case of the psychoanalyst Harry Guntrip. Chapter Seven offers two further such case studies, one of which, the case of Mr. E, was contributed by Jean Hantman.

In the Cultural Realm, Chapter Eight addresses the wider moral problems of modernity from a social evolutionary perspective, including the "postmodern" flight from morality reflected in the de-moralising discourses of psychiatry, psychology, and psychoanalysis and, more broadly, in the de-moralised political discourse of liberalism (as distinct from "neo-liberalism") which has so disadvantaged conscience in its struggle against the highly moralised discourse of its reactionary, superego-driven opponents. Sagan employs his concept of "modernity psychosis" to describe the bizarre forms often assumed by "counter-modernism", the "backlash" against the pressures of social conscience. Chapter Nine offers a critical discussion of the concepts of psychopathy, evil, and the "death drive", as well as the conflict between *Eros* and *Thanatos* that constitutes, in Voltaire's evocative phrase, "a civil war in every soul". Chapter Ten discusses the literalisation and deliteralisation of metaphor in both psychoanalysis and religion and explores some of the theological implications of a revised psychoanalytic theory of human nature in which conscience figures as a distinct structure of the mind, along with id, ego, and superego.

We conclude in Chapter Eleven with an applied psychoanalytic study of the Lyle Kessler play and Alan J. Pakula film, *Orphans*, that wonderfully illustrates both the destructive and the reparative forms of sacrifice: the sacrifice of the other effected through identification with the superego and projective identification of split-off childhood pain into the scapegoat; and the integration and containment of childhood pain that liberates conscience, a healing capacity for sympathetic identification with the suffering of others and creative self-sacrifice on their behalf. As animals burdened with awareness of our finitude (we are all "dead end kids" after all), the only alternative to masochistic submission to death, or attempting to magically evade it by inflicting it upon others, is learning how to integrate dying into our living through creative self-sacrifice. As Eagleton (2010, p. 27) points out, it is through acquiring a capacity for self-dispossession in life that we become finally able to die.

If I had to summarise the essential argument of this book in one sentence it would be this. *It is important not to confuse conscience with either God or the superego, for people are often led by the superego and what they take to be God to act unconscionably.*

PART I

CLINICAL REALM

CHAPTER TWO

On the nature and varieties of guilt

... for here there is no place that does not see you. You must change your life.

—Rainer Maria Rilke, *Archaic Torso of Apollo*

At a roundtable (Carveth, Cavell, Eigen, Greenberg & Lewis, 2007) addressing the question "What is guilt?" at the Philoctetes Center for the Multidisciplinary Study of Imagination in New York, philosopher/psychoanalyst Marcia Cavell opened the discussion with the admission that "This awful subject has been on my mind for many years, beginning consciously, oh, some thirty years ago when my analyst said to me, 'If only you could feel the right *kind* of guilt!' I didn't know what she meant and I don't think I ever asked her what she meant, but I was deeply puzzled." Had she asked her analyst for clarification, I doubt she would have received a very illuminating answer, at least not one likely to satisfy a philosophic mind. In alluding to important distinctions between different types of guilt her analyst was, I suspect, operating more on intuition than reasoned understanding. From the beginning of the discipline, psychoanalysts have been as puzzled as Professor Cavell or anyone else in this area.

Defined legally, guilt is the state of having violated a law; defined morally, it is the state of having transgressed a moral norm. In either case, guilt entails the idea of a *debt* one is obliged to *repay*. Criminals who have completed their sentences are said to have "paid their debt" to society. In *The Genealogy of Morals* (Second Essay, "Guilt, Bad Conscience, and Related Matters"), Nietzsche (1887) writes: "Have these genealogists of morality up to now allowed themselves to dream, even remotely, that, for instance, that major moral principle 'guilt' [*Schuld*] derived its origin from the very materialistic idea 'debt' [*Schulden*]? Or that punishment developed as a *repayment* ...?"

It is not rare for people judged to *be* guilty not to *feel* guilty. And sometimes people *feel* guilty though no one (other than themselves, on some level of consciousness) has so judged them. There is no necessary coincidence between legal or moral guilt and psychological guilt. Discrepancies may arise for various reasons. For example, I may have been judged guilty, but I may believe myself to be innocent and therefore do not feel guilty. Or, I may have been judged guilty, but I may believe the laws or moral norms that have been applied are invalid or unjust. Sometimes I may judge myself guilty and feel guilty even though no one else has so judged me. This may be due to my feeling that the laws or norms by which others judge are too lax, or because others are not aware of my sins or crimes. When people feel guilty despite being unaware of having committed any crimes or sins, psychoanalysts suspect the existence of real or imagined transgressions that are repressed and unconscious to the ego, but not to the superego that is punishing them with (persecutory) guilt, nor to the conscience that is calling them to face their (depressive) guilt and make reparation. While some people feel guilt though unaware of any crimes, others are quite aware of their crimes yet appear to feel no guilt. It is commonly thought that psychopaths have no capacity to feel guilt. I will argue (Chapter Nine) they are merely skilled in the arts of silencing both superego and conscience.

Often people are unaware that they are feeling guilty, feeling something else instead. Freud (1930a) writes, "It is very conceivable that the sense of guilt ... is not perceived as such ... and remains to a large extent unconscious, or appears as a sort of *malaise*, a dissatisfaction, for which people seek other motivations" (pp. 135–136). Here Freud introduces us to the insufficiently appreciated idea of the *guilt-substitute*. From a psychoanalytic perspective, unconscious persecutory guilt may take the form of a wide range of such substitutes: anxiety states, hysterical and psychosomatic symptoms, depression, patterns of self-defeat and self-harm (masochism), among others—conditions that, on the surface, often appear to have nothing whatever to do with issues of morality and guilt. Such less recognised forms of guilt are discussed in Chapter Five.

As I argue in Chapter Four, Freud equated the unconscious need for punishment expressed in patterns of self-torment and self-sabotage with an unconscious sense of guilt that operates in people's lives without any accompanying consciousness of guilt. By equating guilt and self-punishment, Freud missed the opportunity to discriminate the two fundamentally different types of guilt that were subsequently distinguished by Melanie Klein and her followers: namely, *persecutory* guilt on the one hand, and *depressive* or *reparative* guilt on the other (Alford, 1989; Grinberg, 1964). If I injure someone and while he bleeds I self-flagellate, that is useless *persecutory* guilt; but if I put down my cat-o'-nine-tails and get busy bandaging, that is *reparative* guilt. Persecutory guilt is narcissistic; it is all about me. Depressive or reparative guilt reflects concern for the other. It is commonly heard today that guilt is a useless and harmful emotion that we should get rid of. But that applies only to persecutory guilt (in which I include shame), which is utterly narcissistic and irrelevant to the needs of the injured party. In reparative guilt we manage to get our minds off ourselves long enough to take note of the needs of the injured other and to seek to help repair the damage done. The unconscious need for punishment that Freud described as unconscious guilt is a manifestation of only one of the two main types of guilt: persecutory as distinct from depressive or reparative guilt.

Shame, depression, and masochism are forms of self-torment—aggression turned against the self. Though painful, they are narcissistic states, essentially asocial, reflecting a preoccupation with the self, its inadequacy and badness, and a relative lack of concern for the other. Though shaming performs useful controlling functions for the group since people will often conform in order to avoid these painful states, shame, depression, and masochism focus upon the self, not the other. In this they differ from what Klein (1948) called *depressive anxiety*, which Winnicott (1963) renamed the *capacity for concern*. Here one cares less about the self than about the damage one may have done to another and what one might yet be able to do to repair it. In contrast to such concern for the other, depression, masochism, and shame are self-centred, self-punitive, and asocial forms of persecutory guilt. Depressive *anxiety*, unlike clinical depression, reflects concern for the other; it is prosocial and generates reparative guilt leading to creative acts of apology, healing, and restitution for the hurt one has inflicted and the damage one has done.

Because he did not distinguish between these two types of guilt, when Freud (1930a) bemoaned the increasing burden of guilt accrued through repression of antisocial impulses owing to the need to preserve civilised order, such impulses then being turned against the self via the superego, he had only persecutory guilt in mind. Consequently, he was unable to see that while society certainly needs less persecutory guilt (i.e., superego), it needs much more reparative guilt (i.e., conscience). Without this distinction the rebel against the persecutory superego may wind up in revolt against conscience as well, a regressive phenomenon not unknown among, for example, the youth counterculture of the 1960s. Furthermore, the failure to distinguish these two types of guilt prevented Freud from recognising how persecutory guilt (self-punishment; superego) serves as a *defence* against or an *evasion* of the depressive guilt (conscience) leading to reparation. People may prefer to indulge for years in orgies of self-punishment brought about in a myriad of subtle and not-so-subtle ways rather than consciously own up to their faults, wrongdoing, sins, and crimes, confess, and repent through acts of genuine contrition and reparation.

As much psychopathology is grounded in unconscious guilt and self-punishment, the path of contrition is the way to mental and spiritual health. Although over a century and a half ago, this was understood by Kierkegaard (1849), it is still a truth rejected by mainstream psychiatry, psychology, and psychoanalysis which have been and still are committed to the de-moralisation and medicalisation of emotional disturbance—though occasional dissenting voices have been heard (Frattaroli, 2001, 2013; Szasz, 1961). Though many of those who have recognised the root of many forms of mental suffering in moral wrongdoing (the religious term for which is "sin") have been religious, there is in my view no need for religion in order to comprehend the moral dimension of emotional disturbance and the significant role of persecutory guilt in many, if not most, of its manifestations. In this matter I share the opinion of Sir Arthur C. Clarke: "One of the great tragedies of mankind is that morality has been hijacked by religion. So now people assume that religion and morality have a necessary connection. But the basis of morality is really very simple and doesn't require religion at all.

It's this: 'Don't do unto anybody else what you wouldn't like to be done to you.' It seems to me that that's all there is to it" (Matt, 1999).

In a 1915 letter to Putnam, Freud wrote: "I consider myself a very moral human being who can subscribe to Th. Vischer's excellent maxim: 'What is moral is self-evident'" (in Freud, E.L. [Ed.], 1961, p. 307). While many ordinary people, religious and irreligious alike, may conduct their lives according to what they take to be the self-evident values embodied in conscience, until recently they have enjoyed little support for this practice from what for many years has been the extreme social constructivism and moral relativism that have dominated social science in which morals are human creations constructed in radically different ways by different sociocultural groups. Even today such moral relativism is sometimes invoked to oppose judgement of, for example, forced clitoridectomy as practised in parts of Africa and the Middle East—though usually such relativism is not extended in any consistent fashion to such phenomena as rape and child murder in our own society, let alone to the moral perspective that morally condemns moral judgement.

Today such relativism has been relativised and the existence of a universal moral ethic is widely recognised, not just by the religious and by ordinary decent human beings in their private lives, but also by secular philosophers and social scientists. Despite wide variation in culturally specific folkways, mores, and laws, in one form or another the *Golden Rule* (ethic of charity or reciprocity) is universally recognised, though by no means universally practised: "Therefore all things whatsoever ye would that men should do to you, do ye even so to them: for this is the law and the prophets" (*Matthew* 7:12 *KJV*). Though formulated differently in different cultural and religious contexts and in different philosophical frameworks—*viz.*, the Kantian categorical imperative: "Act only according to that maxim whereby you can at the same time will that it should become a universal law" (Kant, 1785, p. 30)—in essence it is the same ethic. Your act is only justified if you are willing to live in a world where everyone acts this way, a world in which you are not a special case, where the same rules apply to you as to everyone else:

> Brahmanism: "This is the sum of Dharma [duty]: Do naught unto others which would cause you pain if done to you." *Mahabharata*, 5:1517; Buddhism: "Hurt not others in ways that you yourself would find hurtful." *Udana-Varga* 5:18; Confucianism: "Do not do to others what you do not want them to do to you." *Analects* 15:23;

Islam: "None of you [truly] believes until he wishes for his brother what he wishes for himself." Number 13 of Imam *Al-Nawawi's Forty Hadiths*; Judaism: "What is hateful to you, do not to your fellow man. This is the law: all the rest is commentary." *Talmud,* Shabbat 31a; Zoroastrianism: "Whatever is disagreeable to yourself do not do unto others." *Shayast-na-Shayast* 13:29. (*Shared Belief in the "Golden Rule" (a.k.a. Ethics of Reciprocity)*)

Social scientists influenced by George Herbert Mead (1934) view this universal ethic as grounded in the equally universal human capacity for empathic imagination of the experience of the other. According to Mead, the capacity to "take the role of the other" arises with symbolic functioning and is therefore universally human. There are no human groups without language and language is a system of shared symbols: I must know that the word I choose has substantially the same meaning for you as for me. I imaginatively put myself in your shoes, so to speak, in order to choose the signifier most likely to elicit the response I seek. It is this same capacity for "role-taking", a capacity more fundamental than the role-playing it allows, that generates the fundamental ideas of reciprocity, mutuality, fairness, and justice. In every playground in every culture and every historical period the words are heard in a myriad of different languages: "That's not fair! You had your turn, now it's mine!"

But it is entirely possible to recognise that it is the other's turn and just not give a damn—or insist the other had his turn bringing the sled up the hill so I can have mine going down. Language generates empathy not sympathy. For Kohut (1959) introspection and empathy are the data-gathering techniques that define the field of psychoanalysis. Self psychologists have often stressed that their empathic technique is not to be equated with sympathy and support. Beyond self psychology, empathy is widely seen as a primarily cognitive, data-gathering act of trial identification (Mead's "role-taking") in which one imagines oneself in the other's shoes, so to speak, so as to try to understand what he or she may be thinking, intending, wanting, and feeling. But coming to know how the other feels (empathic identification) is not at all the same thing as the sympathy (sympathetic identification) that moves beyond *knowing* to *caring* (in Chapter Eleven this distinction is illustrated through an analysis of the Lyle Kessler play and Alan J. Pakula film *Orphans*). The psychopath usually has a well-developed capacity for empathy that he employs to understand the minds of those he seeks to manipulate for his own ends. The sadist must empathise with his victims in order to enjoy their suffering. So for moral action to occur empathy is not enough. It is one thing to know that others suffer; quite another to care and desire to relieve their pain. Our patients are often rightly suspicious of our empathic technique for they know that empathy and caring are two quite different things. To move significantly beyond empathy to genuine sympathy and reparative action requires, as I will argue in Chapter Eleven, the integration and containment of one's childhood pain as opposed to splitting it off and inducing (projectively identifying) it into the other, the scapegoat.

Just as the universal ethic of reciprocity or charity is now commonly acknowledged so, as a result of secularisation in Western societies, it is widely believed that fundamental ethical values require no religious foundation. We do not need "god" in order to know right from wrong—unless we define knowing right and wrong as the essence of faith and conceive of "god" as a loving conscience. According to St. Paul, "He that loveth not knoweth not God; for God is love" (1 John 4:8 KJV). The idea that "god" is love, or that love is "god", is an equation to which few secular humanists are likely to strenuously object, despite preferring to drop the "god-talk" altogether, feeling that a loving conscience is "god" and good enough for them. This is an attitude with which I have long suspected Jesus might have sympathised, having advised us that "by their fruits ye shall know them" (Matthew 7:20 KJV)—unless he meant to include church attendance and pious proclamations among the fruits, which I very much doubt. In my view, and possibly that of the mature Dietrich Bonhoeffer (1951) who wrote in the Letters and Papers from Prison about "religionless Christianity", Jesus was less a "religious" man than a conscientious critic of religion, for which the religious had him tortured and crucified. In this connection it is worth noting the statement that, although unreferenced, is commonly attributed to Gandhi: "I like your Christ. I do not like your Christians. Your Christians are so unlike your Christ." In terms of the distinctions I have been developing, religion is aligned with the superego, while Jesus (like Gandhi, Schweitzer, Bonhoeffer, Martin Luther King, Mandela, and innumerable others from vastly differing cultural, religious, and irreligious traditions) are aligned with conscience. This is not to deny that sometimes religion and the superego may be conscientious, only that they are not necessarily so and in actuality often are not. In the final chapters I will argue that while religion is a matter of belief (the head), faith is a matter of love (the heart). Meaningful devotion to what one loves and holds sacred occurs in what Winnicott (1971) called the "transitional area", participation in which requires a "willing suspension" of *both* belief and disbelief.

At the heart of emotional suffering is guilt stemming not merely from wrongful acts, but also from antisocial wishes and emotions of hate, revenge, envy, greed, and lust. While it is important to distinguish feelings and actions the notion, commonly held by psychoanalysts, that guilt is justified only in relation to the latter is in my view unfounded. Though immoral acts merit substantially more guilt than immoral feelings, the truth is that feelings such as destructive envy and hate are judged to be wrong by both the conscience and the superego, though the former is more interested in constructively transcending them while the latter simply wants to punish. Since such feelings are rooted less in psychobiology than in childhood pain and phantasy they are analysable and potentially resolvable.

When repressed, such guilt generates the torments of the damned. When it becomes conscious it can be worked through in such a way that through repentance and reparation relative mental peace and well-being may sometimes be restored. On the other hand, the refusal to acknowledge guilt that leads to its repression precludes reparation and results instead in self-punishment. Such self-torment may be no more consciously recognised as such than the reasons for it. People in this situation do not consciously recognise that the pain they are suffering is self-inflicted, nor their reasons for inflicting it. They are, in the psychoanalytic sense, unconscious; out of touch or unacquainted with themselves; deeply in need of the sort of introduction to themselves provided by psychoanalytic therapy.

Since value judgement lies outside the means-end calculations that are the province of rationality, one cannot properly speak of rational or irrational moral judgement or guilt. Therefore, we need instead to distinguish guilt that is justified or valid from the standpoint of conscience from guilt inflicted by the superego that may not be justified at all in this sense. Here we begin to see the advantages to be derived from distinguishing conscience from superego. Freud himself, regrettably, chose to conflate them, making conscience a superego function. In this way, he deprived psychoanalysis of any basis for discrimination between guilt that is valid, merited, or justified by the standards of conscience, and guilt that is not.

The superego often inflicts guilt for wishes, feelings, and actions that by the standards of conscience (that is, the ethic of charity grounded in identification with the nurturer and the need to give back love for love received) one should not feel guilty about. If one feels guilt for having consensual, sexual intercourse with the partner one cherishes—and setting aside the possibility that the guilt derives not from the sex but from perverse phantasies accompanying it—then a puritanical superego is likely at work, a result of early socialisation and internalisation of standards one may now consciously reject. This is unjustified guilt inflicted not by conscience but by an anti-erotic superego. In order for change to occur, the anti-sexual attitudes must be rendered fully conscious, critically evaluated in terms of their origins and effects, and altered or transcended. Such superego modification (or, as I prefer, its disempowerment and displacement by conscience) may entail separation from and mourning of a "puritanical" internal object—though as Sagan (1988) has pointed out, the Puritans were actually not "puritanical" in regard to their ideas about sexuality in the context of marriage.

But by no means is all guilt unjustified. If the guilt arising from intercourse with one's partner is not due to a puritanical upbringing but arises from unconscious immoral wishes and phantasies then, to some degree, such guilt is justified by the standards of a loving conscience. But the superego often fails to distinguish wishes and phantasies from actions. While, for example, sadistic acts towards a loved object certainly merit guilt, wishes and phantasies that are not acted upon deserve much less, particularly to the degree that they find a sublimated outlet that may even enhance the object's as well as the subject's pleasure. Well-sublimated transgressive desire should be compatible with conscience, however much the superego, itself an essentially sado-masochistic structure, may be alert to opportunities to inflict pain even for thoroughly sublimated wishes and phantasies. Here is an instance of the perversity of the superego: it glories in sadistically punishing any evidence of sadism.

Some guilt is entirely justified. Our conscience informs us we have done wrong and deserve to feel guilty. Although our "culture of narcissism" (Lasch, 1979) has tended to regard all guilt as unjustified, useless, and therefore to be got rid of, the truth is that a capacity to bear and constructively deal with the guilt arising from wrongdoing and even from wrong feeling is a *sine qua non* of maturity and mental and spiritual health. We *should* feel such guilt; we *should* bear it; we *should* experience contrition; we *should* apologise; we *should* make reparation; we *should* seek to change in positive ways (repent) and seek therapeutic help if necessary to do so; and we *should* seek and accept forgiveness, provided our contrition and repentance are genuine.

But people often find the narcissistic injury entailed in admitting their faults unbearable. A few years ago I clipped out a letter to the editor from a local newspaper in which a woman reported she was unhappy with the quality of the values education her daughters were receiving in their local school. Though she had not been a churchgoer since her teens, she had been looking around for a Sunday school but was frustrated by the fact that, wherever she went, the priests, ministers, and pastors would always imply in their sermons that she was a sinner—and, she protested, she was not! I put that letter on file in the College library for my students, but I do not think many of them got the point. What is the point? One need not be "religious" to raise one's eyebrows at what, on the surface at least, appears to be moral obtuseness: anyone with any degree of developed conscience is likely to be more or less constantly aware of their myriad moral failures and shortcomings whether or not they employ the language of "sin" to describe them.

The inability to bear facing one's faults closes off the avenue of contrition and reparation. When the conscientious path is blocked in this way it seems the superego takes over and self-torment replaces reparative guilt and we flagellate the self instead of bandaging the injured other. It has been difficult for us to see this because Freud (1916d, 1920g, 1923b, 1924c and 1930a) equated guilt and self-punishment and failed to see that the latter often functions as a defence against the former, functioning essentially as a *guilt-substitute*, a consequence of the evasion of mature guilt. Grinberg (1964) called such narcissistic self-torment "persecutory guilt" (in which I include shame) and distinguished it from the "depressive guilt" that manifests a capacity for conscientious concern for the other. Such self-punishment may well be a response to genuine wrongdoing, but in failing to make reparation to the other and indulging instead in sadism towards the self, it entails further abuse of both the other and the self. Although shame serves important social control functions it is a form of persecutory as distinct from reparative guilt in that it is entirely narcissistic entailing little concern for the other. A crucial moment in emotional growth occurs when narcissistic subjects begin to feel ashamed of their inability to get their minds off themselves long enough to be able to experience genuine concern and guilt.

In addition to distinguishing justified and unjustified guilt, and self-punitive and reparative guilt, we must distinguish guilt that is conscious from guilt that has been rendered unconscious through repression and related defensive processes. While conscious guilt can be justified or unjustified by the standards of conscience, being conscious it is open to reality-testing and modification. If I find myself feeling guilty about something that my conscience tells me I need not feel guilty about, then I should stop feeling guilty. If my guilt does not subside then a deeper analysis is indicated. Perhaps my guilt really stems from another, unconscious source that truly merits guilt. Perhaps I have pleaded guilty to a lesser charge, telling myself my guilt stems from enjoying sex with my partner when, unconsciously, in phantasy, I have been enjoying sex with someone else's partner, or with incestuous objects, or objects opposite to my heterosexual or homosexual identification, etc. Here analysis and the making conscious of the deeper sources of the guilt are needed. Becoming conscious of these sources may permit modification and modulation of the hitherto repressed desires and phantasies or their sublimation, perhaps even their acceptance on the level of fantasy and play. According to Stoller (1979, 1985) and Kernberg (1991a, 1991b, 1993), exciting sexuality entails a transgressive element. Kernberg suggests that if a couple's sex life is not to deteriorate into boredom the puritanical superego of each must not be permitted to ally with and reinforce that of the other, both partners managing instead to contain and, in sublimated forms, play with the transgressive elements of their sexuality in order to form and maintain a lively sexual bond.

Conscious guilt that has been subject to reality-testing and found justified by the standards of conscience may lead to contrition, apology, and efforts at reparation. But if such guilt proves unbearable (most likely because it constitutes an unacceptable insult to narcissism) it will likely be repressed or projected. Because the superego knows all and is always on the lookout for an opportunity to inflict pain, the inevitable consequence of refusing to suffer conscious guilt is painful self-punishment inflicted by the superego—unless such punishment is instead inflicted via projection on a scapegoat. Guilt and the need for punishment should not be equated, since the latter serves as a defence against and substitute for the former when depressive guilt is found unbearable and repressed. When guilt is repressed the alleged sins or crimes that generate it are also unconscious and, hence, unavailable for critical evaluation by secondary process thinking. But if guilt and its grounds can be rendered conscious they become open to rational examination. It may turn out that the sins or crimes exist, at least in part, only in phantasy and not in reality. In becoming conscious, guilt can be subjected to reality-testing and its different types, origins, and functions can be discriminated. Morally unjustified guilt should be able to be transcended; if not, then its deeper sources need to be explored. Only when guilt is repressed will self-torment and/or scapegoating automatically take its place.

Vignette: Ms. A

Ms. A, whose father tended to lose interest in the older child in favour of the newborn, had benefited from this at the expense of her older siblings for five years when her sister was born and her father became enthralled with the baby. When the patient was eight, her three-year-old sister drowned. The parents barely spoke of the event. The father, who had always suffered from anxiety, never recovered from the loss and some years later suffered a paranoid psychotic breakdown. When a couple of years after her sister's death, when the patient was ten, she screamed at her younger brother "I hate you!", her narcissistic mother smugly and smilingly responded, "That is what you said to your sister the day she died." The patient had no memory of having said that to her sister but, now, the thought entered her mind that perhaps she had killed her. For years the patient punished herself by depriving and sabotaging herself in myriad ways. On becoming conscious of this in her analytic psychotherapy she recognised she was not responsible for the death and, consequently, became more able to defend herself against the sadistic superego that had been accusing her of murder. Her persecutory guilt diminished, but did not disappear. She had not killed her sister, only been partially gratified as well as devastated by her death. Only by facing and beginning to bear the depressive guilt arising from her jealousy and envy was she able to recover some of the loving feelings she had had for her sister and begin to be able to mourn. She and her siblings began to discuss placing a headstone on the unmarked grave.

The patient had at times half-believed that she had caused the drowning of her sister. But even when the omnipotent phantasy was analytically dispelled and the patient recognised that, in reality, she had had nothing to do with her sister's death, the guilt arising from her jealousy and envy remained. According to Juliet Mitchell (2000), where there are siblings "murder is in the air" (p. 20). Until Ms. A became able to bear the guilt arising from her sibling rivalry, and from her hatred of her narcissistic and at times sadistic mother, she continued to suffer from a wide range of inhibitions, symptoms, and anxieties. I am in no way implying that her hatred was in any way "primary" or a pure product of a death instinct or an aggressive drive, as its grounds in her family experience were quite evident. But only after she was finally able to recover her love for her sister was she able to begin to replace the persecutory guilt of unconscious self-punishment with depressive or reparative guilt and free herself from her pathological, talionic identification with her dead sibling. In repairing and restoring her damaged internal object she was able, through identification, to begin to repair and restore herself. In Chapter Six I hypothesise that it was precisely Harry Guntrip's inability to free himself in this way from his pathological identification with his dead brother Percy that was at the root of his chronic "exhaustion illness".

It seems that the guilty must suffer. Either we suffer consciously, bear our guilt, and strive to make reparation or, if we refuse, suffer myriad forms of self-punishment. Evasion of such self-punishment through projection and scapegoating leads only to deferred self-punishment, for the unconscious superego is aware of this deflection of responsibility and unconsciously ensures that we ultimately suffer for it. In my view, manifest appearances to the contrary, no one really gets away with anything. If jail is avoided, observe the hellish marriage, the hateful kids, the psychosomatic illness, the bizarre accidents ... and make sure to keep observing "unto the third and fourth generation" (*Numbers* 14:18 *KJV*). I say this not to affirm some notion of "karma" but simply to report that, based on my clinical psychoanalytic experience, people who from a superficial point of view appear to be getting away with their transgressions are, from a deeper, psychoanalytic standpoint, seen to be inevitably paying a price. In my view it is simply a fact that one will go on being tormented by the superego until one reconciles with one's conscience.

The apparent absence of conscience in some people is due to defences against it. The Athenians were not lacking in conscience, but merely restricted its application to their fellow citizens, excluding the slaves.

Nations make mass slaughter possible by dehumanising the enemy. In my view, even severe psychopaths have conscience (i.e., understand the Golden Rule, know right from wrong, and experience some desire to return love for love received), but it is deeply buried. Consciously they feel the rules apply only to the others, not themselves: *they* must be treated justly, others just do not count. Yet conscience exists; occasionally, perhaps in dreams, nightmares, or other forms of the return of the repressed, its smothered murmurings can faintly be heard emanating from the basement where it is bound and gagged. Without some minimal degree of maternal care a human being will not survive physically or be sufficiently psychologically functional to be able to do much harm. It follows that anyone who has survived childhood, learned language, and adapted sufficiently to be able to function socially to any degree, however antisocially, will have identified to some extent with the object or objects whose care has enabled such functioning. That is, such a person will have a degree of conscience, however minimally expressed, repressed, or defensively split off. Current tendencies to reify the concept of an entirely conscience-less "primary psychopath" (Meloy, 2007b) have evoked a range of critical responses (Carveth, 2007a; Watson, 2008; see Chapter Nine).

In addition to persecutory (self-punitive) and depressive (reparative) guilt, there are a range of other types: borrowed, defensive, survival, existential, induced, and collective guilt, each of which may, of course, be conscious or unconscious.

In *The Ego and the Id* Freud (1923b) states that the difficult analytic task of unmasking the repressed roots of the unconscious sense of guilt and rendering them conscious is occasionally made somewhat easier when the unconscious sense of guilt is a *borrowed* one—"when it is the product of an identification with some other person" (p. 50, fn.). Here we have a type of unjustified guilt stemming not from any wrongdoing on the part of the guilty subject but from his or her unconscious identification with the guilt of a significant other. Fernando (2000) argues that the child who develops a borrowed sense of guilt has usually been the target of externalisation on the part of a narcissistic parent who cannot bear to own it and who trains the child to accept it instead. The child's acceptance of the guilt as his own serves to defend against conscious perception of the badness of the significant other and eases fears of abandonment.

Borrowed guilt is not the only type of unjustified guilt that is defensive. Fairbairn (1943) was perhaps among the first to draw attention to what he called "the moral defence against bad objects" in which children blame themselves for their parents' deficiencies and wrongdoing:

> If the delinquent child is reluctant to admit that his parents are bad objects, he by no means displays equal reluctance to admit that he himself is bad. It becomes obvious, therefore, that the child would rather be bad himself than have bad objects; and accordingly we have some justification for surmising that one of his motives in becoming bad is to make his objects "good". In becoming bad he is really taking upon himself the burden of badness which appears to reside in his objects. By this means he seeks to purge them of their badness …. (p. 65)

"They would love me if I weren't bad." The moral defence preserves the child's omnipotence, warding off the unbearable recognition of helplessness. Guilt after trauma entails an attempt to reduce helplessness: the idea that one could have prevented it may be preferable to the idea that the traumatic events were random and senseless. The moral defence also serves to preserve the needed tie to the loved objects by shifting the blame from the object to the self. In the tradition of "Modern Psychoanalysis" (Spotnitz & Meadow, 1976) this is known as the narcissistic defence.

Although in his review of the literature on borrowed guilt Fernando (2000) does not include Fairbairn's (1943) contribution, the phenomena they describe are related. But whereas the borrowed guilt arising from externalisation by a narcissistic parent entails the child's identification with the parent's guilt, in Fairbairn's moral defence (Spotnitz's narcissistic defence) the child does not identify with the parent's guilt; instead he absolves the parent and blames himself. If the parent is unloving the child does not accuse himself of being unloving but of being unlovable. It is true that in both cases the child ends up accusing himself of being bad in order not to have to see the parent as bad, but different dynamics underlie this common outcome.

To feel guilt and a need for punishment for surviving would appear to be entirely irrational and unjustified. Certainly magical thinking that fails to distinguish thoughts or words from actual deeds is often involved. Waylon Jennings is said to have suffered lifelong survivor guilt because he gave another musician his seat on a plane that subsequently crashed, killing his friend Buddy Holly and everyone else aboard. At the time, Holly had quipped, "I hope your old bus breaks down," to which Jennings replied "And I hope your plane crashes," a remark said to have haunted him for the rest of his life (M. Gray, n.d.). Aristotle is reputed to have defined luck as the arrow hitting the person next to you. Unfortunately, such luck often comes at a high cost in survivor guilt. Sometimes this arises from simple relief that it was another who suffered instead of oneself. Sometimes it is connected to related feelings of triumph. Sometimes it arises in connection with unconscious death wishes one may have harboured towards those who did not survive, leading to the feeling that one has murdered them. Sometimes, upon analysis, it emerges that the guilt is connected to what one may have actually done in order to survive, not just to what one felt like doing, or imagined having done.

Kierkegaard (1849; R. May, 1950, Chapter Two) drew our attention to two types of existential guilt that are universal, unavoidable, and not in themselves neurotic. They entail a kind of catch-22. On one hand, there is the guilt arising from our failure to develop our potentials; on the other, the guilt precisely for doing so. Self-development involves disruption of a pre-existing equilibrium and this can entail a kind of betrayal of older relational covenants. If we do not grow we fail ourselves; if we do we risk failing others. Hence existential guilt, like the existential anxiety that accompanies our freedom, is unavoidable; neither are in themselves neurotic. For Kierkegaard, much neurotic guilt and anxiety arise from our evasion of the existential guilt and anxiety that are simply a part of the human condition but which, nevertheless, we often refuse to bear.

Freud himself draws our attention to another source of inevitable and, in this sense, existential guilt: that arising from the primordial and inextinguishable ambivalence which characterises all human relations that reach any depth—with, Freud (1921c) insists, "the solitary exception of the relation of a mother to her son" (p. 100), an odd expression of his personal psychology to be examined more closely in the next chapter. The point is that wherever we love, we also hate, something that is hardly surprising given the fact that, as Eagleton (2010) points out, "[L]ove is a laborious process which requires a perilous risking of ourselves" (p. 34). But Eagleton points to yet another, perhaps the most primordial type of existential guilt: "to be implicated in a calamity without having done wrong" (pp. 34–35). For Theodor Adorno, "If we ... knew at every moment what has happened and to what concatenations we owe our own existence, and how our own existence is interwoven with calamity, even if we have done nothing wrong ... if one were fully aware of all things at every moment, one would really be unable to live" (Adorno as quoted by Eagleton, 2010, p. 34).

No wonder analytic work is difficult for we are in the business of helping people transform "hysterical misery into common unhappiness" (Freud, in Breuer & Freud, 1893–95, p. 304), that is, into the existential pain, refusal of which resulted in the neurosis in the first place. Wilfred Bion (1962) elaborated on this existential element in Freud's work. The Symingtons (1996) describe his attitude as follows: "The phenomenon of someone moving from evading pain to acceptance of suffering is in direct opposition to the pleasure principle. Yet this movement is quite central to Bion's theory of development. ... He says that the crucial determinant in mental growth is whether the individual 'decides' to evade frustration or to tolerate it" (p. 6).

In *The Genealogy of Morals*, Nietzsche (1887) drew attention to what he called "the will to power of the weak".

> That lambs dislike great birds of prey does not seem strange: only it gives no ground for reproaching those birds of prey for bearing off little lambs. And if the lambs say among themselves: "these birds of prey are evil; and whoever is least like a bird of prey, but rather its opposite, a lamb—would he not be good?"—there is no reason to find fault with this institution of an ideal, except perhaps that the birds of prey might view it a little ironically and say: "*we* don't dislike them at all, these good little lambs; we even love them; nothing is more tasty than a tender lamb." (Nietzsche, 1887, First Essay, 13)

In direct battle with the strong, the weak will lose. But if the weak invent a morality in which strength is evil—"Blessed are the meek: for they shall inherit the earth" (*Matthew* 5:5 *KJV*)—and induce their enemies to believe it, the strong will fall on their own swords. According to Shakespeare, "Conscience [read superego] doth make cowards of us all" (*Hamlet*, Act III, scene 1). Hence, one motive for inducing guilt in others is to undermine their self-respect and so disempower and control them.

It is common for people tormented by guilt to employ interpersonal projective identification (Bion, 1962; Sandler, 1987) or emotional contagion (Spotnitz & Meadow, 1976) to induce their guilt in others. Sometimes this is done merely to evacuate unbearable guilt. At other times it serves as a communication in the service of being understood. Sometimes guilt is induced in the hope that the other may be able to contain and detoxify it and return it in a symbolically processed form leading to understanding and transformation (Bion, 1962). As noted above, sometimes people suffering from unbearable guilt inflicted by a harsh superego defend themselves by identifying with the superego and developing what Racker (1957) called a "mania for reproaching" (p. 141). Instead of owning their sins, they become the righteous punishers of sinners, projecting the latter role onto scapegoats who may be rendered more easily dominated and controlled through guilt induction.

Karl Jaspers (1947), writing immediately after World War II on *The Question of German Guilt*, argues that "Every human being is fated to be enmeshed in the power relations he lives by. This is the inevitable guilt of all, the guilt of human existence. It is counteracted by supporting the power that achieves what is right, the rights of man" (p. 34). Jaspers goes on to conclude that:

> Every German is made to share the blame for the crimes committed in the name of the Reich. We are collectively liable. The question is in what sense each of us must feel co-responsible. Certainly in the political sense of the joint liability of all citizens for acts committed by their state—but for that reason not necessarily also in the moral sense of actual or intellectual participation in crime. Are we Germans to be held liable for outrages which Germans inflicted on us, or from which we were saved by a miracle? Yes—inasmuch as we allowed such a regime to rise among us. No—insofar as many of us in our deepest hearts opposed all this evil and have no morally guilty acts or inner motivations to admit. To hold liable does not mean to hold morally guilty. (p. 61)

Jaspers is not writing about *guilt-feeling* but about *objective guilt*—that is, about guilt that by the standards of conscience we *should* be feeling, whether or not we actually do. Above and beyond the guilt due to our personal wrongdoings and failures of *response-ability* is that arising from the misdeeds of our communities. Sometimes the latter is misplaced from the collective to the personal domain. For C. Wright Mills (1959) the sociological imagination entails recognising the degree to which personal troubles may be manifestations of public issues. I believe there exists in Western society a kind of free-floating guilt, more or less unconscious, that we tend to attribute to our failings as individuals but that also has to do with collective wrongs—such as the fact that those of us in the West who enjoy some degree of material security do so on the basis of unconscionable capitalist exploitation of the poor both at home and abroad, not to mention our ongoing mutual commodification due to the market relations in which we are enmeshed.

CHAPTER THREE

Conscience *vs.* superego and the bestialising of the id

In his neglected classic, *Freud, Women and Morality: The Psychology of Good and Evil*, the psychoanalytic sociologist Eli Sagan (1988) elaborated a theory of conscience and superego as distinct psychic functions developing in different ways and at different times. Whereas Freud (1933a, p. 65) viewed conscience as one of the three functions of the superego (the others being self-observation and maintenance of the ego ideal) and saw it as arising at around five or six years of age with the shattering of the Oedipus complex due to fear of castration by the rival, Sagan posited a pre-Oedipal origin of conscience grounded in the infant's love for and identification with the primary nurturer. For Sagan, conscience and superego frequently conflict. As we have seen, he cites Mark Twain's (1885). *The Adventures of Huckleberry Finn* to illustrate his point: "Huck's dilemma" is that while his conscience requires him to protect his beloved runaway slave companion, Jim, the racist superego he has internalised from his culture demands that he turn him in to the authorities. After an agonising mental struggle, Huck finally comes to accept that he is "going to hell" and defies his punitive superego in favour of his loving conscience. From this example alone, we may suspect that while often associated with divinity, the superego that threatens "hell-fire" may more accurately be viewed as demonic and the conscience as the opposing power of love—as *Thanatos* and *Eros* respectively. As Paul Gray (1994, p. 110) pointed out, Freud (1920g) himself characterised certain types of severe resistance as having a "hint of daemonic power" (p. 36), even referring to a superego that can at times amount to "a pure culture of the death instinct" (Freud, 1923b, p. 53). Erikson (1958) described the scrupulosity driven by the overweening superego of *Young Man Luther* that led him through a series of crises to the final, liberating "revelation in the Tower": that we are justified not by works intended to satisfy the demands of the law (superego), but by faith in the forgiving power of love (conscience).

It was not until relatively late in his work that Freud turned his attention from the "lower" to the "higher" mental faculties—from his early preoccupation with the drives, to the ego, and finally the superego. In advancing from id to ego psychology, he introduced the concept of the ego ideal and later that of the superego, both concepts addressing the moral function but in different ways. Whereas the ego ideal as "the substitute for the lost narcissism of his childhood in which he was his own ideal" (Freud, 1914c, p. 94) generates the desire to think well of oneself by living up to valued ideals, the superego as "heir to the Oedipus complex" (Freud, 1923b, p. 48) is more about punishment for failure to do so and for unacceptable sexual and aggressive wishes and actions. Its standards are internalised from the wider culture via the parents and its punitiveness is driven by id aggression turned away from the Oedipal rival under the threat of castration and back against the ego.

Freud finally subsumed the ego ideal within his concept of the superego and increasingly emphasised the latter's punitiveness, especially as manifested in the moral masochism of those who turn its sadism upon themselves, a view that dominated psychoanalytic thinking for many years. Eventually Schafer (1960) advanced the idea of a "loving and beloved superego" and Furer (1967) posited its role as a comforter, views quite distinct from Freud's consistent emphasis upon its cruelty. Despite certain promising beginnings (Spitz, 1958), Freudian ego psychology failed to posit a conscience originating in the pre-Oedipal phase, separate and distinct from the superego that Freud viewed as coming into existence at around age five or six when the Oedipus complex "is literally smashed to pieces by the shock of threatened castration" (Freud, 1925j, p. 257).

Although Klein is not central to Sagan's theorising, her work supports his general argument. Kleinians have long distinguished persecutory guilt, which amounts to self-torment, from depressive guilt which instead of being all about the self (as in shame and self persecution) is about caring for and making reparation to the other. The dating of the move from the paranoid-schizoid and narcissistic position into the depressive position and "the capacity for concern" (Winnicott, 1963) is controversial, but there is no doubt that conscience, as depressive position concern for the other, arises far earlier than the Freudian superego. As Sagan pointed out, it has long been difficult to comprehend how a mental function (the superego) formed from aggression turned back against the self under the threat of castration and operating in Freud's (1930a) words "like a garrison in a conquered city" (p. 123) could be the seat of conscientious concern for others.

Though increasingly emphasising its destructive and irrational potentials, even referring to a superego that can at times amount to "a pure culture of the death instinct" (Freud, 1923b, p. 53), Freud nonetheless tended to associate morality with the superego and immorality with the id. He never quite clearly grasped the fact that in order to be truly moral and to really grow up we must overcome the immoral morality of the merely conventional (often racist, sexist, heterosexist, classist, childist, etc.), authoritarian, and tyrannical superego. If, like Huckleberry Finn, we overcome the punitive and immoral superego at all, we do so by listening and responding instead to the humane and loving voice of conscience.

Freud, of course, was not entirely blind to these issues. In *Group Psychology and the Analysis of the Ego* (1921c) he wrote of the destructive consequences that often follow when the individual puts a group leader in the place of the superego. (a point later confirmed experimentally in Milgram's (1963) classic studies on obedience.) Here Freud views the superego of the individual as a conscience capable of resisting both authority and the sadism of the id, but one that is prone to being usurped by a superego offered by a group or its leader. Regrettably, he failed to fully appreciate and elaborate upon the significance of this distinction. Given his theory of the origin of the superego in internalisation of the culture and identification with the castrating Oedipal rival, he could only have viewed such internal moral conflict as a matter of one internalised superego conflicting with another. Without any concept of a conscience, a moral compass, grounded in our earliest experiences of attachment and love apart from and capable of opposing both early aggressive impulses and later social internalisations, we are left with moral relativism: moral conflict is a matter of competing internalised value orientations in the absence of any other authority to which to appeal.

Psychoanalysts naïvely committed to rationalism are unlikely to grasp the problem here. They imagine a simple appeal to reason will sort it out. But reason can only describe but not resolve *ultimate* moral conflicts. It can only appear to do so if and when an ultimate value can be shown to be *penultimate*. For example, the apparent value judgement, "It is good to stop smoking" can be turned into a penultimate effectiveness statement: it is good to stop smoking because that promotes health. But this just moves the problem back a step: why is it good to be healthy? Answer: because greater health is likely to lead to a longer life. But why is it good to live a longer life? Answer: because life is better than death. Why? Answer: *it just is*. Here we have the *ultimate* value judgement which can no longer be deferred. Reason is of no help with such judgements. One cannot reason with people who disagree with one about such fundamental matters; one can only seek to convert, silence, or eliminate them, or be converted, silenced, or eliminated by them, or agree to disagree. Here one is reminded of Freud's (1915a, p. 164) story of the terminally ill godless insurance man whose family sent a minister to attempt a deathbed conversion: the insurance man remained godless but the minister left well insured.

In *Civilization and Its Discontents*, Freud (1930a) emphasised the prosocial role of the superego in preserving social order by inhibiting and turning our aggression against ourselves, leading to a build-up of punitive guilt (which he does not distinguish from depressive or reparative guilt and concern) and our growing discontent in civilisation. While Freud himself explained the formation of the superego as entailing identification with the hated and feared, as well as loved, Oedipal rival, such that one now turns rivalrous aggression back against the self, beating the self as if one were the rival, Anna Freud (1936, pp. 109–121) named this process "identification with the aggressor". We have not always devoted enough attention to the common variant of this mechanism in which we seek to escape being the target of the critical superego by defensively identifying with it, projecting the guilty self onto another, the scapegoat. Because of the tendency to view the superego as a prosocial force it has not always been easy to keep in focus its antisocial manifestations, such as that in which to escape being reproached and punished by the superego we *become* it and reproach and punish others, making the lives of the scapegoats onto whom the guilty self is projected a living Hell, all in the name of ideals, ethics, and the law. The novelist John Connolly (2001) captures this dynamic in his description of the Reverend Faulkner, a serial killer, who claims, "I have nothing to answer for. The Lord did not send demons to kill the firstborn of Egypt … he sent angels. We were angels engaged in the Lord's work, harvesting the sinners" (p. 426). Hantman (2008) describes this process as a central aspect of the psychology of the "normopath" who can become psychopathic in his or her persecution of unconventional and deviant others.

To draw attention to the neglected immorality and destructiveness of the normative, not just the abnormal, superego, Sagan pointed to Robert Jay Lifton's important study (1986) of *The Nazi Doctors* who, for the most part, appear to have been more normopathic than severely psychopathic. In Sagan's words, they were "profoundly corrupt but nevertheless dedicated and idealistic people" (p. 11), severely misguided ideologues who thought of the death camps as a necessary element in a project of public health that, like surgery, aimed to eliminate diseased parts that threatened the health of the whole: they did their work, as Sagan would say, "under the banner of the superego", as did those who laboured in "the killing fields" under the Khmer Rouge, and as do most terrorists. Sagan writes: "One cannot read Lifton's book without being profoundly aware that we are not involved here with the psychological process of rationalisation, wherein a person who wishes to perform sadistic acts and cannot admit to that desire invents a reasonable explanation for his actions. … Without an ideology that they were performing a moral action—without the superego—the whole extermination process would have been impossible" (p. 11). Though we would prefer and our theory has inclined us to think of them as sadistic, id-driven psychopaths, Lifton (1986) describes their ordinariness: "Neither brilliant nor stupid, neither inherently evil nor particularly ethically sensitive, they were by no means the demonic figures—sadistic, fanatic, lusting to kill—people have often thought them to be" (p. 5). In response to this unwanted finding a survivor friend of Lifton's remarked: "But it is *demonic* that they were *not* demonic" (p. 5). In this connection we are moved to ask, were demons responsible for the fire-bombing of Dresden or for dropping a first atom bomb on Hiroshima, then a second on Nagasaki, without giving the Japanese a prior opportunity to witness a test? Or were they too, like the Nazi doctors, doing their work "under the banner of the superego"? Chris Hedges (2012b) writes:

> On this day [Monday, August 6] in 1945 the United States demonstrated that it was as morally bankrupt as the Nazi machine it had recently vanquished and the Soviet regime with which it was allied. Over Hiroshima, and three days later over Nagasaki, it exploded an atomic device that was the most efficient weapon of genocide in human history. The blast killed tens of thousands of men, women and children. It was an act of mass annihilation that was strategically and militarily indefensible. The Japanese had been on the verge of surrender. Hiroshima and Nagasaki had no military significance. It was a war crime for which no one was ever tried. The explosions, which marked the culmination of three centuries of physics, signalled the ascendancy of the technician and scientist as our most potent agents of death.

While sadism and dreams of erotic reward stemming from the id may play a part, the terrorist is most often driven by an authoritarian superego that entirely overpowers conscience. Since the superego is fuelled by the drives as well as by internalised values and ideologies, there is no denying the influence of the id in its operations. Just as there is a scale of differing degrees of psychopathy (Hare, 2003), no doubt there exists a continuum or "complemental series" (Freud, 1916–17, p. 361) ranging between the two poles of ideologically driven and psychopathically driven destructiveness. In contrast to the fanatical ideologues around him, Hitler himself was more psychopathically pragmatic. Metaxas (2010) writes: "Since Hitler had no religion other than himself, his opposition to Christianity and the church was less ideological than practical. That was not the case for many leaders of the Third Reich. Alfred Rosenberg, Martin Bormann, Heinrich Himmler, Reinhard Heydrich, and others were bitterly anti-Christian and were ideologically opposed to Christianity, and wanted to replace it with a religion of their own devising" (p. 169), a savagely anti-Christian blend of the old Germanic paganism, occultism, racism and a decadent will to power. This is not to say that Hitler had no ideology, or that the ideologues around him had no psychopathy. It is merely to argue that the ingredients that go into the witches' brew of extreme human destructiveness vary in quantities and proportions. Psychoanalysts have tended to emphasise the role of the drives and ignore the role of values, ideals, and ideologies in the constitution of evil. This is because Freud tended to associate human destructiveness with the "beast" in us (the somatically rooted drives of the id), rather than with what is uniquely human about us (ego and superego), despite the fact that the beasts are never really beastly, only humans are.

* * *

In "The Uniqueness of Man", Sir Julian Huxley (1941) argued that now that the battle waged on behalf of Darwin by his grandfather, Thomas Henry Huxley, had been won, we could afford to turn our attention to what a unique and truly bizarre kind of animal we are, both biologically and psychologically. It is my experience that, today, any mention of this line of thought, any stress on the discontinuity between humanity and the rest of nature, any emphasis upon our uniquely symbolic consciousness, is likely to bring down on one's head a chorus of criticism of the supposed arrogant anthropocentrism entailed in any such claim and its blindness to humanity's ecological destructiveness. Such critics generally fail to realise they themselves are now making the case for "the uniqueness of man": the uniquely destructive consequences for both human beings and their ecosystems that follow from our relative freedom from the instinctual controls and biological determinants governing the behaviour of other species.

We seem reluctant to recognise the uniqueness of our destructiveness. We like to think of it as "inhuman" when, regrettably, it is one of the things most characteristically human about us. We engage in massive projection of this uniquely human destructiveness on to animals that, unlike us, mostly fight and kill to survive and protect their young, not to impose their favoured abstract ideologies upon one another, nor to amass great wealth while impoverishing others, nor to enjoy sadistic pleasure. The latter requires the uniquely human capacity for empathy, by which I do not mean sympathy but the purely cognitive capacity for what George Mead (1934) called "taking the role of the other"— imagining oneself in the other's shoes, as it were. Without this capacity the sadist would be unable to enjoy the other's pain or humiliation. Empathy and sympathy are two quite different things. People say, "But my cat is sadistic! Look at how it tortures and toys with the mouse it has captured!" But take away the mouse and substitute a crumpled bit of paper and the cat will do the same thing. It enjoys batting around the mouse or the ball of paper, but not because it attributes suffering to either. Sadism is a uniquely human capacity that we prefer to think of as "inhuman".

Look at our everyday language. I will try to be gender inclusive.

> "He's a real animal!"
> "She's a parasite."
> "He's a leech."
> "She's a bitch."
> "He's a snake in the grass."
> "She's a bloodsucker."
> "His behaviour was beastly."
> "She's a cow."
> "He's a dirty dog."
> "She's a vulture."
> "He's a total rat."
> "She's a vixen."
> "He's a pig."
> "She's a black widow."
> "He's a cockroach."

Then there are the famous human "monsters" we "bestialise":

> "Julius Streicher: the Beast of Franconia"
> "Ilse Koch: the Beast (Witch, Bitch) of Buchenwald"
> "Clifford Olsen: the Beast of British Columbia"
> "Ilsa: She-Wolf of the SS"

Freud (1930a) too engages in such projection and it seriously derails his thinking about human destructiveness and our discontent in civilisation: "Men are not gentle creatures who want to be loved, and who at the most can defend themselves if they are attacked; they are, on the contrary, creatures among whose instinctual endowments is to be reckoned a powerful share of aggressiveness. ... *Homo homini lupus*" (p. 110)—"Man is a wolf to man" (Plautus). He goes on to say that all this "reveals man as a savage beast to whom consideration towards his own kind is something alien" (p. 111). Naturally, I am in no way disputing the fact of the human aggressiveness, destructiveness, and sadism to which Freud calls our attention, only his characterisation of it as bestial or animalistic, when it is obvious that animals themselves do not behave in these ways, only humans do. Freud and we are engaged in projection onto animals of the dark, uniquely human traits we do not wish to acknowledge in ourselves.

Such projection led Freud to argue that our raw passions of sex and aggression arise from biological, somatic sources—from our animal bodies. He resorts to a biological rather than a psychological or existential conception of human passion. It is common to blame Freud's "apparent" reductionism and biologism on James Strachey's mistranslation of Freud's *Trieb* by the English term "instinct" instead of "drive". It is true that the *Triebe* or drives differ from animal instincts in being far more open to learning and social influences in their aims and objects, which can be displaced, reversed, etc., and are to a considerable extent acquired rather than biologically fixed or pre-programmed. (I will not belabour the point that the concept of instinct as a biologically fixed and pre-programmed force is controversial even insofar as lower animal life is concerned.) But translation issues aside, in "Instincts and Their Vicissitudes" Freud (1915c) insists the drives arise from a *somatic* source—not the brain but a bodily zone—despite his admission that he could never specify the precise somatic source of the aggressive drive. This should have caused him to question his whole concept of the drive as "a concept on the frontier between the mental and the somatic, as the psychical representative of the stimuli originating from within the organism and reaching the mind, as a measure of the demand made upon the mind for work in consequence of its connection with the body" (Freud, 1915c, pp. 121–122).

We are left with Freud's mind/body dualism. As we have seen, from Plato he borrows the metaphor of the rider and the horse. Reason (ego) and morality (superego) constitute for Freud the human rider who must attempt to guide the powerful horse, the beast (id) upon which we are precariously perched. While the image is vivid and evocative of our profound sense of conflict, it is ultimately misleading. As I have indicated, I consider the structural model of id, ego, and superego invaluable, especially when supplemented by a fourth structure, the conscience. The problem is not with the id conceived as a repository of human, sexual, and aggressive "passions". The problem is only the conception of the human passions of sex and aggression as somatically-based drives. For our sexual and aggressive passions do not in fact "bubble up" from our animal bodies but "trickle down" from our uniquely human minds. As both Sartre (1943) and Erikson (1950) recognised, human passions do not arise from the body; rather, human beings employ their bodies as means to the end of sexual and aggressive and other forms of self-expression. Freud thought of our sexuality as originating in the body and finding expression in the mind when the reverse is true: human sexuality originates primarily in the symbol-making mind that generates the conscious and unconscious images, fantasies, and scenarios that constitute the human erotic imagination (Stoller, 1985). This latter view is far more in keeping than the former with the hermeneutic, clinical psychoanalytic exploration of the stories, the meaning-laden narratives, of which human sexuality is comprised.

Not only does Freud reduce meaning-laden human sexuality to something originating in a bodily zone, at least in his metapsychology as distinct from his clinical psychology he reduces the multi-channel universe of human motivation to the two channels of sex and aggression and their various combinations. Friendship, for example, becomes sublimated sexuality, while sexuality itself always remains the source and is seldom itself seen as a sublimated or disguised manifestation of something else, such as will to power, or a manifestation of a desperate effort to hold oneself together in the face of fragmentation. Sexual driven-ness is metapsychologically understood as a manifestation of drive, while clinically we know it often amounts to a manic defence, an attempt to employ sexual excitement to ward off unbearable feelings of depression, guilt, anxiety, emptiness, or fragmentation—or to what Kohut (1977) called a "disintegration product", a turning to sexuality or aggression in the face of the absence or failure of a good, containing human connection. Although unreferenced by Kohut, this understanding had been achieved decades earlier by Fairbairn (1941) who wrote: "Autoerotism is essentially a technique whereby the individual seeks not only to provide for himself what he cannot obtain from the object, but to provide for himself an object which he cannot obtain" (p. 34). If psychoanalysis has whitewashed the superego, it has bestialised and blackened the id. Despite Freud's (1900a) early discovery of order and meaning in what he would later call the id, the strange logic, structure, lawfulness, and creativity of the primary process, the evolution of his later ego psychology with its mind/body dualism led him to associate all human order and meaning with ego and superego and to reduce the id to "a chaos, a cauldron of seething excitations" (Freud, 1933a, p. 73).

In Burston's (2007) view, it was Erikson's deep, filial loyalty to Sigmund Freud, not so much to his daughter Anna who had trained him, that caused him to downplay and even obscure the depth of his revisionist departures from Freudian, ego psychological ortho-doxy. In extending Freud's stages of epigenetic development through adolescence, youth, young adulthood, the middle years to old age, Erikson implied a far greater capacity for development and change beyond childhood than Freud acknowledged. In addition to signifi-cantly broadening and moralising the conceptualisation of the conflicts and crises of each stage, for Erikson the bodily zones that for Freud were the *sources* of the drives became instead simply *vehicles* for vary-ing modes of human relatedness. All in all, despite his deep respect for the master, Erikson was in fundamental disagreement with what he described as Freud's "centaur model of man" as a creature half beast and half human:

> The id Freud considered to be the oldest province of the mind, both in individual terms—for he held the young baby to be "all id"—and in phylogenetic terms, for the id is the deposition in us of the whole of evolutionary history. The id is everything that is left of our organisation of the responses of the amoeba and of the impulses of the ape, of the blind spasms of our intra-uterine exist-ence, and of the needs of our postnatal days—everything which would make us "mere creatures." The name "id," of course, des-ignates the assumption that the "ego" finds itself attached to this impersonal, this bestial layer like the centaur to his equestrian underpinnings: only that the ego considers such a combination a danger and an imposition, whereas the centaur makes the most of it. (Erikson, 1950, p. 192)

Agreeing with Erikson's characterisation of the Freudian view, Guntrip (1971) regards the theory as "astonishing and unrealistic, in its assump-tion that human nature is made up, by evolutionary 'layering,' of an ine-radicable dualism of two mutually hostile elements" (p. 50). Erikson's critique of Freud's conception of the fundamental human conflict as one between the forces of nature and those of culture, his view of our sociality as something not in itself biologically grounded but rather superimposed upon our biology, and his projection of our distinctively and perversely human aggression onto the "beast", was presented with such discretion and politeness that it never had the impact on the field that it deserved.

Freud himself may have begun to recognise some of the problems with his psychobiology when in 1920 he finally, though implicitly rather than explicitly, broke with Darwin and his own earlier drive theory and resituated psychoanalytic theory on the basis of a new Greek dualism that echoed the work of his pre-Socratic precursor Empedocles for whom all of reality reflects the struggle between *philia* (love) and *neikos* (strife). The fact that Freud chose to give capitalised Greek names to his two new forces, *Eros* and *Thanatos*, is an indication that he was moving far beyond his earlier biological reductionism, subsuming the earlier sexual drive in a far wider "principle" of life, integration, and connectedness, while counterposing this to the utterly un-Darwinian notion of a "drive" towards death.

This is not the place to trace Freud's own and his follower's struggles to interpret in shifting ways the meaning of *Thanatos* (see Chapter Nine). Nor to explore the pessimistic consequences for social theory of Freud's biologising of human passion: if our antisocial passions are biologically given and hence ineradicable, then the perpetual conflict between civilisation and human nature that Freud describes is unsurpassable. For Sagan (1988), the notion of a fundamental conflict between civilisation and our drives is difficult to credit given the fact that for Freud all the energy belongs to the drives; from what source could civilisation derive the power to oppose them? Freud's answer, of course, is from the drives themselves, especially the aggressive drive that, turned against the self, takes the form precisely of an anti-sexual and anti-aggressive superego that aggressively opposes and punishes sexuality and aggression. But even if we find Freud's answer more plausible than does Sagan, we may still appreciate the latter's raising the psychoanalytic question: what, on a deeper level, is Freud really talking about? Beneath the manifest story of a frustrating civilisation demanding instinctual renunciation and engendering in us resentment and discontent, Sagan discerns the latent image of our first boss, first tyrant, first oppressor: the pre-Oedipal mother who, in the other of her split incarnations, is our first nurturer, rescuer, soother—figures underrepresented for many years in Freudian discourse due to its flight from mother to father, from the pre-Oedipal (mere foreplay) to the Oedipal (the main event).

In an early paper (Carveth, 1984a) I pointed out that "… our attitude toward the … the Hobbesian problem concerning the conflict between the individual and the social order, may itself, like all other human attitudes, have been significantly influenced all along by unconscious phantasy" (p. 87):

> On the oral level and in a positive mode society may be seen in terms of the displaced imago of the good mother of infancy, the Madonna who feeds, nurtures and provides that symbiotic union that vanquishes all spectres of anxious solitude; whereas in the negative mode it takes on the character of the destructive mother image, the menacing witch who threatens to smother, swallow, starve or poison. On the anal level and in a positive mode society may appear as the sympathetic other who receives and applauds our earliest gifts and creations; whereas in a negative mode it is the rigid taskmaster who expects the impossible, sadistically imposes incomprehensible demands and shames us when we fail to meet them, who dominates and overwhelms our incipient autonomy and to whom we either submit with sullen resentment or resist with stubborn retention and angry expulsion. Finally, on the phallic-oedipal level, society may be experienced as the oedipal parent whom we secretly long to possess but whom, out of guilt and anxiety arising from this forbidden wish and anticipation of its punishment by the rival, we must resist and reject. Although in a positive mode social adjustment may represent fulfilment of the oedipal wish to possess and be possessed, a person's hostile and anxious sensitivity to the possibility of being dominated, trapped and emasculated by the social order may reflect his fear of the consequences of such an incestuous consummation. The metaphor of socialisation as a bed of Procrustes is all too suggestive of castration. (p. 88)

In the hands of Melanie Klein and her followers our fundamental conflict is seen not to be between mind and body, civilisation and drive, but between *Eros* and *Thanatos* which, for all intents and purposes, are the passions of love and hate grounded, as Sagan argues, in pre-Oedipal identifications with the nurturer on the one hand and the aggressor on the other, matters of the human heart and mind, irreducible to the body or the animal in man. The animal in man is not the problem. Nor is the problem the conflict between an antisocial animalistic id *vs.* a prosocial human ego-superego. If the past century has shown us anything, it is the involvement of human reason (ego) and human ideals and ideologies (superego) in the perpetration of evil. The problem is not the animal in man, it is the conflict in our hearts and minds between our love and our hate, between our employment of our uniquely human capacities for reason, idealism, and empathy in the service of sympathy and nurturance or of sadistic aggression and revenge.

* * *

Whereas Freud identifies conscience with the superego arising with the waning of the Oedipus complex, followers of Mead ground it in the capacity for role-taking that arises with symbolic functioning some time during the second year of life. But while role-taking is the basis for *empathic identification* with others this is quite distinct from the *sympathetic identification* at work in conscience. Advancing beyond Freud's emphasis on the centrality of the Oedipus complex (the triangular conflict emerging after, not before, the achievement of ambivalence, self and object constancy, or the depressive position) and focusing far more on pre-Oedipal issues (despite her misleading labelling of pre-ambivalent triangular conflict as "Oedipal" when it is at best "pseudo-Oedipal" in the Freudian sense), Melanie Klein (1957, 1964) associated morality with the move out of the narcissistic, paranoid-schizoid position into the depressive position where true guilt (as distinct from persecutory anxiety and shame) and the drive towards reparation arise. Regrettably, feeling the need to exaggerate her continuity with Freud, Klein not only described pre-ambivalent triangular conflicts as Oedipal (when ambivalence towards the rival is the essence of the Freudian Oedipus complex), but also used the term superego to refer both to the internal persecutory bad part-object of the paranoid-schizoid position and the conscience, the capacity to experience guilt leading to reparation that emerges with the depressive position. Klein's depressive position with its "depressive anxiety", reformulated by Winnicott (1963) as the "capacity for concern", emerges with the overcoming of splitting and achievement of love for and introjection of the whole good object; it must not be confused with depression which is a paranoid-schizoid phenomenon reflecting splitting (the self being regarded as all-bad or, in the manic defence against depression, as all-good). While her dating of the developmental shift from the paranoid-schizoid to the depressive position as between three and six months is now widely questioned, it certainly occurs long before Freud's dating of superego formation at five or six years of age due to hate retroflected against the self under threat of castration.

Like Klein, Sagan finds the roots of what will become conscience in the very earliest stages of development in the infant's early identifications with the primary nurturer. Herein lies the origin of conscience: the obligation to give love for love received. This is the positive talion: love for love. It constitutes what Alford (1989) calls the reparative morality operative in Klein's depressive position. In the capacity for concern lies the origin of sympathetic as distinct from merely empathic identification; at this point it becomes possible not just to imagine how the other feels, but to care. But since even with the best caring imaginable frustration and pain are inevitable, and since according to Klein and Bion the absent good breast is felt by the infant as a present bad, attacking breast, so we also internalise a persecutory object, an aggressor, with which we identify in both directing rage against ourselves and inflicting it upon others. Here we have the negative talion: hate for hate, an eye for an eye. This constitutes what for Alford is the talion morality operative in the paranoid-schizoid position. Freud describes superego formation this way: id aggression towards the rival is turned against the self as identified with the rival; one now beats oneself as if one were the hated object.

For Sagan, Freud's deficient understanding of the roots of conscience arises from his deficient psychology of women; more specifically his almost phobic theoretical flight forward to the Oedipal and away from the overwhelming (divine and demonic) pre-Oedipal maternal imago (Dinnerstein, 1976). Many readers of *Future of an Illusion* (1927c) and *Civilization and its Discontents* (1930a) will have been jolted when Freud repeatedly refers to the infant's and child's dependency as his or her need for a … *father's* protection. Whereas his father died while he was in his forties, Freud's mother lived on into her nineties; he visited her every Saturday morning—and kept her on a pedestal. According to Margolis (1996), "Freud's idealisation of his mother persisted throughout his life" (p. 14)—an idealisation that, in her view, "defied reality" and involved "denial of hostile feelings toward his mother" (p. 17) for the enormous pressure constituted by her intense narcissistic investment in her "golden Sigi" whom she apparently idolised (as her symbolic phallus?) rather than loving for himself. With reference to Freud's tendency to self-concealment, Margolis writes: "We would surmise … that what Freud found it necessary to conceal, even from himself—perhaps above all from himself—was not his love, but his repressed hate for his mother" (p. 19).

In *Group Psychology and the Analysis of the Ego*, Freud (1921c) writes: "The evidence of psycho-analysis shows that almost every intimate emotional relation between two people which lasts for some time— marriage, friendship, the relations between parents and children— contains a sediment of feelings of aversion and hostility, which only escapes perception as a result of repression." But then he feels the need to add the qualifier, "Perhaps with the solitary exception of the relation of a mother to her son" (p. 100)—almost as if he could not bear to let the generalisation stand as it implied the existence of an element of hostility in the relation of mother and son. He could not conceive of a bad mother. Note that the danger situations of childhood all concern the *absence* of something good: the breast; the mother's love; the phallus; the superego's love—never the *presence* of something bad. It was Karl Abraham (1911) who through analysing certain paintings by the Italian artist Giovanni Segantini ("The Bad Mothers", 1896–97) achieved the breakthrough (U. May, 2001), and it was his analysand, Melanie Klein, who added the presence of a persecutory, bad breast-mother to the catalogue of infantile danger situations.

The desire to nurture others as we ourselves have been nurtured, to help as we have been helped, and to love as we have been loved, is what we mean by conscience. People who have survived infancy and childhood and who are at all functional have been loved, however inadequately; so they know what love is and, having received it, on some level understand the obligation to give it back. This is the true basis of morality and it arises far earlier than the Freudian superego. For Sagan (1988), conscience arises in identification with the loving, comforting, and nurturing pre-Oedipal mother (though certainly fathers and others can serve in this capacity) and in our primordial tendency to turn passive into active. He describes "those delightful circumstances, familiar to all parents, when the infant first endeavours to feed the mother back" (p. 169). He cites Spitz's (1958) observation of a six-month-old child: "The mother, holding the child in her lap, is feeding the child from the bottle and introduces the nipple into his mouth. The child accepts it, sucks, and *at the same time pushes his finger into the mother's mouth*" (p. 391; Spitz's emphasis). At a little over a year: "There are no problems with his drinking milk from a cup, but when he is offered cake, noodles, etc., he is more interested in offering these to his mother than in eating them himself" (p. 391). Such observations are reinforced by more recent experimental infant research. In "The Moral Life of Babies"

Bloom (2010) writes that "A growing body of evidence … suggests that humans do have a rudimentary moral sense from the very start of life. With the help of well-designed experiments, you can see glimmers of moral thought, moral judgement and moral feeling even in the first year of life" (p. 1). A biological basis for morality has been posited by some evolutionary biologists and sociobiologists (Wilson, 1998).

The "good-enough" mother mirrors the affect states of her child and the child mirrors her back. Such mirroring, mutuality, or reciprocity is echoed in Chomsky's (2007) claim that "… the most elementary of moral principles is that of universality, that is, if something's right for me, it's right for you; if it's wrong for you, it's wrong for me. Any moral code that is even worth looking at has that at its core somehow." The essence of the ethic of reciprocity is movingly expressed in the words of the No. 59 Chorale of Bach's (1734-35) *Christmas Oratorio*:

> *Ich komme, bring und schenke dir,*
> *Was du mir hast gegeben.*
> (I come, bring and give to Thee
> That which Thou hast given me.)

According to Klein (1964), "Feelings of love and gratitude arise directly and spontaneously in the baby in response to the love and care of his mother" (p. 65). Unfortunately the mother who comforts and nurtures is at times inevitably replaced in the infant's experience by a mother felt as torturing and depriving. "The infant's feelings seem to be that when the breast deprives him, it becomes bad because it keeps the milk, love, and care associated with the good breast all to itself" (Klein, 1957, p. 183). Bion (1962) writes: "Let us suppose the infant to have fed but to be feeling unloved. Again it is aware of a need for the good breast and again this 'need for a good breast' is a 'bad breast' that needs to be evacuated" (p. 35). In other words, the absent good breast is felt by the infant as a present bad attacking breast that necessarily generates perse-cutory anxiety, rage, and the vicious cycle of rage projected, leading to further persecutory anxiety, more aggression, and so on. To the extent that the inevitable phantasy of persecution is given substance by real, "surplus" frustration due to "not good-enough" parenting the resulting pathology is intensified.

Fortunately, the primitive talion reaction that entails giving hate for hate is paralleled by an equal tendency to give love for love. Although the punitive superego as aggression retroflected from the Oedipal rival against the ego takes shape only at the end of the Oedipal phase, it is grounded in earlier identifications with the persecutory part-object mother. As she hurt me, so I seek to hurt her and others who, in transference, represent her. Love begets love; and hate, even imagined hate, begets hate. In the early relationship with the mother in phantasy and reality lie the origins of love and hate, healing and hurting, comforting and tormenting. For Klein it is the infant's overcoming of the splitting of love and hate and introjection of and identification with a whole good object that generates depressive anxiety, mature guilt, and the drive towards reparation as distinct from persecutory anxiety and self-torment.

Owing to its patriarchal bias and relative repression of the pre-Oedipal phase and the pre-Oedipal mother, Freudian psychoanalysis failed to comprehend the roots of conscience in the early mother-infant attachment. As a result it had no adequate grasp of the conflicts between the superego that is developed much later and the conscience that embodies a moral standpoint, *charity*, from which the former must often be judged immoral. For the superego is a product not just of aggression turned against the self but of internalisation of the culture. And the culture that is internalised has to varying degrees been an unjust and immoral culture that results in an immoral superego.

With language comes the capacity to make distinctions and to categorise. Regrettably human beings have a tendency to distinguish those who count from those who do not. The suffering of the latter is regarded as not quite fully real or significant. Among the citizens of Athens few if any voices were raised demanding the slaves be included in their democracy. Erikson (1968) described the problem of *pseudo-speciation*: "First each horde or tribe, class and nation, but then also every religious association has become *the* human species, considering all the others a freakish and gratuitous invention of some irrelevant deity" (p. 41). The ethic of charity apparently does not pertain to those who are not "like us". The dictum that "[W]hat is moral is what you feel good after and what is immoral is what you feel bad after" (Hemingway, 1934, Chapter One) does not apply when immorality goes unrecognised because it involves a category of others excluded from the moral community (slaves, women, people of colour, Jews, immigrants, homosexuals, children, animals).

To postmodern sociocultural relativism, as for the classical Freudian theory that failed to recognise the conflict between superego and conscience, the idea of an immoral superego makes no sense since the socially constructed superego is itself the judge and there is no other judge to judge it—other than another socially constructed superego. There is no judge among all these judges to judge which is the righteous judge. Freudian psychoanalysis is left with moral relativism. But there is indeed a higher authority to judge both the superego and the culture that produces it: the conscience, originating in love for and identification with the nurturing parents, elaborated through the development of capacities for concern, empathy, sympathy, and reparation, and forming the necessary basis for genuinely moral action and justified guilt.

Freud (1925j, 1931b, 1933a) argued that the feminine superego is weak because unlike that of the male it is not driven by the threat of castration, an idea that has been felt by feminists as an insult. Since women are not exempt from depression and masochism they are certainly not free from aggression retroflected against the self, one of the two major components of the superego. But to the extent that the claim may contain an element of truth, it could refer to a relative weakening in women of the other element of the superego: internalised societal ideology. If by the weakness of their superego we mean that women are less prone to be dominated by internalised societal ideology, much of which is immoral by the standards of conscience, then the insult looks more like a compliment. In rejecting the Freudian view of their defective moral sense there is no need to idealise women in order to recognise they may have a moral advantage: the very weakness of their superego (as internalised ideology) may make it more difficult for it to drown out the still small voice of conscience. As Gilligan (1982) observed, while the moral reasoning of men has tended to be about protection of individual rights from infringement by others, that of women tends to be about what one owes to the other with whom one is in relationship, a difference that echoes that between superego and conscience. One might argue that those without much conscience had better at least have a superego, but it is doubtful this would help for, without conscience, the subject will likely identify with the punitive superego and self-righteously channel aggression away from the self onto the sinners whom it is his mission to punish.

In addition to the conflicts between id, ego, and superego with which we have long been familiar, our patients suffer from conflict between superego and conscience. A good deal of the confusion we experience in this field stems from our failure to distinguish these agencies and our use of a single term, guilt, to describe their very different effects. Whereas the superego generates an essentially narcissistic need for self-punishment resulting in various forms of painful self-torment and shame—or, alternatively, the infliction of such torment upon a scapegoat—the conscience gives rise to a wish to make creative reparation towards the injured other. The superego is fuelled by aggression; the conscience by attachment, concern and love. In subsuming the function of conscience along with self-observation and maintenance of the ego ideal into one mental structure, the superego, Freud foregoes conceptualising conflict between competing moral demands as between superego and conscience, forcing us instead to think of *intrasystemic* conflict within the superego.

The analysis of competing, sometimes incompatible, moral values and demands has not figured large in the psychoanalytic literature, despite the ubiquity of such conflicts in human life. There is mounting evidence, for example, that many soldiers diagnosed with post-traumatic stress disorder suffer from guilt arising in the context of obedience to a superego shaped by familial and military authority that required them to engage in actions condemned by conscience (Filkins, 2012). In the abstract of a recent workshop reviewing preliminary findings of a study of active-duty marines, psychiatrist and retired Navy captain William Nash (2012) writes: "The name given to the guilt and remorse troops feel when they see or do bad things during war is Moral Injury. Failure to recognize and acknowledge exposure to military or civilian carnage in Iraq and Afghanistan sets up troops for post-traumatic stress, a severe and often debilitating anxiety disorder that affects 1 in 5 combat troops. ... Service members who don't talk to loved ones, clergy or some other confidant will become convinced that what they did is unforgivable, leading to recognized symptoms of PTSD, such as withdrawal, self-condemnation and avoidance." Although it is possible to conceptualise such conditions as resulting from intrasystemic conflict between conflicting superego elements, some demanding actions condemned by others, given psychoanalytic understanding of the role of internalisation of parental and social authority in superego formation in addition to id aggression turned against the ego, it makes sense to conceive of such situations as ones of conflict between superego and conscience. Moral injury often arises from obedience to an authoritative superego that commands unconscionable acts.

The fundamental ideas of reciprocity, fairness, and justice grounded in the universal ethic of charity that is the essence of conscience, eventually led in the West to the extension of rights to many categories of others who previously did not count. One need not subscribe to the neo-liberal ideology of progress or blind oneself to the continuing reality of racist, sexist, heterosexist, capitalist, and childist (Young-Bruehl, 2012) forms of exploitation and domination to acknowledge that there have been moral advances: though, to our shame, we must acknowledge slavery still exists, we have at least made substantial progress towards its abolition; though racism is a continuing reality, America now has a black man in the "White" House; despite the current resurgence of misogyny, women have made some substantial gains, though violence, abuse, and injustice have in no way been eliminated; homosexuals can now marry, even in Iowa, and even when they "come out" they can become psychoanalysts, at least in some locales; while widespread child abuse and neglect remain, infanticide is greatly diminished though not a thing of the past. A good deal has been accomplished during the past two centuries, though today these gains are increasingly threatened by the regressive trends set in motion by the rise of neo-liberalism in the 1970s, religious fundamentalism and fanaticism, and other counter-modern forces and "backlash" that at times take the form of what Sagan (2001) calls "modernity psychosis" (see Chapter Eight). While we owe moral and social progress to conscience, today as in the past it is opposed by the reactionary superego.

* * *

Writers such as Schafer (1976) and Brenner (1994, 1998, 2002), among others, concerned to avoid reification of psychoanalytic concepts such as id, ego, and superego, prefer to focus upon the compromise-formations comprising such mental "structures". In this approach "conscience" and "superego" are abstractions referring to compromise-formations composed of libido and aggression, *Eros* and *Thanatos*, identifications with the nurturer and the aggressor, in varying proportions. Hence, to speak of *the* superego and *the* conscience is to commit "the fallacy of misplaced concreteness" (Whitehead, 1925). But just as Freud did not consider *Eros* and *Thanatos* as themselves compromise-formations but as the forces entering into the fusions or compromise-formations that constitute most human behaviour (while also recognising the reality of de-fusion or splitting), he did not, unlike Charles Brenner (1994, 1998) and other post-Freudian ego psychologists, describe the superego as a compromise-formation. Over time Freud increasingly described it as a sadistic force, even referring to a superego that represents a "pure culture of the death instinct" (1923b, p. 53).

In my view, *Thanatos*, hatred, identification with the aggressor, and the superego are parallel terms, as are *Eros*, love, identification with the nurturer, and conscience. I see these as Freud himself saw *Eros* and *Thanatos*, as the forces that enter into compromise-formations, not as compromise-formations themselves. Having become aware of the implications of "Huck's dilemma" only to retreat from the concepts of the superego and the conscience in order to minimise the danger of reification is, to my mind, unnecessary and contraindicated; to do so would deprive us of the new understanding of the important conflicts between these "agencies" opened up by Sagan's distinction, a type of conflict to which we have hitherto been relatively blind. Psychoanalysis is supposed to be about "the mind in conflict" (Brenner, 1982), but here is a whole region of mental conflict to which we have paid insufficient attention because, following Freud, we assimilated conscience to superego and, hence, have had difficulty recognising conflicts between them. In calling for the disempowerment and displacement of the superego in favour of the conscience, I am simply affirming as the *telos* or goal of psychoanalysis the relative dominance of love over hate. This in no way implies the naïve idealism that holds out as a real possibility the complete vanquishing of hate by love, but only the belief that progress in establishing a *relative* dominance of love over hate is a realisable clinical and social goal for an albeit perpetually conflicted (or "fallen") humanity.

Given Freud's depictions of the normal superego as driven by id hatred towards the Oedipal rival turned back against the ego, plus internalised cultural ideology, I prefer not only to reinforce Sagan's (1988) distinction but to conceive of the therapeutic task as that of the disempowerment or displacement of the superego in favour of the conscience. The distinction between the superego and conscience is implicit in the Kleinian distinction between the paranoid-schizoid and the depressive positions. In the former, the superego is an internal, persecutory, bad object generating persecutory anxiety (primitive guilt, shame, and self-punishment). The Freudian superego formed through identification with the aggressor is a post-Oedipal evolution of this pre-Oedipal persecutor. Advance into the depressive position involves transcending the narcissism, the self-centredness of the schizo-paranoid position (whether it takes the form of a preoccupation with how wonderful or how terrible we are), through the development of the capacity for concern for *others*—that is, development of the capacity to get our minds off ourselves long enough to notice and care about the effects we have had or are having upon them. To exchange self-punishment for reparative action, persecutory for depressive anxiety (i.e., guilt as concern rather than shame and self-torment), is to transcend the superego in favour of the conscience. The "loving and beloved superego" (Schafer, 1960), or the "mature" as opposed to the "archaic" superego, is a post-Oedipal development of the pre-Oedipal conscience.

In *Civilization and Its Discontents*, Freud (1930a) quotes Goethe as saying, "He who possesses science and art also has religion; but he who possesses neither of those two, let him have religion!" (p. 74). Allow me to offer an analogous epigram: "He who possesses conscience has no need of either religion or a superego; but he who lacks conscience, let him have religion and a superego!" I hasten to add that, in reality, religion and the superego are poor compensations for a missing conscience. Fuelled as the superego is by hate and internalised cultural ideology it is just not up to the job. And we are all too aware of the unconscionable forms frequently taken by religion—such as, to take but one example, the Nazified Lutheranism of the so-called "German Christians", resistance to whom led Dietrich Bonhoeffer on his way not only to the conspiracy to assassinate Hitler but also towards "religionless Christianity" (Metaxas, 2010).

According to Alexander (1925), "The super-ego … is an anachronism in the mind. It has lagged behind the rapid development of civilised conditions, in the sense that its automatic, inflexible mode of function causes the mental system continually to come into conflict with the outer world" (p. 25). The therapeutic task, he writes, "is carried out by limiting the sphere of activity of the automatically-functioning superego, and transferring its role to the conscious ego" (p. 25). Two years later, Ferenczi (1928) agreed: "Only a complete dissolution of the superego can bring about a radical cure" (p. 100). While "limiting the sphere of activity of the automatically-functioning superego" is both a worthy and a viable goal, "transferring its role to the conscious ego" is not, since reason cannot provide us with moral guidance. And while given the cruelty and rigidity of the superego Ferenczi's call for its total elimination is understandable, in light of Klein's theory of *positions*, not stages, we recognise that advance into and working through of the depressive position does not entail eradication of paranoid-schizoid processes but only their significant transcendence. However much progress has been achieved through the therapeutic disempowerment and displacement of the superego by conscience, even the most well analysed and mature will have to continue to struggle against internal bad objects, including the superego and the torment it inflicts. Conflict between superego and conscience (like that between PS and D), is an inherent characteristic of the human mind that we have hitherto been unable to adequately address because we have lacked the concept of conscience as the necessary fourth element in the structural theory of the mind.

Because, following Freud, most psychoanalysts have conflated the superego with conscience and identified it as a prosocial force despite awareness of its destructiveness in the clinical domain, they feared its critique and disempowerment would amount to the promotion of psychopathy. Hence they have called for superego modulation and maturation (the "liberal" view), instead of its displacement by conscience (the "radical" alternative). In other words, instead of reconciling themselves to the destructiveness of the superego and seeking to quarantine, contain, and disempower it, at the same time seeking to strengthen and reinforce the conscience as the authentic moral centre of the personality, they have sought to convert it from being bad to being good and, at the same time, to strengthen, not the conscience, but the rational ego. In this liberal vein, Britton (2003) advocates rational critique of the authoritarian superego by a strengthened ego and emancipation of the superego from capture by a sadistic internal object. In other words, for Britton the superego is not itself an intrinsically bad object, only captured by one or more of them and therefore potentially redeemable. He proposes liberating it from such bad objects and, at the same time, subjecting it to critique and monitoring by a strengthened ego. But while strengthening the ego is certainly a worthy goal, even an enhanced ego cannot serve as a conscience because, being merely rational, it cannot make value judgements. And while a modulated superego can provide moral guidance, the values on the basis of which it guides can only be truly moral if they are derived from conscience; for if they are merely derived from parents and society they are as likely to be immoral as moral, at least until the establishment of the "kingdom of God" on earth, an event for which I, for one, am not prepared to hold my breath. Hence even the liberal solution that preserves the superego and seeks to rehabilitate it requires recognition of a separate conscience to guide the rehabilitation project and to ensure that what results is a moral rather than an immoral superego.

These psychoanalytic issues have parallels in religion. Religion is a human phenomenon that, however much it may have at times promoted conscience, has as often, or more often, been allied with the superego. While the theological liberal will seek to reform religion (Kierkegaard's "Christendom") to bring it into line with the often crucifying call of conscience (Kierkegaard's "Christianity"), the theological radical will more likely conclude, like the later Dietrich Bonhoeffer, that religion must be replaced by conscience, however the latter may be symbolically expressed (see Chapter Ten). It must be noted here that, unlike Bonhoeffer, Kierkegaard (1850) associated "religion" with Christianity, not with Christendom; hence while they shared a common goal, one (Kierkegaard) sought to achieve it by the reassertion of "religion" and the other (Bonhoeffer) by its replacement by a "religionless" Christian faith.

Against the immoral moralism of the superego, Alexander and Ferenczi, like Bion (1962) and Britton (2003) more recently, grounded morality in *thinking*. They viewed mature moral functioning as thinking through the consequences of one's actions for oneself and others— that is, in rational ego functioning. We might formulate their dictum as: "Where superego was, there ego shall come to be." In contrast to such rationalism, Sagan recognises that conscience arises not from *reason* but from *feeling*, from what Jean-Jacques Rousseau called "pity"—sympathy or fellow-feeling. According to Rousseau (1754):

> There is besides another principle that has escaped Hobbes, and which, having been given to man to moderate, on certain occasions, the blind and impetuous sallies of self-love, or the desire of self-preservation previous to the appearance of that passion, allays the ardour, with which he naturally pursues his private welfare, by an innate abhorrence to see beings suffer that resemble him. I shall not surely be contradicted, in granting to man the only natural virtue, which the most passionate detractor of human virtues could not deny him, I mean that of pity, a disposition suitable to creatures weak as we are, and liable to so many evils; a virtue so much the more universal, and withal useful to man, as it takes place in him of all manner of reflection; and so natural, that the beasts themselves

sometimes give evident signs of it. Not to speak of the tenderness of mothers for their young; and of the dangers they face to screen them from danger …. (Chapter Two)

Given the fact/value disjunction, the confinement of reason and science to the descriptive field of the *is* and its incompetence with respect to the prescriptive field of the *ought*, we recognise that conscience is fundamentally grounded in non-rational, emotional processes of attachment, sympathy, concern, and love, not in the head but the heart—for, as Pascal (1669, Section 4) famously put it, "[T]he heart has reasons reason cannot know." Even while recognising the limits of reason, the later Freud placed his confidence in secondary process thinking, regarding feeling, like primary process and the unconscious, with suspicion, associating it with madness rather than valuing it as a source of existential orientation, potential wisdom, and creativity. It is owing to this suspicion of feeling and overestimation of reason that even those psychoanalysts who recognise the destructiveness of the superego have for the most part felt no need to posit a separate conscience, thinking that the ego itself can serve as a sufficient moral guide.

* * *

It can only be the socially uncritical attitudes of mainstream psychoanalysis that account for the fact that in his recent book, *You Ought To! A Psychoanalytic Study of the Superego and Conscience*, in the course of discussing the role of internalisation in superego formation, Bernard Barnett (2007), like most psychoanalysts, appears largely blind to the fact that the superego will inevitably function as the agent of cultural ideology— of all the various forms of domination and immorality pervading the culture—at least to the extent that it is not opposed by a conscience having some degree of cultural autonomy. In the course of discussing the superego as a mischief maker, the role of the severe superego in psychopathology, Barnett mentions identification with the punitive superego rationalising aggression towards the other, the scapegoat, onto whom the subject's guilt has been projected. But he tends to see the severe or sadistic superego as entailing the "corruption of the superego systems … (i.e., a reversal of normal civilised values) …" (p. 116), whereas history provides plenty of evidence that the socially normal superego is itself both corrupt (i.e., sexist, classist, etc.) and tyrannical, while a humane and loving conscience is the exception rather than the rule.

Freud himself, as we know, thought much of what appears as "moral" behaviour is pseudo-moral, grounded in social anxiety rather than genuinely felt values. In ironic reference to Kant, Freud (1933a) writes: "The stars are indeed magnificent, but as regards conscience God has done an uneven and careless piece of work, for a large majority of men have brought along with them only a modest amount of it or scarcely enough to be worth mentioning" (p. 60). Freud thinks of conscience as a superego function and thereby considers it rare because formation of a truly internalised superego is rare, most people conforming merely out of fear. He does not consider the possibility that the relative absence of conscience might be due to its displacement by the superego. In contrast to Freud who treated superego and conscience as synonymous, in the subtitle of his book Barnett distinguishes them but does not think through and elaborate clearly upon the distinction. In places he seems to consider conscience as a conscious moral function in contrast to the superego as the unconscious conscience, but he does not clearly spell this out nor adhere to it consistently. In my view this is just as well since the voice of conscience, like that of the superego, may be repressed. Barnett makes no reference to Sagan's differentiation of the superego as grounded in identification with the aggressor and fuelled by aggression from the conscience grounded in identification with the early nurturer and motivated by attachment and love.

Barnett discusses "blind obedience" among the Nazis, though without referencing Milgram's (1963) studies on obedience that experimentally validate Freud's (1921c) concept of the usurpation of individual conscience by an authoritative leader. While offering a useful discussion of the *SS*, Lifton's (1986) work on the Nazi doctors, and the mechanisms of "psychic numbing" and "doubling" that enabled them to split off an "Auschwitz self" from the self they resumed at home, Barnett does not fully grasp the fact that their abominable work was enabled and driven by the superego. As we have seen, the tendency to find the roots of evil in the id, rather than the superego, is deeply ingrained in psychoanalytic thought, but Lifton's work challenges this bias. It is not as if Barnett is oblivious to the role of the superego in such behaviour, but only that he views it, as have most psychoanalysts, as a "criminal" or "pathological" superego, which allows us to continue to think that "in health" the "normal" superego is humane and so to dodge the uncomfortable truth that *normally* the superego is not humane, which is why it comes into conflict with the conscience, provided the conscience can make itself heard over the ideological clamour of the superego. Moreover, in my view, the mechanisms of psychic numbing and doubling are far more pervasive in so-called "normal" life than we have wanted to acknowledge. For example, few psychoanalytic societies enjoy a history free of scandal involving once eminent colleagues who, like the Nazi doctors, have been guilty of "doubling".

Barnett, like most analysts, views the developmental transformation of the primitive, harsh superego into a more humane and reasonable version as a process of superego modification. In Sagan's terms, this would involve exchanging a sadistic superego composed predominantly of identifications with the aggressor for a more loving and forgiving superego composed to a greater extent of identifications with the nurturer. In this "liberal" perspective that dominates in mainstream psychoanalysis, the superego, as we saw in Britton's (2003) work, is not irredeemably bad—not the Devil himself, but merely "possessed" by him (the bad internal persecutory objects). Through a kind of therapeutic "exorcism" the superego may be liberated from its demons, being thus transformed into Schafer's (1960) "loving and beloved" superego. But the very valuation by which we prefer the allegedly loving over the sadistic superego itself arises from conscience. And the loving superego is nothing other than the conscience, a conscience that will always be in conflict with a hating superego that can never be entirely eliminated, any more than the bad internal objects, or the paranoid-schizoid position itself, can be eliminated. In the "radical" view adopted here, the superego is an intrinsically persecutory, bad internal object of the paranoid-schizoid position that can never be redeemed but only contained and disempowered—just as *Thanatos* can never be eliminated but only contained and overpowered by a strengthened *Eros*. From the beginning psychoanalysis has only glimpsed but ultimately failed to clearly grasp the antisocial nature of the superego, scapegoating the id in its place. Those who speak of superego modification generally consider that what needs modifying is a pathological superego, not a normal one, failing to see that the normal superego is itself "pathological" and that, therefore, the superego is a pathologically normal—that is, a "normopathic" (Hantman, 2008) phenomenon.

Those committed to avoiding abstract, macroscopic psychoanalytic concepts in favour of the microscopic psychological processes underlying them, prefer to avoid speaking of superego, or conscience, or the modification of either, but to simply describe behaviour as the outcome of the relative balance of identifications with the aggressor and the nurturer of which it is comprised. As I have indicated, I am less worried about the danger of conceptual concretisation. In any case, the concepts of "identification" and "compromise-formation" are themselves abstractions and vulnerable to reification. Ultimately, the flight from abstraction is faced with an infinite regress since in science we can never do without or transcend it.

When the superego (identification with the aggressor, hatred, *Thanatos*) is disempowered, it can no longer drown out the voice of conscience (identification with the nurturer, love, *Eros/Agape/Caritas*). Against this position it is sometimes argued that the strictness and firmness of the superego is required as against the supposed softness and excessive tolerance of conscience grounded in identification with the nurturer, and that we cannot allow the paternal law to be displaced by maternal love. But as I have tried to indicate, both nurturance and authority can be provided by each gender. Men are capable of providing nurturance and, for Dinnerstein (1976), it was urgent that they begin to assume much more of this responsibility. And, traditionally, our first authority, first tyrant, has not been the father but the pre-Oedipal mother. It is a mistake to think that because it is grounded in nurturance the conscience must of necessity be lacking in the power to confront and demand change. Although differing in quality, taking the form of depressive rather than persecutory anxiety, the pangs of conscience can be as painful as the lashings of the punitive superego and perhaps even more persistent. While the superego mostly generates useless self-torment and self-sabotage, the conscience often motivates constructive, reparative action and change. In a much-quoted but unreferenced statement, Gandhi is reputed to have claimed, "The human voice can never reach the distance that is covered by the still small voice of conscience."

* * *

In her recent book, *The Quest for Conscience and the Birth of the Mind*, Annie Reiner (2009) distinguishes between the superego and the conscience which she views as having separate lines of development. Regrettably, both Reiner and James Grotstein who writes an introduction to her book appear unaware of Eli Sagan's development of this very distinction some two decades earlier. Unlike Sagan who, like Klein and Winnicott, grounds conscience (as distinct from the critical superego) in early feelings of love and concern rather than in reason, Reiner follows Bion in finding the basis for conscientious development beyond the rigid, pseudo-moral superego in *thinking*. For such thinking to occur it is necessary, she believes, for the subject to experience a "psychological birth" beyond the merely physical one, a "resurrection" of the true self that has early on been split off in favour of various degrees of false self development owing to virtually universal deficiencies of containment on the part of the early nurturers.

Such metaphors as "second birth" and "resurrection" suggest the author's embrace of a type of "spirituality" that she, like Symington (1994) and others, is at pains to distinguish from the conventional forms of religiosity she devalues. In her view there is false, literalistic religion and there is true, sophisticated spirituality. She goes so far as to cite Nietzsche's notion of the "Superman"—Grotstein prefers "Overman" and "Higher Man" (no "Higher Woman"?)—and "his" advance "beyond good and evil" as conventionally defined (the superego's pseudo-morality) towards the more highly evolved, "authentic" spirituality of those special people ("Mystics", "Messiahs", etc.) who have managed to cast off their false selves and experience a "transformation in O", "O" being defined as "ultimate reality, absolute truth, the god-head, the infinite, the thing-in-itself" (Bion, 1970, p. 25).

There is no denying the difference between concrete, magical, and fundamentalist forms of belief, on the one hand, and demythologised, "spiritual," existentialist and/or psychoanalytic interpretations of religion as metaphor, on the other, whether one values the demythologising strategy as a way of getting at the existential and psychological kernel of truth buried in an outmoded mythological form of expression or, like Freud (1927c, p. 31; 1930a, p. 73), holds it in contempt as a fancy way of denying that one no longer really believes. But in my view there is an entirely other and more significant way of approaching the issue: namely, to ask whether one's mythologised or demythologised, supernatural and magical or entirely secular, religious or irreligious, outlook has the effect of strengthening or weakening one's conscience, either promoting conscientious behaviour or not. "By their fruits ye shall know them" (*Matthew* 7:20 *KJV*), not by the verbiage in their heads or issuing from their mouths.

In addition to following Bion in his mysticism of "O", Reiner is uncritical of his peculiar type of neo-platonic rationalism that posits "the thought without a thinker" (p. 8) and in which "the proto-mental realm" (the mind of God?) is the place where un-thought thoughts patiently await the arrival of a thinker to think them. Reiner posits that it is through a process of spiritual development in which the false self is overcome and the true self resurrected that the subject may acquire the capacity to think and to encounter and bear truth and so develop a maturing conscience. In this view, authentic conscience (as distinct from superego) is a spiritual attainment of one who evolves "beyond good and evil," like Nietzsche's "Overman" or Bion's "Mystic" and "Messiah".

While Eli Sagan also sees the necessity to distinguish conscience from superego, his view of the matter, like Melanie Klein's, foregoes such "spiritual" overtones and is developed in secular humanist and psychological terms. Following both Klein and Sagan we can say that while conscience does develop into more complex and sophisticated forms as maturation occurs, it is there virtually from the beginning in the infant's simple preference for pleasure (good) over pain (bad) and his love for the nurturing good part-object and, later, good whole-object (whether these part- and whole-objects are mothers, fathers, or other carers). For Sagan, conscience is grounded in the infant's love for the person who has loved and nurtured him and in his wish to love her/ him back. In his view and in mine, whatever its "spiritual" manifestations, we can expect to find the mature operation of such conscience in one's personal moral development and one's concern and commitment to oppose and remedy the wrongs and injustices committed by both the self and others.

While Reiner fails to acknowledge Sagan's priority, she implicitly validates his distinction between superego and conscience. In addition, she advances our understanding by insightfully following Winnicott's (1960b) theory of the true and false selves, correctly associating conscience with true self development and recognising, with Fairbairn (1952), how this is almost universally derailed for, as Reiner puts it, "[T]hat which we generally consider to be a 'good-enough mother' may not be good enough" (p. 125). Through the process Fairbairn called "the moral defence" the inadequately contained and nurtured child blames himself for the parental failures since "It is better to be a sinner in a world ruled by God than to live in a world ruled by the Devil" (Fairbairn, p. 66; quoted by Reiner, p. 69). This defence lays the basis for major moral confusion: what is bad is good and what is good is bad; what is true is false and what is false is true. One has now lost one's existential compass.

Feelings arising from the true self, especially aggression in reaction to parental failure, are split off; the unconscious aggression fuels the hostile superego. But whereas Reiner thinks that in these circumstances conscience, like the true self, fails to develop, I think it is repressed but still in existence and generates an existentially valid sense of guilt distinct from that generated by the superego: an existential guilt, if you will; a guilt for failing to be one's self, for failing to *be*, and for being false. Such existential guilt is in addition to the inevitable guilt arising from trauma. Our current preoccupation with trauma largely ignores an inconvenient truth: that traumatised people, whatever other effects they suffer, necessarily experience rage, mostly repressed and turned against the self. Such self-directed aggression generates a valid sense of guilt precisely because it entails identification with the abuser and results in self-abuse. Abuse is abuse, and it is wrong, whether directed against the self by an immoral superego or against others.

* * *

If Freud erred in failing to distinguish conscience from superego, what about the "ego ideal"? If he had not absorbed both conscience and ego ideal into the superego, might the ego ideal have served as something of a conscience capable of opposing the superego? In this connection, Burston (2007) writes that "by the early to mid-sixties Erikson felt the manifest inadequacy of Freud's theory of conscience" (p. 63). Actually, Erikson's dissatisfaction with the superego as a negative conscience and his search for a positive conscience to offset it was evident as early as *Young Man Luther* (Erikson, 1958), a book that given Luther's own internal struggle between law and gospel, superego and conscience, inevitably brought the problem to the fore. For Freud conscience initially consisted of two intrapsychic agencies, the superego containing primarily negative injunctions and prohibitions internalised as "heir to the Oedipus complex" and generating guilt and self-punishment, and the ego ideal as "heir to primary narcissism" composed of identifications with idealised figures and generating shame when the ego appears to fail to live up to its ideals. Erikson attempted to undo Freud's later merging of the two under the single term superego, reinstating the ego ideal as the positive and the superego as the negative conscience.

Aside from the fact that failure to live up to one's ego ideal inevitably results in superego attack for this very failure, the problem with Erikson's attempt to balance the superego as a negative conscience with a reinstated ego ideal as a positive one is that both generate immature, essentially narcissistic states of self-punishment on the one hand and shame on the other. Both reflect a preoccupation with the self rather than genuine concern for others. But in Kleinian theory and Sagan's work we are offered a solution. Both shame and self-punishment operate on the narcissistic, paranoid-schizoid level, as distinct from the depressive anxiety or capacity for concern that obtains on the level of the depressive position. So in addition to the superego (aggression turned against the ego) and ego ideal (narcissism projected into the future or onto idealised others), there is the conscience capable of transcending the narcissistic self-preoccupation characteristic of both self-punishment and shame in favour of depressive anxiety (Klein, 1948), reparative as distinct from persecutory guilt (Alford, 1989; Carveth, 2006a; Grinberg, 1964), or concern for others (Winnicott, 1963).

Erikson was quite right to identify the failure to adequately comprehend conscience as a central problem in psychoanalytic theory. Regrettably, owing to the bias against Kleinian theory characteristic of American psychoanalysis until recently, and the unavailability of Sagan's work until the late Eighties, the solution they offer has gone unrecognised. In the Kleinian perspective the superego has its roots in the persecutory part-object of the paranoid-schizoid position and, hence, can no more be completely eliminated than the paranoid-schizoid position itself. It remains as a permanent regressive potential, however successful one may be in achieving and working through the depressive position where conscience as depressive anxiety or the capacity for concern arises. But if in following Kleinian theory one is forced to abandon the utopian notion of permanent dissolution of the superego in favour of conscience, Kleinian theory remains fundamentally revolutionary rather than reformist; it seeks to promote a fundamental psychic transformation: emancipation from enmeshment in paranoid-schizoid processes and advance into the new world of depressive position functioning and a flexible capacity to draw upon what is creative and life-enhancing in both positions.

Like the values comprising the superego, the ideals comprising the ego ideal are mostly derived from the culture. In the culture of Nazism, for example, the masses were pressured to accept and emulate Nazi ideals. That culture certainly had its opponents and conscientious objectors. Is it enough to say that Dietrich Bonhoeffer resisted the Nazi superego and ego ideal out of loyalty to the very different values

and ideals composing his superego and ego ideal? Or is it necessary
to posit in addition the operation of a conscience? We know that
superegos with differing content can conflict, and so can opposed ego
ideals. We can envisage a situation in which a person's superego might
conflict with his or her ego ideal. For example, one's superego might be
harshly critical of and punitive towards wrongdoers, while one's ideal
might pull in the direction of tolerance and forgiveness.

But like the superego which, for Freud, is comprised of two elements
(id aggression turned back against the ego and socially internalised
values), the ego ideal has a dual composition: on the one hand it is "the
substitute for the lost narcissism of his childhood in which he was his
own ideal" (Freud, 1914c, p. 94) and, on the other, it too is shaped by
socially internalised ideals. If we view conscience as grounded in object
love as distinct from narcissism, in depressive or reparative rather than
persecutory guilt, it is hard to equate it with the ego ideal. *The ego ideal
is a narcissistic structure.* Having been forced by reality to transcend the
"purified pleasure ego" (Freud, 1915c, p. 135) in which everything that
is good is me and everything that is bad is not-me and, hence, having
to admit that there is bad in me and good in the not-me, I am forced to
acknowledge my imperfection. But according to Freud (1915c) such is
my attachment to infantile omnipotence that I am unwilling to surrender the idea of perfection altogether, so I project it into the future as an
ideal. Here is the origin of the ego ideal: I admit I am not perfect now
but, by god, one day I will be.

In measuring myself against my ideal my attention is focused on
me, not on the other. But love requires me to move beyond myself and
develop a "capacity for concern" for the *other* (Winnicott, 1963). Certainly people can turn away from badness towards goodness because
they want to be able to see themselves as good. That would be the narcissistic motive. The utilitarian would say we want to see ourselves as
good because it is pleasurable to be able to do so and painful to have
to see ourselves as bad. But conscience wants more than this: it wants
me to turn away from wrongdoing out of loving concern for the other.
I would argue that conscience also reflects my concern for my "true"
as distinct from my "false self". While the latter, like the ego ideal,
involves the narcissism of the imaginary or specular "ego" as self-
image (Lacan, 1977), the development of the former requires toleration
of the separation, the "cut", "lack", and "loss" (holes in the hands, the
feet, the side)—the transcendence of narcissism or "acceptance of castration" (crucifixion)—entailed in accession to the symbolic.

If both the superego and the ego ideal were shaped by, say, Nazi values, would there be anything in the self to resist? Opposition could hardly come from the id and the pleasure principle since collaboration was rewarded and resistance led to the camps or the gallows. And the reality-oriented ego could hardly object for as an enlightened hedonist it would realise this. Was Dietrich Bonhoeffer simply a masochist, or a narcissist? Did he do what he did only or primarily in order to see himself as good, to bask in a positive self-image? Or did he also do it out of genuine love for his country, its people, and its Jewish, Roma, handicapped, and other victims? Our motives are always mixed, but I believe whatever forces may also have moved him, including id aggression towards those he felt had betrayed his nation, he acted out of conscience, out of his identification with the nurturer. Bonhoeffer's life (Metaxas, 2010) offers a case study in the conflict between superego and conscience. A lifelong Christian pacifist, preoccupied with doing his duty to his God, his family, his country, his church, and his students, he is drawn reluctantly but relentlessly by his conscience into growing opposition to his increasingly Nazified church and, eventually, into the underground opposition to the Reich and, finally, into the plot to assassinate Hitler.

Further examples of conflict between superego and conscience are not hard to come by: a strict superego demands loyalty to both paternal and papal authority while a Protestant conscience can "do no other" than nail ninety-five theses to the church door at Wittenberg (Erikson, 1958); a conscience opposed to mass murder is gradually overpowered by an ideologically indoctrinated superego justifying terrorism; a peasant rabbi insisting the law is made for man not man for the law falls foul of religious authority; a profession barring homosexuals from its training and practice "under the banner of the superego" finally succumbs to increasingly vocal voices of conscience and is forced to attempt to overcome its heterosexism; a woman is torn between a superego demanding fulfilment of her professional responsibilities and a nagging conscience grounded in loving concern for the welfare of her child (as well as internalised maternal ideals that, in this case, constitute superego pressure in the same direction as her conscience); a superego demanding corporate loyalty is gradually overcome by a conscientious need to blow the whistle on corporate crime. This last example illustrates both conflict between superego and conscience and the frequent conflict between self-preservative ego interests and the conscientious need to do what is right at whatever personal cost. When constituted authority backs wrong over right, the price of rectitude can be high indeed. With respect to the question as to which of the competing voices is that of the superego and which that of conscience, we need only remember that the superego is formed through internalisation of social authority and loaded with id aggression turned against the self, while the conscience is grounded in early experience of attachment and love. While conscience is an expression of *Eros*, the superego is a manifestation of *Thanatos*, aggression turned against the self and threatening punishment for failure to adhere to culturally internalised standards and ideals. Superego and ego ideal are narcissistic forms of self-preoccupation rather than concern for others. Certainly the superego can demand concern for others, but the fear-driven and forced "concern" that then results is not heartfelt; it does not express genuine sympathy and identification with the nurturer.

In *Les Misérables* (Volume Five, Book Fourth, "Javert Derailed"), Victor Hugo (1862) offers a moving illustration of the conflict between superego and conscience. The policeman/superego, Javert, comes finally to be touched by conscience, discovering "that one cherishes beneath one's breast of bronze something absurd and disobedient which almost resembles a heart!" As a result, "A whole new world was dawning on his soul: kindness accepted and repaid, devotion, mercy, indulgence, violences committed by pity on austerity, respect for persons, no more definitive condemnation, no more conviction, the possibility of a tear in the eye of the law." Confronted with the "terrible rising of an unknown moral sun", Javert, who until now has been entirely identified with the superego, chooses suicide.

CHAPTER FOUR

Self-punishment as guilt evasion

In the final section (VII) of *Civilization and Its Discontents*, Freud (1930a) states that the primary intention of this work is "to represent the sense of guilt as the most important problem in the development of civilisation and to show that the price we pay for our advance in civilisation is a loss of happiness through the heightening of the sense of guilt" (p. 134). According to Freud, "Men are not gentle creatures who want to be loved, and who at the most can defend themselves if they are attacked," but are, on the contrary, "creatures among whose instinctual endowments is to be reckoned a powerful share of aggressiveness ..." (p. 111). It follows that if a Hobbesian "war of each against all" in which life is, of necessity, "nasty, brutish and short" is to give way to civilised order, such "cruel aggressiveness", this "primary mutual hostility of human beings" (p. 112), must in some way or another be inhibited.

As I point out in Chapter Six, it was only in the face of the devastation of the war and his growing clinical experience of masochistic self-destructiveness that Freud (1920g) finally overcame his resistance to acknowledging aggression as an equally fundamental part of human nature as sexuality and announced his final dual drive theory of *Eros* and *Thanatos*. He then proceeded to project the naïve optimism he had earlier shared with Enlightenment thought onto the Bible, arguing that the idea of an aggressive drive "contradicts too many religious presumptions and social conventions. No, man must be naturally good or at least good-natured" (Freud, 1933a, p. 103). Here Freud fails to recognise that the optimism of his own earlier thought which he now mocks belongs not to the Bible but to the anti-religious Enlightenment his own loyalty to which had prevented him from seeing what the Bible had recognised all along, namely that human beings are "fallen" creatures perpetually torn between the forces of love and hate, construction and destruction. As to whether our hate and destructiveness are innate or acquired, I have elsewhere (Carveth, 1996) advocated an existentialist position that, while acknowledging the influence of both nature and nurture, views aggression as irreducible to either factor or even to their combination. The frustration arising from the birth of a sibling can generate hostility causing intense guilt or guilt-evading self-punishment, yet such hostility can hardly be viewed as a simple drive (however biologically based the aggressive *reaction* to frustration may be), or attributed to environmental failure, although parental behaviour can either mitigate or intensify it.

Freud offers us three options by which the inhibition of primitive sexual and aggressive passions required to preserve civilised order may be achieved: repression, suppression, and sublimation. Since most of us do not possess the strength of character for conscious suppression and self-mastery without self-deception, and lack the talent for much sublimation, the majority will fall back on repression, with the disguised return of the repressed that this inevitably entails. A major manifestation of the disguised return of our repressed aggressiveness is in the operations of the punitive superego that retroflects id aggression away from the object world and back against the ego. Each act of repression of aggression adds to the aggressiveness of the punitive superego, resulting in diverse forms of self-punishment, the "moral masochism" Freud (1916d) described in "the criminal from a sense of guilt", "those wrecked by success", and other self-sabotaging and self-tormenting character-types.

Freud (1916d, 1920g, 1923b, 1924c, and 1930a) equates the unconscious need for punishment expressed in patterns of self-torment and self-sabotage that result from retroflected aggression with an *unconscious* sense of guilt, that operates in people's lives without any accompanying *consciousness* of guilt. Freud (1930a) points out that even where, as in some cases of obsessional neurosis, "[T]he sense of guilt makes itself noisily heard in consciousness ... in most other cases and forms of neurosis it remains completely unconscious, without on that account producing any less important effects" (p. 135).

When the sense of guilt "makes itself noisily heard in consciousness", it often turns out that the ostensible sins of omission or commission with which it is consciously linked bear only the remotest connection to the true, unconscious sources of the guilt feeling—the true crimes, if you will, whether these be acts or merely wishes and phantasies. In *The Ego and the Id*, Freud (1923b) writes,

> In certain forms of obsessional neurosis the sense of guilt is over-noisy but cannot justify itself to the ego. Consequently the patient's ego rebels against the imputation of guilt and seeks the physician's support in repudiating it. It would be folly to acquiesce in this, for to do so would have no effect. Analysis eventually shows that the super-ego is being influenced by processes that have remained unknown to the ego. It is possible to discover the repressed impulses which are really at the bottom of the sense of guilt. Thus in this case the super-ego knew more than the ego about the unconscious id. (p. 51)

In pointing out that such over-noisy self-reproach often bears little relation to its true unconscious sources, Freud comes close to recognising the *defensive* nature of such self-reproach, disconnected as it is from its unconscious grounds.

Freud (1930a) writes, "Our patients do not believe us when we attribute an 'unconscious sense of guilt' to them" (p. 135). But this does not deter him. "In order to make ourselves at all intelligible to them, we tell them of an unconscious need for punishment, in which the sense of guilt finds expression" (p. 135). The self-damaging or self-tormenting behaviours are observable, and although at first patients may be unconscious of the role they themselves are playing in bringing such suffering on themselves, they can often come to recognise their own unconscious agency in their misfortune when it is pointed out to them. Since Freud assumes that self-punishing behaviour is driven by and a manifestation of guilt and since conscious guilt is absent, he postulates the existence of unconscious guilt, equating this with the unconscious need for punishment.

Just as the sense of guilt (which Freud most commonly views as fear of the superego) may not be conscious in the moral masochist, so

"[I]t is very conceivable", Freud (1930a) writes, "that the sense of guilt produced by civilisation is not perceived as such either, and remains to a large extent unconscious, or appears as a sort of *malaise*, a dissatisfaction, for which people seek other motivations" (pp. 135–136). Here we are introduced to the important concept of the *guilt-substitute*. Just as the unconscious operations of the punitive superego (which Freud equates with unconscious guilt) may find expression in the patterns of self-punishment seen in manifold forms of masochism, so they may appear in various forms of *malaise*, dissatisfactions, discontents, and mysterious neurotic afflictions, many of which appear to have little or nothing to do with issues of crime and punishment, but may nevertheless be the work of the unconscious punitive superego.

As instances of such *malaise* and mysterious neurotic afflictions I include the states of fragmentation and depletion of the self that Kohut (1971, 1977) described in the "self disorders" of the "Tragic Man" that he claimed has replaced the "Guilty Man" of the Freudian era, as well as the range of "hystero-paranoid" and psychosomatic syndromes (discussed in Chapter Five) that, although widely conceptualised in terms of defect, deficit, failures of mentalisation, etc., resulting from parental or "selfobject" failure, are nevertheless experienced as *tormenting* by those who suffer from them. Like more obvious forms of self-punishment, these states function, I believe, as guilt substitutes. In this view, the tragedy of "Tragic Man" has less to do with deficits in psychic structure *per se*, than with the latent ongoing self-annihilation, the manifest traces of which appear as defects in the ego or the structure of the self.

In "The Economic Problem of Masochism", Freud (1924c) writes: "Patients do not easily believe us when we tell them about the unconscious sense of guilt. They know well enough by what torments—the pangs of conscience—a conscious sense of guilt, a consciousness of guilt expresses itself, and they therefore cannot admit that they could harbour exactly analogous impulses in themselves without being in the least aware of them. We may, I think, to some extent meet their objection if we give up the term 'unconscious sense of guilt,' which is in any case psychologically incorrect, and speak instead of a 'need for punishment,' which covers the observed state of affairs just as aptly" (p. 166). In the same essay, writing of the "negative therapeutic reaction", Freud places the adjective *unconscious* in quotation marks in referring to "patients to whom … we are obliged to ascribe an 'unconscious sense of guilt'" (p. 166). He does so because he views as problematic the notion that a feeling or affect, as distinct from its associated ideation, could be unconscious. Only a few years later, in *Civilization*, Freud (1930a) is struggling with the same issue. He associates the unconscious sense of guilt with fear of the superego and refers to it as an "unconscious anxiety" and continues, "or, if we want to have a clearer psychological conscience, since anxiety is in the first instance simply a feeling, of possibilities of anxiety" (p. 135). Strachey feels compelled to add a footnote here: "Feelings cannot properly be described as 'unconscious'" (p. 135).

Freud's uneasiness about his concept of unconscious guilt had to do with the question of whether an affect can properly be said to be unconscious, not with his equation of unconscious guilt with the unconscious need for punishment. Today the idea of defences against affects is widely accepted (Modell, 1971; Westen, 1999; Wurmser, 2000). Here I am not concerned with the question of whether the sense of guilt may be unconscious, for I believe it certainly can be, but rather with the problematic equation of guilt, conscious or unconscious, with the need for punishment. Although Freud suggests that we could "give up the term 'unconscious sense of guilt,' which is in any case psychologically incorrect, and speak instead of a 'need for punishment'" (p. 166), he in fact does not do so. Instead, he continues to use these terms and concepts interchangeably, with the consequence that the role of self-punishment in the evasion of guilt, rather than as an expression of it, has been obscured.

Although, in theory, Klein (1935, 1940, 1948) follows Freud in his association of guilt with self-punishment, her actual descriptions of the depressive position (1946, 1948) reflect a conception of guilt not as self-punishment but as the subject's depressive *anxiety* that his or her hate may have damaged or destroyed the good object and/or the good self, leading to efforts at reparation. Here guilt is conceived not as self-directed hate, the punitive superego, but as what Winnicott (1963) called "the capacity for concern". It was Grinberg (1964) who greatly clarified matters by offering us the crucial distinction between "depressive guilt" (concern on the level of the depressive position) and "persecutory guilt" (self-torment in the paranoid-schizoid position), although the function of the latter in defending against the former was not a focus of his work.

While guilt as depressive anxiety, conscience, or concern as distinct from the need for punishment may be unconscious, it is an open question whether such unconscious guilt is best conceived as repressed concern, or as concern that is prevented from coming into being by defences against cognitive appraisals that would generate it (Erdelyi, 1985). But if the defence against depressive guilt, or against recognition of circumstances meriting it, is at all extended over time, this would seem to indicate the anticipation that it will prove to be unbearable and, hence, the beginning of a regression in which the superego resorts to self-punishment (persecutory guilt) as a substitute for and a defence against the depressive guilt or concern that might lead to reparation. Although in principle it should be possible to punish oneself and simultaneously make reparation to the other, there seems to be a tendency, as described in Freud's (1914c) U-tube theory, to invest in either the object (object love) or the self (narcissism), to attend to the wounded other or allow him to bleed while self-flagellating instead of bandaging. Here we encounter the question of whether paranoid-schizoid and depressive dynamics can operate simultaneously or necessarily oscillate.

I am, of course, in no way seeking to cast doubt upon Freud's important discovery of the role of the unconscious need for punishment in psychopathology, merely seeking to draw attention to the fact that not distinguishing between persecutory and depressive guilt and equating the need for punishment with guilt as such obscures the defensive function of self-torment or persecutory guilt in the *evasion* of depressive or reparative guilt. Freud (1924c) writes:

> The satisfaction of this unconscious sense of guilt is perhaps the most powerful bastion in the subject's (usually composite) gain from illness—in the sum of forces which struggle against his recovery and refuse to surrender his state of illness. The suffering entailed by neuroses is precisely the factor that makes them valuable to the masochistic trend. It is instructive, too, to find, contrary to all theory and expectation, that a neurosis which has defied every therapeutic effort may vanish if the subject becomes involved in the misery of an unhappy marriage, or loses all his money, or develops a dangerous organic disease. In such instances one form of suffering has been replaced by another; and we see that all that mattered was that it should be possible to maintain a certain amount of suffering. (p. 166)

All that matters is the subject's need to suffer; there is little or no attention to the suffering of the object. This is masochism and narcissism, self-persecution, not guilt as concern potentially leading to reparation.

While the theme of regression from the depressive to the paranoid-schizoid position, resulting in persecutory rather than depressive anxiety or guilt, has long been a prominent one in the Kleinian literature, more recent writers in this tradition (Eskelinen De Folch, 1988; Riesenberg-Malcolm, 1980; Safán-Gerard, 1998) have emphasised the ways in which self-punishment or expiation serves as a defence against unbearable depressive guilt. Conscience involves the depressive anxiety or capacity for concern for the object that characterises the depressive position and motivates the desire to make reparation; it is a manifestation of attachment and love (*Eros*). The unconscious need for punishment reflects the narcissism, shame, persecutory anxiety, and guilt of the paranoid-schizoid position; it is a manifestation of aggression and hate (*Thanatos*). As a persecutory substitute for depressive guilt, the unconscious need for punishment should not be conflated with what it evades. Far from representing depressive guilt, concern, and the drive towards reparation, such self-persecution results from fixation in or regression to paranoid-schizoid dynamics: it represents an inability to bear, and a defence against, depressive anxiety. Failure to make a clear distinction between these two types of guilt leads to the type of confusion in which, for example, the project of emancipation from the punitive guilt inflicted by an excessively restrictive, anti-sexual and anti-aggressive superego may be conflated with liberation from guilt as concern, as it was by some elements of the so-called Freudian Left (Robinson, 1969) and the youth counterculture of the 1960s and early '70s. This conflation of guilt as concern and responsibility with guilt as self-torment may be one reason why a project of emancipation from punitive guilt at times degenerated into a project of emancipation from guilt as such and thus into a pathologically narcissistic and ultimately sadomasochistic regression.

In an insightful paper addressing both clinically and theoretically the issue of defences against unbearable guilt, Safán-Gerard (1998) points out that whereas Freud saw fear of the superego as motivating an unconscious need for punishment as expiation, "[W]ithin the Kleinian framework guilt is a 'marker' of development signalling a capacity for concern for the object" that "typically initiates reparative efforts toward the external as well as the internal object" (p. 352). But because she associates such concern with *conscious* guilt, she conceives of defences against such concern as resulting in *unconscious* guilt: "The person may attempt to restore the object or manically defend against an acknowledgement of his or her attacks on it. When guilt is short-circuited in this defensive way, it remains unconscious and has various consequences" (p. 352). But short-circuited guilt (concern) is not replaced by unconscious guilt (concern)—at least not for long—for unconscious guilt (concern) either becomes conscious and leads to reparation, or it is regressively replaced by the unconscious need for punishment. In other words, object relating (guilt as concern for the object) is replaced by narcissism (shame, self-torment, and self-punishment); and love (conscience, concern, and guilt) is replaced by hate (the attacking superego, moral masochism, hatred turned against the self).

When conscience becomes cognisant of wrongdoing, such judgement will result either in depressive guilt or concern leading to reparation, or if such guilt is found unbearable and evaded, the superego will generate an unconscious need for punishment. Safán-Gerard's detailed clinical discussion of the case of David confirms this point. He continually attempts to "cure" himself of guilt, but her "interpretations of the patient's defences against the experience of guilt provide an *anchor* that prevents or delays a shift back to the paranoid-schizoid position where guilt seems to turn into persecution" (p. 375).

Safán-Gerard writes:

> How we understand guilt's unbearability will determine the stance we take with our patients, and each stance has its own pitfalls. If we believe that guilt results from an unrealistically harsh superego, our aim will be to help the patient free himself or herself from this excessively demanding superego. An analyst who, in an attempt to help free the patient from excessive guilt, interprets the patient's expressions of guilt as being *merely* the result of the patient's harsh superego, is bypassing an opportunity to help the patient experience guilt, restore his or her objects, and thus replace the internal damaged object with a reconstituted one. An interpretation based on this notion can exacerbate the patient's manic defences against depressive anxiety and lead to a "flight into health." On the other hand, if we believe that guilt is a necessary response to an awareness of the individual's own destructiveness, our goal will be to help the patient bear the guilt so that reparation for the fantasised or real attacks on his or her objects can take place. (p. 352)

Those who seek to soothe the patient's superego—to "de-guilt" patients by suggesting they have nothing to feel guilty about—fail to realise that what they are dealing with is usually only the pseudo-guilt of self-torment. In addition, they fail to recognise that self-torment always has its real or imagined unconscious grounds that must be brought to consciousness and worked through. Although Freud failed to distinguish persecutory and depressive guilt, far from repudiating or negating patients' self-reproaches, he sought to help them recognise the wishes, phantasies, beliefs, and actions that underlay them. In Freudian psychoanalysis and its Kleinian development, far from soothing the psyche or the self and dismissing self-reproach as unfounded, the analyst seeks to make conscious its unconscious, real or imagined, grounds. Sometimes, as we saw in the case of Ms. A, the apparent unconscious grounds for self-reproach are irrational: she had not murdered her sister, only wished to do so, and had been gratified as well as traumatised by her sister's death and by her mother's sadistic reproach. But it was only when she faced and began to bear the guilt arising from her destructive envy and hate that she was able to recover some of her love for her sister and begin to mourn.

There is little doubt that the unconscious need for punishment and the unconscious operations of the punitive superego occupy a central place in psychopathology. Where an unconscious need for punishment exists, the unconscious superego clearly regards the subject as culpable and, hence, as deserving of punishment. But to refer to this unconscious superego judgement and the self-punitive activity that results from it simply as guilt, failing to recognise the guilt-evading function of the self-torment, obscures the fact that such self-punishment forecloses the experience of depressive anxiety or concern for the object and the resulting drive to make reparation. When Freud (1924c) refers to the "torments—the pangs of conscience" by which "a conscious sense of guilt, a consciousness of guilt, expresses itself" (p. 166), one must question whether such pangs represent authentic guilt or the self-torment that so often defends against it. Experiencing the pangs of conscience either initiates reparative efforts that tend to reduce self-torment by restoring some positive self-esteem (in which case they are genuine pangs of *conscience*), or leads to chronic, conscious or unconscious, self-punishment (in which case they are pangs inflicted not by conscience but by the punitive superego). In my view, bearing guilt does not mean suffering perpetual pangs, but acknowledging and seeking insofar as possible to repair the damage done, in this way restoring one's good objects and one's self-esteem, yet living in the awareness of the badness that inevitably accompanies one's goodness.

Whether or not one is able to bear awareness of the badness that inevitably accompanies one's goodness depends on one's level of narcissism. The excessive narcissism that cannot bear acknowledgement of any fault is characteristic of the paranoid-schizoid position. Due to splitting, the admission of any fault spreads like ink in the water and blackens the self *in toto*, and to prevent this situation, which can carry a suicide risk, fault must be denied and usually projected onto the others, the scapegoats. Quoting Anna Freud's (1936) view that "true morality begins when the internalised criticism, now embodied in the standard exacted by the superego, coincides with the ego's perception of its own fault" (p. 119), Arlow (1982) writes, "It takes very little to remind us how difficult it is to perceive, much less to acknowledge, one's own fault" (p. 233).

To view guilt exclusively as the unconscious superego activity resulting in self-punishment is to blur the crucial difference between the *subject's* self-torment and the capacity for concern for the *object*. Unconscious self-punitive activity is narcissistic. Authentic guilt moves beyond narcissism towards object love. It only leads to theoretical confusion when we employ the same term to refer to such different realities as the narcissistic, paranoid-schizoid phenomena of self-torment and shame on the one hand, and the object-oriented, depressive-position phenomena of guilt and concern on the other. Whether we opt to confine the concept of the superego to the former and refer to the latter as conscience (as I prefer), or distinguish between the archaic, paranoid-schizoid superego fuelled by hatred expressed in self-attack and the mature, depressive-position "superego" fuelled by object love and concern and generating reparative guilt, the point at issue concerns the need to recognise *the ways in which archaic superego function (self-punishment) defends against conscience or mature superego function (guilt, repentance, and reparation)*. It is as if in the face of real or imagined transgression (sins of commission or omission) the subject must suffer mental pain: if the depressive position is unattainable and depressive guilt unbearable, there appears to be no alternative to regression to schizo-paranoid self-torment.

Unlike Freud and Strachey, I do not find the notion of unconscious or repressed feelings or affects, such as guilt, problematic. One may *be* guilty but unconscious of the fact that one's conscience or superego or both consider one so. One may *be* guilty and *feel* guilty but remain unconscious of the fact that one has such feelings of guilt. But frequently, instead of coming to consciously or unconsciously *feel* guilty (whether such guilt is justified or not is another matter), the subject often unconsciously seeks punishment. Such self-punishment, I submit, usually serves as a defence against the process of coming to feel depressive guilt, even unconsciously. Ironically, one of the best defences against depressive guilt (concern) is the mobilisation of painful "guilt" feelings, the persecutory guilt in which *pangs* of "conscience" (read superego) replace *acts* of conscience—that is, acts of reparation as distinct from orgies of self-tormenting, persecutory guilt feeling. Painful pangs of conscience will either lead to constructive reparative activity or be revealed as the self-tormenting persecutory guilt that substitutes for genuine concern. By its fruits you shall know it. If guilt results in reparation towards the object, it is depressive anxiety, concern, or guilt in the depressive position. If it results in self-torment, it is persecutory, schizo-paranoid guilt.

Vignette: Ms. B.

PATIENT: I feel *terrible*! I feel *so guilty* about what I said to X the other day!

ANALYST: You're feeling awful, I understand, but is there more to it?

PATIENT: Like what?

ANALYST: Well, do you have a plan for dealing with it?

PATIENT: Well … no … not really … that's just the way I talk … the way I am.

ANALYST: Oh, so you just feel badly.

PATIENT: Isn't that what I said?

ANALYST: Well, no ... you said you felt guilty.

PATIENT: Isn't that the same thing?

ANALYST: Doesn't guilt usually involve more than that?

PATIENT: Like what?

ANALYST: (silence)

PATIENT: You mean, like, for example, apologising? Deciding not to do it again?

ANALYST: (silence)

PATIENT: I'm not sure I can do that … it's just … me.

ANALYST: Problem is, we know what happens, you feel terrible and then …

PATIENT: The headaches.
ANALYST: … a migraine starts, or suddenly you're into a squabble with your husband and then it starts.
PATIENT: That's true.
ANALYST: Guilt is so unbearable and change is so frightening you'd rather escape them by punishing yourself instead?

Where shame, persecutory anxiety, and unconscious self-punishment fail to entirely prevent guilt (concern) from arising, the repression of such guilt feeling prevents it from becoming conscious. The feeling of guilt that might accompany the state of being or being judged to be guilty is absent, either because, being found unbearable, its development has been short-circuited through mechanisms of self-torment, the pain of which is somehow preferable to unbearable guilt feeling, or because guilt feeling has been mobilised but repressed. In the latter case, continued repression would appear to promote an eventual defensive regression in which unconscious depressive guilt comes to be replaced by self-punishment.

Instead of proposing that we reserve the term *guilt* for pangs of conscience that lead to reparation as distinct from pangs that substitute for reparation, I think it makes more sense to distinguish superego and conscience and the types of guilt corresponding to each. Riesenberg-Malcolm (1980) and Safán-Gerard (1998) have shown how unconscious self-punishment or expiation serves to evade and defend against the experience of guilt as concern. The failure to make this distinction obscured the defensive function of unconscious self-torment and its role in the chronic evasion of the mental suffering, depressive anxiety, reparative guilt, and remorse that must be confronted and contained in working-through the depressive position. Frequently, when conscience judges us guilty, we evade *feeling* guilty by going directly to self-punishment. Unfortunately, evading guilt feeling in this way precludes the rational evaluation of such guilt that would enable us to decide whether to accept and make reparation for it, or reject it as unjustified.

Although Freud (1914c, 1921c) was aware of the role of libido in the development of the ego ideal, his increasing emphasis upon the punitive aspect of the superego resulting from id aggression turned back against the ego, together with his decision to subsume the ego ideal under the concept of the superego (Freud, 1923b), resulted in the widespread tendency to conceive of guilt as self-punishment rather than anxiety regarding the effects of one's real or imagined destructiveness upon the good objects (and the good self) one loves. Guilt has been equated with self-punishment rather than anxious concern and remorse. Our discontent in civilisation arises not through an increase of depressive guilt or concern, but through a heightening of the unconscious need for punishment that defends *against* reparative guilt. An advance in civilisation through a heightening of the capacity to confront and bear reparative guilt leads to a decrease, not an increase, in the persecutory anxiety that is at the core of our discontent. Our unhappiness in civilisation is a product of our hatred turned against ourselves in the form of a persecutory superego. Mature guilt, understood as depressive anxiety or concern, is not a product of the punitive superego but of the conscience or the "loving and beloved superego" fuelled not by hatred but by love.

At the conclusion of his meditation on human destructiveness, on the last page of *Civilization and Its Discontents*, Freud (1930a) writes, "And now it is to be expected that the other of the two 'Heavenly Powers,' eternal *Eros*, will make an effort to assert himself in the struggle with his equally immortal adversary" (p. 145). Despite his association of guilt with the punitive superego rather than with the conscience or loving superego, Freud understood that faced with a superego that sometimes represents a "pure culture of the death instinct" (Freud, 1923b, p. 53) our only hope lies in the power of love. Conscience, concern, and reparative guilt are functions of *Eros*, not *Thanatos*. The enlarged capacity to experience and bear guilt (i.e., to love and thereby have conscience) that is a mark of civilisation reflects the healing, not the deepening, of our cultural malaise. As Freud (1930a) himself suggests, this "dissatisfaction, for which people seek other motivations" (pp. 135–136) is a *guilt-substitute* and one, I submit, that is rendered unnecessary when the guilt it replaces is confronted and accepted. For with genuine contrition, repentance, and reparation, forgiveness and healing become possible.

Ury (1998) insightfully drew attention to the contradiction in Freudian theory between its developmental affirmation of superego formation as a sign of maturity and its clinical recognition of the role of the superego in psychopathology. She writes:

> There is a tendency in psychoanalytic literature to view the nature of guilt in two contradictory ways. The first is often found in the theoretically derived developmental premise of the tripartite structural model of intrapsychic differentiation, which states that

unconscious guilt emerges from an internalised superego, which presupposes a structured and mature ego. An assumption follows that the "capacity for guilt" is a higher and more adaptive form of mental functioning: it is healthy, civilised, and mature, and equated with notions of repair and concern. It is also often interchanged with the concept of conscience. The second view of guilt is to be found in clinical formulations of pathology where the destructiveness of guilt in psychic functioning is highlighted, especially in relation to the sadism of the superego. Despite the observation that guilt is usually, if not always, associated with destructive pathology, the developmental framework that positions guilt as a mature affect is left intact. This contradiction begins with Freud, who suggested that guilt is not only the height of civilisation, but also a deep-seated, intractable form of aggression. (p. 51)

Ury proposed to resolve this problem by distinguishing between *guilt* as a superego function observed in pathological states of self-torment, and *conscience*, as an ego function involving thought and anticipation of the consequences of our actions for others and ourselves. In this she follows Alexander (1925) and Ferenczi (1928), the latter of whom, as we have seen, went so far as to argue that, as conscience is an ego function, the aim of psychoanalysis is the complete dissolution of the superego.

As I have argued the point above, here I will only reiterate that conscience cannot be conceived primarily as an ego function since, although thinking through the consequences of potential action is an important aspect of moral functioning, reason cannot generate but only explore the implications of value judgements that it must obtain from outside itself. Aside from this, to my mind there are two main problems with Ury's proffered solution. First, it requires us to abandon our everyday association of guilt with normal and healthy experiences of the voice and pangs of conscience—that is, for what Grinberg (1964) calls *depressive* as distinct from *persecutory* guilt. Second, in excluding the operations of mature conscience from the experience of guilt and identifying the latter exclusively with the pathological states of self-torment that Grinberg calls persecutory guilt, Ury, like Freud himself, makes it difficult to see that persecutory guilt frequently functions as a defence against reparative guilt—that is, it functions as a *guilt-substitute*. I do not wish to surrender to the widespread inclination in our "culture of narcissism" (Lasch, 1979) to derogate guilt as pathology instead of recognising it as an essential component of maturity and mental and spiritual health. In addition to the persecutory superego that inflicts self-torment, there is the conscience that generates reparative guilt and with which we can be reconciled when, having inevitably fallen and failed, we own up to our guilt, repent, and attempt to make reparation. Ury's wish to rename Schafer's (1960) loving and beloved superego as conscience and by superego refer to the inner persecutor is congruent with my own thinking. But I prefer to follow Grinberg's distinction between the two types of guilt, rather than surrender the term to its persecutory variant.

Why is guilt at times so unbearable that it must be short-circuited through unconscious self-punishment? One answer is that the subject, caught up in paranoid-schizoid splitting or polarisation, feels it cannot admit any wrongdoing or badness without being revealed as a poisonously all-bad object. In other words, there is a difficulty in the area of self and object constancy, in holding both bad and good simultaneously, in being able to acknowledge the badness without forgetting the goodness and so achieving ambivalence. In the pre-ambivalent, paranoid-schizoid position, to admit any imperfection is to reveal oneself as hopelessly defective. Among other significant problems it causes, the inability to be bad while at the same time being good—not needing to be all-good as the only alternative to being all-bad—interferes with the subject's enjoyment of the pleasures of playful transgression and leads to a flattening, an impoverishment, in the domain of sexual and other forms of play and creativity. As Stoller (1974) and Kernberg (1991a) have both emphasised, "Sadomasochism, an ingredient of infantile sexuality, is an essential part of normal sexual functioning and love relations, and of the very nature of sexual excitement"—as are "bisexual identifications, the desire to transgress oedipal prohibitions and the secretiveness of the primal scene, and to violate the boundaries of a teasing and withholding object" (Kernberg, 1991a, p. 333).

It is for these reasons that Safán-Gerard (1998) recommends a technique in which analysts remind patients of their goodness whenever they seek to confront or interpret their badness. She suggests two additional reasons for patients' inability to bear the guilt for aggression towards good objects in the present. One is the unconscious linking of such attacks with similar attacks on other objects and with "omnipotent unconscious attacks on the primary object and their fantasised devastating effects"—effects imagined to be beyond repair. Another has to do with the fact that *guilt is evidence of love*: the awareness of such love threatens narcissistic, schizoid, and psychopathic patients by bringing to their attention their separateness, love, and consequent dependency and vulnerability (p. 355).

In the paranoid-schizoid position, the sadistic superego reigns. Whatever the surface effectiveness of the defensive denial, displacement, or projection of blame, the superego demands its pound of flesh for the full range of real and imagined, sexual and aggressive, sins of commission and omission towards objects and part-objects. It generates the unconscious need for punishment (persecutory guilt) that Freud equated with unconscious guilt but that I have argued functions as a defensive evasion of (depressive or reparative) guilt. Unlike therapies that collude with such evasion, psychoanalysis works against it, both by making unconscious guilt conscious, and by reawakening conscience through analysis of the self-tormenting unconscious superego activities by means of which (depressive or reparative) guilt is evaded. Because the need for punishment substitutes for and defends against genuine guilt, learning in analysis how to face and bear one's guilt (i.e., working though the depressive position) is the road to freedom from the grip of the unconscious need for punishment, and from the pressing need for soothing of the pain arising from self-torment, a point relevant to the understanding of the wide range of addictions. For, however effective on the surface, such soothing, whether derived from substances, "selfobjects", or other sources, cannot eradicate the savage god or demon, the sadistic superego and its punitive operations. By blocking development of conscience, which some prefer to call the mature superego, of guilt as concern and reparation, such soothing sets up a vicious cycle in which the subject is left at the mercy of a sadistic superego inflicting self-torment, resulting only in an increased need for soothing.

While it is true that no one can feel guilt about the damage one has done or wished to do to others without simultaneously feeling ashamed of the fact that one is the sort of person who has done or wished to do such damage, the reverse does not follow. It is possible to experience shame without guilt—that is, to be so self-obsessed that one loses sight of the object altogether except as a mirror or audience or resource for the self. In this sense, while it may be incorrect to say that guilt is a more mature emotion than shame, in that mature people continue to experience both, it is certainly true that the person who can experience guilt is more mature than the person who can experience only shame. In such a mature person, despite shame for the self, concern for the object (i.e., reparative guilt) is maintained. On the more primitive level of the paranoid-schizoid position one may experience predominantly shame—one can be suffused with shame without having to cease one's self-obsession long enough to feel any concern for the object. On the other hand, one may mature to the point of becoming ashamed of one's narcissism and incapacity to experience guilt. This is perhaps a turning point initiating an advance to a level of object-relating, the depressive position, at which the capacity for concern is finally achieved. While my analysis differs in emphasis from that of Wurmser (1981), his distinction between shame and guilt is congruent with that elaborated here: "Shame protects an integral image of the self; guilt protects the integrity of an object" (p. 67). He associates shame with "primary process thought—the language of the self" and guilt with "secondary process thought—the language of object relations" (p. 67).

This is not to say that guilt may not seem at times to be a defence against shame, as Fairbairn (1952) recognised in describing "the moral defence" in which the unloved child attempts to escape traumatic helplessness through the illusion of control afforded by blaming the self for the parental failure to love. In order to escape intolerable shame in the face of one's unmet needs and one's helpless dependence on others who cannot be controlled, one resorts to an illusion of guilt, which at least moves the trauma into the field of one's own defensive omnipotence. There is no doubt that this mechanism exists and is important in psychopathology. But, far from constituting an argument for reducing guilt to an underlying shame, it merely points to a spurious or unjustified guilt, for such pseudo-guilt that functions as an escape from a painful state of shame reflects no concern for the object; its function is purely defensive. The very idea that the phenomenon of human guilt could be reduced to such pseudo-guilt and in this way made subordinate to shame is itself a symptom of a widespread desperation to somehow find a way to sidestep the real guilt that is an inevitable part of mature object-relations. The motive for this wish to reduce guilt to shame is simply the wish to sidestep both the conscience and the superego and continue to live in a culture of narcissism with a psychology that evades the developmental demand that we move beyond issues of shame and the self and take up the cross of object-relating and the inevitable struggles with guilt that such relating entails.

Towards the end of his perceptive essay on shame, Karen (1992) writes of a patient whom he says wants to know "the real me" but is afraid to find out. She is afraid to face "the shameful fact that she is a shrew to her husband and children ... [and suffers from] the desperate fear that she will be found in the wrong" (p. 69). He points out, "To stop running and experience the shame is to give herself a chance to recognise that being in the wrong for acting like a shrew does not mean that her husband isn't also in the wrong in his way, nor does it make her into a poisonously deformed and unlovable thing" (p. 69). Beyond this, it is necessary to add that only if she faces and learns to bear her depressive guilt, repents, and ceases to be a shrew will she be able to overcome the self-tormenting shame, the persecutory anxiety, that is her substitute for depressive guilt.

This is not the place to discuss the complex technical issues involved in the clinical handling of these problems. Suffice it to say that persons suffering from a persecutory superego are all too ready to hear its confrontation and interpretation as accusation or attack and to flee from or, alternatively, submit to and even be gratified in being, as they imagine, attacked in this way. But the fact that the sadistic superego can turn interpretations of the sadistic superego to its own purposes does not mean that the sadistic superego does not exist or need, eventually, to be interpreted. It merely means that it must be approached tactfully, skilfully, and strategically. It is here that respect for patients' resistances is most important. Patients suffering from the severe neuroses have good reasons for evading depressive guilt by resorting automatically to self-torment: fixed in the paranoid-schizoid position as they are, any admission of fault appears to confront them with a traumatic and unbearable sense of badness, inadequacy, and shame.

Safán-Gerard (1998) offers a number of technical suggestions in this regard that can help the analyst attempting to confront guilt-evasion avoid being caught in an enactment of blaming that only enables the patient to project the critical superego into the analyst, to thereby feel confirmed in victimhood, and further avoid responsibility. In this connection, Wurmser (2000), informed by the work of Paul Gray (1994) on defence analysis, advises us "to avoid, as much as is possible, falling into the role of a judging authority, to avoid fulfilling in reality, much less creating, the transference of superego functions, and rather, ... to analyse them" (p. ix). While much of his critique of the use of direct drive interpretation by the early Kleinians, and Kernberg's use of confrontation focused especially on splitting, may be valid to a degree, for such techniques can intensify resistance to the point of impasse, Wurmser fails to note that "the contemporary Kleinians of London", whom Schafer (1997) calls "Kleinian Freudians" precisely to emphasise the continuity of their work with mainstream Freudian psychoanalysis, long ago replaced such techniques in favour of their own very subtle forms of defence, resistance, transference, and superego analysis. As a consequence of his rejection of contemporary Kleinian themes, Wurmser's (1987, 2000) work on the dynamics of "flight from conscience" is hampered by his insufficient differentiation between paranoid-schizoid and depressive phenomena. He employs the term *conscience* to describe both the persecutory and the loving superego; and fails to distinguish conscience (depressive guilt or concern) from persecutory anxiety and the unconscious need for punishment. Progress in this field will only come when in psychoanalysis we recover the crucial differentiation between superego and conscience or, as it was known for several centuries during the Reformation, between law and gospel (Pelikan, 1984; see Chapter Ten).

"A person will spend his whole life writhing in the clutches of the superficial, psychological symptoms of guilt unless he learns to speak its true language" (Carroll, 1985, p. 15). The challenge facing the guilt-evading subject is that of facing and bearing its guilt, integrating as a part of the tragic dimension of human existence the reality of our primordial ambivalence, and accepting as an aspect of "common human unhappiness" the need to shoulder the burden of responsibility to make reparation, and to change, that genuinely facing our guilt entails. Facing and bearing guilt opens the path towards restoration of a sense of inner goodness through reparative processes mediating identification with surviving (Carveth, 1994; Winnicott, 1969), comforting, forgiving, good internal objects. If advance in civilisation entails an increased capacity to confront and bear guilt, then a first step may be to learn to speak its true language, not least by ceasing to confuse it with the self-torment that represents its evasion.

CHAPTER FIVE

Less recognised manifestations of guilt: the old and new hysterias*

One of the many important lessons Freud learned from Charcot during his period of study at the Salpêtrière (Oct. 1885–Feb. 1886), was that male hysteria exists. "What impressed me most of all while I was with Charcot", Freud (1925d) writes in his *An Autobiographical Study*, "were his latest investigations of hysteria, some of which were carried out under my own eyes. He had proved, for instance, ... the frequent occurrence of hysteria in men. ...." (p. 12). But when Freud brought the news of male hysteria back to Vienna he got a cold reception. He writes: "One of them, an old surgeon, actually broke out with the exclamation: 'But, my dear sir, how can you talk such nonsense? *Hysteron* (*sic*) means the uterus. So how can a man be hysterical?'" (p. 15). But the fact is that men certainly can be hysterical, as Freud knew from the case with which he was most familiar: himself (his famous hysterical fainting episodes provide merely one example). Although he often tried to conceptualise his persistent symptoms as arising from what he called an *actual* as distinct from a *psycho*neurosis, a condition of an essentially somatic order supposedly without

---

*Both Jean Hantman and Naomi Gold assisted in the writing of the paper (Carveth & Carveth, 2003) upon which this chapter is based.

psychological meaning, the concept of the actual neurosis was dropped by subsequent psychoanalysis because no cases of it were found. At other times, Freud was able to acknowledge both to himself and others the hysterical and psychoneurotic nature of certain of his symptoms.

But the resistance to recognition of male hysteria persisted. The concept received little attention in Freud's own later work, or in that of his colleagues and, as Elaine Showalter (1997) has pointed out, despite its early recognition of the fact of male hysteria, psychoanalysis came essentially to collude with the wider cultural feminisation of hysteria in which a man might be said to be hysterical if he was homosexual, but otherwise his hysteria would be redefined as "shell shock", "battle neurosis", "post-traumatic stress disorder", or some other more "manly" condition. In speaking of hysteria, I reject such feminisation and seek to reinforce Freud's and Charcot's original discovery. While its feminisation is a significant aspect of our culture of interest to sociologists and feminist theorists, hysteria itself is not a gender-specific disorder. I for one have seen rampant evidence of male hysteria in my practice. Hysterical and psychosomatic symptoms ranging from mild to severe seem to be ubiquitous.

What then is hysteria? For Freud it took three main forms: anxiety hysteria (panic attacks), phobia, and conversion hysteria. The latter is a condition in which one presents symptoms that mimic those of organically-based medical illnesses but that have no organic basis. The classic example of this is the so-called "glove anaesthesia" in which the paralysis of the hand does not follow known nerve pathways but corresponds instead to the mental concept of the hand as distinct from the wrist or the rest of the arm. Hysterics are not malingerers: they do not consciously fake organic illness, but unconsciously mimic it. Hysteria is not to be confused with psychosomatic disease in which one suffers from a genuine medical illness or dysfunction, but one believed to be caused to a significant extent by psycho-emotional factors. Psychosomatic illness is not "only in one's head"; it is clearly in one's body; objective signs of tissue pathology are evident. By contrast, hysterical symptoms, although psychologically real and painful enough, have no organic basis: they are products of mimesis. Because their symptoms are not consciously faked, but unconsciously mimicked, hysterics are not malingerers, but neurotic sufferers.

The symptoms of both conversion hysteria and psychosomatic disease are painful and tormenting to patients suffering from them (and, of course, there are cases reflecting a mixture of the two, as in the case of Mr. C, described below). Why, the psychoanalyst must ask, do we bring such suffering and torment upon ourselves? The answer, I believe, is that we (both hysterics and psychosomatics) have an unconscious need for punishment. But why do we unconsciously seek punishment? We do so because on one level we judge ourselves guilty of some real or imagined crime, but instead of consciously confronting such judgement, rationally evaluating it and either rejecting it as unfounded or accepting its validity, bearing guilt, and seeking to make reparation, we repress it and succumb to the unconscious superego's demand for punishment—the unconsciously self-inflicted suffering entailed in hysterical, psychosomatic, and other neurotic symptoms. Those of us who consider the admission of sin and wrongdoing an intolerable insult to our narcissism and find conscious guilt unbearable are forced to resort to symptom-formation. The suffering entailed in our symptoms gratifies the superego need for punishment and, at the same time, evades unbearable conscious guilt. But the price of this refusal to render moral judgement conscious is loss of the opportunity to subject it to rational assessment and conscientious judgement leading either to conscious acceptance and the bearing of conscious guilt, or to conscious rejection and superego modification in the light of conscience.

It is precisely to avoid the question (why do we bring such suffering upon ourselves?), and the answer to which it leads (an unconscious need for punishment), and the further question to which this answer gives rise (what is our real or imagined crime?), that we resist so vociferously the premise that grounds this unwanted series of questions and answers: the idea that we do in fact bring such suffering upon ourselves. If we are to evade the issue of "crime and punishment", we must evade the fundamental idea that we are the agents, not merely the victims, of our hysterical and psychosomatic misery. To represent ourselves essentially as passive victims of these afflictions rather than as agents inflicting them upon ourselves for understandable reasons is to "de-moralise" our understanding of such conditions and ourselves. But however much we seek such de-moralisation, both as suffering individuals and as a cultural community increasingly committed to a de-moralising postmodern discourse, the fact remains that, like it or not, there is a moralist alive and well in each of us, a conscience (however buried), as well as an often harsh and sadistic superego. De-moralise as much as we like consciously; deny agency, responsibility, and guilt as much as we will. All that applies only to consciousness. Unless wrongdoing and even wrong feeling are consciously and conscientiously confronted and worked through via repentance, restitution, and reparation, the unconscious superego will continue to accuse and to demand its pound of flesh. The de-moralising cultural and personal discourses that repress or otherwise evade agency, responsibility, and guilt end up producing the demoralising conditions (depression, masochism, hysteria, paranoia, psychosomatic disease) that result from the activity of the unconscious superego that these discourses deny: de-moralising leads to demoralisation.

Most of us, to one degree or another, are fugitives from guilt—whether our guilt evasion takes a hysterical, a psychosomatic, or some other psychopathological form. We cling to the de-moralising discourses that we fabricate for ourselves, sometimes with the help of de-moralising therapists, and the de-moralising discourses offered by our postmodern culture, in a desperate attempt to believe we are victims of mysterious afflictions rather than moral agents afflicting ourselves with suffering for our real or imagined crimes. And we do this because we refuse the burden of moral agency: the need either to consciously bear guilt if conscience considers it merited, or consciously confront and disempower the accusing superego in the light of conscience if it is not. It matters little whether our hysteria takes the old-fashioned form of the paralyses, tics, and fainting episodes, etc., that characterised the hysterias of the late nineteenth and early twentieth centuries, or such more contemporary forms as so-called "environmental illness", "multiple chemical sensitivity", "chronic fatigue syndrome", "fibromyalgia syndrome", etc., the dynamics remain essentially the same. However much what Edward Shorter (1992) calls "the legitimate symptom pool" may vary from time to time and place to place—for example, a legitimate symptom in one cultural situation is the Koro complaint that someone has stolen or reduced the size of one's penis—the underlying dynamics remain constant: unconscious superego accusation for real or imagined crimes, leading to a need for punishment, that takes the form of hysterical, psychosomatic, paranoid, and other forms of psychological and/or physical suffering.

What does characterise the new, as distinct from the old hysterias, is their more obvious reliance upon defensive externalisation and, hence, the paranoid element in their structure. It is for this reason that I employ the term *hystero-paranoid* to describe states of feeling persecuted by supposed environmental agents (toxins, moulds, parasites, etc.) or molestation by satanic cults or by aliens. The role of hostility, its projection, and its return in the form of delusions of external or internal persecution is emphasised here precisely because these factors have been underemphasised in most previous discussions of hysteria.

* * *

In *Hystories: Hysterical Epidemics and Modern Media*, Showalter (1997) explored a range of conditions—chronic fatigue syndrome, multiple personality disorder, recovered memory, satanic ritual abuse, alien abduction, Gulf War syndrome—that she viewed as modern forms of hysteria as distinct from the old conversion and anxiety hysterias characteristic of the nineteenth century *fin-de-siècle* and associated with the names of Charcot, Janet, Breuer, and Freud. Against the widespread claim that hysteria is a thing of the past, having disappeared owing to the rise of feminism or a level of psychological sophistication incompatible with the formation of hysterical symptoms except perhaps among culturally "backward" populations, Showalter argued that, on the contrary, far from having died, hysteria is alive and well in the form of the psychological plagues or epidemics of "imaginary illnesses" and "hypnotically induced pseudo memories" that characterise today's cultural narratives of hysteria (pp. 4–5).

Although she provided a rich description of the new hysterias—the "hystories" or hysterical stories of chronic fatigue, alien abduction, and so on—Showalter did not pretend to offer a depth-psychological account of the psychodynamics underlying these conditions beyond identifying the role of suggestion on the part of physicians and the media in their creation and dissemination. Her definition of hysteria as "a form of expression, a body language for people who otherwise might not be able to speak or even to admit what they feel" (p. 7) and as "a cultural symptom of anxiety and stress" arising from conflicts that are "genuine and universal" (p. 9) was accurate enough as far as it went. From a psychoanalytic point of view, however, it did not go far enough.

Although she did not appear to share Juliet Mitchell's (2000) insight that "… there is violence as well as sexuality in the seductions and rages of the hysteric" (p. x), Showalter did call attention to the centrality of externalisation (i.e., projection) in these conditions. She wrote: "Contemporary hysterical patients blame external sources— a virus, sexual molestation, chemical warfare, satanic conspiracy, alien infiltration—for psychic problems" (1997, p. 4). In recognising the paranoid element in hysteria, albeit without theorising the connection, Showalter contributed to the evolution of a deeper understanding. In the following, I will fasten upon this externalising feature and offer a psychoanalytic understanding of both the old and the new hysterias (including so-called multiple chemical sensitivity, environmental illness, and fibromyalgia syndrome) as subtypes of a more general *hystero-paranoid syndrome*.

Whereas traditional psychoanalytic accounts have emphasised the role of Oedipal and pre-Oedipal sexual wishes and conflicts in hysteria, seldom associating it with aggression and paranoia, I believe such overlooked psychological factors as unconscious aggression, envy, hostility, malice, destructiveness, and the resulting persecutory guilt and need for punishment occupy a central place in both the old and the new hysterias. Following the conception of the unconscious need for punishment as a defensive evasion of unbearable depressive guilt rather than its equivalent, I see hysterical, psychosomatic, depressive, masochistic, and other self-tormenting conditions as defensive alternatives to facing and bearing depressive or reparative guilt.

Although this analysis has much in common with both Showalter's *Hystories* and Edward Shorter's (1992) *From Paralysis to Fatigue*, it is necessary to correct their occasional blurring of the important distinction between hysteria and psychosomatic conditions and their use of the term "somatisation" in the description of both. Showalter, for example, notes correctly that "[O]n the whole, Freudians make strict distinctions between hysterical symptoms and psychosomatic symptoms" (p. 44) yet refers to "psychosomatic conversion symptoms" (p. 36). She muddies the waters further by describing the conversion symptom as a particular form of "symbolic somatisation" (p. 44). But somatisation is a process in which psychological and emotional forces contribute to the development of genuine organic disease; symbolisation, if it is operative at all (and I believe it often is), takes a different form than in hysteria where physical symptoms and dysfunctions have no discoverable organic basis but are formed through a psychological process of *mimesis*. Showalter made no secret of her difficulty with these concepts: "How psychiatrists tell the difference between hysterical and psychosomatic symptoms is hard for a layman to figure out" (p. 44). Though no doubt there are cases involving both psychosomatic and hysterical processes, psychosomatic symptoms are symptoms of objective medical disease thought to result from a process of somatisation in which psychological and emotional forces affect the immune system and operate in conjunction with various organic and constitutional predispositions to produce disease. By contrast, hysterical symptoms involve no objective organic pathology but entail the unconscious mimicry of organic disease and dysfunction—as distinct from their conscious imitation as in malingering.

Whereas many writers on psychosomatic disease see it as entailing the failure or foreclosure of symbolisation, I believe a symbolisation process may yet be at work in it, as the following case vignette suggests.

Vignette: Mr. C

Mr. C had been suffering for some years from an objectively observable, painfully tormenting rash covering much of his body surface. It had proved resistant to a myriad of medical treatments. Recently, in addition, he had been experiencing frequent "accidents", a few of which had been life-threatening. It turned out that for years, as the eldest son of a large family, he had been saddled with the sole responsibility for looking after his aging parents, his chronically depressed mother and his bitter, manipulative, narcissistic father. His own business was suffering owing to his need to make frequent trips to another country to attend to their real and imagined needs. His siblings, in the meantime, were happily leading their own lives and quite content to have the patient free them from their own responsibilities *vis-à-vis* the parents.

When asked in the first session whether he ever felt angry over this state of affairs, Mr. C looked curious and reported that his friends had sometimes asked him the same thing. Over the next few sessions he proceeded to become angrier and angrier, and as he did so his rash began to diminish. He had been raised within a particularly concrete and magical version of Christianity. The rash, it turned out, had made him feel he was "burning in hell" in punishment for his hitherto unconscious death wishes towards his parents and his anger at the siblings who saddled him with the responsibility for looking after them. As his rage and death wishes became conscious and began to subside as he started to take constructive action to end his masochistic submission to exploitation, the rash gradually disappeared. But because Mr. C was as yet unable to consistently experience and bear depressive guilt, his rash was quickly replaced by other forms of self-sabotage and self-punishment. Having freed himself from masochistic submission to parents and siblings, he proceeded to enter a relationship with an exploitative and manipulative woman.

As a result of clinical experiences of this sort, I am not at all convinced that the difference between conversion and somatisation boils down to the presence of symbolism in the former and its absence in the latter, though it is possible that different types or levels of symbolisation may be involved in the two conditions. Showalter (1997, p. 7) quoted Mark Micale (1994, p. 182), who wrote that "[H]ysteria is not a disease; rather it is an alternative, physical, verbal, and gestural language, an iconic social communication". Psychosomatic illness *is* disease, but it, too, appears, at least sometimes, to involve interpretable unconscious meaning.

According to Mitchell (2000), "Hysteria's many manifestations have shown some striking similarities throughout the ages—sensations of suffocation, choking, breathing and eating difficulties, mimetic imitations, deceitfulness, shock, fits, death states, wanting (craving, longing)" (p. 13). Under the category of mimetic imitations falls the hysterical utilisation of the body in the simulation of organically based disease and somatic dysfunction. In the theatrics of "conversion", physical illness is dramatically mimicked—once again, unconsciously, not consciously as in malingering—and somatic dysfunction (difficulty swallowing, paralysis, contractions, non-organic limp, paraplegia, etc.) lacking any discoverable organic basis is displayed. The type of hysteria known as hypochondria involves subjective suffering and the conviction that one is medically ill in the absence of objective evidence of disease or injury.

Psychosomatic illness involves somatisation as distinct from conversion or mimetic imitation. In somatisation, manifest psychological distress of various sorts (such as Mr. 'C's rage, death wishes, and consequent persecutory guilt) is blocked from consciousness and feeling, either because the subject is lacking in the necessary words and psychological understanding to express it (see Sifneos, 1996, on "alexithymia"), or because it is found to be unbearable and consequently foreclosed and somehow channelled into the body. In either case it results in real organic disease, such as Mr. 'C's objectively observable burning rash, that functions as a self-punitive and persecutory alternative to unbearable depressive guilt. But the foreclosure of the experience of depressive guilt does not always entail a foreclosure of symbolisation. The pain arising from his organic rash symbolised to Mr. C that he was "burning in hell" for his sins, his failure to "honour" mother and father, and his Cain-like murderous rage towards his siblings. Although, like Showalter, some writers (e.g., Taylor, Bagby, & Parker, 1997) blur the distinction between hysteria and psychosomatic disease by considering all disease psychosomatic on the grounds that all disease involves psychological factors to some degree, this ignores the fact that what distinguishes psychosomatic disease is precisely the prominence of psychological factors in its aetiology.

Although she employed the title *Theatres of the Body* for a book dealing primarily with psychosomatic disease rather than hysteria, Joyce McDougall (1989) recognised the role of symbolisation processes in both the drama of hysterical conversion, the theatrical "neurotic hysteria" in which it is so obvious, as well as in what she called the "archaic hysteria" of psychosomatic disease (p. 54) in which it is often more obscure. The symbolisation entailed in somatisation, as distinct from conversion, may take the archaic form that Hanna Segal (1957) described as "symbolic equation" as contrasted with the more elaborated symbolisation processes entailed in "symbolic representation". Far from seeing meaning in hysteria and only a foreclosure of meaning in psychosomatic disease, I believe that in both conditions, whatever additional factors may be in play, unconscious aggression and an unconscious need to suffer serve as alternatives to and defences against unbearable depressive guilt. But whereas the mimicry and theatrics of hysteria embody an hystero-paranoid defence against and substitute for the experience of unbearable depressive guilt, in psychosomatic conditions the need to suffer finds an all-too-real and concrete outlet in the development of organic disease and its attendant discomfort, pain, and torment.

Both classical Freudian and post-Freudian psychoanalysis have emphasised the role in hysteria of such factors as forbidden sexual wishes, unresolved Oedipal conflicts, castration anxiety, the need for attachment, and the compulsion to preserve object ties or a threatened sense of self. In so doing, they have tended to lose sight of the role of aggression and guilt—just as in various branches of contemporary psychoanalytic thought the dynamics of the superego have been lost sight of. I have heard psychoanalytic colleagues, not Freudians or Kleinians but self psychologists and some relational analysts, report that they seldom if ever encounter guilt or the unconscious need for punishment as significant dynamics in the lives of their patients. A technique of empathic attunement to patients' conscious and preconscious experience that views any ideas about their unconscious experience as no more than the analyst's imposition of his or her theories might be expected to ignore these dynamics.

It is not my intent to deny the role of sexuality, attachment, object relations, or issues of identity and the self in these conditions, but merely to refocus attention on factors that I regard as central but that, for a variety of reasons, have widely succumbed to what Russell Jacoby (1975) has referred to as the "social amnesia" in which "society remembers less and less faster and faster" and in which "the sign of the times is thought that has succumbed to fashion" (p. 1). Even while "listening with the third ear" (Reik, 1948) to the latent meanings, messages, motives, and dynamics underlying manifest symptoms and experience, Freud was so centred on sexuality in hysteria that he tended to overlook or downplay the role of aggression. Although in his final dual instinct theory Freud (1920g) eventually made aggression as fundamental as sexuality in his metapsychology, he never reworked his psychology of hysteria in this light.

Mitchell (2000) suggests that another reason for the neglect of the role of aggression (and, hence, of guilt) in hysteria had to do with Freud's and subsequent psychoanalysts' relative retreat from Charcot's and Freud's own earlier recognition of the fact of male hysteria. This led psychoanalysts to collude with the wider cultural equation of hysteria with femininity. Although hysteria could be acknowledged in the "effeminate" male homosexual, gross instances of hysteria in heterosexual men were redefined as "shell shock", "battle fatigue", "posttraumatic stress disorder", etc., while the everyday instances of male hysteria—dizzy spells, fainting (such as Freud's famous faints in Jung's presence), organically ungrounded orthopaedic dysfunctions, and such psychosomatic phenomena as sensitive breasts and swollen abdomens in men whose wives are pregnant, etc.—are somehow overlooked or discounted.

Listening with the third ear does not guarantee recognition of the aggression underlying manifest suffering, but without this distinctively psychoanalytic capacity there is simply no way it will be detected. As a consequence of this failure, patients who experience such suffering remain unempowered by the discovery of their unconscious subjectivity.

For far from being simple victims or martyrs of mysterious afflictions, in reality they are unconscious sadomasochistic agents tormenting themselves for understandable reasons.

* * *

In Todd Haynes's film, *Safe* (1995), Carol White (Julianne Moore) is an affluent but bored suburban housewife who appears, at the outset, to be suffering from a personality disorder of a schizoid type character-ised by identity diffusion, anhedonia, diffuse anxiety, and "emptiness depression". Obsessively preoccupied with maintaining and enhancing her spacious, tastefully furnished and decorated home, she seems oth-erwise unoccupied and lost. She appears curiously detached from both sexuality and aggression. Her stepson's vivid, albeit politically incor-rect, essay on gang violence offends her; she asks, "Why does it have to be so gory'?" In another scene the camera plays over Carol's blank and emotionally detached face as her husband performs intercourse (one cannot call this making love); she pats his back distractedly as he reaches orgasm.

Gradually, in addition to her vague anxiety, joylessness, and detach-ment, Carol begins to develop a range of mysterious physical symp-toms (nosebleeds, coughing fits, difficulty breathing, etc.) for which, after extensive investigation, her doctor is unable to find any physical basis. He refers her for psychiatric treatment, despite her suppressed yet evident hostility and bland resistance to the idea that psychological factors might be at the root of "symptoms" that by now have led her to withdraw entirely from sexual involvement with her husband. As frustrating as he finds this situation, her husband struggles, not entirely successfully, to suppress his irritation. Despite his father's strictures, Carol's stepson still manifests his anger towards her; socialisation into the family culture of politeness and non-aggression has apparently not yet fully taken hold of him.

Encouraged by the suggestions of a friend and a flier found in a health food store from an "alternative healthcare" organisation that she later contacts, Carol comes increasingly to attribute her problems to an environment that she believes contains toxins to which she is chemically sensitive. We witness the worsening of her "environmen-tal illness" or "multiple chemical sensitivity" as she retreats from her home and family to a supposedly chemically "safe" environment pro-vided by this group in the rural south-west; and then, when this proves insufficient, to a specially engineered, igloo-like habitation designed to provide even more effective protection against a world to which she seems increasingly allergic.

Throughout most of this film the director maintains a neutral attitude as to whether Carol's affliction is chemically based, as she insists, or hysterical or psychosomatic, as her physicians seem to think. But towards the end there is a group encounter session at the retreat led by its resident guru in which, one by one, her fellow patients painfully acknowledge that their "environmental illness" had arisen as a kind of unconsciously self-punitive alternative to consciously facing guilt and making reparation for their hitherto unacknowledged hatred, bitterness, longings for revenge, and inability to forgive others and themselves. Carol listens distractedly but appears unmoved by these revelations.

Her "illness" intensifies. At the end of the film we see her recoil anxiously from her visiting husband's parting embrace, apparently a "reaction" to the cologne he was wearing, as he and her stepson prepare to fly home. With what appears to be an oddly contented look on her face, she heads back to her isolated and hermetically sealed capsule.

One of the aspects of the film most interesting to the clinician concerns the way that Peter Dunning, the resident guru/therapist, is depicted. Initially at least, he and his organisation appear to advocate the idea that "environmental illness" is a genuine medical condition caused by toxins that official medicine has so far failed to identify. But over time we detect a subtle shift in the messages he communicates to his patients: he increasingly suggests that their suffering is a consequence less of toxic chemicals than of toxic emotions.

Although Dunning's directions to "think positive" and replace hatred with love have a distinctly "New Age" flavour and strike the psychoanalytically informed viewer as naïve, the overall therapeutic strategy of his retreat could be viewed as ingenious. Instead of directly confronting the patient with the hysterical and paranoid nature of his or her disorder, he adopts what followers of Hyman Spotnitz's (1969, 1976) "modern psychoanalysis" refer to as the techniques of "mirroring" and "joining". He "mirrors" their condition himself: he too suffers from an immune deficiency disease. And instead of attacking the resistance to awareness of the emotional causes of their suffering, he "joins" this resistance and gives the appearance, initially at least, of sharing their understanding of it as caused by a toxic environment. (Much later he will insist that sufferers from "environmental illness" have made themselves sick by attacking their own immune systems, thus making themselves vulnerable to environmental factors.)

Like many psychoanalysts who work with highly resistant, personality disordered, and psychotic individuals, Dunning has the clinical wisdom not to attempt, at the outset and perhaps for a very long time, to differ with or challenge the preferred self-understanding of his patients. But unlike those therapists who never move beyond empathy and the validation of experience and who therefore collude with the very pathology they should be treating, Dunning, like Spotnitz and his followers, eventually comes out of the therapeutic closet, as it were, and invites his patients to face the much resisted emotional basis of their afflictions, which he rightly regards as rooted in the dynamics of unconscious self-attack.

We do not know what becomes of Carol. Perhaps she eventually becomes willing to set aside her paranoid evasion of responsibility and to call herself into question. But this is doubtful, for she seems more than "half in love with easeful Death" (Keats, 1819). But what are the sins, real or imagined, for which she has judged herself deserving of self-execution? Whereas the hatred poisoning the psyche of Nell, one of the other patients in the group, is "hot" and therefore unmistakable, Carol's is cool and easily masked by her apparent meekness and suffering. Being only eleven and, in the great tradition of pre-adolescents, as yet incompletely civilised, her stepson Rory sees it—and hates her back.

* * *

Central to Showalter's (1997) argument is the observation that the hysteria investigated by Breuer and Freud was not the isolated product of a certain historical period. Rather, the same "illness" has mutated into contemporary forms corresponding to changes in the cultural context. Thus, the late-twentieth-century syndromes she described (chronic fatigue syndrome; multiple personality disorder; satanic ritual abuse; alien abduction; Gulf War syndrome) are modern forms of the hysteria once diagnosed in upper-class Victorian women; and they are "psychological epidemics" (p. 1). To Showalter's list of new hysterias, I would add: Carol White's multiple chemical sensitivity or environmental illness; fibromyalgia syndrome; popular concerns with intestinal toxins, parasitic infestation, and colonic cleansing; the Tourette's-like shaking of teenage girls in upstate New York; as well as hysterical exaggeration in situations of real but limited threat, such as the Y2K hysteria, that surrounding anthrax after 9/11, around mad cow disease, moulds, and the SARS epidemic in Toronto—the list goes on and on. I believe it makes sense to classify all these phenomena as subtypes of a more general *hystero-paranoid syndrome*. In keeping with Freud's acknowledgement that the "choice of neurosis" is often beyond the powers of psychoanalysis to explain, so the development of one subtype of the hystero-paranoid syndrome as distinct from another may not be fully accountable in particular cases.

Showalter defined hystories as "the cultural narratives of hysteria" (p. 5). In no way was she accusing patients of merely fabricating, pretending, seeking attention, or malingering. Nor was she stating categorically that there is no organic basis for the perceived symptoms, although, as she pointed out, none of the hundreds of studies investigating these claims had produced any conclusive evidence (except perhaps, in some cases of so-called Gulf War syndrome). Despite this absence of scientific support, sufferers aggressively maintain an unyielding conviction that their symptoms are organically based. Like Showalter, I have no reluctance to acknowledge an organic basis for such conditions if and when consensually validated scientific evidence leads to their medical recognition as diseases.

In *Hysteria: The Elusive Neurosis* (1978), Alan Krohn writes: "It should be stressed that hysterics are not faking, playing games, or simply seeking attention.... The hysteric is neither a malingerer nor a psychopath in that the sorts of parts he plays, feelings he experiences, and actions he undertakes have predominantly unconscious roots—he is usually not aware of trying to fool or deceive" (p. 162). Yet, as Krohn observes, such hysterical theatrics display certain standards of conventionality and reality-testing: "The facility with which the hysteric can utilise roles considered acceptable by his culture attests to his sensitivity to the norms of the culture, the limits of acceptability, interpersonal resourcefulness—in short, his capacity for good reality testing, impulse control, and interpersonal sensitivity" (pp. 161–162).

It is a hallmark of those suffering from the newer forms of hysteria to insist on the existence of objective (as distinct from subjective or psychological and emotional) causes of their perceived symptoms: viruses (as yet neither isolated nor identified by medical researchers); toxin-producing faecal matter impacted in the bowels; radiation emitted by video display terminals; moulds growing on or in the walls of houses;

long-repressed memories of satanic ritual abuse; abduction by aliens; and so on. Indeed, multitudes of people in North America and Western Europe present with long lists of seemingly inexplicable and unrelated symptoms: extreme fatigue, sore muscles, swollen glands, headaches, stomach troubles, rashes, memory dysfunction, and depression. So vehement are the convictions of many of these patients that their conditions have objective rather than subjective origins that Showalter was roundly attacked for suggesting that psychological and sociocultural factors might be involved. Similarly, with respect to so-called "fibromyalgia syndrome", neurologist Thomas Bohr, who with psychiatrist Arthur Barsky "contends that even honouring this bundle of symptoms with a medical label may be doing more to make people sick than to cure them" (Groopman, 2000, p. 86), "has received more than two hundred pieces of hate mail, and has been lambasted by fibromyalgia advocates on the Internet and in newsletters" (p. 91)—despite the fact that "these doctors don't claim that the symptoms of fibromyalgia are not real, only that their origin lies in the mind and not in the peripheral nerves of the body" (p. 86). Showalter remarked that the ferocity of these reactions "has only confirmed my analysis of hysterical epidemics of denial, projection, accusation, and blame" (p. x).

Nevertheless, challenging American Medical Association position papers, some physicians have lent support to the objectifying claims of these patients, maintaining that they are suffering from genuine illnesses to which names such as "chronic fatigue syndrome", "fibromyalgia syndrome", and "multiple chemical sensitivity" have been appended. It is for this reason, Showalter asserted, that the proliferation of these conditions depends both on the media "narratives" that do so much to generate them (hence the "stories" of "hystories") and on the collusion of physicians, researchers, and psychotherapists who either take at face value the patient claims with which they are presented or, in some cases, operating from their own therapeutic agendas, actually help manufacture the maladies in question through processes of subtle and not so subtle suggestion and interpersonal influence. In this connection it is significant that the rheumatologist who first codified the so-called fibromyalgia syndrome now wishes he could make this diagnosis disappear. In an interview reported by Groopman (2000), Dr. Frederick Wolfe is reported as saying: "For a moment in time, we thought we had discovered a new physical disease. . . . But it was the emperor's new clothes. When we started out, in the eighties, we saw patients going from doctor to doctor with pain. We believed that by telling them they had fibromyalgia we reduced stress and reduced medical utilisation. This idea, a great, humane idea that we can interpret their distress as fibromyalgia and help them—it didn't turn out that way. My view now is that we are creating an illness rather than curing one" (p. 87).

The fact that hysterical symptoms as they are presented "have internal similarities or evolve in similar directions as they're retold" does not necessitate the conclusion that an objective event or organic disorder underlies them: "Patients learn about diseases from the media, unconsciously develop the symptoms, and then attract media attention in an endless cycle. The human imagination is not infinite, and we are all bombarded by these plot lines every day. Inevitably, we all live out the social stories of our time" (Showalter, 1997, p. 6). Showalter's literary training served her well in her analysis of "intertextuality", the narrative similarities that believers find so compelling: "Literary critics … realise that similarities between two stories do not mean that they mirror a common reality or even that the writers have read each other's texts. Like all narratives, hystories have their own conventions, stereotypes, and structures. Writers inherit common themes, structures, characters, and images. … We need not assume that patients are either describing an organic disorder or else lying when they present similar narratives of symptoms" (p. 6).

Despite the twentieth century's supposed psychological revolution, "… many people still reject psychological explanations for symptoms; they believe psychosomatic [and hysterical or somatoform] disorders are illegitimate and search for physical evidence that firmly places cause and cure outside the self" (p. 4). The validity of this observation is borne out by the vociferous insistence of hysterical patients themselves who demand that their symptoms, however indefinite and variable, be acknowledged as genuine, organically based conditions. For example, rejecting any suggestion that psychological factors might be involved in her suffering and insisting on the medical objectivity of so-called fibromyalgia syndrome, one patient told Groopman (2000): "I won't see any doctor who questions the legitimacy of what I have" (p. 87). Showalter observed that such patients "live in a culture that still looks down on psychogenic illness, that does not recognise or respect its reality. The self-esteem of the patient depends on having the physiological nature of the illness accepted" (p. 117). It would seem that this disrespect for psychogenic illness is shared by those physicians, including some psychiatrists who, despite the lack of supporting scientific evidence, nevertheless seek to validate such externalising claims. To the extent that psychiatry itself foregoes psychology for biology, psychodynamics for neurochemistry, it might itself be seen as hysterical and resistant to psychoanalysis.

In order to meet the objective of plausibly establishing "cause and cure outside the self", patients must work within the parameters that the culture will allow, for all cultures maintain their own "legitimate symptom pools" (Shorter, 1992, p. 3) and it is a hallmark of hysteria to "mimic culturally permissible forms of distress" (Showalter, 1997, p. 15). This tendency of hysteria to remain within certain bounds of convention was also described by Krohn (1978): "Hysteria makes use of dominant myths, assumptions, and identities of the culture in which it appears. The hysteric may play out a somewhat caricatured version of an accepted role in an effort to enlist caring, attention, help, or to satisfy other needs; however, he rarely goes far enough to be considered substantially deviant … the hysteric characteristically forms his sense of himself around an identity granted a high degree of approval in the culture" (p. 160).

Thus, while symptoms change, and contemporary symptoms are, naturally, congruent with current cultural concerns and preoccupations, their function is the same as it was in the nineteenth century: to manifest an allegedly physical condition "that firmly places cause and cure outside the self" or, more precisely, that solidly places cause and cure within the body but outside the self, thereby expressing pain and conflict in "acceptable" forms of bodily illness without the taint of psychological forces at work (Showalter, p. 4). The adaptive character of hysteria is also described by Shorter (1992), who writes that "hysteria offers a classic example of patients who present symptoms as the culture expects them, or, better put, as the doctors expect them" (pp. 8–9).

But to explain this flight from psychology simply in terms of the cultural stigmatisation of illness recognised as psychogenic is to overlook the deeper reasons for this very stigmatisation. If cause and cure lie not outside but within the self, then such "illnesses" are in some way unconsciously engineered by the patients themselves, although not consciously as in malingering. If so, we are led to ask why hysterics, and we are all hysterical at times and to varying degrees, feel the need to bring pain and suffering upon themselves in these ways. There is no doubt that, as Freud would say, such phenomena are "overdetermined", but among their multiple causes, such as the need to suffer to maintain important ties to internal or external objects, I believe the role of aggression, guilt, and the unconscious need for punishment has received insufficient attention. For today these concepts are distinctly unpopular among many intellectuals, including those post-Freudian and post-Kleinian psychoanalysts who have come to conceptualise psychopathology less in terms of intrapsychic conflict than in terms of structural defects and deficits arising from parental failure, and who conceptualise therapy less as analysis leading patients to insight and self-mastery than as provision of allegedly missing psychic structure through processes of internalisation and identification with the therapist—a kind of reparative re-parenting (Carveth, 1998).

While it is most likely the case that the hystero-paranoid fugitive from guilt has always been with us, the varieties of contemporary psychoanalysis in which the discourse of guilt and self-punishment is played down are poorly prepared to come to grips with the dynamics that underlie this type of suffering. In other words, a psychoanalysis, never mind a psychiatry, that is itself in flight from guilt is in no position to understand the hystero-paranoid fugitive from guilt, for to do so it would have to understand and cure itself. Needless to say, it is the aim of this book to contribute to such curative self-understanding.

Among what are arguably the four most important books on hysteria of the past few years—Elaine Showalter's *Hystories: Hysterical Epidemics and Modern Media* (1997), Christopher Bollas's *Hysteria* (2000), Juliet Mitchell's *Mad Men and Medusas: Reclaiming Hysteria* (2000), and Ronald Britton's *Sex, Death, and the Superego* (2003)—Bollas's work is notable for its single-minded emphasis on sexuality and its relative neglect of the role of aggression in hysterical conditions. Freud himself never revisited his work on hysteria in light of his later positing of *Thanatos* and its outward manifestation as an aggressive drive as the "immortal adversary" of *Eros* in a human nature driven by these two "Heavenly Powers" (1930a, p. 145). For Bollas, as for Freud, "the heart of the matter" of hysteria is "the hysteric's disaffection with his or her sexual life" (p. 12).

Bollas (2000) argues, I think correctly, that "hysteria has disappeared from contemporary culture only insofar as it has been subjected to a repression through the popular diagnosis of 'borderline personality disorder'" (frontispiece): "Thinking the hysteric through the theoretical lenses of the borderline personality had become something of a tragedy" (p. 2). He sets out to recover and elaborate on an earlier psychoanalytic understanding of hysteria. But in so doing he loses sight of the elements of this condition that were at least brought into focus through the theoretical lens of the borderline concept, whatever its inadequacies in other respects—namely, the paranoid-schizoid dynamics of splitting, projection, sadomasochism, disavowed aggression, and hostility, and the resulting unconscious need for punishment. In emphasising the role of aggression in psychopathology I imply no commitment to either the notion of a biologically-given death instinct or a somatically grounded aggressive drive, but merely recognise the fact that frustration, an unavoidable feature of human existence, leads to aggression that then must be directed outwardly in constructive or destructive ways or bottled up and retroflected against the self.

Bollas praises Showalter's work and endorses her view that "[H]ysteria is alive and well in the form of attention-deficit disorder, chronic-fatigue disorder, alien-abduction movements and the like" (p. 178), as well as her emphasis on the role of both clinicians and the media in creating such conditions. Actually, Showalter does not address attention-deficit disorder, or attention-deficit hyperactivity disorder, which I feel Bollas is nevertheless right to include in the list of new hysterias. But in this instance the hysteric is not the child so diagnosed but the parents, teachers, psychologists, and school officials who redefine boredom, dreaminess, fidgetiness, and passive aggressiveness (i.e., being a child) as an organically based disorder in the absence of any evidence of the "minimal brain dysfunction", or whatever, alleged to underlie it. I believe here we have an instance of Munchausen's syndrome by proxy, itself a widespread hysterical epidemic that assumes many different forms. If we define Munchausen's syndrome by proxy as a factitious disorder in which a carer misleads people into thinking someone has an illness when they do not, then there is a real sense in which a good deal of contemporary psychiatry and psychology can be diagnosed as suffering from this disorder—which I do not regard as an illness, but as a form of hysteria. In writing of "the myth of mental illness", Szasz (1961) is essentially arguing that psychiatry suffers from Munchausen's syndrome by proxy.

"It is more than sad", Bollas writes, "that the hysteric's capacity to fulfil the other's desire has meant that many people have dedicated their lives to romances with clinicians, presenting new 'sexy' diagnoses—such as multiple personality disorder—which inevitably earn accolades for the clinicians founding a new term or re-founding an old one, now rendered dramatically potent" (p. 178). Recall in this connection Frederick Wolfe's regret at having pioneered the "fibro-myalgia syndrome" diagnosis. But whereas Showalter did not shrink from the evidence of the dynamics of hatred and paranoid projection in the new hysterias, Bollas writes almost exclusively within a pre-1920 Freudianism that, however enriched by later object relational and Lacanian perspectives and insights, focuses in a one-sided fashion on sexuality. He summarises his theory of hysteria as follows: "The hysteric specifies the body as the agent of his or her demise because its bio-logic brings sexual mental contents to mind" (p. 178). If the hysteric has been displaced in recent decades by the borderline, in Bollas the borderline (schizo-paranoid) is repressed by an old-fashioned view of the hysteric. Even Ronald Britton whose Kleinian orientation one might have expected to sensitise him more to the role of aggression in hysteria, emphasises sexuality. In discussing Sabina Spielrein's contri-bution, Britton (2003, Chapter One) points out that she is not actually concerned with the death instinct, but rather with a death wish meant to consummate a desired sexual union—that is, a force not seeking to separate but to end all separation and to consummate the Oedipus com-plex. But how "sexual" is this really? Is it not really about an aggressive determination to smash all boundaries and seize and merge with the object at whatever cost? If this is sexuality, it is at least as much rage and aggression in the face of frustration and prohibition.

And how sexual is the Oedipus complex anyway? Is it not time for us to admit that rather than being a sexual it is a primarily narcis-sistic project—that Oedipal desire is not fundamentally a desire for sex with the object but the wish to be the apple of his or her eye? In "Is the Oedipus Complex Universal?" the psychoanalytic anthro-pologist Anne Parsons (1964) revisited the Malinowski/Jones debate, reviewed Malinowski's data and the anthropological record in gen-eral, and came to the conclusion that, in an importantly revised form, the Oedipus is universal. Parsons noted that Malinowski observed that in the Trobriand Islands, a matrilineal and matrilocal culture, a boy's hostile rivalry is with his maternal uncle rather than his father. His uncle is the man responsible for raising him, for his father only visits from time to time from his own village (where he is an uncle). Although it is father who has sex with mother the boy's hostility is to the uncle. Marxist theorists jumped on this data and, against Freud, concluded the complex is not about sex but authority and domination. In response, Jones insisted on a very literal reading of Freudian theory and reasserted its sexual basis, arguing the sexual jealousy is merely displaced from father to uncle. If we are true believers in a theory we can usually find mechanisms to explain away discrepant data. Parsons went back to the data and said no to both the Marxists and the Freudian literalists. She found that Malinowski's data contains all kinds of evidence of obsession with brother-sister incest themes in Trobriand culture: myths, jokes, taboo avoidances, etc. No wonder: the culture makes a woman's brother the most important man in her life. Husbands come and go; they are easily divorced. A brother, on the other hand, is the protector of his sister and her children. Parsons concluded: no wonder the boy is rivalrous with uncle; he does not sleep with mother but he is the most important person in her life in many ways. Therefore, the Oedipus complex is not fundamentally about sex, it is about who is most important to whom.

For Lacan (1977) my desire is the desire of the other; it is to be desired. Oedipal desire is not primarily about sex, it is about narcissism: the wish to monopolise the love and attention, to be the apple of the eye, of the desired other. In our culture the boy's rival also sleeps with mother so we thought it was about sex when it is actually about priority. We should not have been surprised, least of all the French. Many women and men, not just the French, can tolerate their spouses merely sleeping with other lovers, as long as they come home to the one who is really important. The Oedipus complex is the universal desire on the part of the child to monopolise the love, look, and attention of the primary object and his/her hostile rivalry with anyone who takes that look, love, and attention away. And it is about the decentring ("castration"), and the narcissistic rage, despair, and other passions experienced when gender and generational and other realities force us to recognise the ultimate impossibility of the narcissistic Oedipal project. No doubt Jocasta mothers and Laius fathers make it worse, but it was sentimental and naïve of Kohut (1977) to think anyone, even with the best, most empathic, and sympathetic parenting imaginable, can get through this without major *Stürm und Drang*. Many parents are so unempathic, unsympathetic, and abusive, such total failures as "selfobjects", that they actually bring other children into the world, cruelly displacing the older child from his or her position of centrality and saddling him or her with annoying rivals.

In contrast to Bollas and Britton, Juliet Mitchell (2000), like Showalter, draws attention to the dynamics of aggression in hysterical conditions. She does so by refocusing our attention on two sets of facts that, although recognised by Freud, were later played down both in his own work and in that of his followers. The first is Charcot's and Freud's early recognition of the existence of male hysteria. Mitchell cites two main reasons for the circumstance that while "… the critical claim that inaugurated psychoanalysis was that men could be hysterical … psychoanalysis too slipped from explaining to endorsing its proclivity in women" (p. x). First, there is "the non-elaboration of the hypothesis of a death drive in general, but in particular in relation to hysteria". Here, by "death drive" I understand Mitchell to be referring, like Britton (2003), not to Freud's (1920g) literal, primary masochism, his biologically-given death instinct, but to a destructive drive, to aggression, violence, and hostility. Mitchell writes: "As with feminists' accounts of hysteria, what is missing [in psychoanalytic accounts such as Bollas's] is that there is violence as well as sexuality in the seductions and rages of the hysteric" (p. x). The feminisation of hysteria extended sexist blindness to female aggression to the hysteric. In addition, the failure to revise the psychoanalytic theory of hysteria in light of the dual drive theory introduced by Freud in 1920, long after his pioneering work on this condition at the turn of the century, contributed to ignoring the role of aggression, whether conceptualised as primary or secondary to frustration, in hysterical conditions.

The second set of initially recognised but subsequently minimised facts concerns "the omission of the key role played in the construction of the psyche by lateral relationships" (Mitchell, p. x), that is, by sibling rivalry in personality formation. Mitchell writes, "When a sibling is in the offing, the danger is that the hero—'His Majesty the Baby'—will be annihilated, for this is someone who stands in the same position to parents (and their substitutes) as himself. This possible displacement triggers the wish to kill in the interest of survival" (p. xi). In the sibling rivalry that inevitably accompanies sibling love, "murder is in the air" (p. 20). Mitchell acknowledges, of course, that such violence may take a "sexual" (in my view in essence a narcissistic) form—"to get the interests of all and everyone for oneself" (p. xi). In connection with the link between violence and hysterical hyper—and pseudo-sexuality, I am reminded of a remark made by a seasoned male clinician in an initial interview with an overtly seductive, scantily clad hysterical young woman: "Why are you trying to destroy me?" Just as Carol White's stepson Rory is not blind to the manipulation and passive-aggressiveness beneath his stepmother's manifest helplessness, this clinician was alert to the destructiveness in seduction.

Like Bollas and Showalter, Mitchell affirms the continuing presence of hysteria in our culture, despite psychiatric attempts to deny it. "It has been fashionable in the twentieth-century West to argue that hysteria has disappeared. To my mind, this is nonsensical—it is like saying 'love' or 'hate' have vanished. There can be no question that hysteria exists, whether we call its various manifestations by that name or something else" (p. 6). For Mitchell, there is nothing intrinsically feminine about hysteria, which she views, like love and hate, as a potential of human nature as such, arguing instead that "[H]ysteria has been feminised: over and over again, a universal potential condition has been assigned to the feminine; equally, it has disappeared as a condition after the irrefutable observation that men appeared to display its characteristics" (p. 7).

Like Showalter and Krohn, Mitchell emphasises hysteria's adaptation to the sociocultural surround: "Hysteria migrates. Supremely mimetic, what was once called hysteria manifests itself in forms more attuned to its new social surroundings. What was once a subsidiary characteristic becomes dominant and vice versa" (p. ix). Nevertheless, "[H]ysteria's many manifestations have shown some striking similarities throughout the ages—sensations of suffocation, choking, breathing and eating difficulties, mimetic imitations, deceitfulness, shock, fits, death states, wanting (craving, longing). ... If the treatments and conceptualisations vary, mimetic hysteria will look different at different times because it is imitating different treatments and different ideas about hysteria" (p. 13). Such hysterical symptoms are well depicted in the case of Carol White in *Safe*, a film that ought to be required study for physicians and psychotherapists working with hysteria.

Referring to the introduction in the *Diagnostic and Statistical Manual-III* (1980) of "histrionic personality disorder" to replace "hysteria", Mitchell comments that "The irony of this triumph of the diagnostic is that the doctors who no longer recognise hysteria's existence continue to refer to it daily." She continues: "Given the history of hysteria, one must surely ask: Is it hysteria itself or its classification—psychiatric, medical or psychoanalytic—that has become redundant?" (p. 15). The same might well be said with respect to psychosomatic illness which many doctors now no longer officially recognise but continue to refer to daily. With respect to Mitchell's point about hysteria, I recall several years ago overhearing from the next cubicle a crusty orthopaedic surgeon dictating notes after seeing a man on crutches: "Get the damn crutches away from this man before he turns into a complete hysteric! He doesn't need them!" When it was my turn to see him, I congratulated him on his use of a language our psychiatric colleagues have largely abandoned.

Many of the varieties of hysteria that Showalter (1997) described exhibit paranoia. She referred to the particular vulnerability of American culture to hysterical movements: "Such movements have centred on the Masons, Catholicism, communism, the Kennedy assassination, and the fluoridation of water. In the 1990s, hysteria merges with a seething mix of paranoia, anxiety, and anger that comes out of the American crucible" (p. 26). She quoted Michael Kelly, who in *The New Yorker* gave the term "fusion paranoia" to the *mélange* of conspiracy theories flourishing in the United States: "In its extreme form, paranoia is still the province of minority movements, but the ethos of minority movements—anti-establishmentarian protest, the politics of rage—has become so deeply ingrained in the larger political culture that the paranoid style has become the cohering idea of a broad coalition plurality that draws adherents from every point on the political spectrum" (Showalter, p. 26, citing Kelly, 1995, pp. 62–64). Showalter observed that this "fusion paranoia" had taken up residence in medicine and psychiatry, allowing for the proliferation of conspiracy theories to explain "every unidentified symptom and syndrome" (pp. 26–27). This point was elaborated by Sherrill Mulhern, an American anthropologist critical of such excesses, who highlighted "… the emergence of conspiracy theory as the nucleus of a consistent pattern of clinical interpretation. In the United States during the past decade, the clinical milieu has become the vortex of a growing, socially operant conspiratorial mentality, which is undermining crucial sectors of the mental health, criminal justice, and judicial systems" (Showalter, p. 27, citing Mulhern, 1994, p. 266).

The close connection between hysteria and paranoia—and even, perhaps, their interdependence—does not appear to have been explicated by psychoanalytic writers, who have tended, implicitly at least, to treat these conditions as discrete entities. It is to rectify this insufficiently theorised linkage that I refer to the psychological conditions I am addressing as *hystero-paranoid*. Consistent with the tendency of psychoanalytic writers to treat hysteria and paranoia as unrelated,

Melanie Klein wrote extensively about anxiety and paranoia, but was "silent on the subject of hysteria" (Rycroft, 1968, p. 64). However, certain insights into the origins of hysteria can be extrapolated from her writings. I contend that there is a relation between hysteria and Klein's paranoid-schizoid position, so much so that hysteria may be viewed as an offshoot of the latter. Schizo-paranoid functioning almost inevitably produces hysterical symptoms, albeit often minor ones that often go unrecognised.

Human beings are never free from the task of managing their primal passions, phantasies, and anxieties, including their aggression, or from the simultaneous need to order and regulate the world of internal objects and form meaningful connections with external ones. Because these tasks of mental life are ongoing and permanent rather than occurring in discrete stages, the mental "positions" Klein expounded are fluid, dynamic states that are present in varying degrees throughout every phase of life. The infant's early pre-ambivalent paranoid-schizoid state characterised by splitting of the object (and the self) into all-good and all-bad part-objects (and part-selves), persecutory anxiety, envy, manic defences, "symbolic equations" (Segal, 1957) and "beta elements" (Bion, 1962), optimally gives way to the depressive position's ambivalence, whole object (and self) relating, guilt, reparation, gratitude, capacity for "symbolic representation", "alpha function", and creativity. But elements of paranoid-schizoid functioning, both healthy and pathological, including the paranoid-schizoid persecutory superego, remain operative in all persons throughout life. In current post-Kleinian theory, development is no longer conceived as a unilinear progression from paranoid-schizoid (bad) to depressive (good) (PS→D), itself a manifestation of PS splitting, but dialectically (PS←→D), with pathology conceptualised as breakdown of the dialectic into a fixation on either pole (Ogden, 1986), for it is now recognised that there is both good and bad in both PS and D.

At this stage in the development of object relations theory, it is unnecessary to adhere to a literal notion of a biologically pre-given aggressive drive, let alone any literal death instinct, in order to credit Klein's insight into the fact that, even with the most attuned and devoted carers imaginable, all infants must encounter some degree of frustration that inevitably generates aggression that, when projected, returns in the form of persecutory anxiety. It is plausible to assume that the cognitively immature infant experiences any frustration as an attack, and any absence of "good" as an indication of the malevolent presence of "bad". It follows that the infant assumes it to be the job of the good part-object to protect and gratify, while experiencing any pain and frustration not merely as an indication that the good part-object is failing at this task, but that it has actually turned into a bad part-object—that is, a persecutor. Needless to say, any "surplus" frustration, beyond the unavoidable existential minimum, arising from objective environmental failure of various types, will only aggravate a paranoid dynamic that is in varying degrees universal.

In the face of frustration and feelings of persecution, the infant reacts with both fear and aggression; projection of the latter leads to further persecutory anxiety. Here, in the realm of disowned aggression, lies the particular insight of Kleinian theory into the development of hysteria. The subject operating in the paranoid-schizoid position cannot escape the feeling of attack, having repudiated its own aggressive and destructive impulses and situated them squarely in the outside world. This move, however, fails to dissolve the aggression. It still exists in all its strength on the outside, which is now rendered threatening and dangerous. The ensuing tangle of conflict is compounded when the subject also projects perceived good objects and impulses in order to protect them from the contamination of badness inside, and introjects or even identifies with perceived external persecutors in an attempt to gain control of them. Segal (1964) comments that "In situations of anxiety the split is widened and projection and introjection are used in order to keep persecutory and ideal objects as far as possible from one another, while keeping both under control. The situation may fluctuate rapidly and persecutors may be felt now outside, giving a feeling of external threat, now inside, producing fears of a hypochondriacal nature" (pp. 26–27). Hysteria may likewise be interpreted as the product of a paranoid-schizoid dynamic in which individuals who have split off and disowned their own aggressive and destructive impulses suffer from fantasies of attack and an abiding sense of being made ill by hostile forces, either within the body (as in "fibromyalgia syndrome" and "chronic fatigue syndrome") or outside it in the environment (as in "environmental illness" or "multiple chemical sensitivity"), but in any case from outside the self.

Hysterical patients tend to regard their symptoms as residing *in* the body but not *of* the self, that is, existing as a foreign, invading force. In paranoid-schizoid functioning subjects may disown or evacuate their internal bad self and objects, project the split-off contents, and as a consequence perceive the external world as independently bad and dangerous. To complicate matters further, in an attempt to manage the external persecutors thus created, they may reintroject them. Segal's observation regarding the introjection of persecutors and subsequent hypochondria (in which the persecutors are felt to be attacking from within the body) illustrates the conjunction between paranoia and hysteria. This dynamic is clearly demonstrated in two Kleinian analyses of the film *Alien* (Carveth & Gold, 1999; Gabbard & Gabbard, 1987). There is an unforgettable scene in the film in which, thinking they had successfully eliminated the alien creature that had plastered itself like a bad breast over the mouth of one astronaut, the crew are enjoying a celebratory meal when the alien stirs and begins to move inside him and then suddenly smashes its way through his chest cage and scuttles off into the interior of the ship. The rest of the film concerns attempts to eject the alien into outer space and the haunting anxiety that it might yet remain inside.

According to Segal (1964), "The projection of bad feelings and bad parts of the self outwards produces external persecution. The reintrojection of persecutors gives rise to hypochondriacal anxiety" (p. 30). While there are grounds for maintaining the distinction between hypochondria and hysteria, and for viewing the former as one type or manifestation of the latter, it is reasonable to extrapolate a reciprocal connection between paranoia and hysteria by way of this connection between paranoia and hypochondriacal anxiety. Both involve projection and a resulting experience of attack and persecution, in one case from without, in the other from within. But the psychoanalytic literature has tended to treat paranoia and hysteria as discrete conditions, and these citations from Segal may be one of the few places where paranoia and hypochondria are explicitly brought together with hysteria.

The splitting characteristic of the paranoid-schizoid position produces an austere, one-dimensional, concrete mode of thinking and an inability to relate to others as whole persons. In Klein's (1935) words, "Where the persecution anxiety for the ego is in the ascendant, a full and stable identification with another object, in the sense of looking at it and understanding it as it really is, and a full capacity for love, are not possible" (p. 154). Conceiving of the world in terms of part-objects and keeping good and bad thoroughly separated allows the subject to feel as though he is protecting good objects from contamination by the badness inside him. But paranoid-schizoid functioning exacts a high price for the manufacture of this apparent "safe" zone through projection of the badness, if not in the form of persecutory fantasies, feelings, and outright paranoid delusions, then in the hysterical and psychosomatic disorders that embody the return of the disavowed badness and simultaneously punish the subject in ways that evade the experience of unbearable guilt.

As we have seen, a central feature of the paranoid-schizoid position is an inability to achieve the types of guilt and remorse that are operative in the depressive position (Meissner, 1978, p. 13) and that reflect attainment of what Winnicott (1963) called "the capacity for concern". Instead of mature "depressive guilt" (Grinberg, 1964) what we find in paranoid-schizoid functioning is either an intensely self-attacking "persecutory guilt" that is entirely narcissistic and reflects little or no concern for the object, or else a variety of tormenting states (including hysterical and psychosomatic conditions) that operate as substitutes for and defences against unattainable or unbearable depressive guilt. In the context of the depressive position, a continual state of rage and feelings of destructiveness will be accompanied by simultaneous feelings of guilt, concern, and the need to make reparation. In the paranoid-schizoid position, however, such destructiveness is split off and projected, resulting in persecutory anxiety and unconscious masochistic needs for expiation through self-punishment (Riesenberg-Malcolm, 1980). Safán-Gerard (1998) describes a patient whose career has collapsed after he leaves his wife and children to pursue one of his numerous affairs. At the end of one session the patient ponders, "I don't know what changed after my separation. Because I used to make good money before. Did I change or did reality change?" (p. 365). This patient's enormous load of unbearable guilt, which he verbally acknowledges but evades in reality since he cannot allow himself to feel or suffer from it, must nevertheless be expiated in some way. In this light, the collapse of his career and his financial difficulties, events that seem to be "just happening" to him, may be viewed as a form of unconsciously contrived self-punishment.

I have argued that the unconscious need for punishment is a manifestation of persecutory guilt which functions to defend against unbearable depressive guilt. Such self-torment is at work in a wide range of psychopathological conditions, including hysterical and psychosomatic disorders. But just as the hysterical or somatising subject takes flight from unbearable guilt into self-tormenting symptoms, so a de-moralising post-Freudian psychiatry and psychoanalysis ignore the dynamics of conscience and superego in favour of preoccupation with one or another form of reductionism in which the meaningful communications of the psyche are reduced to by-products of neurochemical malfunction, or viewed one-dimensionally as the direct result of trauma and deprivation. Even when patients are viewed as victims of bad parenting, a de-moralising psychoanalysis seeks to protect the parents from guilt and responsibility by viewing them, in turn, as victims. The superego aggression that both patients and their de-moralising therapists repress returns in the patients' self-torment and in the moral condemnation directed by such professionals at the abusers of their patient-victims, including those fellow professionals who see the patients as hysterical and point to their guilt evasion. Sometimes such de-moralising is extended to the abusers as well, in which case everyone gets to be a victim and to suffer and enjoy the helplessness intrinsic to that role.

* * *

Unfortunately, the well-intentioned desire on the part of many psychoanalysts to avoid being linked to the world of the cop, the judge, or the priest has not infrequently led to neglect of patients' moral conflicts. The justified aversion on the part of psychoanalysts to morally judging patients has frequently led, in both clinical theory and practice, to a tendency to attempt to sidestep this area altogether. It may also happen that a countertransferential inability to tolerate the painful revelation of a patient's badness unconsciously causes analysts to steer clear of the topic. Analysts are not required to judge whether or not a patient *should* feel guilty about his wishes or actions. In fact, it works against the aim of making the unconscious conscious for analysts to weigh in with their values and opinions about what is right and wrong over the course of a patient's treatment. But for various reasons, many psychoanalysts seem to feel that soothing a patient's conscience or superego is part of their job. It is not uncommon for an analyst to communicate to a patient that he or she has nothing to feel guilty about—for example, in the case of murderous Oedipal fantasies that are, as we know, part of the human condition. But it is one thing to help patients understand the universality of Oedipal aggression and quite another to suggest that such universality obviates the necessity for guilt. Even in the case of wrong actions, not merely wrong feelings or wishes, therapists have been known to attempt to absolve the patient, communicating in some way that there is nothing to feel guilty about.

Setting aside for a moment the fact that, according to the patient's conscience and superego, there is indeed quite a lot to feel guilty about—guilt that must be reckoned with, not avoided—the act of soothing a patient's conscience or superego implies that the analyst has taken a stand in regard to value judgements and has brought his or her own set of moral criteria into the session. Ironically these analysts tend to be quite critical of colleagues who recognise that the patient's judgements (e.g., "I should feel guilty") represent an important aspect of the latter's personality and must necessarily occupy an essential and valid place in the analysis. In examining a patient's moral functioning, analysts should strive as far as possible to maintain the classical stance of technical neutrality that, according to Anna Freud (1936), involves taking a position "equidistant from the id, the ego, and the superego" (p. 28). Admittedly, this is an ultimately unattainable ideal and, for this reason, we should seek to be as conscious as possible of our moral biases as significant aspects of the countertransference. And this includes being honest with ourselves and others about the moral agenda that underlies the entire therapeutic enterprise: that our therapeutic work depends upon and embodies a preference for consciousness over unconsciousness, life over death, love over hate, and constructiveness over destructiveness. In this light the idea of "technical neutrality" is ambiguous, for it is obvious that in important ways we are not and cannot be technically neutral at all.

Nevertheless, many analysts will agree that in seeking to promote the patient's emotional growth (itself something that can only be defined in moral terms) we should not engage in either inappropriate moral soothing or inappropriate moral condemnation. Yet it is my impression that the former departures from this ideal seem more acceptable in today's climate than the latter. Such soothing gives the patient the message that his or her badness should probably be concealed from an analyst who appears to think everything is acceptable, or who just cannot tolerate intense feelings of guilt and remorse. The patient hides his feelings of badness. This type of analyst will aid the patient in further symptom-forming self-punitiveness, rather than helping to bring his unconscious moral conflicts to consciousness where they might be resolved. On the other hand, condemning patients sends the message that they are in the presence of a priestly confessor—not an analyst—who will, ironically, also inadvertently foster additional symptom-forming self-punitiveness instead of conducting an analysis. Once again, patients hide their feelings of badness.

Today, in a culture of narcissism in which the discourse of guilt and reparation is suppressed, the hysterical dynamic in which a destructive wish leads to guilt denied, which leads in turn to an inhibited or symptomatic life, is widespread. One rarely encounters patients who have not been affected in some way by being taught to silence both their rage and their remorse, with the consequence that they spend their lives engaged in hysterical, unconsciously self-punitive behaviour of one type or another. With Showalter, Shorter, Bollas, Mitchell, Britton, and others, I believe that hysteria has in no way disappeared. While the older forms of hysteria, such as *globus hystericus*, are still encountered, and not merely among pre-modern populations, today it more often appears in the newer forms we have reviewed. Because Freud never revised his sex-centred theory of hysteria after he introduced the dual drive theory in 1920, the role of aggression in this condition has not been adequately recognised. As late as 2000, Bollas still viewed hysteria in largely sexual terms. On the other hand, the Kleinians, who emphasise the role of aggression in psychopathology, have, with a few exceptions such as Mitchell (2000), had little to say about hysteria, except for their understanding that hypochondria, a subtype of hysteria, involves a paranoid sense of persecution by bad objects imagined to reside inside rather than outside the body. Aside from Mitchell, the Kleinians have not developed the connection between hysteria and the paranoid-schizoid position—a connection so profound that I regard the various forms of hysteria as subtypes of a more general hystero-paranoid syndrome.

In my view, both the old and the new hysterias involve a paranoid-schizoid retreat from and defence against the depressive position—that is, a retreat from Winnicott's "capacity for concern" into a narcissistic and schizoid non-relatedness, combined with repression and projection of destructive hatred and envy of the object, resulting in a paranoid state of persecution by the bad objects into which the subject's hate has been projected. The resulting paranoid torment serves the archaic superego's demand for punishment for both the schizoid coldness towards and hatred of the object world. Such persecutory guilt serves as a defence against the advance into the depressive position where one must learn how to bear depressive or reparative guilt.

Carol "White", a personality purged by externalisation of all darkness, suffers from a schizoid state of demoralisation resulting from her de-moralising flight from concern and guilt—that is, from human relatedness—and from a paranoid state of persecution resulting from projection or externalisation of her hostility, a state of torment that simultaneously defends against unbearable guilt and punishes her for her evasion, irresponsibility, and hatred. Carol's personal demoralisation, and the de-moralising flight from morality—or object relations—that causes it, mirrors that of the wider culture. Due to the liberal-democratic critique of domination and exploitation it has become more difficult for us to bear the guilt arising from the hateful impulses that remain even when hateful actions are inhibited. If we cannot manage to creatively transform such impulses or learn to bear the guilt to which they give rise, we succumb to guilt evasion through the patterns of unconscious self-torment. Various popular schools of post-Freudian psychoanalysis, unlike its Freudian and Kleinian forbears, all too often retreat from helping patients discover their agency and assume responsibility for their suffering and instead collude with the cultural discourse of victimhood in which persons are held to be products of their traumatic childhoods, parental failures, poorly calibrated neurochemistry, or whatever. Although such therapists are not blaming a polluted environment but toxic neurotransmitters, not alien abduction but the absent father or unempathic mother, they share the defensive externalisation of responsibility with their hysterical patients. Furthermore, should these mothers and fathers ever find themselves in analysis, they too are helped to understand themselves as victims.

What then is the direction forward? Certainly it is neither the path of an instinctual liberation that would seek to return us to a premoral era nor the path of brutal interpretations of guilt. It is not necessary for analysts to be sadistic in interpreting guilt to help people confront it. Neither is it the continuation of our current de-moralising trends that merely intensify the unconscious need for punishment. What is called for is neither the de-moralising nor the re-moralising of psychoanalysis, but rather the *analysing* of the dynamics of conflict involving both the superego and the conscience, so that patients may be aided in transforming their unconscious self-torment into conscientious guilt and helped to find ways to bear it, to make creative reparation, and to change.

Harry Guntrip: a fugitive from guilt?

A major contributor to the de-moralising trend in post-Freudian and post-Kleinian psychoanalysis is Harry Guntrip. Guntrip's (1969) descriptions of the "in-out programme" resulting from the schizoid person's experience of connection as engulfing and separation as abandonment are vivid and useful up to a point. But in focusing upon the roots of the "schizoid problem" (Guntrip, 1971, Chapter Six) or the "disordered self" (Kohut, 1977) in defective early object-relations he, like Kohut, obscured entirely the role of guilt and the need for punishment in these conditions and promoted a cure based on reparative re-parenting rather than analysis and resolution of inner conflict (in this connection see also Hantman, 2004, 2006).

The guilt evasion that characterises both our "culture of narcissism" (Lasch, 1979) and the types of psychoanalytic thought it has generated is mirrored in my view by that of Guntrip himself. In my hypothesis, despite his background as a Christian minister and his years of analysis with two of the most creative analysts in the field, Guntrip managed by the end only a paranoid understanding of himself as a victim of a murderous mother, rather than a man crippled by a need to punish himself for his disowned murderous wishes towards a brother who died and towards the mother he hated and blamed. In the following I offer an

admittedly speculative interpretation of Guntrip's pathology. I have
not analysed him, nor do I claim to have thoroughly studied all available data pertaining to his case. I do not claim that my interpretation is
true, only that it is a plausible account—and one that Guntrip himself,
despite his expertise in analytic theory, notably failed to consider.

* * *

A few months after his death, Guntrip's (1975) "My Experience of
Analysis with Fairbairn and Winnicott" appeared in the *International
Review of Psycho-Analysis*. He describes how he sought analysis for
"vague background experiences of schizoid isolation and unreality"
(p. 743) and a recurrent "exhaustion illness". In the nineteenth century
this would likely have been diagnosed as "neurasthenia"; today it might
be seen as "chronic fatigue syndrome" or a type of depression. Guntrip
sought analysis to overcome his amnesia for what he had decided was
the traumatic cause of his illness. He had been told by his mother that
at the age of three and a half he had walked into a room and saw his
brother Percy lying naked and dead on his mother's lap: "I rushed up
and grabbed him and said: 'Don't let him go. You'll never get him back!'
She sent me out of the room and I fell mysteriously ill and was thought
to be dying. Her doctor said: 'He's dying of grief for his brother'"
(p. 746). For the next year and a half, Guntrip suffered from "repeated
petty psychosomatic ills, tummy aches, heat spots, loss of appetite, con-
stipation and dramatic, sudden high temperatures" (p. 747). Around
the age of five Guntrip replaced self-directed aggression with outright
rebellion, causing his mother to fly into rages and beat him. Gradually, by seven or eight, he developed a life outside the home and, as
her business began to thrive, his mother became less depressed and
hostile. Whereas Guntrip himself viewed his symptoms as attempts to
get his cold mother to mother him (p. 747), my hypothesis is that they
represent forms of hysterical and psychosomatic self-torment for the
phantasy-crime of having killed his brother.

Guntrip describes three subsequent acute episodes of his "mysterious illness", each occurring in the face of a loss of a "brother". In
1927, at the age of twenty-six, a fellow student who had been a brother
figure to him left for another university. Guntrip went home on vacation and attributed his exhaustion illness not so much to the loss of the
friend, but to being with mother. As soon as he left home and returned
to college it disappeared, but it returned in 1938, he now aged thirty-
seven, when "a colleague who had become another Percy-substitute"

left the large congregation to which they had ministered together. At this time Guntrip had "a big dream": "I went down into a tomb and saw a man buried alive. He tried to get out but I threatened him with illness, locked him in and got away quick" (p. 746).

Although in light of this dream Guntrip saw that "I lived permanently over the top of its repression" (p. 746)—that is, Percy's death—it does not seem to have occurred to him (whether or not it occurred to his analysts is unknown) that the dream might reflect a guilty wish to keep the brother he imagined he had killed safely dead and buried. One of the other "mysterious death-threat" dreams that occurred at this time was based on a memory of his mother taking him aged six into the bedroom of his invalid aunt: "I was working downstairs at my desk and suddenly an invisible band of ectoplasm tying me to a dying invalid upstairs, was pulling me steadily out of the room. I knew I would be absorbed into her. I fought and suddenly the band snapped and I knew I was free" (p. 746). Guntrip writes perceptively: "I knew enough to guess that the memory of my dying aunt was a screen memory for the repressed dead Percy, which still exercised on me an unconscious pull out of life into collapse and apparent dying" (pp. 746–747). But Guntrip notably failed to consider the possibility that this "unconscious pull out of life" exercised by the repressed dead Percy may have had to do with Harry's phantasy that Percy desired justice and revenge upon his murderer.

Padel (1996) discusses what he sees as a related dream reported by Guntrip some eleven years later, towards the end of his analysis with Fairbairn:

> I was going home from Edinburgh by train and had a life-size dummy of a man left with me, made of flesh, human but no bones in it. I put it in the Guard's van to get rid of it, and propped it up as it slumped limp. I hurried away so the Guard wouldn't know it was mine. Not that I was doing anything wrong but I didn't want him to know I had any connection with it. I met the Guard in the corridor and suddenly heard it shambling after me, calling out. I felt a queer horror as if it were a sort of fleshly ghost, and said to the Guard, "Quick, let's get away. It's alive. It'll get us." (pp. 756–757)

Guntrip saw the dummy as his passive self and Fairbairn as the guard. Although Guntrip thought he wanted Fairbairn to see this part of himself, Padel points out that "[I]n the dream he tries to get the guard and himself away from the dummy" (p. 757). Padel sees both this and the earlier dream as referring to the time of Guntrip's mother's pregnancy and Percy's birth and to Harry's "anxiety that his anal-phallic phantasies about it might be discovered, whether these were phantasies of creation or of destruction or both" (p. 757). Padel refers to Freud's (1917) symbolic equation, "Stool = phallus = baby", and suggests that the dummy must represent this: "When it came alive, its dreaded hostility needed to be explained by the child's hostility to the living foetus" (p. 760). Padel points out how Guntrip ended his treatment with Winnicott "without ... really attending to Winnicott's focus on the events of Percy's birth", thus, in his own mind, making Percy's death "the centre of his problems and of his treatment" (p. 758). But a sibling's birth is problematic not least because it stimulates death wishes that seem omnipotently realised if the sibling dies. Although without Guntrip's own associations it is impossible to do more than speculate, I suspect the dream may also have represented Guntrip's view of Fairbairn as a "dummy" with no "backbone" who needed to be "propped up" like a flaccid phallus or a dead man by his analysand—and, at the same time, the ghost of the dead Percy come to life and shambling, like a zombie, after him.

In his discussion of "The Taboo upon the Dead", Freud (1912–13) describes the primitive belief that "[A] dearly loved relative at the moment of his death changes into a demon, from whom his survivors can expect nothing but hostility and against whose evil desires they must protect themselves by every possible means" (p. 58) for "the dead, filled with a lust for murder, sought to drag the living in their train" (p. 59). (I have not been able to determine the origin of the, to my mind, quite psychologically plausible idea that the unconscious function of heavy tombstones or *stelae* is to ensure that the dead stay buried and cannot come back to haunt or carry out revenge on the living.) Freud explains these beliefs on the basis of the survivor's projection of the hostile element of a relationship of emotional ambivalence onto the deceased: "The survivor thus denies that he has ever harboured any hostile feelings against the dead loved one; the soul of the dead harbours them instead and seeks to put them into action ... In spite of the successful defence which the survivor achieves by means of projection, his emotional reaction shows the characteristics of punishment and remorse, for he is the subject of fears and submits to renunciations and restrictions" (p. 61).

In my hypothesis, in Guntrip's case the survivor reacted with self-punitive states of inner deadness based on a talion law identification with his dead brother. Hazell (1991) reports that Guntrip occasionally felt a "static lifeless state deep within him" (p. 151). In phantasy the mechanism here would be: "You see, I am dead too, so you needn't kill me," or "You see, I have paid the price for killing you, by becoming dead myself." In this sense the dream dummy would represent Guntrip's passive self, as he thought, but in a way that he never comprehended: an identification with both his dead brother and, via both projection and the brother transference, with Fairbairn. Here survival guilt takes a persecutory form, self-annihilation (the states of inner "deadness") functioning as an alternative to and defence against depressive or reparative guilt.

Although Glatzer and Evans (1977) view Guntrip's mysterious illness as a talion punishment for the unconscious death wishes towards Percy that he projected onto his demonised mother, and although they write of the neglect by both of his analysts of his sibling rivalry, their main focus is upon his infantile megalomania and terror of the all-bad mother imago, whereas I am stressing his possible need to "deaden" himself in a punishing identification with Percy owing to his inability or unwillingness to face and bear depressive or reparative guilt. Although they see the case as pre-Oedipal and refer approvingly to Winnicott's comment to Guntrip that "'You show no signs of ever having had an Oedipus complex'" (Guntrip, 1975, p. 744), their recognition of the role of sibling rivalry in the case belies this idea insofar as we regard the struggle with rivals for the desired object's love as the essence of the Oedipus complex. While some may wish to restrict the complex to rivalry with one parent for the love of the other and refer to the broader rivalry with siblings as a "family complex", I prefer to broaden the concept of the Oedipus complex to include rivalry with any "third"— parent, sibling, "Father Time" who imposes the demand for separation at the end of the hour, death itself—that is, anything that constitutes a "No", a barrier, boundary, prohibition, or obstacle to exclusive possession of the love and attention of the object of desire.

The fourth episode of exhaustion illness occurred in 1957, when Guntrip was fifty-six and the old friend whose departure had provoked the collapse in 1927 suddenly died. When Fairbairn returned to work after a six-month struggle with viral influenza, he told Guntrip, "I think since my illness I am no longer your good father or bad mother, but your brother dying on you" (Guntrip, 1975, p. 747). The fact that the failing Fairbairn had become Percy in the transference led Guntrip to feel he must end the analysis to avoid being "left with a full scale erup-tion of that traumatic event, and no one to help me" (p. 748). But despite continued struggles with his health, Fairbairn lived on for another five years. One wonders whether, if Guntrip had been able to stay and tol-erate deep work on that transference, he might have got to the root of his problem. But he left, and afterwards complained that, while radical in theory, Fairbairn operated in practice as a "'classical analyst' with an 'interpretive technique' when I felt I needed to regress to the level of that severe infancy trauma" (p. 742). It may well be that he had so regressed and, in the face of the regressive Percy-transference, he fled.

Guntrip describes Fairbairn's approach as "broadly oedipal analysis of my 'internalised bad-object relations' world" (p. 747): "He repeatedly brought me back to oedipal three-person libidinal and anti-libidinal conflicts in my 'inner world,' Kleinian 'object splits' and Fairbairnian 'ego splits' in the sense of oedipal libidinal excitations" (p. 743). But it is not at all clear how "Oedipal" this focus really was—at least in the Freudian sense, involving triangular conflict between a child who desires the exclusive love of one parent and both loves and hates the other parent and the siblings as rivals, with all the guilt and anxiety that follow from such longings, death wishes, and attendant phan-tasies. Fairbairn may well not have focused on this (which is central to the hypothesis I am offering here), but more on Guntrip's internal world of sadomasochistic struggles with his mother. Glatzer and Evans (1977) chide Fairbairn for providing Oedipal analysis of Guntrip's pre-Oedipal structure, but I think despite Guntrip's description of Fairbairn's focus as Oedipal it may, in reality, have been pre-Oedipal— but not in the sense that Glatzer and Evans value (a focus on infantile grandiosity and demonisation of the mother), but rather in the sense of focusing on the split endopsychic structure and sadomasochistic strug-gles that follow, in Fairbairn's view, from the internalisation of bad objects. If my hypothesis has any validity, it would have been better if Fairbairn *had* provided Oedipal analysis of Guntrip's death wishes towards his sibling Oedipal rival.

Fairbairn's (1952) theory would have predisposed him to see Guntrip's split internal world as an internalisation of and a reaction to "bad object-relations". He appears to have shared Guntrip's belief that severe maternal failure was at the root of both Percy's death and

Harry's problems: "Both Fairbairn and Winnicott thought I would have died if she had not sent me away from herself" (p. 746). Glatzer and Evans (1977) write in this connection, "No evidence was supplied for this conclusion ... The statements were based on the evidence of the sole witness: a guilt-laden mother" (p. 83). Markillie (1996), a colleague and friend of Guntrip's for over thirty years, writes, "I always felt that her [Guntrip's mother's] bad-object aspects were overemphasised by him in later years" (p. 764). Despite apparent agreement on the part of Guntrip himself, his father, the family doctor, Fairbairn, and Winnicott that the mother's coldness killed Percy, we really have little idea as to the real causes of his death. Hazell (1996) writes, "The most probable explanation, supported by those parts of her [the mother's] explanations which are common to letters and verbal accounts, both in the 1920s and the 1940s, is that Percy died during a febrile convulsion which coincided with teething to bring about what she described as a 'teething fit'" (p. 6). But Hazell then goes on to join the consensus that the mother was to blame: "But, whatever the physical cause of Percy's demise, the sheer lack of maternal feeling for him as an unintended and unwanted second baby must surely have been a strong contributory factor" (p. 6).

In a brief sketch of his family history, Guntrip (1975) writes:

> My mother was an overburdened "little mother" before she married, the eldest daughter of eleven children and saw four siblings die. Her mother was a feather-brained beauty queen, who left my mother to manage everything even as a schoolgirl. She ran away from home at the age of 12 because she was so unhappy, but was brought back .... They married in 1898 but he did not know that she had had her fill of mothering babies and did not want any more. In my teens she occasionally became confidential and told me the salient facts of family history, including that she breast-fed me because she believed it would prevent another pregnancy; she refused to breast-feed Percy and he died, after which she refused further intimacy. (p. 745)

Glatzer and Evans (1977) suggest that, despite Guntrip's apparent sympathy for his mother's plight, on a deeper level he used her confidences to demonise her: "On an intellectual level, then, Guntrip understood his mother's reluctance to have more children, but on an emotional level he exploited these confessions to demonstrate that his mother was not just a failure, but a 'total' failure and a murderess as well" (p. 82).

We, of course, have only Guntrip's reports of Fairbairn's interpretive approach to the case. But with that *caveat* in mind, it seems reasonable to suppose that whereas Fairbairn may have stressed the split, pre-Oedipal, sadomasochistic internal world formed in reaction to bad object-relations experience as the core of Guntrip's problem, and may have viewed his schizoid states as defensive withdrawal from such internal relations with bad objects, Guntrip himself saw all this as a defence against the ego-weakness and inner deadness deriving from the maternal coldness that he believed was also responsible for Percy's death. While Guntrip's desire that Fairbairn acknowledge the mother's badness was gratified, his demand for a regressive transference cure, a kind of re-parenting with Fairbairn in the role of good mother, apparently was not. Fairbairn "regarded his demands as a resistance. The analysis was a stalemate, though it continued for another five years" (Padel, 1996, p. 756). Perhaps if analyst and analysand had been able to study their theoretical and technical disagreement as the rivalry it appears to have been, and if Guntrip had not fled the analysis after Fairbairn interpreted the Percy-transference, what in my hypothesis is the truly Oedipal root of Guntrip's illness—the phantasy of having killed his sibling rival and the need to be dead like him in talion punishment for this crime—might have come to light.

But he went to Winnicott, who, like Fairbairn, seems to have been ready to stress the mother's deficiencies but, unlike Fairbairn, seems also to have offered a reparative re-parenting therapy, countering (magically, I would say) the baleful influence of Harry's "bad" mother by playing the role of the "good" mother whose early existence, to his credit, Winnicott helped Guntrip acknowledge: "He enabled me to reach extraordinarily clear evidence that my mother had almost certainly had an initial period of natural maternalism to me as her first baby, for perhaps a couple of months, before her personality problems robbed me of that 'good mother'" (p. 749). An alternative to a magical, transference cure through paranoid-schizoid splitting, merely countering the "all-bad" with the "all-good" breast, the demonised mother with the idolised analyst, would have been an analytic cure based on achieving a depressive position consciousness of ambivalence towards his objects (mother, brother, analyst) and of guilt for death wishes towards them together with efforts at reparation.

Winnicott appears to have offered direct, non-analytic support to Guntrip, telling him, "I'm good for you but you're good for me. Doing your analysis is almost the most reassuring thing that happens to me. The chap before you makes me feel I'm no good at all" (p. 750). Again, we have no independent knowledge of Winnicott's behaviour, only Guntrip's account. But if my overall hypothesis has any validity, we must wonder about the effect on a man with Guntrip's sibling conflicts of his analyst so openly favouring him over an analytic brother. Guntrip reports that, in addition to providing him with narcissistic gratification of this sort, Winnicott assisted him to more fully understand his ceaseless activity, his "hard talking" in the analysis, and his obsessive record-keeping after sessions, as essentially manic defences—not against internalised, essentially pre-Oedipal object-relations with the bad mother (Fairbairn's hypothesis); not against states of inner deadness formed out of a self-punishing identification with the dead brother (my hypothesis); but rather, in Winnicott's as distinct from Fairbairn's hypothesis (though both were pre-Oedipal), against the core of ego-weakness and unrelatedness stemming from *the earlier mother who failed to relate at all*" (original italics, p. 749). Presumably this "earlier mother" came after the earliest phase of her "natural maternalism".

According to Guntrip, Winnicott said:

> You must have had an earlier illness before Percy was born, and felt mother left you to look after yourself. You accepted Percy as your infant self that needed looking after. When he died, you had nothing and collapsed ... Your problem is that that illness of collapse was never resolved. You had to keep yourself alive in spite of it. You can't take your ongoing being for granted. You have to work hard to keep yourself in existence. You're afraid to stop acting, talking or keeping awake. You feel you might die in a gap like Percy, because if you stop acting mother can't do anything. She couldn't save Percy or you. You're bound to fear I can't keep you alive, so you link up monthly sessions for me by your records. No gaps. You can't feel that you are a going concern to me, because mother couldn't save you ... The gap is not you forgetting mother, but mother forgetting you, and now you've relived it with me. You're finding an earlier trauma which you might never recover without the help of the Percy trauma repeating it. You have to remember mother abandoning you by transference on to me. (p. 749)

The idea of an earlier illness is speculative, as is that of Percy as Harry's infant self. An alternative (equally speculative) hypothesis that neither demonises the mother nor renders Harry her total victim is that the collapse upon Percy's death involved a self-punitive identification with the brother whom, in omnipotent phantasy conflating wish with deed, Harry imagined he had killed. In this view, his chronic overactivity represents a constant fight for life in the face of the constant regressive "ectoplasmic" pull towards death grounded in the primitive superego's demand for Harry's death as the price that, according to talion law, must be paid for the crime of fratricide.

But according to Guntrip, Winnicott "became a good breast mother to my infant self in my deep unconscious, at the point where my actual mother had lost her maternalism and could not stand me as a live baby any more" (p. 750). Guntrip felt Winnicott enabled him to see that "[I]t was not just the loss of Percy, but being left alone with the mother who could not keep me alive, that caused my collapse and apparent dying" (p. 750). When Winnicott died, Guntrip's first thought was, "I've lost Winnicott and am left alone with mother, sunk in depression, ignoring me. That's how I felt when Percy died" (p. 751). But instead of collapsing, over the next few months he experienced a series of dreams leading to two that he regarded as finally breaking the amnesia for Percy's life and death and confronting him with "the 'faceless' depersonalised mother, and the black depressed mother, who totally failed to relate to both of us" (p. 751). He concluded that though Winnicott's death had reminded him of Percy's, the situation was entirely different in that Winnicott had been internalised as a good mother: "*He has taken her place and made it possible and safe to remember her in an actual dream*" (p. 752; original italics).

Guntrip felt he had finally reaped the gains he had sought in his analyses. If Fairbairn had become another good father, Winnicott had replaced his non-relating mother. He had been successfully re-parented. If my hypothesis is correct, he had achieved a kind of "transference cure", not an analytic one. He writes, "It hardly seems worth mentioning that the only point at which I felt I disagreed with Winnicott was when he talked occasionally about 'getting at your primitive sadism, the baby's ruthlessness and cruelty, your aggression' in a way that suggested not my angry fight to extract a response from my cold mother, but Freud's and Klein's 'instinct theory,' the id, innate aggression" (p. 750). The issue of whether such id aggression is innate, although theoretically important, is something of a red herring here. Quite apart from instinct, frustration breeds aggression, and not just the frustration of having a cold mother, but even that of having a sibling born and thus losing one's privileged status as the only child. Human existence *per se* is frustrating. Having to die and knowing it is frustrating. Not being able to have our cake and eat it too is frustrating. One need not be a psychobiological instinct theorist to recognise the frustration that is inherent in the human condition and that is nobody's fault, in addition to the frustration that is. In any case, although far from being a systematic or even a theoretically consistent thinker, Winnicott was far too astute an analyst to be entirely blind to the role of aggression in Guntrip's psychology. But Guntrip seemed able to prevent this evidence of difference between them from disrupting his determination to have a cure through identification rather than analysis.

After acknowledging his wife's role in what he regarded as his cure, Guntrip asks, "What is psychoanalytic psychotherapy? It is, as I see it, the provision of a reliable and understanding human relationship of a kind that makes contact with the *deeply repressed* traumatised child in a way that enables one to become steadily more able to live, in the security of a new real relationship, with the traumatic legacy of the earliest formative years, as it seeps through or erupts into consciousness" (p. 752; original italics). There is no need to deny the significance of trauma to suggest that not all emotional disorder is reducible to this cause and that a good deal of the psychological suffering to which humanity is heir arises from other sources—unless one is prepared to argue that being human is itself traumatic, an existentialist notion I would personally support.

It seems to me that one of the dangers of a personal relations therapy that offers a kind of reparative re-parenting through provision of a "new real relationship" is that it appeals to the therapist's unresolved omnipotence. Guntrip (1971) claims, "At the deepest level, psychotherapy is replacement therapy, providing for the patient what the mother failed to provide at the beginning of life" (p. 191). On occasion, his comments on his work with deeply regressed schizoid patients, some of whom he felt were "literally 'born again'" (p. 196) through a "therapeutic process of re-growth of the personality from the foundations" (p. 191) have caused me to wonder if this former minister may have become excessively identified with Jesus resurrecting Lazarus from the dead. With regard to his becoming a physician, Freud (1927a) wrote: "I do not remember in my childhood any craving to help suffering humanity; my sadistic tendencies were not very strong, and so there was no need for this particular derivative to develop" (p. 393). The passion to heal (*furor sanandi*) often embodies a therapist's unconscious need to engage in manic (magical) reparation for real or imagined crimes. For Freud it was enough to work to transform "hysterical misery into common unhappiness" (Freud, 1895d, p. 305) through the analytic resolution of interior conflict. To me this seems a more modest and potentially achievable therapeutic aim for fallen human beings who must toil by the sweat of their brows outside Eden.

In this connection Guntrip's long-time friend and colleague, Ronald Markillie (1996), writes:

> I think the most critical thing I can say of what he did is that it struck me that he entered into an allegiance with his patients against a bad object which got made even badder in the process. It is possible that this was encouraged early on by Fairbairn's idea that only bad object relationships are introjected ... In consequence, a patient may be left more dependent than ever, unable to make reparation because his part in events cannot be worked through; unable to recognise that if, for example, mother was depressed, she had her reasons and he played some part; unable to explore the realm of his omnipotence. (p. 769)

Regarding Guntrip's terminal carcinoma of the oesophagus, Markillie writes, "I can't remember when the diagnosis was confirmed, for the timing is crucial ... The more I think about it now, the more I believe some denial had been going on for some time ... I know that I have always believed that when he knew what his condition was he turned his face to the wall and ceased the struggle, his last and final collapse" (pp. 768-769).

* * *

In such early writings in the field of pastoral psychology as his *Psychology for Ministers and Social Workers* (1949), Guntrip recognised that "among the most persistent features of neurosis are the tyrannous conscience, the emergence of anxiety in the form of guilt, and the need for self-punishment" (p. 245). But his subsequent personal contribution to psychoanalytic thought displaced the role of conflict, guilt, and self-punishment in psychopathology in favour of a one-sided emphasis upon deficit and trauma resulting from parental failure. There is no need to downplay the role of trauma and deprivation in the genesis of neurosis, the ways in which we may indeed have been victims, in order to see how such experience gives rise to reactive hate, narcissistic rage, and wishes and acts of revenge. Such emotions and acts make us guilty or self-punitive agents.

In *Mental Pain and the Cure of Souls* (1956), Guntrip wrote, "Human beings feel safer, calmer, and less anxious if they can find scapegoats for their troubles. They try if possible to find an external scapegoat—Nazis, communists, capitalists, the government, the political party that is not one's own; or, coming nearer home, their employer, or annoying neighbour, or their minister who didn't visit them or doesn't fill the church or isn't like the last minister, or else even their husband, wife or children" (pp. 26-27). But despite this recognition of our proclivity to scapegoat others as the cause of our troubles rather than acknowledge the degree to which we have brought them on ourselves, from his earliest to his latest writings Guntrip would consistently blame the early carers:

> *All our troubles and sorrows arise out of our deep ineradicable need for love, for good-object relationships*: our fundamental insecurities, fears, anxieties, angers and aggressions, and guilty feelings are all reactions to persons who have frustrated our love-needs ... Thus in the unconscious inner world we are forced to live in a state of tantalised, stimulated, excited needs which are never given any proper satisfaction. This perpetuates the outer situation of infancy in so far as the baby was allowed to get into a state of painful, unsatisfied, hungry craving through lack of proper emotional "mothering". (1956, pp. 62-63; original italics)

Certainly bad relationships, especially those with caregivers in infancy and early childhood, give rise to neurosis. But so does the hate and consequent need for self-punishment arising, for example, from the birth of a sibling. As Mitchell (2000, 2003) has recently reminded the psychoanalytic community, where there are siblings "murder is in the air" (2000, p. 20). This, of course, is not to deny that when relations between siblings are destructive, one has to ask where the parents were. (See in this connection Hantman's (2006) review of Mitchell's (2003) book on *Siblings*.)

Murderous feelings often lead in primary process thinking to phantasies that one has, in fact, murdered or at least maimed or otherwise damaged another, with all the consequent needs for punishment that generally follow. The self-murdering states of chronic fatigue and inner deadness, depletion, and devitalisation that Guntrip viewed as direct outcomes of the deficient mothering of which he believed both he and Percy were victims represent, in this hypothesis, the consequence of the turning of aggression against the self and of superego-driven self-punishment for fratricidal wishes that in phantasy were tantamount to fratricidal deeds. While unconsciously accusing and punishing himself, on the conscious level the murderer became through projection not Harry but his mother.

In his own way, Guntrip lived out his phantasy murder of the brother with each of his analysts: he allowed neither to succeed with him, rendering them impotent, putting them out of commission. Padel (1996) writes of Guntrip's "rivalry with his analysts" and his "intense and compulsive competitiveness" that is "destructive of the other person" (p. 759). Glatzer and Evans (1977), following Abraham (1919), see Guntrip as a specific type of narcissistic characters who offer "nothing more than a pretended compliance, for analysis is an attack on their narcissism ... They expect from analysis interesting contributions to the autobiography they are writing ... They instruct the physician by giving him their opinion of their neurosis, which they consider a particularly interesting one, and they imagine that science will be especially enriched by their analysis" (Abraham, 1919, p. 304, as quoted by Glatzer & Evans, 1977, pp. 84–85). Glatzer and Evans point out that "Guntrip instructed his analysts in what they had to uncover, namely his trauma. And both did his bidding" (p. 85). They write of narcissistic patients who feel they are better than their analysts and for whom "... there is obviously only one person who can conduct their analysis—themselves" (p. 85). They conclude, "One is left with the impression that Guntrip had this grandiose fantasy: the only person who could analyse Guntrip was Guntrip" (p. 87).

Markillie (1996) asks, "Did he ever then have an analysis or is that a name used to name something else? It [Guntrip's (1975) report] reads as if the title should be 'My Self Analysis'" (p. 770). He wonders if both Fairbairn and Winnicott were exposed by Guntrip "to have made such unanalytic comments, and to have mixed promiscuously an analytical role and a colleague-relation to the detriment of the task" and in this way were "made into parents who failed" (p. 770). Once they had died, Guntrip omnipotently analysed himself, remembering the trauma, blaming the mother, exonerating himself.

In reality, of course, Guntrip had not murdered his brother: he only (in my hypothesis) phantasised that he had. The crime occurred in *psychic reality*. But such unconscious beliefs are common in children who have had siblings who died. Guntrip's mother may well have been cold; this would have contributed to the problem. All children experience sibling rivalry, envy, hate, death wishes, and resulting needs for self-punishment (even "only children", see the case of Mr. D in Chapter Seven). If mother is cold such feelings are exacerbated for, when love is a scarce commodity, competition and envy are intensified. Added to all this, of course, is the bad conscience and superego reproach for the hatred towards the mother that Guntrip seems never to have got over.

This analysis in no way denies the trauma of a sibling's death, nor that of maternal coldness. It only refuses to deny the role of envy, hate, guilt, and self-punishment in human psychology. If my hypothesis has any validity, then Guntrip's chronic symptom might have been permanently resolved had he been able to surrender his paranoid-schizoid defensive guilt evasion through projection of blame onto the mother in favour of a capacity to bear the guilt for hating her and for having wished his brother dead. Death wishes towards siblings are a rather normal occurrence and regularly cause trouble enough but have severely pathological consequences when they appear, in primary process phantasy, to have omnipotently produced an actual death.

Although entirely blaming the parents' intolerance of the child's aggression for its repression and turning against the self, at least in his early work Guntrip (1949) was aware of the role of the sadistic superego in psychopathology. He describes it as a "tyrannous internal policeman keeping the child, and later the adult, in a state of constant anxiety" (p. 249). Repressed aggression is "turned back against the bad self and used in self-suppression, self-blame, self-punishment" (p. 251). In this situation, "the conscience or superego becomes a really vindictive, destructive, inner dictator" (p. 251), "a ruthlessly repressive persecuting conscience in a guilt-laden mind as the only alternative to becoming an anti-social person" (p. 252). In this early work, Guntrip sees three possible outcomes of the aggression arising from parental failure: suicide, real or symbolic; homicide or other forms of antisocial behaviour; and the "mania for reproaching" (Racker, 1957, p. 141): "One grave danger involved is that the mind may be driven to seek relief from self-torture by projecting its guilt-laden bad feelings on to other people and attacking its own 'sins' there ... Such an external attitude always hides intense repressed feelings of personal guilt" (1949, p. 252). The latter is itself a form of antisocial behaviour but one in which, as Hantman (2008) has suggested, psychopathy takes a distinctly "normopathic" form.

* * *

It is ironic that the Judaeo-Christian doctrine of original sin is better preserved in psychological form by the non-religious psychoanalysts, Sigmund Freud and Melanie Klein, than by the Christians, Fairbairn, Winnicott, and Guntrip. Eigen (1981) is incorrect to describe Guntrip's object-relations theory as a "profoundly Christian psychology" because it "views hate as reactive to failings by primary objects" and implies that "if love were perfect there would be no hate" (p. 108). Eigen is not incorrect to attribute such views to Guntrip, only in calling them Christian; they are in no way Christian views, and Guntrip was out of step with Christianity in espousing them. In Christianity hate is an intrinsic feature of a fallen and sinful human nature that envies and hates perversely, even in the face of love, including the perfect love extended to man by God. Translated from religious into secular terms, this is Kleinian theory in which the infant comes to hate not only the bad object for its badness, but also the good object out of envy of its very goodness.

Eigen's error echoes that of Freud. In the face of the devastation of Europe brought about by the First World War, together with the masochistic self-destructiveness he had come to recognise in so many patients, Freud (1920g) finally overcame his long-standing resistance to acknowledging aggression as an equally fundamental part of human nature as sexuality and announced his final dual drive theory of *Eros* and *Thanatos*. He then proceeded to misattribute (project) the naïve optimism he had earlier shared with Enlightenment thought onto the Bible:

> Why have we ourselves needed such a long time before we decided to recognise an aggressive instinct? ... We should probably have met with little resistance if we had wanted to ascribe an instinct with such an aim to animals. But to include it in the human constitution appears sacrilegious; it contradicts too many religious

presumptions and social conventions. No, man must be naturally good or at least good-natured. If he occasionally shows himself brutal, violent or cruel, these are only passing disturbances of his emotional life, for the most part provoked, or perhaps only the consequences of the inexpedient social regulations which he has hitherto imposed on himself. (Freud, 1933a, p. 103)

In this passage, Freud seems entirely unaware of the fact that the optimism of his own earlier thought that he now mocks belongs not to the Bible but to elements of Enlightenment thought and the environmentalistic social sciences stemming from it. It was his own loyalty to the anti-religious Enlightenment and his estrangement from the Bible (and the father who beseeched him to return to it) that prevented him from overcoming his own naïvety until after the war and his deepened clinical experience finally made him see what the Bible had recognised all along. In its vision of human beings as fallen, perverse, and broken sinners, even after salvation or redemption, the Bible is far more congruent with Freud's late, dark view of human nature than he was ever prepared to acknowledge. So the problem with Guntrip's thinking in regard to aggression is not that it is Christian thinking but that it, like Freud's early thinking, is in denial of the profound ambivalence of a human nature torn between the forces of construction and destruction, a vision that the Bible had always conveyed and that the later Freud had come to share.

In Freudian drive theory, whether early (sexual *vs.* self-preservative drives) or late (*Eros vs. Thanatos*), the child is seen as coming into the world with inherently antisocial, polymorphous perverse, incestuous, and murderously aggressive drives that simply must, in one way or another, be inhibited or tamed if society is not to deteriorate into a universal war. Despite the fact that in Freudian theory the human *Trieb* is distinct from animal *Instinkt* in that its aims and objects are not biologically hardwired but influenced by experience, the theory is biologically reductionist in its insistence that the *Triebe* arise from a somatic source (not the brain, but an erogenous bodily zone). This grounding of human motivation in the somatic component of human existence, together with its essentially paranoid blaming of human evil on the animal in us rather than upon our uniquely human transcendence of the biological component of our being-in-the-world, is widely regarded today as untenable.

Unfortunately, in rejecting such biologism, the critics of Freudian theory have all-too-often swung to an equally reductive environmentalism. The work of Fairbairn and Guntrip and, to a somewhat lesser extent (because of his very inconsistency as a theorist) Winnicott, are cases in point. What is lost in this pendulum swing is an existentialist recognition of a human situation that, although conditioned by both nature and nurture, is irreducible to either, or to their interaction. We transcend both as a result of our uniquely human type of ego-functioning in which symbolic processes open us to absence, the not-yet and the no-longer (i.e., time), consciousness of both self and other, awareness of both freedom and mortality, and to the ontological anxiety all this generates in us. In the face of such anxiety and the maddening nature of our human condition we experience unavoidable mental pain that is nobody's fault, but that generates rage and a wide range of demonic reactions. Although they obscured and mis-theorised their insight through their biologism, the Freudians and Kleinians were at least aware of the demonic in human nature as intrinsic to our being, and not merely a reaction to victimisation at the hands of others.

It would seem odd that a Christian such as Guntrip would lose sight of the existentialism intrinsic to the Judaeo-Christian anthropology, while secular humanists, such as Freud and Klein, would, albeit in an obscured form, retain something of its intuition of the demonic in human nature. Unlike the former pastor Guntrip, they did not resort to the paranoid projection of sin, but required us to recognise it (albeit translated into secular terms such as narcissism or aggression) in ourselves. In my hypothesis, Guntrip's failure in this regard was due to a personal factor: his guilt was unbearable; it could not be tolerated in the self; it had to be evacuated into the other, the mother. In his reparative re-parenting, personal relationship therapy, Harry would be a better mother to his patients. In his autarchic self-analysis, he would be a better mother to himself. If this represented merely Guntrip's personal tragedy, it would be sad enough, but the fact is that his flight from guilt contributed to a de-moralising trend within contemporary psychoanalysis that, in offering a defence against guilt, deprives its adherents of the opportunity to receive or provide a genuine analysis and the personal maturation this can sometimes make possible.

CHAPTER SEVEN

Two case studies*

The case of Mr. D

During the second year of his analysis, Mr. D, a thirty-year-old academic with a flamboyantly rebellious cultural and political outlook who entered analysis owing to work inhibitions, relational problems, and diffuse anxiety and unhappiness, suddenly started experiencing dizzy spells. For example, he might be in a supermarket when, suddenly, the lights would appear to dim and his field of vision would shrink almost to nothing and he would have to clutch his cart to keep from falling over as the store seemed to slowly begin to move, like a merry-go-round starting up. Although suspecting hysteria, the analyst recommended a complete neurological investigation which yielded nothing. As the analysis continued evidence accrued that the symptoms amounted to a kind of body language in which D communicated the defensive message that he was not at all a phallic, competitive, Oedipally aggressive male but, on the contrary, something rather like the swooning woman of Victorian stereotype. As this interpretation got

---

*The second of these case studies, the case of Mr. E, was contributed by Jean Hantman.

worked through in his analysis the dizzy spells disappeared, never to return.

Some years later, while the analysis continued, D began to experience severe pain in both hip joints. By the time he sought medical help for this, he was at times using a cane. A physician x-rayed the joints and informed him that he had sustained serious damage to both in the course of a mysterious illness he had suffered between the ages of three and five that had been accompanied at the time by rheumatoid arthritis. The physician informed him that double hip replacement surgery would eventually be necessary but, as the technology in this field was improving at a rapid pace, it would be in his interest to postpone the surgery as long as possible with the use of anti-inflammatory medication. He was prescribed a large daily dose which he gradually reduced by about two thirds and maintained at that level for several years. After viewing a television report about sudden bleeds caused by long-term use of such medication, D decided he needed to get a second opinion. He retrieved the original x-rays and took them to the head of the rheumatology department at a local hospital who looked at them and examined him and then informed him there was nothing whatsoever wrong with him. D was dumbfounded. He asked what he was to do with all the medication. The specialist told him to flush it down the toilet. As he had been told he would never be able to run or play sports such as tennis, he asked about this and was told to "start gradually" as he was not in great shape. Incredulous, D sought the advice of another rheumatologist who confirmed the diagnosis that neither the original x-rays nor examination revealed any pathology whatsoever. D stopped taking the anti-inflammatory medication, replacing it with coated aspirin when necessary, and soon dispensed with that. There were no subsequent episodes of hip joint pain. (D cast off his crutches and walked.)

In his analysis, Mr. D came to realise that, once again, he had been communicating, psychosomatically and hysterically, that he was not an intact, phallic, and competitive male, but a wounded, in fact, a crippled man. Though the mystery as to what caused the original physician to see serious pathology in x-rays in which two subsequent specialists could find no pathology whatsoever remained unresolved, what was clear was Mr. D's readiness to identify with and begin to play the part of a defective man. In this connection he recalled his high school football career. He had been a defensive middle linebacker who was talented in his capacity to figure out the play and spot the ball carrier and in the speed with which he could get to him. But he had been unable to launch his body into the air and knock his opponent down, with the self-defeating consequence that he would be dragged for five or ten yards. He recalled both his infuriated coach screaming at him from the sidelines ("Hit him! Hit him!"), and spending a lot of time on the bench.

We can only speculate as to the nature of D's infantile neurosis and the psychosomatic illness it generated. The combination of high spiking fevers and rheumatoid arthritis suggests Still's disease, a condition some view as an autoimmune disorder which may have emotional causes. The patient's mother suffered from periodic severe depression throughout her life and became recognisably alcoholic by the time D was five or six. The illness seems to have manifested around the age of four, when a boy of the same age who had been taken into the family and raised for a year as the patient's informally adopted brother was returned to his family of origin when it refused to allow him to be formally adopted. During the following year D was subject to long stays in hospital and subjected to myriad tests and procedures that sought to determine the causes of his dangerously high fevers and rheumatoid arthritis. This occurred at a time when hospitals were not yet sufficiently enlightened to permit long visitations by family. Mr. D's busy father visited occasionally but his anxious and increasingly depressed mother seldom appeared. Fortunately her elder sister worked nearby and D's favourite aunt visited him daily after work. D's tonsils had been removed the year prior to the onset of the illness, but eventually infected adenoids were identified and removed in an additional surgery and with subsequent cortisone therapy and radiation the symptoms gradually disappeared. By this time, D had missed the first year of school and subsequently felt shy, timid, and out of synch with his peers when he returned to school.

D's childhood illness emerged when a "sibling" who had suddenly arrived in his life during his Oedipal phase, dethroning him from his status as the only child, disappeared from it just as suddenly. On the boy's arrival, D had been told by his parents that he must be very good and nice to the poor little fellow and to uncomplainingly share his toys with him. He recalled that on that first night his mother slept not with father or with him but in the guest room with the newcomer. This was followed by his dim awareness of his mother's serial "illnesses" (several miscarriages) and his growing recognition of her worsening depression and alcoholism. As a little boy, the patient appears to have associated the miscarriages with memories of his father's burial of several of the family canaries in large matchboxes in the backyard. As we have seen, according to Juliet Mitchell (2000), in the sibling rivalry that inevitably accompanies sibling love, "murder is in the air" (p. 20). It may be that Mr. D's repetitive need to enact the role of a swooning woman or a castrated and crippled man had its roots both in his pre-Oedipal relationship with a disturbed mother and in unconscious Oedipal (persecutory) guilt, an unconscious need for punishment, for the "crime" of survival and triumph over both his real, albeit temporary, and potential siblings.

The trauma of hospitalisation, early separation from his primary carers, repeated intrusive procedures, separation anxiety due both to the hospitalisation and his mother's increasing emotional unavailability all generated in Mr. D core feelings of anxiety and inadequacy. He appeared to have interpreted his hospitalisation as a punishment: he had been sent to a kind of Hell for being a bad boy, for repressed feelings of resentment of and death wishes towards his temporarily adopted sibling, and unjustified guilt for his triumph over him and the series of other potential siblings, his mother's miscarriages. His early sense of sinfulness was both counteracted to some extent and reinforced by his early Christian education. As a boy he was devout, a choir boy; the atmosphere in church offered him respite from his increasingly unhappy home, recognition for his singing, and the attention of older mother figures who fussed over him—until his voice broke in early adolescence and his sexual activities and explorations, his intensifying rage towards his alcoholic mother, and his growing intellect combined to alienate him from the Church.

D built up a phallic-narcissistic character structure employing manic defences, grandiosity, anger, and a degree of sadism to defend against and compensate for deep underlying feelings of inadequacy and badness. This character structure led in late adolescence and youth to an angry, iconoclastic, and culturally and politically rebellious stance, as well as to selfish and exploitative behaviour towards the women with whom D attempted to form intimate relationships—women onto whom he transferred his not very well buried hatred of his mother. All this only fed his persecutory guilt or unconscious need for punishment, part of which was unjustified, grounded in childhood phantasy and pain, but part of which was quite justified owing to the rage and narcissism that had emerged from trauma and that had led to destructive behaviour towards himself and others.

Prior to embarking upon a full-scale psychoanalysis, Mr. D had experimented with a wide range of the trendy therapies of the time: Gestalt, transactional, bioenergetic, even primal scream therapy, all to no avail. Only in the course of extensive, three or four sessions per week analysis did his various patterns of self-punishment, self-defeat, and inhibition gradually yield as he came to understand the complex psychodynamics involved. Only then was he finally able to begin to reconcile with his conscience, to sort out which elements of his guilt were justified and which were not, to experience contrition and attempt to make reparation for his misbehaviour, to overcome his anger, and to begin to defend himself against his punitive superego while moving towards forgiveness of both his mother and himself.

While analysis of D's narcissism, his Oedipal conflicts with his father, his excessive phallic aggressiveness covering feelings of castration, and the inhibition stemming from his need to sabotage and punish himself proved helpful, what really seemed to facilitate major character change was receiving his analyst's empathic and sympathetic understanding of his early childhood traumata (the hospitalisation, maternal deprivation, the appearance and disappearance of a "brother"), the self-blame emerging from all this, and the additional guilt arising from the rage, narcissism, and sadism that were consequences of and defences against his childhood pain. Early in his analysis he had a dream featuring a lamb being led to the slaughter and a sad little boy sitting forlornly alone on the curb. He recognised the lamb as the *Agnus Dei*, the "lamb of God", and recognised that as a child he too had been an innocent sufferer, but one who, unlike Christ, had reacted to his pain with rage and a thirst for vengeance. Like most victims of trauma, he had identified with the aggressor and was guilty of wanting to make others suffer as he had.

Experiencing the non-judgemental empathy and sympathy of his analyst enabled Mr. D to develop compassion towards his child self and to begin to reconcile with his troubled conscience, experience contrition for his sins, and defend himself against his sadistic superego. As he did so, his need to thwart self-fulfilment both in his intimate relationships and in his creative life was increasingly overcome. Although for many years he had been an angry atheist, preaching the anti-Christian views of Marx, Nietzsche, Freud, and Sartre, his personal analysis gradually undermined his anger and narcissism and eventually liberated him to make contact once again with the attitudes of gratitude and thanksgiving of his early Christian experience. Mr. D was finally able to allow himself to form a lasting marriage with a woman who physically resembled his mother, but who unlike her was a strong, independent, and mature person able to provide him with the warmth and reliable containment he needed, while helping him remain accountable to his conscience and stand up to his sadistic superego.

Recognition of the analyst's need to provide empathic and sympathetic understanding of childhood pain has tended in recent years to be split off from recognition of the equally important need to help patients reconcile with conscience by acknowledging guilt arising from destructive feelings and acts. The case of Mr. D, like the one that follows (the case of Mr. E contributed by Jean Hantman), demonstrates, I believe, the necessity for both of these elements if analytic therapy is to be genuinely healing.

* * *

The case of Mr. E

By Jean Hantman

A man who began analysis at the age of forty-five had bodily preoccupations since childhood. He was compelled to stare into mirrors to "see if I'm here". He somatised with various illnesses (such as Graves disease) whenever he hated. That is, he developed unconsciously a systematic somatic defence against the feeling of hate. Before he consciously realised that something or someone had stimulated his rage, Mr. E would have a fever, heart palpitations, or diagnosable thyroid alterations. Along with illnesses E had elective surgeries for various ailments leading to vague postoperative medical regimens and prescriptions. He reported that his wife (whom he liked to avoid touching) was annoyed at night when he lined up his multitude of pill bottles, then swallowed his medications in a ritual that drove her to fall asleep before they could be intimate.

Born the fourth of eight children to a cold, inattentive, phobic, and distracted mother, E had only two pleasant memories of childhood.

The first was that at the age of five he contracted an illness that was serious enough for him to miss two months of school but did not warrant hospitalisation. A bed was placed in the living room so his mother could take care of him without having to run upstairs. That time of being ill, which he was told damaged his heart slightly but permanently, was the only time in his life that he had his mother to himself. E's only other nice memory of his mother occurred when his baby brother was born. His brother, the last of the eight children, made the mother happier than the others for no apparent reason. After returning home with the new baby, after five days in the hospital, E sensed in his mother an unusual calm (she was usually depressed and cold, or tense and mean) and he was allowed to sit beside her as she fed his brother. Mr. E felt an inextricable link between disease and attachment, hospitals and affection. He experienced both horror and excitement at signs of illness, as his childhood illness was the only time he had a mother.

A year after the birth of Mr. E, his sister F, the fifth child, was born. This sister was the now consciously identified root of E's history of denied hate, sneaky sadism, guilt-evasion, and psychosomatic illness. For the first half of his analysis, he could recall torturing F in many ways but did not know why. The motivation was a total mystery. He could remember coldly pushing F off the bed, demeaning her, abandoning her on the busy city street when he was six and F was five, all with no conscious recollection of the accompanying feelings or motivation. Why would someone push his sister off the bed? Mr. E could not answer. (Long pause.) "I'm truly puzzled … we all loved each other so much," voicing the myth of the family. He was entirely unaware of any feelings of rivalry, hate, frustration, craving, or envy. He could access only memories of having felt sorry for F for never being as popular as he was and for developing debilitating anxieties and not being able to go to college, while he went on to receive a master's degree and, eventually, a doctorate. As is typical of this dynamic, when murderous impulses are acted on with repression of affect, responsibility and subsequent contrition can be evaded. Then the still-unconscious aggression is turned against the self that continues to deny having acted destructively. The patient enacts the parts of both the criminal *and* the sentencing judge and jury.

In Mr. E's case, however, even his self-torment was always tinged with an excitement that could only be described as sexual, though such excitement was a consequence, not the aim of the violence. (Evidence for this is that the excitement, through analysis, disappeared years before the violence.) In the earlier years of his analysis, during the sequence of denied rage, sadistic action, and evasion of responsibility, Mr. E was quite overtaken physically. His heart fluttered and pounded as his thyroid "kicked up". He got flushed and breathed heavily. He sweated and smiled weakly as his eyes rolled back and his lashes fluttered. During this theatrical demonstration of falling ill, E maintained a cheerful demeanour, impeccable grooming, and meticulous orderliness. His analytic group was perplexed watching the discrepancy between E's alarming medical symptoms, his thrill at being swept away by them, and his determination to be perceived as cheerful and impeccable all at the same time. Psychoanalysts know how hard it is to be a hysteric. It is one of the most exhausting and often permanently debilitating defences against rage that we treat.

What led to E's somatisation? Denied hate. He hated and was unconscious of his homicidal rage towards the person he hated. Someone had been disrespectful; someone threatened to leave him; someone turned down an invitation. Mr. E denied to himself that he wanted to knock these offending people right off the bed. But instead of overtly pushing anyone, in adulthood *he got sick instead of consciously feeling and talking*. By working together for fifteen years, along with help from his analytic group which confronted him with the vast difference between how he perceived himself and how he was perceived, Mr. E and the analyst gradually were able to make conscious the dark rage that underlay his pose of "nothing's wrong", his sneaky aggressive actions, the evasion of responsibility, and subsequent self-punishments via illnesses. Where it used to take E a year of analysis to acknowledge the progression from rage to illness, he came to be able to identify it quickly. He gradually became able to *interrupt the hysterical sequence by substituting feelings and words for symptoms*, that is, to become healthy by becoming real.

His illness and then his progress presented in an unusually clear pattern, which made Mr. E's resistance to seeing and acknowledging his destructiveness and self-attack easier to resolve. The pattern was this: as long as he was working he was able to set aside his symptoms, using the job that he loved as distraction, a manic defence. In the beginning of his analysis (the first phase) this was not the case. He would self-attack for his crimes no matter what distractions were present. In fact, his manic defence, developed some time in the fifth year of his analysis, was actually a significant sign of progress, a defence more evolved and successful than the primitive defences that failed to keep him intact and functioning much at all when he first began analysis.

A pattern emerged some time in the fourth or fifth year when he started becoming asymptomatic as long as he was working every day. Then summer would arrive; he did not work in the summer so he was confronted with idle time, confronted with himself, and he became sick or unconsciously injured himself. The self he was stuck with through the summer felt homicidal, which quickly led to major anxiety, followed by an illness which presented him with the opportunity to completely forget the hate and rage he felt but could neither tolerate nor verbalise for years: Lyme disease (diagnosed but never confirmed by medical tests), fractured ankle, anorexia, symptoms of thyroid disease ultimately leading a doctor to irradiate Mr. E's thyroid gland. Every summer he started to feel what he had been defending against throughout the months on the job—and every summer he quickly became sick or hurt. As autumn approached and he started preparing to return to work his illnesses and injuries mysteriously went away.

As Mr. E began to become conscious of his destructive wishes and dark feelings the pattern changed and he moved into a third phase of his analysis. At first, when realising consciously how consumed he was by anger, paranoia, entitlement and envy, he was able to intellectually acknowledge that he had these feelings, but could neither accept nor tolerate them—that is, he still would not incorporate what he intellectually knew into his life, to become someone with a conscience, someone who felt destructive but without acting on the feelings. In his sessions he would consciously insist that he was beginning to understand his way of flowing from hatred towards others to serious self-attack, but he was still unconscious of the *intensity* of his rage and continued to maintain an ever-so-polite demeanour while controlling others through various manipulations, contemptuous without knowing it, then visibly anxious, as he articulated the details of his history with rage in his sessions. Still denying the intensity and imagining his rage was past, not present, instead of becoming abruptly stricken sometime early in the summer, as he had earlier in his treatment, he now began to feel the stirring of anxiety in the spring, while he was still working.

The analyst and Mr. E were able then to use this spring anxiety to prepare for the summer. The analyst, now having recognition from the patient before, not after he became sick or hurt, was able to analyse and achieve a diminishing of the severity of the physical symptoms. Part of the analytic process during this time was the analyst's attempt to help the patient feel and articulate his rage in the safe environment of the session. Here is an example of the kind of discussion Mr. E and the analyst had in this third phase of the analysis:

PATIENT
(in May):   I had anxiety this weekend thinking about the summer coming up. The closer summer comes the more anxious I'm getting. I have anxiety now.
ANALYST: What will you have this summer, an illness or an injury?
PATIENT: I don't want either!
ANALYST: Consciously.
PATIENT: (Slightly annoyed. Refers to theory accepted but not yet useful.) Well, I can't think of anything I'm angry about.
ANALYST: Who do you want to kill this year?
PATIENT: (More annoyed) I don't want to kill anyone.
ANALYST: Sounds like you wouldn't mind killing me right now. I'm presuming to know how you feel. I'm pushing you for answers to questions that don't make any sense to you.
PATIENT: (Trying to be the ever-cooperative analytic patient) I hate when you sound like my mother.
ANALYST: Are you being a good student now or do you mean it?
PATIENT: (Pauses) Dr. H, something happened. The anxiety is gone.

This was the truth. He had come into the session sweating with brow furrowed, his body posture rigid on the couch and then, after having had a good discussion about aggression, or a harmless aggressive session (i.e., hearing and saying the word "kill" without anyone dying), he was calm. Invited to put his hitherto concealed murderous feelings and guilt into words, encouraged to talk about what he had been taught from childhood were taboo words, wishes, and impulses, he started to resolve his need to unconsciously leak, to act hatefully, and to attack himself through physical symptoms.

During this third phase, the breakthrough, Mr. E's somatisation became weaker and an ability to empathise began. There was an end to hospitalisations. Towards the end of the treatment Mr. E stopped somatising and began instead to obsess for a short period. The symptoms stopped being physical, they were (briefly) mental. "Do we have enough money to get by? Will the house repairs ever be finished?" Etc. And summers would pass with no visits to doctors.

By this time Mr. E had become a great deal more comfortable with his destructive wishes. During the last, fourth phase, the more comfortable he became verbalising *all* of his feelings instead of only the pleasant ones, the more authentic concern he started feeling towards others. This was the first time in his life that his sympathy and compassion were sincere rather than an act, a mimicry of people he had observed expressing concern, but had never himself experienced. He was able to return to school after many years and two master's degrees, having given himself permission to complete a doctorate, the first in his large, extended family to do so. His marriage and relationships with his children became satisfying and harmonious, a dramatic difference from what they had been for so long (mean, distracted, tense, and avoidant).

The four phases of Mr. E's treatment

1. Intense unconscious destructive impulses and feelings that are intolerable lead to depression, anxiety, somatisation (self-attack through illness and injury) as defences against self-awareness, acceptance, guilt, and reparation.
2. Manic defence develops which allows patient to function competently for most of the year and proceed with analysis. Pattern emerges of summer illnesses and injuries which come on abruptly as Mr. E is aimless and idle, not working in the summer and faced with himself. Several years in phase two, which follows this path: manic defence collapses → intense rage, contempt, envy, paranoia, destructive impulses and behaviours move towards consciousness → interrupted by major anxiety → followed quickly by vague (yet diagnosable enough for the doctors) illnesses or injuries. (One summer Mr. E went into hospital as his daughter was about to give birth for the first time, stealing the drama from her and diverting everyone's attention towards him. Another summer his other daughter was getting married and Mr. E fractured his ankle, forcing him to spend the evening of the wedding sitting in a chair in pain, another diversion of attention away from his child.)
3. Phase three is the breakthrough, characterised by a shift from sudden illness/injury in the summer, unconsciously hidden from the analyst until after it happened, to a warning occurring in the

spring, mild anxiety that Mr. E could use in his analysis to prepare for the summer of self-attack, indicating a great strengthening of the transference. Although Mr. E still had not resolved his resistance to acknowledging the intensity of his destructive feelings and wishes, the analysis became productively collaborative, leading to a diminishing of the length of time spent being ill. By the end of phase three, Mr. E had become capable of tolerating his destructive feelings which reduced his anxiety and moved him closer to genuine remorse and the complex verbalisation of a much wider range of feelings. When Mr. E understood the difference between wishing (just words) and acting out (destructive behaviour), he stopped acting out, tolerated feeling, talked, loved.

4. In phase four Mr. E became comfortable being a human being, that is, someone who could feel hate without needing to act on it, feel it intensely, could observe himself (sharpened observing ego) starting to be mean, cold, or avoidant and instead of continuing the destructive behaviour, stopped it, making self-attack unnecessary. He began to feel remorse, to apologise (an action his family found startling, because he had never before apologised, ever), and to offer to make reparation in any way they needed.

Externally, in phase four, Mr. E resolved his resistance to allowing himself to surpass his extended family of sisters and brothers, nieces and nephews, and wrote his dissertation. He could only do this because his unconscious destructive aggression had been liberated, made conscious, and could now be channelled constructively instead of bound up in attack and self-attack. Conscience, depressive guilt, and reparation replaced denial, persecutory guilt inflicted by the superego, and illness.

PART II

CULTURAL REALM

CHAPTER EIGHT

Modernity and its discontents

We live in curious times and amid astonishing contrasts: reason on the one hand, the most absurd fanaticism on the other ... a civil war in every soul

—Voltaire (1789)

The phenomenon of guilt evasion cannot be adequately comprehended exclusively from the standpoint of the psychology of the individual. To attempt to do so would entail a failure of the sociological imagination which seeks to reveal the degree to which private troubles are grounded in public issues (Mills, 1959). Human beings have always been reluctant to face and bear guilt. But economic and socio-cultural forces create conditions that may either encourage or discourage conscience and responsibility. I have argued that from the very beginning psychoanalysis sought to cloak its intrinsic moral ethic beneath a positivist, de-moralising façade, but in recent decades the de-moralising trend intensified leading to neglect of the concepts of guilt and the superego, concepts through which psychoanalysis had earlier managed to address moral issues even while seeking to obscure the fact.

As I have indicated, I think it is no coincidence that the psychoanalytic retreat from guilt and the superego in favour of a preoccupation with the "self" occurred simultaneously with the economic shift from productive industrial to consumer capitalism and the culture of narcissism it creates. This is a culture of release rather than restriction; a culture hostile to regulation and regulators; a culture that tolerates, even encourages, the bending or evasion of rules; a de-moralising culture hostile to moral critique and to whistleblowers; a culture hostile to conscience. (Are any of the "banksters" responsible for the economic crisis of 2007–8 or the more recent manipulation of the Libor rate yet in jail?)

As Lakoff and Wehling (2012) have pointed out, owing to its rationalism and traditional reluctance to moralise, the Left surrenders moral discourse to the Right, which takes full advantage: "Where progressives argued policy—the right to collective bargaining and the importance of public education—conservatives argued morality from their perspective and many working people who shared their moral views voted with them and against their own interests. Why? Because morality is central to identity and, hence, trumps policy." What they mean by the morality of the Right corresponds, in the psychoanalytic terms employed here, to the morality of the superego, while the morality of the Left corresponds to conscience. "Progressive morality fits a nurturant family: parents are equal, the values are empathy, responsibility for oneself and others and cooperation," while "Conservative morality fits the family of the strict father, who is the ultimate authority" and in which "You are responsible for yourself and not anyone else and no one else is responsible for you." Owing to their commitment to de-moralising, their inveterate reluctance to preach what they practise, progressives have failed to overtly bring their values into everyday public discourse, to loudly advocate their moral vision, while "… conservatives have managed to get their moral frames to dominate … on virtually every issue." In my view the de-moralising discourse of both traditional and contemporary psychoanalysis has had similarly destructive effects, not least in its failure to discriminate conscience, the ethic of nurturance, from superego, the ethic of authority, and its failure to fully recognise and confront the destructiveness of the latter. The following, more sociological analysis seeks to place the theme of the flight from conscience within a broader, socio-historical perspective.

* * *

The grandfathers of modern sociology, Comte and Spencer, contributed to a strongly evolutionary approach in social science, "as with many reservations, did Durkheim and Weber" (Bellah, 1964, p. 358). In his own way, so did Marx, for the idea of advance from primitive communism, to the feudal order, to the emergence and development of capitalism, and on to its overthrow by the proletariat and the emergence of socialism, envisages a process of social evolution. Friedrich Engels certainly thought so. In his funeral oration at Marx's graveside he opined: "Just as Darwin discovered the law of evolution in organic nature, so Marx discovered the law of evolution in human history" (Foner, 1973, p. 39).

But by the 1930s, Robert Bellah writes, "[T]he evolutionary wave was in full retreat" (p. 358), at least in its non-Marxian forms. The first edition of Richard Hofstadter's classic, *Social Darwinism in American Thought*, appeared in 1944 and officially registered the demise of those attempts to apply evolutionary thinking in social science that posited competition between individuals and groups as the engine of history resulting in the alleged "survival of the fittest". In becoming linked to and used to justify capitalism, ethnocentrism, and outright racism, the very idea of social evolution fell victim to guilt by association.

Given the resurgence in our contemporary hegemonic, neo-liberal social order of what Henry Giroux (2012) describes as "the punishing values of economic Darwinism and a survival-of-the-fittest ethic", the notion of social evolution is no less suspect in the eyes of most social scientists today. In calling upon sociologists to return from their infatuation with positivism to the study of history and anthropology in order to foster "an historic sense of how recent and how dramatic are the social transformations of the past two centuries" (p. 22), Anthony Giddens (1982) challenges us "to break away from the belief, explicit or implicit, that the modes of life which have developed in the West are somehow superior to those of other cultures" and warns us against those "social thinkers who have given concrete form to this notion in attempting to squeeze human history into schemes of social evolution, in which 'evolution' is understood in terms of the capability of varying types of society to control or master their material environments" (p. 23). In such ethnocentric evolutionary theories, he writes, "Western industrialism inevitably appears at the apex" (p. 23). In its guise as "modernisation theory", such evolutionary thinking assumes "that industrialism is essentially a liberalising force and a progressive one; and hence that the Western societies provide a model for 'underdeveloped' societies to follow" (p. 143). This serves as "an ideological defence of the dominance of Western capitalism over the rest of the world" (p. 144).

Giddens's critique of evolutionary or modernisation theory rests on the premise that Western industrialism appears at the apex "since it has undeniably unleashed a material productivity vastly greater than that of other societies which have preceded it in history" (p. 23). But the material productivity associated with industrial society is not restricted to its liberal capitalist form but characterises its fascist, totalitarian socialist, and totalitarian capitalist incarnations as well. So what if the standard by which we evaluate societies were to be political, not merely material—namely, their relative progress towards achieving a stable, social democratic order characterised by universal suffrage, the protection of human rights and liberties, a multi-party system with protection of minority rights, as well as progress towards economic in addition to political democracy? What if human emancipation from the varied forms of tyranny and domination—by patriarchy, the capitalist ruling class, the unfettered market, the colonial powers, the totalitarian state (whether in its fascist, socialist, or capitalist incarnations)—becomes the criterion of evolutionary success? Of course, both material productivity and human emancipation from domination are values; hence an evolutionary scheme based on either is in no way "value-free". But I for one have no objection to being accused of moral bias by those who have a continuing attachment to the varied forms of domination.

In the mid-1960s, Talcott Parsons attempted to revive evolutionary thinking in social theory along these lines. In his paper on "Evolutionary Universals in Society", Parsons (1964) wrote: "Slowly and somewhat inarticulately, emphasis in both sociological and anthropological quarters is shifting from a studied disinterest in problems of social and cultural evolution to a 'new relativity' that relates its universals to an evolutionary framework" (p. 491). Defining an evolutionary universal as "a complex of structures and associated processes the development of which so increases the long-run adaptive capacity of living systems in a given class that only systems that develop the complex can attain certain higher levels of general adaptive capacity" (p. 493), Parsons identified six such evolutionary universals that "are closely interrelated in the process of 'breaking out' of what may be called the 'primitive' stage of societal evolution" (p. 496), the stage in which the primary form of social cohesion is the kinship system. These are: (1) a well-marked system of social stratification transcending "the role in primitive societies of *ascription* of social status to criteria of biological relatedness"; (2) "a system of explicit cultural legitimation of differentiated societal functions" (p. 496); (3) bureaucratic organisation; (4) money and the market complex; (5) generalised universalistic norms; and (6) "the democratic association with elective leadership and fully enfranchised membership" (p. 514).

As Jackson Toby (1977) points out, "Parsons does not treat social evolution as inevitable. In order for differentiation to occur, crucial problems must be solved, and these problems emerge at every level. ... An adequate solution to a problem posing an obstacle to further evolution is not necessarily discovered. If it is not found, the society does not evolve further; it may disintegrate as [classical] Greece and ancient Israel did" (p. 9). But, writing in 1977, Toby observes:

> Societal evolution can hardly be called an idea whose time has come. Many sociologists would say it came in the nineteenth century—and went, along with Herbert Spencer. Parsons is attempting to breathe new life into the theory despite a contemporary preference for explanations of the immediate present over explanation of long-run trends. Thus, many sociologists—and not just radical sociologists—cannot muster enthusiasm for a theory of social change so detached from current anxieties that it disregards the latest war and the next presidential election. His focus on the long view makes Parsons seem complacent about the present. As Keynes put it, in the long run we are all dead. But Parsons' theory of societal evolution is not just a retooled version of the romantic faith in the inevitability of progress—despite the congratulatory tone that [at times] creeps into his analysis. (p. 20)

But beyond the factors Giddens and Toby posit for the retreat from evolutionary thought, in light of the psychoanalytic concept of "resistance" one may suspect a deeper source: flight from the burden of responsibility such thinking places on us to *evolve*, that is, to seek to overcome the moral compromises we have made with the *status quo*, with the varied forms of domination, and the pressure it places on us to renew our commitment to the struggle for modernity—defined not in terms of material productivity but in those of human emancipation, achievement of a stable and inclusive social democracy, and the exchange of relations of domination for those of mutual recognition.

The "congratulatory tone" Toby finds in Parsons is evident, to my mind, not so much in his discussion of the evolutionary "breakthrough" and enhanced adaptive capacity of the "democratic revolution" as in his overly optimistic attitude to the American society of the 1960s and early '70s. Toby writes that Parsons "discusses some of the current tensions in American society not as evidence of declining adaptive capacity but as due to transitional strains ... [and] denies he has an ethnocentric value preference for American society ... [which] he believes ... has simply proceeded further along the evolutionary path than even its European counterparts" (pp. 17–18). Toby asks, "If Parsons is right and that is what is happening, why are so many intellectuals so sour about the United States? Why the complaints about poverty, the erosion of community, the power elite, immorality, bureaucracy, student unrest?" (pp. 18–19). But Parsons, who died in 1979, "does not find a worsening capacity to adapt", "does not observe moral deterioration", and "... does not find increasing polarisation between the rich and the poor, the owners and the proletariat, but instead growth of professional and white collar groups that cannot easily be categorised in terms of the rhetoric of traditional Marxism. In the polity, he does not find power more centralised, but rather more dispersed to electorates and more subject to veto groups" (Nielsen, 1991, p. 19).

Certainly, from today's perspective, all this seems naïve, to say the least. Already in the early Seventies the Watergate scandal was unfolding leading ultimately to Nixon's resignation in 1974. As we have seen, observers, such as the psychoanalyst Rangell (1974, 1976, 1980, 1997, 2000) and the psychoanalytically informed social historian Lasch (1979), were already detecting what Rangell called "the syndrome of the compromise of integrity" at work, not merely in "the mind of Watergate", but also in what Lasch considered "the narcissistic personality of our time" characteristic of the "culture of narcissism". Those of us who were coming of age intellectually in the Sixties and Seventies were confronting conflict all around us—racial, gender, generational—and found Parsons's focus upon societal equilibrium and consensus out of synch with our experience. But while his evolutionary social theory failed to help him properly assess contemporary trends in his own society, his emphasis on the importance of democracy did prove successful in enabling him to accurately predict the disintegration of the Soviet Union a decade after his death. Parsons recognised that his positing of "the democratic association with elective leadership and fully enfranchised membership" (p. 514) as one of the six evolutionary universals leading to a society's enhanced adaptive potential required him to assert the following:

> I must maintain that communist totalitarian organisation will probably not fully match "democracy" in political and integrative capacity in the long run. I do indeed predict that it will prove to be unstable and will either make adjustments in the general direction of electoral democracy and a plural party system or "regress" into generally less advanced and politically less effective forms of organisation, failing to advance as rapidly or as far as otherwise may be expected. One important basis of this prediction is that the Communist Party has everywhere emphasised its function in *educating* the people for the new society. In the long run its legitimacy will certainly be undermined if the party leadership continues to be unwilling to *trust* the people it has educated. In the present context, however, to trust the people is to entrust them with a share of political responsibility. This can only mean that eventually the single monolithic party must relinquish its monopoly of such responsibility. (pp. 518–519)

This prediction was made in 1964, a quarter of a century before the fall of the Berlin wall in 1989. Accurate prediction has not always been easy to achieve in social science; perhaps this instance of it adds a degree of credibility to Parsons's evolutionary model.

On the other hand, if we accept Parsons's view that a viable democracy is essential in the long run for a society's evolutionary success, the deterioration and corruption of American democracy in recent years (and I hasten to add that things are not that much better in Canada which has recently been preoccupied with an unfolding scandal involving widespread electoral fraud and other forms of corruption) suggests that the fate Parsons foretold for the Soviet system might well turn out to be that of his own society as well. In 2003 Sheldon Wolin was already writing in *The Nation*: "The war on Iraq has so monopolised public attention as to obscure the regime change taking place in the Homeland. We may have invaded Iraq to bring in democracy and bring down a totalitarian regime, but in the process our own system may be moving closer to the latter and further weakening the former." In what Wolin (2008) considers the "inverted totalitarianism" that has come to characterise the "managed democracy" of American society, "What is absent is the political, the commitment to finding where the common good lies amidst the welter of well-financed, highly organised, single-minded interests rabidly seeking governmental favours and overwhelming the practices of representative government and public administration by a sea of cash" (p. 66).

It was all too easy for my generation to dismiss Parsons with the clichés of the time, viewing his evolutionary social theory as "a product of a conservative and nostalgic mind", condemning it for "its basic legitimation of capitalism and bourgeois Western values" (Nielsen, 1991, p. 217) and dismissing it as reactionary ideology disguised as social science. In reality, as Nielsen points out, Parsons "was from very early a fearless critic of totalitarianism", whether in its communist, fascist, or peculiarly American McCarthyist, incarnations. According to David Riesman, "Parsons had no sympathy for the right at all" and in Neil Smelser's view "[P]eople who call Parsons 'conservative' do not understand him ..." (Riesman and Smelser as quoted by Nielsen, p. 227). For Nielsen, although "[Parsons] had very little sympathy for Marxism ... one might say that he had more respect for Marx than for Marxism ... it would be very inadequate to portray him ... as a mindless and eager defender of capitalism." According to Robert Bellah, "The notion that Parsons was primarily concerned with the defence of capitalism is simply historically wrong" (pp. 227–228). Jeffery Alexander states, "I do not think that there is any great opposition between Parsons' theory and democratic socialism" (p. 229). Nielsen concludes that, although "... his political orientation had a clear anti-utopian cast and was solidly grounded in the values of a liberal tradition ... Parsons is not only located on the left side of the liberal tradition, but ... it is not unreasonable to consider him as a part of the modern leftist tradition in a broader sense. This does not deny that Parsons was a liberal, but it emphasises the idea that he shared many values with ... the humanistic Left" (p. 230).

But despite his essentially social democratic values, Parsons's optimism, patriotism, and perhaps his theoretic bias towards consensus over conflict prevented him from recognising the emerging threats to American democracy represented by the success of neo-liberal ideology, beginning in the Seventies and continuing until the economic crisis of 2007 and beyond. What intellectual in the early Seventies would have anticipated the power and impact of Ayn Rand's (1962) banal and simplistic "philosophy" of selfishness? But notions that "greed is good", that the individual pursuit of self-interest will result, as by the intervention of an invisible hand, in the greater good of all, that the growing profits of the corporate elite will "trickle down" to the masses, and so on, turned out to be remarkably successful in undermining opposition to the growing inequality in American society, the corruption of its democratic institutions, and the emergence of a plutocratic oligarchy. As long as it is felt to be bad, greed conflicts with conscience; but redefining it as good undermines both the conflict and the conflict-driven urge towards progressive social change.

If, with the social evolutionists, we opt to view societies as living systems, then we must remember, as Parsons himself points out, that like the societies of classical Greece and ancient Israel, they can die as well as live; they can become ill; they can deteriorate, degenerate, and regress instead of progressing. In *Civilization and Its Discontents*, Freud (1930a) suggests "we may expect that one day someone will venture to embark upon a pathology of cultural communities" (p. 144). Perhaps, then, we can conceive of societies as capable of becoming neurotic, masochistic (we already know they can be sadistic), self-sabotaging, even suicidal. Perhaps a society can suffer from something akin to an autoimmune disease and begin to work against itself. Henry Giroux (2012) writes:

> Neo-liberalism is once again imposing its values, social relations and forms of social death upon all aspects of civic life. One consequence is that the United States has come to resemble a "suicidal state", where governments work to destroy their own defences against anti-democratic forces; or as Jacques Derrida has put it, such states offer no immunity against authoritarianism and in fact emulate "that strange behaviour where a living being, in quasi-suicidal fashion 'itself' works to destroy its own protection, to immunise itself against its 'own' immunity … What is put at risk by this terrifying autoimmunity logic", he grimly stated, "is nothing less than the existence of the world …."

* * *

Like Talcott Parsons (1964) and Robert Bellah (1964, 2011), sociologist and psycho-historian Eli Sagan sought in a series of important monographs (1974, 1979, 1985, 1988, 1991, 2001) to elaborate an evolutionary social theory and, like Parsons, with whom he shared a prominent Boston psychoanalyst for a number of years, Sagan wanted to establish his social theory on a sound psychoanalytic foundation. Although agreeing with Durkheim that sociology cannot be reduced to psychology, like Freud himself, Sagan felt there can be no sociology that does not involve key psychological assumptions regarding the nature of human nature and human motivation. As Robert Alun Jones (1986) put it: "… if social facts thus cannot be *completely* explained by psychological facts, it is at least equally true that even the most determinedly 'sociological' explanations necessarily rely upon certain assumptions, explicit or otherwise, about how individual human beings think, feel, and act in particular circumstances" (p. 81).

For Freud, the essential fact about the human mind and about human nature is the fact of conflict. If Marx is the foremost conflict theorist of society, Freud is the conflict theorist of the mind. Perhaps Ernst Kris (1938) offered the best short definition of psychoanalysis: "*the* psychology of the innermost mental processes of man in conflict" (p. 140). Taking his work as a whole, we have seen that Freud advances two fundamental models of psychic conflict, both of which are solidly grounded in Greek thought: on one hand he borrows Plato's metaphor of the rider and the horse to frame a vision of conflict between mind and body, culture and nature: a human ego-superego (reason and morality) *vs.* an animalistic id (bodily-based drives of sex and aggression). It is this early model that, projectively (and therefore, in my view, erroneously) locates the roots of human destructiveness in the somatically-based drives, in the alleged "beast" in man, rather than in his uniquely human ego and superego.

On the other hand, the later Freud offers us a vision of conflict between the forces of life and death, integration and disintegration, construction and destruction. It is this latter aspect of his thinking that Melanie Klein builds upon in her vision of a fundamental conflict, not between mind and body, but *within the human mind and heart*, a clash between the psychological passions of love and hate. Talcott Parsons was among the few major sociological thinkers to make a serious effort to incorporate psychoanalytic insight; had he been able to do so more thoroughly he might have been less inclined to minimise regressive trends in his own society, recognising with Freud that *Eros* is always accompanied by *Thanatos*, progressive tendencies by regressive ones, modernism by "countermodernism" (Berger, 1977, p. 71). The very extension of democracy that Parsons rightly appreciated about America should have dispelled complacency and rendered him more alert to modernity's other face—fascism—especially given his earlier encounters with McCarthyism.

More or less independently of Melanie Klein, Eli Sagan's work advances a comparable psychological, as distinct from psycho-biological, vision in which human beings are fundamentally torn by competing *identifications*, with the aggressor on one hand and the nurturer on the other. If we have survived and are in any way functional, we have been nurtured, however inadequately, so we know what love is, and we know we have received it, however minimally. We have also endured varying degrees of basic (inevitable) and surplus (beyond what is inevitable) frustration. As Klein explained, we have experienced such frustration as a persecutory attack (for the absent good object is experienced as a present bad, attacking object) and this has generated in us varying degrees of reactive rage and aggression which, projected, add to our paranoid sense of persecution, our persecutory anxiety, which in turn stimulates further aggression.

Freud regarded conscience as one of the functions of the superego arising around five years of age as aggression is turned away from the Oedipal rival out of fear of castration and, in an identification with the aggressor, back against the self. In contrast, Sagan (1988) views conscience and superego as distinct psychic functions and posits an early origin of the former in the child's pre-Oedipal identification with the nurturer. In light of modern empirical infant research (e.g., Bloom, 2010) we now know that conscience originates far earlier than Freud's Oedipal phase. The Kleinians have long distinguished persecutory guilt, which like shame entails self-torment, from depressive guilt, which is about caring for and making reparation to the other. Sagan derived essentially the same distinction from the work of the classical scholar, E. R. Dodds (1951) on the transition in ancient Greece from a predominantly shame culture to one centred predominantly on guilt. As Sagan points out, it is difficult to comprehend how a mental function such as the superego—which is about aggression turned back against the self under the threat of castration and that operates, in Freud's words, "like a garrison in a conquered city"—can be the seat of conscientious concern for others. Whereas the superego is fuelled by hate, the conscience is grounded in attachment and love.

The fundamental principle of reciprocity that governs the psyche, the need to give back what one has been given, manifests not only in our need to repay the love we have received through loving, but also in the *lex talionis* whereby we repay aggression with aggression. As Klein understood, the roots of Freud's Oedipal and post-Oedipal superego lie in early pre-Oedipal identification with the aggressor, the persecutory part-object, which she regarded as a persecutory pregenital superego. In Sagan's vision, as in Freud's, all individual and social behaviour is a *compromise-formation* embodying varying mixtures of these inclinations and identifications, a compound in which each component of the conflict achieves partial expression. Since the need to nurture as one has been nurtured forms, for Sagan, the basis of conscience, we can say that our fundamental conflict is that between our inclination to aggression (all too often appearing in the form of an attacking pre- or post-Oedipal superego) and our conscience.

In Sagan's, as in the Kleinian view, whatever its ultimate origin, aggression is mostly driven by anxiety. Because we fear being eaten, we cannibalise others. Because we fear being beheaded, we take heads. Because we fear being sacrificed, we sacrifice others. Because we fear being enslaved we enslave. Because we fear being dominated and exploited, we dominate and exploit. Because we fear death, we inflict it upon the other. This is not to deny the existence of other motives for cannibalism, head-hunting, human sacrifice, slavery, domination, and exploitation. As Freud pointed out, most human behaviour is "over-determined". But while material interests and motives such as greed and the lust for power certainly contribute to the causation of such behaviours, the need for defences against persecutory anxiety is of central importance. Following Freud's insight into the fact that aggression can be directed not only outwards against others (sadism) but also turned inward against ourselves (masochism), and into the destructive inclinations (*Thanatos*) that always accompany construction (*Eros*), Sagan (2001, ch. 22) is alert to the ways in which revolutionary aggressors are often self-destructive. He points out, for example, that during the French Revolutionary Terror, by placing other Jacobin leaders under suspicion Robespierre guaranteed that he himself would be "fed" to the insatiable cannibal-guillotine.

But aggression (*Thanatos*), whether sadistic or masochistic, is inevitably opposed by the ultimately inextinguishable voice of conscience (*Eros/Agape*). Out of the resulting conflict arise varying forms of displacement or substitution and, at times, of sublimation, the redirection and elevation of a drive towards a more creative and prosocial outlet. Cannibalism (oral aggression) gives way to head-hunting (anal collecting) which, in turn, gives way to the forms of ritual human sacrifice. Then an advance is made in which the enemy is no longer killed but kept alive in order to be exploited (slavery), until slavery is eradicated and the anxiety-driven need to dominate and exploit is manifested in varying forms of racism, sexism, class domination, heterosexism, and as the late Elisabeth Young-Bruehl (2012) recently reminded us, in the domination and exploitation of children.

In history, Sagan traces a pattern of social development in which the anxiety and aggression occasioned by the break-up of tribal and kinship-based social organisation motivates varying forms of defensive tyranny. Whereas Parsons and Bellah posit five stages of social evolution (the primitive, the archaic, the historic, the early modern, and the modern), Sagan inserts between the primitive and the archaic a stage that he calls complex society in which he finds the origins of both tyranny and the state. The kinship system had managed to more or less contain the paranoid anxieties to which human beings are perpetually prone, but with its break-up intense separation and persecutory anxieties emerged. The rise of the first individual, the omnipotent god-king at the head of the early state, served as an attempt to assuage such anxieties through religion, the symbolic enactment of authority, and magical practices involving ritual human sacrifice.

Sagan sees a pattern of moral progress in the West as the critique of tyranny is intensified and nurturing concern extended to include formerly disenfranchised and maltreated populations. The ever-widening application of the principles of conscience led finally to the emergence of constitutional democracies with an ever-extending franchise, the socialist critique of capitalism, the civil rights movement, and the women's movement. More recently it has manifested in movements advocating the rights of lesbian, gay, bisexual, and transgender people, and of children, as well as an ecological conscience that condemns our exploitation of nature and animal life as well as one another.

But such moral progress is in no way automatic or guaranteed. A move forward under the influence of *Eros* stimulates regressive pressure from *Thanatos*. Modernisation results not only in advances towards a stable democratic society but also in the emergence of Nazism, Stalinism, and other forms of totalitarianism. In addition to progress and regress, there is paralysis; and there is backlash. Sagan sees America as encountering "a failure of nerve" in the late 1960s when Lyndon Johnson's "war on poverty" and his plans for "the Great Society" stalled. What emerged instead was the neo-liberalism of Thatcher and Reagan that functioned ideologically to interrupt and incapacitate the operations of conscience. Sagan views moral progress as a potential outcome of felt *conflict*: conscious moral conflict can function as the engine of sublimation. But when such conflict is repressed, no longer conscious, it is deprived of its power to motivate progressive social change. If I am unaware of conflict, I am not motivated to resolve it. A range of defences can be employed to circumvent conscience when we feel we cannot bear to go where it demands we go or do what it demands we do. I argue (Chapter Nine) that even the psychopath is not lacking in conscience, only skilled in the arts of binding and gagging it. On the social level, in addition to censorship, exile, imprisonment, and execution, conscience can be silenced by a wide range of defences, including the power of ideology to redefine as morally good what had previously been seen as evil or unjust.

Beyond moral paralysis lies backlash. Being deprived of socially legitimated scapegoats removes a major defence against anxiety. In Kleinian theory the term projective identification refers to the defensive process whereby I unconsciously "dump" my unbearable pain into another whom I induce to suffer it. But if I can no longer get away with this—if I am no longer allowed to project and scapegoat in this way—then the unbearable pain returns from repression. Sagan employs the term "modernity psychosis" to describe the aberrant behaviour to which people are often driven by their anxiety and aggression when inflicting it upon others is socially condemned rather than legitimated. Modernisation removes from play whole categories of formerly socially legitimated scapegoats: women, Jews, people of colour, immigrants, homosexuals, and children. Whom today are we allowed to hate, dominate, and destroy? And if the answer is no one, then what are we to do with our hate? The pressure to find new external enemies is intense in this situation. The truly bizarre antics of the radical right, the Tea Party, the popularity of proto-fascist talk radio hosts, etc., are manifestations of modernity psychosis, of backlash against the rights of women, black people, lesbian, gay, bisexual, and transgender people, immigrants, and children. In such counter-revolutionary reaction we see identification with the aggressor at work.

* * *

A few years prior to the revolution of 1789, Voltaire wrote, "We live in curious times and amid astonishing contrasts: reason on the one hand, the most absurd fanaticism on the other … a civil war in every soul" (cited in Sagan, 2001, p. 406). In Sagan's view, that internal civil war first burst on the scene during the French Revolutionary period that witnessed "Glorious triumphs: Constitutionalism, the Rights of Man, the Sovereignty of the People", only to be followed by "the Terror, the millions sacrificed to the paranoid fantasies of Napoleon" and almost a century of failure to establish democratic stabilisation in France (Sagan, 2001, pp. 1–2). Sagan asks if there is a deep irrational connection between these contrasting events: "Was the Terror, as well as the Rights of Man, the result of the Enlightenment?" He quotes Nietzsche who writes, "Whoever pushes rationality forward also restores new strength to the opposite power, mysticism and folly of all kinds" (*The Will to Power*, quoted in Sagan, 2001, p. 1).

Nietzsche was a great psychologist—so great that Freud claimed to have stopped reading him so his own creativity would not be overpowered. But this particular insight into the dialectical relationship between the rational and the irrational in man, such that an increase in the one simultaneously stimulates an increase in the power of its opposite, was certainly developed by Freud. His central concept of the *disguised return of the repressed* holds that whenever in the name of reason and social adaptation we repress the irrational and antisocial in ourselves we can expect to see their return in the disguised form of neurotic or psychotic symptoms of various sorts—unless we are able to forego repression, relegation to the unconscious, by employing the more mature and creative mechanisms of conscious suppression without self-deception, or sublimation, the redirection of dangerous or destructive impulses towards more acceptable, creative, and prosocial outlets.

The Freudian revolution taught us that we are not unitary subjects but divided selves, profoundly conflicted, ambivalent, torn between the opposing constructive and destructive tendencies of *Eros* and *Thanatos* that Melanie Klein came to understand as those of love and hate, our wish to create and our urge to destroy, our identification with the loving nurturance to which we owe our lives, and our competing identification with the forces of frustration, aggression, and persecution. In the Kleinian model of the human mind each of these conflicting drives and identifications dominate in one or the other of the two layers, zones, or "positions" that make up our mental structure.

In the more primitive layer, hate and paranoia predominate. It is a Manichaean world, profoundly split between the forces of good and evil. Here, life is a jungle in which evil predators seek the destruction of all goodness and in which the jungle law, kill or be killed, prevails. This is the paranoid position in which the subject's own hate and aggression are projected onto the others who in this way are perceived as persecutors. Paranoid anxiety prevails. Narcissism, utter self-centredness, predominates, since in a jungle survival is the priority and there is little time or energy for concern or care for others. And it is a schizoid position in that both self and others are split into all-good, idealised, or all-bad, demonised figures. It is a world in which one resorts to magic and illusions of omnipotence in order to ward off evil and overcome anxiety. Gods and devils may be placated by means of various forms of sacrifice of human or animal scapegoats.

The advance into what Klein called the depressive position entails the achievement of ambivalence, the capacity to see "both sides now", the good and the bad in both self and others, without splitting. Persecutory anxiety gives way—not to depression, for clinical depression involves splitting, viewing the self as all-bad and, hence, occurs in the paranoid-schizoid position—but to *depressive anxiety* which reflects one's new capacity for concern for the welfare of both the other and the self. The fear that in one's paranoid delirium one may have done irreparable damage now generates a reparative drive, no longer characterised by magic and omnipotence but by an enhanced sense of reality vis-à-vis the self and others now viewed as whole rather than part-objects. Whereas in the more primitive, schizo-paranoid position shame and other forms of self-punishment predominate, in the depressive position we become capable of mature guilt as concern for others and for the genuine welfare of the true self. Useless self-flagellation for one's sins now gives way to positive efforts to repair the damage done and to change.

What Sagan (2001, ch. 24) calls "the politics of the impossible" are characteristic of the paranoid-schizoid position. This is the politics of perfection, of utopia, where "the lion shall lie down with the lamb", "the state shall wither away", and I shall finally be able "to hunt in the morning, fish in the afternoon, and criticise after dinner". And when this utopia turns out to be unrealisable, someone must be blamed and liquidated and we soon wind up in the dystopia of death camps and gulags that inevitably follow from the all-good, idealising, and subsequent demonising of the paranoid-schizoid position. Fortunately, to the extent that we can advance into the depressive position we become more able to reconcile ourselves to a "politics of the possible" in which perfectionism is sacrificed (rather than people sacrificed to perfectionism) and we learn to live in that imperfect realm between the All and the None called the Some—where some imperfect solutions can be found and imperfect institutions created, and where imperfect people (neither saints nor absolute sinners) can manage to live imperfect lives in an imperfect society with a terrible form of government, social democracy, that is simply better than all the rest.

The trouble with democracy is that its progressive universalisation of human rights deprives us of socially acceptable scapegoats; there are no longer any quasi-legitimate targets for our sadism, no socially approved whipping boys—at least within our own society. To be clear, there is no absence of scapegoating; what is increasingly absent is its social legitimation. People are told it is wrong. There are laws against it. This does not prevent it from happening. But it prevents it from happening in a conflict-free manner. Conscience can be silenced, but it cannot be eradicated; in late modernity it is difficult if not impossible to scapegoat in good conscience. When universalisation of rights and freedoms is applied on an international scale we are even more at a loss as to what to do with our aggression. When no one can legitimately be dominated, no one legitimately devalued, my wish to externalise my aggression via projection and scapegoating is opposed by conscience. Even a silenced conscience, a conscience blocked from consciousness, speaks unconsciously in the many ways psychoanalysts understand. One of the ways such repressed conscience speaks is through extremism. The very need to stifle conscience sometimes drives one to loudly assert and aggressively act out the feelings and impulses it opposes. With no legitimate outlet, my rage and aggression threaten to turn on me in the form of self-attack, self-devaluation, even self-destruction—a threat that increases my tendency to avoid such acting-in by acting-out in extreme ways.

Sagan (2001) writes, "Modernity, pregnant with the possibility of great moral advance, also engenders an almost unbelievable psychological burden" (p. 456). In *Escape from Freedom*, Erich Fromm (1941) pointed out that as modern man "becomes more independent, self-reliant, and critical", he simultaneously "becomes more isolated, alone and afraid" (quoted by Sagan, 2001, p. 405). The evolution of society involves a long struggle with separation anxiety beginning with the break-up of the kinship system that contained the anxiety of primitive man. Subsequent social forms attempted to bind and contain this anxiety through a range of social structures, religions, magical practices, and defences. The breakdown of the feudal system and the early modern monarchies, and the growing pressures on people to become individuals, to separate and to individuate, to take on the burden of self-responsible individuality and identity, has been the source of widespread anxiety, frustration, and anger, leading to attempts both to "escape from freedom" into some old or new form of collectivism, and to reassure the self of its validity, frequently by invalidating and dominating some category of others.

The ever-widening extension of democracy, especially when it includes social democratic demands for economic justice, equality, and mutual recognition, threatens to undermine defensive domination altogether. What are men to do when they can no longer dominate women, or children, people of colour, gay people, or poor people? What are women to do when they can no longer dominate children? The backlash against modernisation takes such forms as persistent doubt regarding the citizenship of a president; US Senate committees refusing to allow women to offer testimony regarding issues affecting women's health; hate radio hosts calling women "sluts" for wanting access to birth control; and the extreme violence of religious fundamentalists of every stripe. As Robert Reich (2012) recently put it, "A party of birthers, creationists, theocrats, climate-change deniers, nativists, gay-bashers, anti-abortionists, media paranoids, anti-intellectuals, and out-of-touch country clubbers cannot govern America."

As Dostoevsky's Grand Inquisitor understood, the demand that one forge one's identity as an individual, as opposed to merely occupying a ready-made, ascribed status in the tribe, group, or estate to which one has been assigned by fate, is a harsh demand, even cruel if it asks more of people than they are capable of. For many it would seem, the sense of self remains ontologically insecure unless bolstered by a compensatory assertion of superiority to some category of despised others. As Terry Eagleton (2010) points out, "The kind of others who drive you to mass murder are usually those who for some reason or other have come to signify the terrible non-being at the core of oneself" (p. 100). For the Nazis this included not only the Jews, but Roma, gay men and women, left-wingers, the mentally and physically handicapped—all those "thought to pose a threat to the purity and unity of the German nation and the so-called Aryan race" (p. 99). While American fascism has not yet come quite this far, the underlying dynamics of the current backlash against women, homosexuals, left-wingers, racial minorities, and youth are, I believe, essentially the same. As Eagleton puts it, "Human beings will often go to quite barbarous lengths to carry on being themselves" (p. 98)—especially when "being themselves" requires the ongoing devaluation and domination of others in order to cover up inner vacuity. As Sagan points out, whenever you ask someone to surrender a defence against anxiety or depression (i.e., mental pain), however destructive that defence may be to the self and others, you are asking for trouble.

* * *

Through its restored and enhanced social safety-net, income redistribution, economic justice, and innovative forms of decentralisation, a stable, democratic socialist society might provide, on a more advanced evolutionary level, some of the senses of community and security that have been lost in the course of modernisation. The problem is that the very evolution towards such a society provokes almost psychotic levels of anxiety among those reliant on defensive devaluation and domination. On the concluding page of *Civilization and Its Discontents*, his meditation on the disturbance of our communal life by the forces of human aggression and self-destruction, Freud (1930a) writes: "And now, it is to be expected that the other of the two 'Heavenly Powers' … eternal *Eros*, will make an effort to assert himself in the struggle with his equally immortal adversary" (p. 145). Beginning in the autumn of 2011 we witnessed a remarkable rebirth of conscience, of identification with the nurturer, in the form of the growing critique of Wall Street and its ideological justifications. "This is not recession, it's robbery!" declared a sign made from a used pizza box in Zuccotti Park. "Banks got bailed out, we got sold out." "Robin Hood was right!" "Dear capitalism. It's not you, it's us. Just kidding, it's you!" Despite the eventual and often brutal dismantling of its encampments by police employed to serve and protect the interests of the corporate state, the Occupy movement was clearly a success in enabling people to finally voice a moral critique of the extreme concentrations of wealth and the obscene levels of inequality that had emerged in many of the Western democracies, together with widespread corruption in government, financial institutions, and the press, and the erosion of the welfare state.

As Eli Sagan has pointed out, Maximilian Robespierre was a "... genius of moral critique.... He began his political life as one of the greatest democratic voices of all time .... His vision of what the future democratic society had to be was extraordinary ...." (p. 494). And he was committed not just to political, but also to economic democracy. He wrote: "What is the final object of society? It is to maintain the imprescriptible rights of man. What is the first of these rights? That of existence. ... All mercantile speculation that I make at the cost of my fellow human being is not commerce, it is brigandage, it is fratricide" (Robespierre quoted in Sagan, 2001, p. 496). Here we certainly see identification with the nurturer. But *Eros* must always contend with *Thanatos*. Such was Robespierre's utopianism, his perfectionism, that he winds up demonstrating a "complete willingness to overthrow all liberal and enlightenment concepts and rules of justice" and to embrace "the unambivalent use of judicial assassination, and subsequent execution, to eliminate political opposition" (p. 502).

While the Marxism of the Bolshevik party clearly reflected nurturing concern for the exploited and suffering masses, its insistence, after 1917, on imposing a one-party state (or rather regressing to one), had the effect, as Leon Trotsky himself had predicted prior to his own conversion to Bolshevism, of promoting a "substitutism" in which the party would substitute for the proletariat, then the central committee for the party, and finally the leader for everything and everyone else. We can see the effect of identification with the aggressor even in the early stages of this process and not merely in the monstrous behaviour of Stalin. Isaac Deutscher's biographies of both Trotsky (1954, 1959, 1963) and Stalin (1949) reveal the compound nature of their personalities. As Julius Martov, the Menshevik leader, left the first meeting of the council of soviets after October 25, 1917, in disgust at the way the Bolsheviks had seized political power (not in a revolution but a *coup d'état*), Trotsky bid farewell to his former mentor and friend exclaiming: "You are miserable, isolated individuals. You are bankrupt. You have played out your role. Go where you belong: to the dust heap of history!" (Trotsky quoted in Deutscher, 1954, p. 259).

One of the most painful passages in Deutscher's profound study of Lev Davidovich Trotsky concerns the prophet's maltreatment of his devoted son Lyova. The streak of authoritarianism and cruelty revealed here probably played a role in Trotsky's inability ever to entirely appreciate and acknowledge the fundamental error entailed in

Bolshevism's substitution of the so-called "proletarian democracy" of a one-party state for democracy understood precisely as a multi-party system devoted to the protection of minority rights and lawful dissent. A psychoanalyst might well speculate that unconscious guilt over his sadism may have contributed to Trotsky's masochism, his neurotic, self-defeating inhibitions against using the many opportunities he was given, not least by Lenin in the weeks before his death, to defeat Stalin before it was too late.

The radicalism of the 1960s New Left was suspicious of Marxist, Leninist, Trotskyist, Stalinist, and Maoist authoritarianism, sceptical about its slippery, Orwellian notion of "democratic centralism", insisting instead on at least the rhetoric of democracy, albeit in its quasi-anarchist, "participatory" form. Whereas in early twentieth century radicalism outright authoritarian trends (no doubt bolstered by confidence in one's positive knowledge of the laws of history) hampered progressive action motivated by conscience, in the 1960s, as Chris Hedges (2011) points out, such self-defeating tendencies took the form of the narcissistic self-indulgence and sexism of elements of the male leadership. Although his critique of 1960s radicalism is extreme and unfair—it succeeded, after all, in ending the war in Vietnam—Hedges was correct to point out that "[T]he Occupy Wall Street movement ... is rooted in the moral imperatives of justice and self-sacrifice ... values closer to King than Abbie Hoffman. It seeks to rebuild the bridges to labour, the poor and the working class. ... It denounces the consumer culture and every evening shares its food with the homeless, who also often sleep in the park."

Two decades ago, Charles Taylor (1991), like Christopher Lasch a decade earlier, and Chris Hedges more recently, was worried about "the dark side of individualism ... a centring on the self" (p. 4). Citing de Tocqueville, Taylor wrote: "A society in which people end up as the kind of individuals who are 'enclosed in their own hearts' is one where few will want to participate actively in self-government. They will prefer to stay at home and enjoy the satisfactions of private life, as long as the government of the day produces the means to these satisfactions and distributes them widely" (p. 9). This results in what de Tocqueville called "soft" despotism—not a tyranny of terror and oppression, but mild and paternalistic. But following the economic crisis of 2007–8 the governments of the day were no longer producing the means to these satisfactions and distributing them widely. Faced with the prospect of austerity imposed by the 1% upon the 99% they had robbed, many of the latter began to protest and, as a result, "soft despotism" began to turn hard; the velvet glove of the security and surveillance state began to come off and the steel fist underneath began to be revealed and felt. Most recently we have witnessed the corporate state arming itself against mass protest, not only by further militarising police forces, but also through such measures as legitimating complete, humiliating strip searches for the most minor infractions.

The Occupy movement refused to specify clear "demands", insisting instead on offering simple and consistent moral critique of a morally bankrupt established order. Though there was no shortage of elders recommending the virtues of Marxism to the democracy movements— often without pointing out that the idea of a *dictatorship* of the proletariat originated not with Stalin or Lenin but with Marx—most occupiers seemed to have little confidence in any overarching theory of history as an infallible guide. The fringe Stalinist, Trotskyist, and Maoist sects handing out their pamphlets seemed almost pathetically frozen in a time-warp; they were good-naturedly ignored by the occupiers, welcome to attend, just like the homeless or anyone else. The movement's refusal to rely upon and identify specific "heads" which could be decapitated by authority, or might themselves co-opt and dominate the movement, was ingenious. This was a movement of a different sort in which our sleeping conscience appeared to show signs of awakening and making itself heard.

The key question, it seems to me, is whether this upsurge of moral critique of the existing order can mature, modulate the idealism and anarchism of soft "participatory democracy", and face the need for practical political and labour organisation of various types, without at the same time succumbing to either assimilation into a corrupt establishment or to the cynicism, authoritarianism, and manipulativeness of the old hard left. In the face of the corruption and increasingly undemocratic nature of the existing political system, what is needed is concerted political action to reform it, and then to employ it in pursuit of social justice. Despite his blind spots, Talcott Parsons, like Eli Sagan, understood the need for well-functioning democratic institutions devoted to "the politics of the possible" through which genuinely positive social change can sometimes be effected by imperfect people, here, in the imperfect world outside Eden, a world in which multi-party politics is accepted because it is recognised that sane people of goodwill can

nonetheless have fundamental disagreements. In order to bring about
the radical reforms needed to restore democracy, in addition to conventional political and labour mobilisation enhanced by utilisation of all
the resources of modern social media, it will be necessary to engage in
non-violent resistance of varying types. Chris Hedges (2012a) recently
outlined Ralph Nader's view of Occupy Wall Street with which I am in
agreement:

> The Occupy movement arose by embracing a rejectionist atti-
> tude toward politics, but in the end that is lethal. … It is a form
> of ideological immolation. If they won't turn on politics, poli-
> tics will continue to turn on them. Politics means the power of
> government—local, state and national—and the ability of corpo-
> rations to control departments and agencies and turn government
> against its own people. Not engaging in politics might have been
> a good preliminary tactic to gain credibility so they could avoid
> being tagged with some "-ism" or some party, but it has worn out
> its purpose.

CHAPTER NINE

Psychopathy, evil, and the death drive

In the late 1960s and '70s a romantic sensibility emphasising the themes of instinctual liberation, de-repression, and the validation and indulgence of narcissistic needs was influential in popular culture and psychoanalysis alike. For the latter, this entailed a relative de-emphasis of its classical concern with themes of guilt and self-punishment—that is, with the dynamics of the superego—in favour of a preoccupation with promoting the patient's "transmuting internalisation" (Kohut, 1977) of the analyst's "empathic responsiveness" (Bacal & Newman, 1990) and related "relational" dynamics thought to contribute to the healing of psychological defects and deficits in the "self". In Kohut's (1977) view, "Guilty Man" had been replaced in our culture by the "Tragic Man" who, far from suffering from a self riddled with conflict and guilt, was increasingly unsure of his or her possession of any viable sort of "self" at all. The flight from conscience and superego was to continue for several decades, despite attempts by Menninger (1973) and Rangell (1974, 1976), among others, to remind us that intrapsychic conflict often results in compromises between ego and superego as distinct from those between ego and id—that is, in corruption of conscience and character as distinct from neurosis (though we generally see complex combinations of these phenomena). Rather than comprehending the "fragmentation-prone self" of "Tragic Man" as in part at least an outcome of the fragmenting unconscious operations of a sadistic superego, such self-states were understood as resulting entirely from failures of provision of essential "holding" and "responsiveness" from the past and present "selfobject" milieu. Intraspsychic dynamics were, in other words, displaced by a focus upon intersubjective and interpersonal relations.

After some decades in which both popular culture and psychoanalysis were more interested in the ways people have been injured than in the ways they can be injurious, the pendulum began to swing in the opposite direction and we became fascinated by literary and cinematic depictions as well as social scientific accounts of cold, unattached, apparently conscienceless deceivers, manipulators, and killers. The recent spate of popular books, such as Robert Hare's (1993) *Without Conscience: The Disturbing World of the Psychopaths Among Us*, Martha Stout's (2005) *The Sociopath Next Door: The Ruthless Versus the Rest of Us*, and Paul Babiak and Robert Hare's (2006) *Snakes in Suits: When Psychopaths Go to Work*, together with a range of popular television series, such as *The Sopranos*, *Criminal Minds*, *Dexter*, and *Breaking Bad*, is indicative of the fascination with psychopathy in contemporary popular culture. But in contrast to Rangell's and most other psychoanalytic views of compromised integrity as an outcome of psychic conflict, in much of the recent scientific literature psychopathy is viewed as biologically determined to a significant degree. The notion of "the bad seed", so dramatically presented in the William March (1954) novel of that title, Maxwell Anderson's successful and long-running Broadway play adaptation, and the Academy award-nominated film (1956) of the same name—was for decades dismissed as fiction by environmentalistic social scientists, but today it has found new scientific credibility.

It seems psychosocial scientists are either inclined to deny the existence of evil or, if forced to acknowledge it, to attempt to explain it in deterministic terms, a strategy that far from explaining it may actually, as Eagleton (2010) points out, explain it away: if evil is a determined outcome of biological or psychosocial forces, is it really evil? If we have in the past tended to view psychopathy one-sidedly as an outcome of environmental trauma and deprivation, today it is increasingly seen as a product of nature as much as nurture. As usual in social science, voluntaristic or existentialist views emphasising the degree of agency, choice, and responsibility that are retained despite the force of circumstance are left to the religious or philosophically minded, those unburdened by any *a priori* commitment to various one-sided types of determinism.

Building on the work of Cleckley (1976), Hare (1993, 2003), and others, J. Reid Meloy (1988, 2001, 2007a, 2007b and Meloy & Shiva, 2008) has developed what he calls a psychoanalytic view of psychopathy. The collection of papers he edited, *The Mark of Cain: Psychoanalytic Insight and the Psychopath* (2001), offers an historical review of past psychoanalytic contributions in this area, although these papers mostly predate the discovery of biological factors in severe psychopathy and focus more on psychological and environmental factors in its less severe manifestations. His *The Psychopathic Mind* (1988) approaches the issue of causation from multiple perspectives, emphasising the severe pathological narcissism of the psychopath and his/her biologically based attachment disorder.

Meloy (2007b) points out that, some eighty years later, "[W]e define the psychopath's personality … in essentially the same twofold manner" as did Freud in 1928, stressing "his pathological narcissism and his cruel aggression". Freud's attitude towards the psychopath may also be gleaned from Paul Roazen's (2005) last book, *Edoardo Weiss: The House that Freud Built*. With respect to a patient about whom Weiss had consulted him, Freud wrote: "In the most unfavourable cases one ships such people, as Dr. A., across the ocean, with some money, let's say to South America, and lets them there seek and find their destiny" (Freud as quoted by Roazen, p. 94). As Roazen points out, "As early as 1907 Freud was contrasting 'scoundrels' with 'neurotics' …" (p. 98), but without, as far as I know, emphasising biological factors in the genesis of the "scoundrel".

We must take care not to oversimplify the relationship between psychopathy on the one hand, and criminality or antisocial personality disorder on the other. There are many people who display psychopathic traits who are not criminals and do not qualify for the diagnosis of antisocial personality disorder; many criminals do not display much psychopathy; and some criminals do not have antisocial personality disorder. Criminal gangs are wary of severe psychopaths for their extreme narcissism makes them unreliable and untrustworthy gang members. In his recent review of the concept of "antisocial personality disorder", Meloy (2007a) writes: "A substantial body of research has shown that, at most, only one out of three patients with antisocial personality disorder has severe psychopathy. … Psychopathy is not synonymous with behavioural histories of criminality or the categorical diagnosis of antisocial personality disorder, although it is often a correlate of both in severe cases" (pp. 2–3). Meloy (2007b) summarises his view of the psychopath by underlining three factors: no attachment, underarousal, and minimal anxiety.

The truth is that all of us at times display compromised integrity without displaying severe degrees of either narcissism or psychopathy. It is possible to be a wrongdoer, what used to be called a sinner, without being either very psychopathic or very narcissistic, although malignant narcissism is a defining feature of severe psychopathy. On the other hand, I would argue that there can be no significant wrongdoing without at least some degree, however mild, of narcissism and psychopathy, for without these our attachment to, our identification with, and our empathy and sympathy or concern for others—in short, our conscience—would restrain us.

I titled the paper on which this chapter is based "Degrees of Psychopathy vs. 'The Psychopath'" (Carveth, 2007a) in order to draw attention to the problem of *reification*. In this regard there is a notable difference between Meloy's (2007a) essay on antisocial personality disorder and his "A Psychoanalytic View of the Psychopath" (2007b). Although in both he refers to degrees of psychopathy ranging from mild (10–19) to moderate (20–29) to severe (30 or above) on the Hare (2003) scale (Meloy, 2007a, p. 2), in the latter he claims that "the more severe the psychopathy, the more psychobiologically rooted is the cause" (Meloy, 2007b, p. 8) and proceeds, on this basis, to separate out the "primary psychopath" from those who, by comparison, seem barely to merit the diagnosis of psychopathy at all.

Though Meloy (2007b) refers to Lykken's (1957) differentiation between "secondary (anxious) and primary (nonanxious) psychopaths" (p. 6), in an adjacent sentence he states categorically that "Anxiety is minimal or absent in psychopathy" (p. 6), a statement that implies that the anxious, secondary psychopath is not really a psychopath at all. Similarly, he states categorically that "… his [the psychopath's] personality is organised at a preoedipal or borderline level" (p. 13), which is no doubt true of the "primary psychopath" who, again, now seems to be the only psychopath worthy of the name. On the next page Meloy states explicitly that "The neurotically organised psychopath appears to be an oxymoron" (p. 14) and goes on to indicate that "There is no tripartite structure (id, ego, superego) to the psychopath's personality.

Internalised objects remain part-objects ..." (p. 14) and defences remain primitive. Without casting doubt upon Meloy's conceptualisation of the paranoid-schizoid nature of the primary psychopath's personality, it is nevertheless important to note that in Kleinian theory an archaic superego is operative in the paranoid-schizoid position (which is why the persecutory superego can at best be disempowered and displaced by conscience, not eliminated altogether). The central role in psychopathy of the persecutory superego is stressed in many of the papers collected in *The Mark of Cain*. The absence of the more mature Oedipus complex and superego described in Freudian ego psychology does not mean the absence of either pre-Oedipal triangular conflict or an archaic superego in psychopathy.

As Meloy's (2007b) paper proceeds it becomes more and more clear that he is conceiving the primary psychopath as *the* psychopath as such. The concept of *degrees* of psychopathy is being displaced in favour of a dichotomous or polarised conception in which the primary, non-anxious, biologically-based psychopath is the psychopath *per se*, and the secondary, neurotic, or anxious psychopath is not really a psychopath at all.

Here we are encountering in the field of psychopathy a problem afflicting the whole field of psychodiagnosis: the tendency for the conception of degrees or *continua* of pathology to collapse into polarised or reified syndromes. But this is merely a particular instance of the wider problem of human consciousness as such. As what George Steiner (1969) calls "language animals" we try to understand the baffling complexity and flux of our experience by making distinctions, carving out and naming categories, and employing metaphors. As Lakoff and Johnson (1980) pointed out, metaphor is not an exceptional or poetic device but the very basis of human thought. We can only know one thing by comparing or contrasting it with another. But our "live" metaphors tend to go "dead" (Carveth, 1984b), our distinctions and categories tend to turn into reified or falsely concretised concepts, with all the consequences in racism, sexism, etc., we know all too well. The problem of reification of psychoanalytic concepts has been addressed earlier in this book. While Schafer (1976) and Brenner (1994, 1998, 2002), among others, are so worried about the danger of reification of the concepts of id, ego, and superego that they prefer to speak only of the compromise-formations comprising them, I have indicated my preference to work at the molecular rather than the atomic or subatomic level of analysis, continuing to employ the concept of these mental "structures", even adding a fourth, the conscience—but all the while striving to remember the metaphorical nature of these concepts.

Instead of speaking of the mild, moderate, and severe *degrees* of narcissism and psychopathy displayed by neurotics, borderlines, and psychotics, we are instead inclined to speak of "narcissists" and "psychopaths". But note that I just committed the very fallacy I am criticising in the work of Meloy and most other contributors to the recent literature on psychopathy. Instead of speaking of mild, moderate, and severe levels of psychopathology, I resorted to the falsely concretised notions of "the neurotic", "the borderline", "the psychotic". Naturally, this sets the stage for people to come along and write books about the neurotic's "psychotic core" or the micro-psychotic episodes suffered by "the borderline"—notions made necessary by our refusal of the continuum concept in favour of what Albert North Whitehead (1925) called "The Fallacy of Misplaced Concreteness" (p. 25). Frank Sirotich (personal communication) kindly drew my attention to the fact that earlier claims (Harris, Rice & Quinsey, 1994) that psychopathy is a taxon, a discrete class or category, have recently been reviewed and negated by Edens, Lilienfeld, Marcus, and Poythress (2006) who provide taxometric evidence supporting a dimensional as opposed to a categorical conception of psychopathy.

In contrast to the tendency towards reification, most of the psychoanalytic essays collected in *The Mark of Cain* (Meloy, 2001) are written in the spirit of the *one genus hypothesis* that Harry Stack Sullivan (1953) formulated as follows:

> We shall assume that everyone is much more simply human than otherwise, and that anomalous interpersonal situations, insofar as they do not arise from differences in language or custom, are a function of differences in relative maturity of the persons concerned. … I have become occupied with the science, not of individual differences, but of human identities, or parallels.… I try to study the degrees and patterns of things which I assume to be ubiquitously human. (pp. 32–33)

These psychoanalytic papers view psychopathy as, for example: an outcome of "the interplay of attachment, identifications, affect, and intellectual development" (Loretta Bender); of affect hunger (David

Levy); of the inhibition of love by rage (John Bowlby); of superego pathology due to projected aggression in response to frustration (Phyllis Greenacre); of a "narcissistically disturbed relationship with the mother during early childhood" (Kate Friedlander); of "superego lacunae" due to intergenerationally and unconsciously transmitted immoral and anti-social behaviours (Adelaide Johnson); of an inflated ego ideal (Helene Deutsch); of inadequate "holding" and "containing" of the aggressive impulses of the child by the mother (Donald Winnicott); of the "defensive search for painless freedom from objects" (Seymour Halleck); of the "impulse-feeling-defence triad of greed-envy-devaluation" in which "the psychopath spoils that which he hungrily wants" (Betty Joseph); of the aim of "reunion with the omnipotent object" and preservation of the grandiose self through domination and devaluation of the other (Ben Burston); and of pathological narcissism, superego deficits, and sadism (Otto Kernberg).

In brief commentaries, Meloy expresses his reservations regarding many of these papers, arguing that they overestimate the role of psychodynamic and environmental factors, overemphasise conflict and anxiety, confuse secondary and primary psychopathy, and ignore the biological determinants of the latter. For example, in response to John Lion who emphasises the importance in treatment of the emergence of the psychopath's sadness and depression as his narcissistic defences are confronted, Meloy indicates that this applies only to "the patient who has sufficient anxiety and attachment capacity to make the treatment endeavour worthwhile". He argues that "[I]f the psychopathy is severe and biologically rooted, such emotional states will not occur" and "The therapist may find, instead, that his time has been squandered by a chameleon" (p. 265). Similarly, against Betty Joseph's emphasis on the psychopath's defences against anxiety, guilt, and depression, Meloy argues that "... neurotic personality organisation must be achieved to nurture such socialised feelings" and that "... this level of personality will not exist in the more primitive, less conflicted primary psychopath" (p. 227).

In the course of his analysis of the character of Heathcliff in Emily Brontë's *Wuthering Heights*, Neville Symington (1980) affirms Melanie Klein's (1934) view that:

> One of the great problems about criminals, which have always made them incomprehensible to the rest of the world, is their lack

of natural human good feeling; but this lack is only apparent. When in analysis one reaches the deepest conflicts from which hate and anxiety spring, one also finds there the love as well. Love is not absent in the criminal, but it is hidden and buried in such a way that nothing but analysis can bring it to light. (Klein, quoted by Symington, in Meloy, 2001, p. 289)

While Meloy appreciates Symington's insights into "the countertransference aroused by these patients", the "collusion, disbelief, and condemnation" that Symington sees as "superego defences against our own sadism", he suggests that Symington "overestimates the emotional and moral development of psychopathic persons" (p. 283). Is this to say that Heathcliff, like others in whom love is not absent but only buried, is not a psychopath at all? Or is it to suggest he is only mildly or moderately as distinct from severely psychopathic?

Given Meloy's reservations regarding the relevance of psychodynamic factors in what amounts in his view to "true" psychopathy, one wonders why he bothers to collect these psychoanalytic papers in the first place? Is it primarily to point out their irrelevance in light of the new evidence of the biology of psychopathy? Are they primarily of historical interest, indicators of where we were and, in light of recent biological evidence, how far we have come? And why does he title his recent paper "A Psychoanalytic View of Psychopathy" when its main thrust is to emphasise the role of biological rather than psychological and psychodynamic factors in psychopathy?

Although Meloy at times employs the language of degrees, of more or less anxiety and attachment capacity, of levels of personality organisation, of "the more primitive" and "the less conflicted", his point is that the sorts of psychological factors outlined in the papers collected in *The Mark of Cain* are of limited relevance with respect to biologically determined primary psychopathy. This theoretical move separates off the "true psychopath" from other types of narcissistic and antisocial personalities, but at the cost of ignoring the concept of degrees of psychopathy and thereby constructing "*the* psychopath" as essentially Other, if not "beyond the pale", a creature who is reptilian in his or her coldness and incapacity to become truly attached and, thus, as Symington suggests, setting him or her up as a target for projection of our own disowned sadism.

If this construction of "the psychopath" sets him up as a target of *projection* then it may also set him up as a target for *injection*, of the lethal type. Because the so-called primary psychopath is alleged to have no remorse and to be incurable, we may come to feel justified in remorse-lessly killing him—especially now that, owing to DNA evidence of his guilt, we have less cause to worry about the possibility of executing an innocent person. In this sense, the diagnosis of primary psychopathy might serve to rationalise enactment of our own homicidal inclinations: it may serve to help us kill the killers—and, in so doing, become them.

On the other hand, the biological theory of primary psychopathy might have the opposite effect—not of scapegoating the psychopath but of exonerating him. After all, if his condition is biologically deter-mined, what sense does it make to hold him responsible and to punish him for a condition entirely outside his own control? To the argument that psychoanalytic understanding is equally deterministic and that free will and responsibility are no more negated by a biological than by a psychoanalytic view of the determinants of personality and behav-iour, I have already pointed out that Freud's (1916–17) psychic deter-minism, the view that "[T]he ego is not even master in its own psychic house" (p. 285), was always complemented by his equally important revelation of the remarkable degree to which we are, in fact, the uncon-scious agents of our fates, as Schafer (1976, pp. 153–154) has so clearly articulated.

However much the conscious ego might, like Freud, embrace deter-minism and, hence, claim, rightly or wrongly, to be a product of forces beyond its control, both the conscience and the superego, like Sartre (1943), appear to be existentialist. Despite the powerful force of circum-stance, our conditioning by biology, history, class, culture, and upbring-ing, for Sartre (1946, p. 34) we are nevertheless "condemned to be free", at least in the limited sense that as long as our consciousness is not elim-inated or subjected to control through physical or chemical techniques (which, in effect, render us things rather than persons), we retain that minimal degree of psychological freedom to refuse at whatever cost and to "make something out of what is made of [us]" (Sartre, 1969, p. 45), if only by reflecting upon and choosing our attitude to this.

Conscience and superego insist upon our agency and hold us to account; often the superego, out of its desire to reproach and punish, does so to an irrational degree. As Schafer (1976) has explained, some-times we excessively claim responsibility, and sometimes excessively disclaim it. But however much responsibility may be excessively dis-claimed, my clinical experience has over the years convinced me that in the long run nobody gets away with anything. However repressed or split off, conscience sees and knows all, like the biblical God who "called unto Adam.... Where *art* thou?" (*Genesis* 3:9 *KJV*) and who "said unto Cain, Where is Abel thy brother?" (*Genesis* 4:9 *KJV*). In François Chifflart's illustration for Victor Hugo's *La Conscience* that serves as the cover of this book, conscience is appropriately depicted as an all-seeing eye. Unless one reconciles with conscience, faces and learns to bear one's guilt, and makes reparation, the enforcer-Gestapo-superego is only too happy to mete out punishment—a process wonderfully conveyed in symbolic form by Hieronymus Bosch in the third panel of the triptych, *The Garden of Earthly Delights* (*circa* 1490–1510), in which the punishments of the damned are portrayed.

If you think psychopaths, unlike ordinary neurotic-level sinners, have no conscience, nor any superego to enforce its dictates and that, therefore, they can get away with anything, note how many of them wind up in jail; note the effect of their psychopathy on their families ("visiting the iniquity of the fathers upon the children unto the third and fourth generation") (*Exodus* 20:5 *KJV*). Read about the life and times of Lord Conrad Black of Crossharbour. It is true, as the traditional folk song has it, "You can run on for a long time, run on for a long time, but sooner or later, God [read the superego] is going to cut you down." According to a Canadian Broadcasting Corporation documentary (2005), "The Life and Times of Conrad Black", Conrad "broke into the principal's office, stole the exam papers and offered them for sale" to other boys. Though expelled (and later honoured as an old boy for reasons not hard to guess), he ran on for a *long* time. According to Dietrich Bonhoeffer (1953), "It is one of the most astounding discoveries, but one of the most incontrovertible, that evil—often in a surprisingly short time—proves its own folly and defeats its own object" (p. 141).

It was in 1927, in *The Secret of Father Brown*, that G. K. Chesterton wrote the following, which rather succinctly, and without either dehumanising or exonerating wrongdoers, summarises the concerns I have been elaborating:

> No man's really any good till he knows how bad he is, or might be; till he's realised how much right he has to all this talk about "criminals", as if they were apes in a forest ten thousand miles away; till he's got rid of all the dirty self-deception of talking about low types and deficient skills; till he's squeezed out the last drop of the

oil of the Pharisees; till his only hope is somehow or other to have captured one criminal, and kept him safe and sane under his own hat. (p. 466)

Now, of course, it can be argued that Chesterton is writing here about criminals and garden-variety scoundrels, not psychopaths, as it could be argued I was doing when writing above about Lord Black. On the other hand, the continuum concept suggests that all wrongdoing entails some degree of both narcissism and psychopathy. Exchanging a theory of degrees of psychopathy for a reified conception of the true psychopath increases the risk of projection and scapegoating—which was Chesterton's point.

It is not my aim to cast doubt on the validity of the science reviewed for us by Meloy and others regarding biological factors in severe psychopathy, but rather to express, in the spirit of Max Weber, my anxiety regarding its potential unintended social consequences. Sociologists in the 1960s developed a critique of asylums and the "institutionalisation" they were found to create. No one anticipated that governments would welcome such research as an opportunity to cut spending with the consequence of homeless ambulatory schizophrenics living in cardboard boxes in neighbourhoods adjacent to the hospitals that used to give them asylum. What worries me is what might well be the unintended consequences of the new biological research on psychopathy, namely:

1. The utilisation of such evidence to form a reified or falsely concretised conception of *"the* psychopath" that invites projection and scapegoating.
2. The denial of a psychopathic dimension of human personality *as such* that takes the form of a continuum from mild to moderate to extreme, an idea that forces us to confront the degree of psychopathy in ourselves instead of projecting it onto the Other and condemning and possibly persecuting (or even executing) it there.

Meloy (2007a) has himself written of the countertransference reaction to psychopathy that Lion (1978) calls "therapeutic nihilism" and Symington (1980) calls "condemnation":

Instead of arriving at a treatment decision based on a clinical evaluation, including an assessment of the severity of psychopathy, the clinician devalues the patient as a member of a stereotyped class of "untouchables." The clinician does to the patient with antisocial personality disorder what the patient does to others. Symington (1980) called this *condemnation* and it psychoanalytically reflects the clinician's identification with this aspect of the patient's character. (p. 10)

Is the tendency to reify the concept of "the primary psychopath" a manifestation of such condemnation?

Naturally I am in no way implying that potential misuse of scientific truth in any way justifies irrationalist evasion or denial of such truth. As Meloy and others correctly emphasise, the frightening reality of severe psychopathy must be faced, including the scientific evidence of significant biological factors in its causation. I am in no way positing nurture against the new evidence of the role of nature in the genesis of severe psychopathy, but only arguing against the tendency to reify "the psychopath" as such. For just as the frightening reality of severe psychopathy must be faced, so must the frightening potential uses of this diagnosis. In my view, one way to work against such misuse is to adhere scrupulously to the continuum concept which, in reminding us of the lesser degrees of psychopathy we share with those who manifest it in more severe forms, makes it more difficult for us to project and to scapegoat others for what we refuse to see in ourselves. Two millennia ago a perceptive analyst offered the following insight into projection:

> And why beholdest thou the mote that is in thy brother's eye, but considerest not the beam that is in thine own eye? Or how wilt thou say to thy brother, Let me pull out the mote out of thine eye; and, behold, a beam *is* in thine own eye? Thou hypocrite, first cast out the beam out of thine own eye; and then shalt thou see clearly to cast out the mote out of thy brother's eye. (*Matthew* 7:3-5 KJV)

* * *

A person may score high on the psychopathy scale, even be diagnosed as a primary psychopath, and yet not be that particular type of malignant narcissist, the antisocial sadist, who is inclined to evil. Not all wrongdoers are severely psychopathic, and while most severely or even moderately psychopathic people are wrongdoers, perhaps even contributing to evil outcomes, not all are evil in themselves. Here we must distinguish between evil as an outcome of human action and as a characteristic of a person. People who are not evil may involve themselves in committing evil. Not all the perpetrators of the Holocaust or the horrors committed under Stalinism or Maoism were evil. "Monstrous acts are by no means always committed by monstrous individuals" (Eagleton, 2010, p. 143). To qualify as evil it is not enough to do evil, one must *intend* to do it and *enjoy* it; there must be, as Eagleton (2010) holds, an element of "*jouissance*, or obscene enjoyment" (p. 77) in its practice. To qualify as evil it is not enough to be severely psychopathic, one must also be sadistic—that is, one must positively seek and enjoy the suffering one inflicts upon one's victims. But even this requires qualification. Eagleton points out that "Two actions may look the same, but one may be evil and one may not. Think, for example, of the difference between someone who practices sadism for erotic pleasure in a consensual sexual relationship, and someone who forces excruciating pain on another person in order to assuage his own nauseous sense of nonbeing" (p. 152).

In this connection, Eagleton quotes John Rawls: "What moves the evil man is the love of injustice: he delights in the impotence and humiliation of those subject to him and relishes being recognised by them as the author of their degradation" (p. 94). Many even severely psychopathic people are too pragmatic for that: they are entirely out for number one and do not object to hurting or even killing those who get in their way, but hurting and killing is not their primary aim. We must, as Eagleton suggests, distinguish the merely vicious from the positively evil (p. 95): while for Kant "[E]vil lies in our propensity to deviate from the moral law … evil is a lot more interesting than that. And not all such deviations are worthy of the name" (p. 95). In so arguing one restricts the term to what Kant called *radical evil*, the enjoyment of "wickedness for wickedness's sake". As Eagleton points out, Kant did not think this was possible on the grounds that "[E]ven the most depraved of individuals must acknowledge the authority of the moral law" (p. 95) which, even if true seems beside the point, for to acknowledge the authority of the moral law in no way rules out violating it for the sheer hell of it.

In famously referring to "the banality of evil", Hannah Arendt (1963) did not mean to suggest that evil is banal, only that certain of its perpetrators, thoughtless bureaucrats like Eichmann, are. While, following Kant, she had expected to encounter radical evil in Eichmann, she was surprised by his banality. But while acknowledging that evil may be perpetrated by people for whom this is not a primary aim and who may even be banal, the term evil, as a descriptor of human beings as distinct from what their actions produce, should be restricted to the types of people who intend to perpetrate evil and who obtain obscene, perverse enjoyment in doing so and who, therefore, are anything but banal.

However malignantly narcissistic the severely psychopathic may be, they differ from the severely sadistic psychopath—that is, the evil—in that their narcissism is not so all-encompassing that they experience a deep hatred for *being* as such. In fact, they find the world of sufficient interest that they are determined to get what they want of it by any means necessary. The evil, on the other hand, are consumed by a hatred of all otherness and wish to reduce it to nothing. Their narcissism is such that they cannot bear the existence of anything outside the self. Recently Britton (2003) has described the narcissistic disorders this way: unable to tolerate otherness the schizoid withdraws from it, the borderline seeks to colonise it, and the hysteric strives to impersonate it. But we need to supplement Britton's list to include five additional strategies: the psychotic who denies it; the pervert who seeks to defeat or castrate it; the sadistically psychopathic who attempts to destroy it; the neurotic who acknowledges and feels guilty towards it; and the healthy who loves and sacrifices himself for it when it is good, and hates and fights it when it is evil.

In traditional theology the only being that can be said to be *causa sui*, entirely self-caused and autonomous, is God, who is thus the object of intense envy by the severely narcissistic, not least by Satan, who cannot bear to acknowledge their dependence on anything or anyone outside themselves. As Eagleton (2010) says, "Pure autonomy is a dream of evil" (p. 12). Unable to realise their autarchic dream to be everything, they seek to destroy everything that is not them and are sometimes even willing to destroy themselves in the process. It may well be true, as Eagleton says, that "Only the good are capable of dying" (p. 22) and that, owing to their fanatic clinging to themselves and incapacity for self-dispossession, "The damned are those who are dead but won't lie down" (pp. 49–50). But I think there is one condition under which they can let go: when everything and everyone else goes with them.

Freud (1915c) attributes a good deal of this psychology to the infant whose first attitude towards otherness, he says, is one of hatred: "Hate, as a relation to objects, is older than love. It derives from the narcissistic ego's primordial repudiation of the external world with its outpouring of stimuli" (p. 138). For Freud (1914c), "'His Majesty the Baby', as we once fancied ourselves" (p. 90) is loathe to surrender his omnipotent sense of being the all and everything. Even when forced by reality to do so, he engages in the rearguard action Freud (1915c, p. 135) called the "purified pleasure ego" in which he employs projection (to export the bad) and introjection (to import the good) to in this way sustain the illusion that at least all that is good is me, and all that is not-me is bad. In this light, the sheer destructive envy and hatred of all otherness characteristic of evil would appear to be simply a form of malignant infantilism. In positing an innate hostility to otherness, what he calls a "xenocidal impulse", Britton (2003, Chapter Eight) is close to Freud.

But if this is occasionally Freud's infant, it certainly is not Klein's, nor mine. For Klein the infant's first relation to otherness is love, but such love is quickly and inevitably joined by hatred and envy. Like Klein, I believe it makes sense to assume the infant arrives with a kind of instinctual pre-orientation towards a good breast. Klein writes: "The newborn infant unconsciously feels that an object of unique goodness exists, from which a maximal gratification could be obtained and that this object is the mother's breast" (Klein, Heimann, Isaacs & Riviere, 1952, p. 265). But the infant soon encounters frustration, even with the best, most attuned and responsive carers imaginable. Given his lack of accurate reality-testing, he inevitably experiences all frustration as an attack. Hence, the good breast is inevitably and quickly joined in the infant's experience by a bad, persecutory breast. Even with the best care imaginable, the infant will become paranoid. In all this there is no need whatever to posit a literal "death instinct" understood in Freud's (1920g) original sense as a biologically-given (and utterly non-Darwinian) drive towards death that under the influence of the life drive may be deflected outwards as aggression. While Klein certainly referred to the death instinct in this connection (though she appeared to mean different things by it at different times), on almost every page that she cites it to explain the infant's sense of persecution and fear of annihilation as a consequence of his projection outwards of the death drive, she also provides an alternative and, to my mind, far more acceptable explanation: namely that the absent good breast is experienced by the infant as a bad, attacking breast—that owing to the infant's cognitive immaturity all frustration is experienced as persecution.

In this view, although our first orientation to the world is a loving expectation of encountering love, which if we survive at all we clearly do encounter (else we would be dead or vegetating in a far ward of some asylum), we also inevitably encounter frustration which we experience as persecutory, as an attack to which we respond with hate, leading to a persecutory fear of retaliation, generating further hate, such hate being projected outwards intensifying the sense of persecution, generating more hate, and so on in a vicious, persecutory cycle. Our initial loving is soon accompanied by hating; we become ambivalent, divided, conflicted. The relative balance in a person between loving and hating is, no doubt, a complex outcome of constitutional as well as environmental factors.

Regrettably, John Bowlby did our discipline a great disservice, misrepresenting Klein by suggesting that her emphasis on phantasy denies entirely the role of the real external carers, a view reiterated by authors of secondary sources who, apparently, felt justified in writing about Klein without actually reading her. In an interview (Bowlby, Figlio & Young, 1986), Bowlby states:

> ... as you know, in 1897 Freud, having initially attributed troubles to real life experiences, then said these things hadn't happened; they were fantasies. Different analytic traditions no doubt varied a bit in this regard but Ernest Jones was very averse to attributing any great importance to real life experiences; Melanie Klein was very averse. My own analyst, Joan Riviere, who was a close friend of Melanie Klein's, went on record, I think in 1926 or '27, as saying that analysis was not concerned with the external world; it was concerned only with the internal. So you see, although Melanie Klein was concerned with human relationships (I don't use the word object relationships, I think it's misleading) and parent-child interaction and all that sort of thing, it was the internal world on which she put all the emphasis and, effectively, she turned her back on real life experiences. (p. 37)

It is disappointing, to say the least, to witness someone—who was capable a quarter of a century earlier (Bowlby, 1958) of writing in a careful, scholarly way about Klein—fall into such a gross misrepresentation of her work. In Klein's actual writings the role of the real external carers is constantly emphasised. It is only by encountering real love and nurturance that the infant's inevitable paranoid phantasies of persecution may gradually be counteracted. Strachey's (1934) theory of the therapeutic action of psychoanalysis follows directly from Klein's view: only by encountering the analyst's non-judgemental, more tolerant, and forgiving attitude may the harsh, persecutory superego gradually be modified. The more frustration, trauma, and pain encountered in childhood, the more reactive aggression will be directed outwards and inwards, unless such pain is to some degree contained by being able to be communicated to empathic, sympathetic, and responsive carers. In "A Contribution to the Psychogenesis of Manic-Depressive States", Klein (1935) writes: "The fact that a good relation to its mother and to the external world helps the baby to overcome its early paranoid anxieties throws a new light on the importance of its earliest experiences. From its inception analysis has always laid stress on the importance of the child's early experiences, but it seems to me that only since we know more about the nature and contents of its early anxieties, and the continuous interplay between its actual experiences and its phantasy life, are we able fully to understand *why* the external factor is so important" (p. 169). Passages such as this are to be found throughout Klein's work.

Freud's description of an infant full of hatred for otherness and reluctant to surrender his omnipotence, his insistence that he is the all and everything, or at least that all that is good is himself and all that is not himself is bad, is a description not of a normal but of an emotionally disturbed infant. In my view, ignorance of impotence is not omnipotence. The infant is unaware of his limits, but that is not at all the same thing as a denial of his limits or a delusion of limitlessness. While early ignorance of limits is normal, a delusion of omnipotence is a pathological grandiose phantasy formed precisely as a manic defence against an overwhelming sense of helplessness and insignificance experienced by a neglected, uncontained, or traumatised child. Similarly, while there is a phase in emotional development characterised by splitting, keeping good apart from bad in regard to both one's objects and one's self, and employing projection to export badness outside the self and introjection to import goodness into it, failure to surrender such defensive manoeuvres as development proceeds is a pathological outcome: in Kleinian terms it is fixation in and failure to transcend the narcissism, splitting, and paranoia of the paranoid-schizoid position.

* * *

According to Eagleton, "You can believe in evil without supposing that it is supernatural in origin" yet, in his view, "Evil … is indeed metaphysical, in the sense that it takes up an attitude toward being as such, not just toward this or that bit of it. Fundamentally, it wants to annihilate the lot of it" (p. 16). In psychoanalytic terms, this is severe, pathological narcissism and sadism. Descriptively, the person displaying it is in a paranoid-schizoid state, a pathologically intensified version of what normal infants, children, and all of us from time to time experience in the paranoid-schizoid position. In this position, experience is ordered entirely through binary oppositions or splitting. Both self and other are either all-good or all-bad, idolised or demonised. Since in the paranoid-schizoid position life is a jungle, one is either the killer or the killed, predator or prey, alive or dead. States of mania defend against depression, and sometimes depression defends against mania. One is either manically alive or entirely dead. Sometimes one plays dead as a defence against psychotically inflated states of manic vitality.

Eagleton writes, "In the end, evil is indeed all about death—but about the death of the evildoer as much as that of those he annihilates" (p. 18). In writing thus, he refers to the "non-being at the core of one's own identity", the "aching absence" that is a foretaste of death and that the evildoer seeks to project into the other rather than learning how to bear and creatively transform. "[O]ne way of fending off the terror of human mortality is to liquidate those who incarnate this trauma in their own person. In this way you demonstrate that you have authority over the only antagonist—death—that cannot be vanquished even in principle" (p. 100). For Eagleton:

> … evil is not just any old kind of sadism. It is the kind of cruelty which seeks to relieve a frightful inner lack. … A lot of people in acute pain would rather be dead. And some of those who are spiritually dead rejoice in witnessing this torment because it confirms their own ascetic contempt for human existence. So their relish for other people's afflictions has a reason. … There is a kind of sadist who makes others howl in order to transform them into part of his own nihilistic nature. Evil brings false comfort to those in anguish by murmuring in their ear that life has no value anyway. Its enemy, as always, is not so much virtue as life itself. If it spits in the face of virtue, it is because, as Aristotle and Aquinas were aware, virtue is by far the fullest, most deeply enjoyable way to live. (p. 106)

Eagleton is correct to suggest that "In psychoanalytic terms, evil is thus a form of projection" (p. 107), but it would be better to draw on the Kleinian rather than the Freudian tradition here and to say that evil entails a form of interpersonal *projective identification* in which the subject not only *imagines* as residing in the other that which he repudiates in himself, but actually *induces* the other to experience and even enact what is projected. Eagleton attributes this understanding to Schopenhauer (1818) who "saw evil deeds as motivated by a need to obtain relief from … inner torment … by inflicting that torment on others" (p. 107). But the problem we encounter here is the same one we met in defining evil in terms of sadism: like sadism, interpersonal projective identification, the induction of others to suffer our pain is, to one degree or another, a universally human practice. From human sacrifice, to animal sacrifice, to kicking the cat or taking out one's frustration on one's spouse or child, scapegoating is ubiquitous. Thus to qualify its perpetrator as evil in contrast to the rest of us more ordinary sinners, such scapegoating must take a particularly vicious, virulent, and murderous form. Eagleton comes closer to its essence when he describes evil as a process of "leeching life from others in order to fill an aching absence in oneself" (p. 71).

Eagleton associates the aching absence in the self, the inner deadness that the evil seek to inflict on the other, with the Freudian death drive. But Eagleton's version of *Thanatos* is a long way from Freud's (1920g) for whom it was, at least initially, a literal biologically-given drive to return to an inorganic state. In marked contrast, Eagleton views the death drive as a response to the ego's pain and frustration in the face of its perpetual conflicts with id, superego, and reality: "Savaged by the superego, ravaged by the id, and battered by the external world, the poor bruised ego is understandably in love with its own dissolution. Like some badly mutilated beast it finds that its only final security lies in crawling off to die" (p. 108). But this makes the death drive a *reaction* to pain, not a primary instinctual drive; it makes it an understandable response to unbearable suffering. This might well be a plausible account of the origin of a death *wish*, but it is certainly not how Freud himself defined the death *drive* in *Beyond the Pleasure Principle*. In addition, this view of the death drive as a reaction to pain appears inconsistent with Eagleton's own tendency to view it in universal terms, as a primary given of human nature, and not merely a secondary reaction to painful experience. He writes, "At the core of the self is a drive to absolute nothingness. There is that within us which perversely clamours for our own downfall" (p. 108) and this, Eagleton claims, is the true scandal of psychoanalysis, not its theory of infantile sexuality.

There is no doubt that *Thanatos*, understood as a superego-driven masochistic tendency towards self-defeat, exists in all of us; but the point is that in some of us such masochism is far more intense than in others and this cannot be understood in such universalising terms but only in light of the particular conditions that have generated such "surplus" destructiveness in some and not in others. This distinction seems crucial for anyone interested in utilising psychoanalytic think- ing to inform socio-political critique which requires us to differentiate between human nature as such and human nature as shaped under par- ticular historical, familial, and personal conditions. As Marx (1867) put it, "He that would criticize all human acts, movements, relations, etc., by the principle of utility, must first deal with human nature in general, and then with human nature as modified in each historical epoch" (p. 668).

For Lacan (1994), "The Holy Spirit is the entry of the signifier into the world. This is certainly what Freud brought us under the title of death drive" (p. 48). According to Slavoj Žižek (2003), for Lacan "the Holy Spirit stands for the symbolic order as that which cancels (or rather suspends) the entire domain of 'life'.... When we locate ourselves within the Holy Spirit, we are transubstantiated; we enter another life beyond the bio- logical one" (p. 10). Eagleton thinks of the death drive in such universal terms: "There is something potentially self-thwarting or self-undoing about humanity. ... Man is Faustian Man, too voraciously ambitious for his own well-being, perpetually driven beyond his own limits by the lure of the infinite" (p. 31). According to Sartre (1943), to whom French psychoanalysis seldom acknowledges its debt, human consciousness is doubly "nihilating". To know this cup I must first know it is not me. I place a nothingness between myself as the knowing subject and the object I seek to know. Second, I must know the cup is not the table upon which it rests, so I place a second nothingness between them. As the squid injects ink into the water, human consciousness brings nothing- ness (gaps, lacks, cracks, holes, fissures, distinctions, differences, and boundaries) into the world. As Kenneth Burke (1968) points out, our symbolic consciousness constitutes us as "inventor[s] of the negative" (p. 9), enables us to imagine "what is not" and compare it to "what is", to posit various "Thou shalt nots" and, as Sartre (1943, pp. 33–85) says, to "secrete a nothingness" between our situation and our reaction to it (i.e., ourselves)—an act of "nihilation" that transforms "reaction" into "action" in the proper sense. At the point at which, like Helen Keller in that moment of realisation that words refer to things and that everything has a name (Cassirer, 1944, pp. 33–36), we cross the emergent evolutionary boundary between the prehuman and the human condition, we acquire the freedom to refuse; to delay our response to stimuli; to replace an overt response by a covert symbolic action (i.e., to think); to distance ourselves from immediate influences; to compare what is with what was, will be, or might be; to deny the truth; and to repress our wishes—even to die rather than submit to the force of circumstance.

For Eagleton the "language animal's" (Steiner, 1969) capacity for abstraction and its ability therefore to imagine and, hence, desire the infinite is at the core of the death drive: "This creature cold shoulders all finite things in his hubristic love affair with the illimitable. And since infinity is a kind of nothingness, the desire for this nothingness is an expression of ... the Freudian death drive" (Eagleton, 2010, p. 31). Reflecting upon the suicide of his friend, Sylvia Plath, and his own subsequent attempt, Alvarez (1971) describes awakening in an intensive care unit and proceeding to diagnose his narcissism. Realising that he had found fault with life because it failed to meet his expectations, he decided to set his expectations aside and accept life on its, rather than his, terms. A central element of the capacity for abstraction that Eagleton associates with the death drive is narcissism which, as Lacan more than any other psychoanalytic theorist realised is a matter of unconsciously substituting something dead, a mere mirror-image or "false self", for the living "subject" or "true self". But, again, it is essential to remember that while narcissism is a universal human problem, some of us are more narcissistic than others. The degree of one's narcissism has much to do with the particular conditions of one's infancy and childhood, as well as with the societal surround which either inflames the pathology (consumer capitalism), or encourages one to cure or at least contain it (socialism).

As Lacan understood, the Fall (up not down) into language (the Symbolic) at some point in the second year of life opens up an avenue of potential liberation from domination by the (Imaginary) ego of the mirror-phase. But it does so by inflicting a metaphysical wound (in hands, feet, side ...) that prefigures the grave (and for many narcissistic men, the vagina), a wound that must be allowed to remain open if the madness (narcissism) stemming from attempts at closure is to be avoided. It is the emergence of human consciousness into this field of negation that Kristeva (1982) describes as "abjection"—the opening of the wound that, in health at least, bleeds perpetually, or of a loss that cannot, and must not ever, be finally mourned (Derrida, 2001). It is this very wound and loss that constitute our freedom and our *Angst*, the foreclosure of which constitutes our narcissism, the only cure for which is "acceptance of castration" (Lacan, 1977). As Žižek (2003) says, "The problem with the Fall is thus not that it is in itself a Fall, but, precisely, that, *in itself, it is already a Salvation which we misrecognize as a Fall*" (p. 87; original emphasis).

But if one is unable to bear this wound, too addicted to the wholeness of one's Imaginary ego to be able to tolerate castration then, as Eagleton points out, one will seek to stuff "this aching absence … with fetishes, moral ideals, fantasies of purity, the manic will, the absolute state, the phallic figure of the Führer" (p. 100), etc. But salving the wound in the self in these ways requires wounding others: "The non-being at the core of one's own identity is, among other things, a foretaste of death … one way of fending off the terror of human mortality is to liquidate those who incarnate this trauma in their own person" (p. 100). We either learn how to carry our cross or crucify others (and also, ultimately, ourselves). In psychoanalytic terms, we either learn how to bear mental pain or we inflict it unconsciously upon scapegoats via interpersonal projective identification, or upon ourselves in neurotic, psychosomatic, and psychotic pathology. As we have seen, for Bion (1962) as for Freud (1920g), we must move "beyond the pleasure principle" and learn how to accept and bear the existential pain, refusal of which caused the pathology in the first place. Learning to bear this pain requires those acts of ongoing self-dispossession which, as Eagleton (p. 24) points out, are the ways we rehearse in life for the ultimate act of self-surrender in death. "Only the good are capable of dying. … In this sense, how you die is determined by how you live. Death is a form of self dispossession which must be learned in life if it is to be successfully accomplished. … Being-for-others and being-toward-death are aspects of the same condition" (p. 24).

While conscience requires us to learn how to bear our existential pain instead of inflicting it on others, the superego delights in punishing us for our inevitable failures in this regard. Eagleton writes: "In punishing ourselves for our transgressions, this reproachful power stakes up in us a lethal culture of guilt. Yet since (masochistic creatures that we are) we also rejoice in the superego's scolding, we can come to hug our chains, finding a perverse source of pleasure in our very guilt. And this succeeds in making us even more guilty. This surplus guilt then brings the high-minded terrorism of the superego down on our heads with even greater vindictive force, with the result that we feel even more guilty, and thus even more gratified, and so on" (p. 109). As Freud (1930a) explains, every bit of aggression repressed for the sake of morality and civilisation is taken over by the superego and turned back against the self, thus increasing our guilt and reactive aggression. In extreme cases, we may wind up with a superego that amounts to "a pure culture of the death instinct" (Freud, 1923b, p. 58). As Eagleton explains, "The death drive is not just content with seeing us tear ourselves to pieces. With boldfaced insolence, it commands us to enjoy the process while we are at it. It wants us to be perverts as well as suicides" (2010, p. 110).

But in arguing that for psychoanalysis both desire and the drive to destruction are "nothing personal" but "purely formal, utterly impersonal, and implacably inhuman" (p. 113), Eagleton draws upon certain excessively abstract and universalising types of psychoanalytic and philosophic discourse to the neglect of psychoanalytic traditions more attuned to the particular, personal, and social conditions that shape desire. As the clinical psychoanalysis that analyses people as well as texts understands, human desire and self-destruction do not simply emerge from "an anonymous network into which we are inserted at birth" (p. 113), but from highly particular experiences and relations with specific individuals, usually called mother, father, brother, and sister, that are very personal indeed. It is odd to find the Marxist concern with the particularities of historical experience subordinated here to vague, universalising abstractions. Both Marx and Freud find conflict rooted in historical experience, not in ahistorical chains of signifiers. And to say that, as opposed to the view of St. Thomas Aquinas, "For Freud, there is that at the core of the self which has no solicitude for us at all" (Eagleton, 2010, p. 113) is to risk forgetting that, for Freud (1930a, p. 144), *Thanatos* has *Eros* as its constant companion.

On the question of death we are on firmer ground when instead of consulting the philosophers we rely on another of Eagleton's favourite sources, the Bible, which informs us that "the wages of sin is death" (*Romans* 6:23 *KJV*). Far from self-destruction emerging from "purely formal, utterly impersonal, and implacably inhuman" (p. 113) anonymous networks of signification, it is the price we pay for the sins we refuse to confess and the guilt we refuse to bear and for which we decline to make reparation. For in thus turning our backs on conscience we are prey to the superego which is only too happy to make of our lives a living hell, a death-in-life that Eagleton describes as "the vampire-like existence of the living dead" and that he contrasts with "a benign kind of death-in-life which is the 'death' of yielding oneself as a gift to others ... [something] that the damned cannot do. For them, the self is too precious to be given away" (p. 114)—for, as Žižek (2000) puts it, "Only a lacking, vulnerable being is capable of love: the ultimate mystery of love, therefore, is that incompleteness is, in a way, *higher than completion*" (p. 147). The damned refuse to be saved since, as Eagleton, following Kierkegaard, points out, "... this would deprive them of their adolescent rebellion against the whole of reality. Evil is a kind of cosmic sulking. ... Only by persisting in its fury and proclaiming it theatrically to the world can evil provide damning evidence of the bankruptcy of existence" (pp. 116–117). But, again, this is too general and insufficiently psychoanalytic. Evil is grounded in transference. It is not really a rebellion against the whole of existence but against the parents whose images are projected onto the whole of existence. It is not that evil refuses to die because to do so "would be to let the cosmos off the hook" (p. 117), but because it would let the parents off the hook.

Following Kierkegaard, Eagleton goes on to suggest that the reason the despairer "cannot consume himself, cannot become nothing ... cannot be rid of himself" (Kierkegaard, 1849, p. 141) is because the damned "are more fearful of nothingness—of the total abandonment of the self—than of their own acute distress" (Eagleton, 2010, pp. 114–115). Yes, but it is not "nothing" they fear; it is something they imagine as far worse than their distress. However painful it may be, at least such distress is self-administered and, in that sense, within the province of their own omnipotence. We know that people often prefer self-inflicted pain to trauma that is entirely outside their control. Whereas the Winnicottians may suspect that what is feared is a breakdown that has already occurred (Winnicott, 1974), I think what we are up against here is sheer paranoia. The damned have a superego that is "a pure culture of the death instinct", that is, that is loaded with murderous aggression—*their* murderous aggression as well as that introjected from others. This aggression is projected outwards in phantasy creating a paranoid anticipation of complete annihilation by God or the Devil should they rest in doling out torture to themselves and to the others who projectively represent themselves. The irony is that should they manage to genuinely let go, they would discover, not annihilation (that is a more likely consequence of the refusal to let go), but rather their paranoid anxiety and depression yielding to guilt, remorse, sadness, and mourning for all the harm they have done to themselves and others and then, hopefully, to contrition and efforts at reparation, leading finally to some measure of self-forgiveness and peace.

CHAPTER TEN

Resurrecting "dead" metaphors in psychoanalysis and religion

... not of the letter, but of the spirit: for the letter killeth, but the spirit giveth life.

—II Corinthians 3:6 KJV

As early as 1895, in the *Studies on Hysteria* (Breuer & Freud, 1893–95), Josef Breuer expressed a prescient concern regarding a tendency towards the literalisation of metaphor in psychoanalytic theory. Influenced, no doubt, by the more general apprehension regarding the abuse of language shared by many leading Central European thinkers of that period (Steiner, 1969; Szasz, 1976), Breuer wrote:

> It is only too easy to fall into a habit of thought which assumes that every substantive has a substance behind it—which gradually comes to regard "consciousness" as standing for some actual thing; and when we have become accustomed to make use metaphorically of spatial relations, as in the term "sub-consciousness", we find as time goes on that we have actually formed an idea which has lost its metaphorical nature and which we can manipulate easily as though it was real. Our mythology is then complete. All our thinking tends to be accompanied and aided by spatial ideas, and

215

we talk in spatial metaphors .... If, however, we constantly bear
in mind that all such spatial relations are metaphorical ... we may
nevertheless speak of a consciousness and a subconsciousness. But
only on this condition. (pp. 227–228)

A century later, Leavy (1983) expressed a similar concern: "It is only
when we stop to think about it that we can see what a momentous step
this is, to give more than lip service to recognising that our traditional
metaphors—even 'repression' itself—might not be the most informative ones. Indeed, it gives us something of a jolt to acknowledge that
they are metaphors—alternative descriptive words—in the first place,
and not determinate, positive facts of the natural order" (p. 48).

The experience of analysands and analysts alike is unconsciously
shaped by metaphors and contrasts that, having become literalised,
have assumed the status of myths. The deliteralisation of such "dead"
or "frozen" metaphors and oppositions—a practice resembling what
poststructuralist literary and philosophical theory called "deconstruction" (Derrida, 1978, 1981; Meisel, 1981; Sturrock, 1979)—often results
in those "jolting" experiences of insight that characterise important
phases of psychic development in general and the psychoanalytic process in particular. At the same time, we must heed Breuer's (Breuer &
Freud, 1893–95) warning regarding "the danger of allowing ourselves
to be tricked by our own figures of speech" (p. 228) and take care not
to literalise this metaphor of psychoanalysis as "deconstruction" of literalised metaphor and contrast. It too must be prevented from claiming, as mythologies inevitably do, an absolute and exclusive validity by
implicitly invalidating all other conceptions of analysis (as, for example,
"holding", "containing", provision of "selfobject function", the building up of a "good internal object", exchanging maladaptive for "more
adaptive defences", "sublimation", etc.).

Like every metaphor, the metaphor of analysis as promotion of
insight through deliteralisation is in no way complete or even adequate
to describe a multifaceted reality. But it would be a mistake to conclude
that such a focus upon the cognitive dimension of analytic work must
necessarily entail neglect of the role of affect. Having once been considered separate mental functions, today cognition and affect, though
analytically distinguishable, are regarded as ultimately inseparable. All
cognitions have some affective valence; and affect arises in response
to cognitive appraisals—that is, in the context of what the sociologist

W. I. Thomas called one's "definition of the situation" (Bruyn, 1966). If one hears what one takes to be an insult anger may immediately flare up, only to dissipate just as quickly if one realises one misheard the remark. Affect is generally dependent upon one's definition of the situation.

The painful affects that bring analysands to analysis will often begin to moderate in intensity and, sometimes, dissipate altogether when the unconscious definitions of the situation, the narratives or phantasies upon which they are based are brought into the light of consciousness and subjected to reality-testing, modified, or even set aside. Once conscious, the concretised or "frozen" metaphors (links) and contrasts (splits) through which such stories are constructed can be deconstructed and begin to "melt". To vary the metaphor, it is through the "enlivening" or "resurrection" of "dead" metaphors (identities) and contrasts (antitheses) that the compulsive repetitions constituting psychopathology can be overcome. In a sense, this is only to state in non-Kleinian language what Kleinian (and to a lesser extent Freudian) analysis has always implicitly understood: psychoanalysis is the process through which the analysand is helped to become conscious of the hitherto unconscious narratives (phantasies) that shape thought and action. For as long as we persist in confusing the inner world of phantasy with the outer world of reality we will continue, despite our conscious intentions, to shape the latter to conform to the former through the self-fulfilling prophecies that constitute our compulsion to repeat.

* * *

Metaphor may be defined as the "application of a name or descriptive term or phrase to an object or action to which it is imaginatively but not literally applicable (e.g., a glaring error, food for thought, leave no stone unturned) …" (Sykes, 1982, p. 636). Similarly, in a paper on "Metaphor and the Psychoanalytic Situation", Arlow (1979) states that: "The word metaphor comes from the two Greek words meaning 'to carry over,' and refers to a set of linguistic processes whereby aspects of one object are carried over or transferred to another object so that the second object is spoken of as if it were the first" (p. 367). According to Bruyn (1966): "A metaphor is an implied comparison between things essentially unlike one another. It is so much a part of language we hardly notice it; for example, the 'leg' of a table, or the 'face' of a clock" (p. 133). In his 1963 Massey Lectures, *The Educated Imagination*, the distinguished Canadian literary scholar Northrop Frye writes that:

> As soon as you use associative language, you begin using figures of speech. If you say this talk is dry and dull, you're using figures associating it with bread and bread-knives. There are two main kinds of association, analogy and identity, two things that are like each other and two things that are each other. You can say with Burns, "My love's like a red, red rose," or you can say with Shakespeare: "Thou that art now the world's fresh ornament/And only herald to the gaudy spring." One produces the figure of speech called the simile; the other produces the figure called metaphor. (pp. 10–11)

Whereas in a metaphor the comparison between the two elements is only implied, in a simile it is explicitly stated in words such as "like" or "as": "... the kingdom of heaven is *like* to a grain of mustard seed; as dead *as* a doornail; life, *like* a dome of many-coloured glass" (Sykes, 1982, p. 985). Whereas the simile and the metaphor are closely related figures of speech, the former is in an important respect a less hazardous one. Because the comparison is explicit in a simile, it is less likely to be mistaken for an identity. As Frye (1963) points out: "... [Y]ou have to be careful of associative language. You'll find that analogy, or likeness to something else, is very tricky to handle ... because the differences are as important as the resemblances. As for metaphor, where you're really saying 'this *is* that,' you're turning your back on logic and reason completely, because logically two things can never be the same thing and still remain two things" (p. 11).

To social scientists and psychoanalysts concerned with what Wittgenstein (1958) called the "bewitchment of our intelligence by means of language" (p. 47), the metaphor is of central interest. Not only is psychoanalysis "the talking cure" based upon the method of free association, but according to Arlow (1979, p. 382) transference and metaphor are two words for a single associative process. The process Freud referred to as regression from logical, reality-oriented, "secondary process" thinking to the alogical, phantasy infiltrated, "primary process" type of mentation characteristic of dreams and psychosis is paralleled in the tendency for metaphor to regress through literalisation from the more differentiated level at which similarities are regarded as merely relative and comparison takes the form of analogy, to the less differentiated level at which similarities are absolutised and the representations of different objects are identified or merged. This process of dedifferentiation is described by Bruyn (1966) as a regression from "live" to "dead" metaphor:

> Students of language such as Colin Turbayne (1962) are aware of stages in the life of the metaphor. The first stage involves giving a name to something that belongs to something else. Initially, this is generally thought to be inappropriate or "going against the ordinary language." Examples would be Newton's calling sounds "vibrations," or we would imagine, Comte calling enduring social relationships "structure" [or Freud calling a human motive an "instinct"]. The second stage is when the inappropriate name becomes appropriate, or in effect, a true metaphor. Other people besides the creator of the comparison acquiesce in the make-believe, yet still understand it to be only a comparison, not a complete identity. The third stage is when the metaphor is used so often that the difference is forgotten. The term then, as Turbayne would say, has moved from a "live" metaphor to a "dead" one. The identity is accepted. (pp. 136–137)

Once such literalisation has occurred and a "live" metaphor has been regressively transformed into a "dead" one, one no longer compares the "leg" of a table, let us say, to the leg of a person (or the human motive to an "instinct"; or the mental "apparatus" to a machine; or a woman to a castrated man) but literally thinks of the supports of a table as its legs (of a motive as an instinct; of the mind as a machine; of a woman as a castrate). "In the myth there is no recognition of difference or comparison; the identity is complete" (Bruyn, 1966, p.137).

The distinction between *live* and *dead* metaphor (or myth) finds parallels in a range of psychoanalytic traditions. Bion's (1962) distinction between *alpha* and *beta* elements (the former have undergone "alphabetisation") overlaps to some extent Segal's (1957) distinction between *symbolic representation* and *symbolic equation*. While alpha function and symbolic representation characterise Klein's (1946) *depressive position* (D), beta elements and symbolic equation characterise her *paranoid-schizoid* (PS) position—such "positions" constituting the two mental organisations or structures (not developmental stages) that for Klein constitute the mind. Whereas on the level of the depressive position the distinction between the metaphorical and the literal is maintained and each form of conceptualisation and communication is employed in its proper domain (because what Freud called "secondary process" thought is maintained here), on the more primitive, paranoid-schizoid level the distinction is blurred or lost altogether and the subject treats the metaphorical as the literal and vice versa (because here Freud's "primary process" mentation prevails). Such blurring or loss of boundaries is characteristic of mental life in the paranoid-schizoid position where separation between self and object is tenuous at best.

In conceptualising metaphor as "live" or "dead" we need to avoid the false and unintended association of "dead" metaphor with states of relative emotional "deadness" and "live" metaphor with more "lively" states. For in reality "dead" or concretised metaphor, like paranoid-schizoid processes in general, can lead to states of great emotional intensity, while "live" metaphor, like depressive position phenomena in general, may produce more muted or modulated, even at times "deadened", emotional states. For example, if the metaphor "life is a jungle" is taken literally, then daily existence becomes a very intense matter of life or death.

Just as it is necessary to overcome the splitting entailed in older notions of PS as all-bad and D as all-good by recognising the good in PS and the bad in D and the dialectical interdependence of the two positions or mental levels, so the merits of the primary process and of "dead" metaphor and contrast (e.g., emotional intensity, passion, the inspiration phase in creativity) and the demerits of the secondary process and of "live" metaphor and contrast (e.g., excessively moderate, dispassionate, or "dis-affected" states) must be kept in mind. Loewald (1971, 1981), among others, emphasised the creative potential of primary process thought and the adaptive potential of regression, especially when secondary process functioning has becomes too distant from its vital roots in the unconscious. At the same time, it seems important to recognise PS and D, "dead" and "live" metaphor and contrast, primary and secondary processes, as the terminal poles respectively on a continuum, the "intermediate area" of which may be viewed, following Winnicott (1955), as a "transitional process" in which metaphor and contrast are neither completely "dead" nor fully "alive". This "transitional area" includes types of mental functioning that cannot clearly or consistently be assigned to either PS or D and that seem somehow to overlap or fall between these categories. It is commonly recognised that use of transitional phenomena requires a "willing suspension of disbelief", but in actuality it requires suspension of *both* belief and disbelief. Both vital experience of the arts and transitional faith in and worship of the sacred exist between the poles of dogmatic literalistic belief and an entirely rationalist scepticism that, having been achieved, is temporarily suspended on entry into the transitional area and resumed again on exit.

The association of non-literalised or "live" metaphor with secondary process mentation (corresponding approximately to Lacan's (1977) Symbolic order) and of literalised or "dead" metaphor with the primary process (Lacan's Imaginary order) appears to be supported by Rogers (1978) who says of the latter: "It employs symbolism in a crudely associative way … [which] differs from what people usually consider symbolism in that similarities are not realised as mere similarities but treated as identities" (p. 17). Rogers cites Fenichel in support of this view of the primary process: "The object and the idea of the object, the object and a picture or model of the object, the object and a part of the object are equated; similarities are not distinguished from identities; ego and nonego are not yet separated" (Fenichel, 1945, p. 47). As Wittgenstein (1958, para. 115) put it, "A picture held us captive and we could not get outside it, for it lay in our language and language seemed to repeat it to us inexorably."

Yet it would be a mistake to define primary and secondary process thinking exclusively in terms of absolute versus relative similarity (i.e., in terms of "dead" or "live" metaphor respectively). For primary and secondary process are equally concerned with the question of difference; either *absolute* difference in the case of the primary process antitheses that constitute splitting, or *relative* difference in the case of secondary process distinctions. Hence, in deliteralising various metaphors we must guard against the opposite fallacy: that of literalising various contrasts. For primary process mentation appears to be characterised as much by absolute antithesis as by absolute identity, by "dead" contrast as much as by "dead" metaphor. Bion (1959) recognised this in viewing psychopathology as an outcome of "attacks on linking" (i.e., denial of all similarity, absolute difference, or splitting), but without emphasising that it also takes the form of "attacks on separating" (i.e., denial of all difference, absolute similarity, or fusion).

Although any two objects are inevitably similar in some respects while being different in others, it appears that individuals are frequently induced to repress either similarity or difference (*splitters* repressing similarity, *linkers* repressing difference) or both (at different times and/ or on different levels of consciousness) by painful affects of anxiety and depression (Brenner, 1982) associated with an expanded range of infantile danger situations. Freud's (1926d) list of danger situations must be expanded to include the danger of impingement or annihilation by bad objects, in addition to loss of good ones. As we have seen, Freud's difficulty in conceiving the primary object as a bad part-object all-too-present, as distinct from a good part-object that could be lost, seems to have been grounded in resistance to the idea that the early relation to the mother could be anything but good—that is, in idealisation as a defence against recognition of the hated, persecutory maternal part-object.

It is important to recognise that the representations of danger (based on perception, memory, phantasy, or their combination) that arouse signal affects are themselves composed of literalised metaphor and contrast. As the analysis of transference and resistance and of their unconscious cognitive-affective foundations, psychoanalysis may be viewed as simultaneously deliteralising and relativising the associations (metaphors) and dissociations (antitheses or splits) that characterise the fixated and regressed individual's relatively undifferentiated and unintegrated mental functioning.

Of particular relevance for psychoanalysts interested in the concepts of "ego defect" and "deficit" in "psychic structure" is Lakoff and Johnson's (1980) discussion of the metaphor *the mind is a brittle object*, commonly expressed in statements such as: "Her ego is very fragile. He broke under cross-examination. She is easily crushed. The experience shattered him. I'm going to pieces. His mind snapped" (p. 27). Those less inclined to literalise this metaphor are perhaps also less likely to regard certain narcissistic, borderline, and psychotic patients as unanalysable, or at least not on the grounds of their allegedly defective, deficient, or broken mental "apparatuses". However, that does not mean that there may not be other reasons to consider such people unanalysable. Lemaire (1970) explains the Lacanian rationale for doing so as follows: "The neurotic has effected the transition to the symbolic order, whereas the psychotic … never effected it completely" (p. 7). Whereas, in neurosis, repression effects the forgetting of an already established symbolisation (and, hence, the regression from "live" or secondary process to "dead" or primary process metaphor and contrast, in principle reversible through the analytic process), in psychosis "foreclosure" or "repudiation" has precluded accession to the principle of symbolisation (and, hence, to "live" metaphor and contrast) as such: "The impossibility of re-evoking the foreclosed experience arises from the fact that the psychotic never really had access to the principle of symbolisation" (p. 231). In this view, in order to be "revivified", metaphor must once have been "alive".

On the other hand, those who reject the disjunction between neurosis and psychosis in favour of something like a continuum—perhaps sharing Sullivan's (1953) "one genus hypothesis" that "everyone is much more simply human than otherwise" (p. 32)—will seek explanations for the challenge these patients pose for psychoanalysis that avoid the odious implication that they are less than fully human. Although acknowledging that "[O]ne encounters patients who, one feels, never had attained (even before the schizophrenia became overt) any full differentiation between metaphorical and concrete thought" (pp. 579–580), Searles (1962) lays major emphasis upon the role of regression which he conceptualises as a process of "desymbolisation". "By the term I refer to a process, seemingly at work in the schizophrenic patient, whereby the illness causes once-attained metaphorical meanings to become 'desymbolised'; and in the grip of the illness, the individual reacts to them as being literal meanings which he finds most puzzling" (p. 580). For Searles, it is not that the schizophrenic's thinking is concrete or literal or that he is unable to employ metaphor, but rather that in his thinking "… there is a lack of differentiation between the concrete and the metaphorical" (p. 561)—that is, that the metaphors he employs, being "dead" or literalised, are unrecognised by him as such. In this condition, his thinking is neither truly metaphorical (in the sense of "live" metaphor), nor truly concrete: "… just as the schizophrenic is unable to think in effective, consensually validated metaphor, so too is he unable to think in terms which are genuinely concrete, free from an animistic kind of so-called metaphorical overlay" (p. 561).

It is not unusual in the history of psychoanalytic theory for a psychic process originally regarded as pathological to be eventually recognised as characteristic of normal mental development. An example would be the extension of the concept of identification from its pathological role in melancholia (Freud, 1917e) to the status of a central process in normal ego and superego development (Freud, 1923b). Similarly, so ubiquitous are "dead" metaphors and contrasts, or undifferentiated and black and white thinking respectively, in "normal" mentation that if schizophrenia were simply equated with the use of literalised metaphors and contrasts we would all have to be considered mad—a theory that, despite its considerable plausibility, has certain obvious drawbacks in that some of us, evidently, are crazier than others. It would seem that, as is so often the case in psychoanalysis, we are thrown back for our definitions of normal and pathological upon quantitative considerations and concepts such as Freud's (1916–17, p. 347) "complemental series". In this view, instead of absolute contrasts between normality and neurosis, and between neurosis and psychosis—antitheses which themselves reflect regressive splitting—only a relative differentiation is recognised depending upon the prominence of "dead" metaphors and contrasts (i.e., primary process) in an individual's experience, among other factors.

In this vein, Searles (1962) complains that: "Most of the writings on this subject [schizophrenic thought disorder] do not attract the psychotherapist, for they possess a certain static, fatalistic quality, portraying this aspect of schizophrenia as though it ... sets the schizophrenic hopelessly apart from his fellow human beings" (p. 561). In focusing upon the defensive function of desymbolisation in warding off various painful affects, Searles enables us to view schizophrenia as meaningful action (Schafer, 1976) and not merely as a manifestation of a defective or deteriorated mental "apparatus" as those "possessed" by the metaphor, *the mind is a brittle object*, would have it. Searles writes:

> Usually the loss of ego boundaries is regarded as a final, grievous result of the schizophrenic process, and in a sense this is so. But I have found it of the greatest value, in my therapeutic work, to realise that this loss of ego boundaries is one of the most vigorously formidable defence mechanisms which comprise the schizophrenic process. This latter view is not only accurate, but is particularly conducive to our approaching the chronic schizophrenic patient not as being solely a grievously broken object for our compassion, but as being also, like every other living person, a creature imbued with limitless energy and the unquenched potential, therefore, for limitless growth and change. (p. 566)

It can only serve to further counteract such objectification and the therapeutic pessimism that accompanies it if we also recognise that such defensive desymbolisation is motivated by a range of infantile anxieties which themselves arise on the basis of our representations of danger—that is, from literalised metaphors and contrasts amenable to analytic deconstruction.

When the metaphor of analysis as metaphor-analysis—as the transformation of "dead" metaphors into "live" ones—is itself subjected to metaphor-analysis, some significant issues are brought into focus. For example, the question arises as to why analysis should be identified exclusively with the deliteralisation of "dead" metaphors and not of "dead" contrasts or antitheses as well? The view of analysis as relativising absolute similarity by drawing attention to repressed difference neglects the complementary analytic task of relativising absolute difference (splitting) by drawing attention to repressed similarity. A one-sided view of the analytic process as deconstructing absolute similarity is likely motivated by a "masculine" bias in favour of difference, which may in turn be motivated by unconscious fears of symbiotic merger, impingement, annihilation, undifferentiation of self and object, loss of self-cohesion, castration, or the fear of "femininity". This conception of pathology as symbiosis or "attacks on boundaries" and the corollary model of therapy as boundary-making would appear to underlie the rigid insistence upon the achievement and preservation of a clear analytic "frame" that was characteristic of the work of Langs (1978) and his co-workers. On the other hand, an equally one-sided view of the analytic process as deconstructing absolute difference, splitting, or "attacks on linking" (Bion, 1959) may be motivated by the "feminine" or erotic bias in favour of symbiosis, similarity, and "containment" that we see at work in therapies that prefer connection, the empathically attuned therapeutic relationship, and the transmuting internalisation it is thought to facilitate over confrontation, clarification, interpretation, insight, separation-individuation, and mourning in the analytic cure. This bias is likely motivated by unconscious fears of object loss, loss of love, castration, and superego condemnation, each of which in turn may threaten loss of self-cohesion.

Some people (the "linkers") have a "feminine" bias towards similarity: they want everything to touch, merge, and be the same, and have little tolerance for differences. If they succeed in sublimating this bias toward *Eros*, they become the creative unifiers or integrators. Others (the "separators") have a "masculine" bias towards difference: they want to differentiate and keep things apart and have little tolerance for similarity and merger. If they succeed in sublimating this bias towards *Thanatos*, they become the creative discriminators or distinguishers. But, ultimately, neither bias, to the extent that it entails a defensive repression of one or the other component of what Freud (1905d) regarded as our inherent bisexuality, can alone result in the achievement of optimal psychic functioning because this requires attention to reality in its entirety, both similarities and differences. Hence, a more adequate conception of analysis is as both metaphor-analysis and contrast-analysis: it promotes both the transformation of absolute similarity into relative similarity (by pointing to implicit difference), and the transformation of absolute difference (splitting) into relative difference (by pointing to implicit similarity). For just as different things can never be absolutely the same and yet remain different, so different things can never be absolutely different, without being similar in at least some respects. Hillman's (1972) conclusion that "Analysis cannot constitute this cure until it, too, is no longer masculine in psychology" (p. 292), needs to be supplemented by the recognition that an opposing perspective that is exclusively "feminine" is no better. We are cured when we are no longer only either "masculine" or "feminine" in psyche—that is, when we manage to stop "essentialising" or privileging one element of our "bisexual" nature at the expense of the other.

Needless to say, the reason the terms "masculine" and "feminine" are placed in quotation marks throughout this chapter is to indicate that the equations in which they figure belong to the Imaginary and Symbolic orders (Lacan, 1982). In other words, they refer to image and symbol rather than to anything biological, to what is imagined to be masculine or feminine in the order of human culture and not to what an "essentialising" perspective might regard as being literally, as opposed to metaphorically, the case. In a "contextualising" or semiotic perspective that restricts itself to the realm of *psychic reality* as the proper domain of psychoanalytic concern, the human subject is seen to be inevitably only figuratively masculine or feminine and never literally so. In bringing to light the repressed "bisexuality" upon which the fictions or tropes that constitute our sexual identities are founded, psychoanalysis reveals the constructed, dramatic, and imaginal quality of human identity (the "ego" or "self") as such. However inclined we may be to take ourselves seriously in our roles as masculine and feminine actors—and no one is recommending we switch parts or leave the stage—we are wise to remember that, as in all of our performances, in our sexual dramas we are never a man or a woman "in the way a table is a table" (Sartre, 1943). We forget or repress this awareness only at the cost of falling into what Sartre described as "bad faith" or the "spirit of solemnity", a phenomenon that I have discussed as a defensive regression involving the literalisation of metaphor and contrast, and which Lacan explained as the narcissistic alienation of the "ego" maintained by the primal and ongoing repression of the otherness within me (the unconscious) which would give the lie to my cherished identity and which, fortunately, periodically leads me to forget or mistake my lines.

The tendency for one or another image of absolute similarity or difference to hold us captive arises either from genuine ignorance of other possibilities or from a defence against the affects of anxiety and depression associated with the full range of infantile danger situations. We can only speculate about the factors contributing to a person's bias towards similarity, *Eros*, and "femininity", or towards difference, *Thanatos*, and "masculinity", and the resulting personality orientations towards saying "Yes" (agreeing, linking, and merging) on the one hand, and saying "No" (disagreeing, breaking links, separating, and individuating) on the other. Factors such as, for example, the role of a depressed and withdrawn mother in the early development of the "linkers" and the corresponding role of an impinging, intrusive, and dominating mother, or a more general need to "dis-identify from mother" (Greenson, 1968), in the early formation of the "separators" might be important. However, such pure types are non-existent because *Eros* and *Thanatos*, integrating and disintegrating tendencies, "femininity" and "masculinity", inevitably coexist in a greater or lesser degree of fusion; because both types of danger situation may motivate both personality orientations; and because both orientations may coexist on different levels of the personality structure and even serve to defend against each other.

As was suggested, it seems that such biases are reflected in psychoanalytic theory itself. Although a predisposition towards union may lead to a preference for a metaphorical concept of analysis as mothering, an inclination towards separation may underlie acceptance of a model of analysis as fathering. But despite its patriarchalism in other respects, it seems apparent that the bias of the "linkers", those predisposed to privilege similarity over difference, finds expression in the classical theory of the infantile danger situations, a theory that in focusing upon *loss* (of the object, its love, the phallus, superego approval) implicitly downplays those dangers having more to do with the object's overwhelming or malevolent *presence* than with its *absence*. The Freudian myth of man's eternal longing to "refind" (Freud, 1905d, p. 222) the lost object of primary identification and re-establish the oceanic bliss or Nirvana of primary narcissism (Freud, 1920g, 1930a; Grunberger, 1979) is only half the story: it needs to be complemented by insight into the equally primordial and eternal wish to "re-lose" or "re-destroy" the primary object, the primary identification (Greenson, 1968), and Eden itself, regarded as a dubious paradise, more as a prison or a coffin than a haven. And despite their matriarchalism in other respects, in the work of theorists such as Klein, Winnicott, and Mahler, the Freudian bias towards *Eros* (a reflection of Freud's idealised image of the mother-infant relation) is balanced to some extent by insight into wishes to destroy links, resist impingement, separate, individuate, and guard autonomy, wishes associated with *Thanatos* understood as the psychic desire to separate in the service of independence or self-cohesion, whether this aim leads in the direction of literal life or death. It is perhaps at least partly in this bias of the Freudian tradition towards *Eros* (only partially corrected in 1920 with the introduction of the final dual drive theory) that the explanation lies for its relative failure to recognise the importance of (i.e., its relative repression of) the role of the destructive mother-image in the genesis of various types of psychopathology and, consequently, its tendency to privilege anxieties concerning loss over those having to do with impingement, annihilation, or merger.

The association of integrating tendencies, metaphor, libido, *Eros*, and "femininity" on the one hand, and disintegrating tendencies, contrast, aggression, *Thanatos*, and "masculinity" on the other, need imply no commitment to an "instinct" or "drive" theory of these phenomena—a view that in identifying the human motive with a biological urge itself literalises a metaphor. To make use of Freud's psychological observations of our dual desires to merge and to separate, to create and to destroy links, we need not overstep the proper boundaries of psychoanalytic concern with *psychic reality* (the realm of meaning, myth, and motive) and embrace the implausible biological speculations in which the metaphorical "forces" of *Eros* and *Thanatos* are both literalised and allegedly explained. Just as certain suicidal individuals literalise their longings for metaphoric death and rebirth and for radical separation from a self metaphorically conceived as hopelessly spoiled, and confuse such mythical quests (which, far from being "natural" are themselves founded upon metaphor) with a wish to literally die, so on the level of theory Freud reifies both the human wish for connection or integration and the longing for separation or disintegration and reduces *Eros* to sexual instinct and *Thanatos* to a literal biological drive towards death. Understood on the purely psychological level, however, Freud's (1940a) reflections concerning the twin desires to unite (metaphor) and to separate (contrast) possess enduring value: "The aim of the first of these basic instincts [*Eros*] is to establish ever greater unities and to preserve them thus—in short, to bind together; the aim of the second [*Thanatos*] is, on the contrary, to undo connections ..." (p. 147).

The connection between metaphor and the longing to "refind" (Freud, 1905d, p. 222) the lost object is discussed in a literary context by Frye (1963) whose distinction between two phases of human consciousness echoes Freud's discussion of primary identification and its loss. "The first ... was a state of identity, a feeling that everything around us was part of us, and the second is the ordinary state of consciousness, or separation, where art and science begin" (Frye, 1963, p. 9). Following Wallace Stevens, Frye locates "the motive for metaphor" in our longing to recapture "that original lost sense of identity with our surroundings ..." (p. 9) and in "... a desire to associate and finally to identify, the human mind with what goes on outside it" (p. 11). But when Frye goes on to assert that "[T]he only genuine joy you can have is in those rare moments when you feel that although we know in part, as Paul says, we are also a part of what we know" (p. 11), his own bias towards similarity is revealed. For to play on a title of Balint's (1959), in addition to the thrills of regression and fusional experience (aside from its terrors), there are the joys of separation in which, as a part of what we know, we feel, sometimes with elation and at others with anxiety or despair, that we are inevitably also *apart from* what we know.

In this connection it is interesting to note that whereas Frye emphasises the fusional aim of metaphor, Searles (1962) suggests that "Perhaps the reason why so many metaphors have a peculiarly poignant beauty is because each of them kindles in us, momentarily, a dim memory of the time when we lost the outer world—when we first realised that the outer world is outside, and we are unbridgeably apart from it, and alone" (p. 583). The resolution of these apparently contradictory views of metaphor as on the one hand unifying and on the other separating lies in recognition that Frye is referring to the fusional quality of "dead" or literalised metaphor which conveys a sense of absolute similarity purged of all difference, whereas Searles refers to the sense of difference maintained by "live" metaphor in which similarity is recognised as only relative. A "live" metaphor symbolises both our lost identity with the other and our sense that it *is* lost.

But I have expressly avoided saying that "live" metaphor symbolises the fact that the outer world is lost, for such metaphysical statements descend from phenomenology or psychology as the description and analysis of experience, to ontological assertion about the nature of ultimate reality. Whereas Frye narrowly escapes this descent into metaphysics by speaking of the *feeling* of unity or *sense* of identity with our surroundings—even though his bias towards similarity is clear from his statement that "the only genuine joy you can have is in those rare moments" of mystic union—Searles succumbs to a tragic, existential ontology that epistemologically privileges separation and difference over union and similarity when he refers to the time "when we first realised that the outer world is outside, and we are unbridgeably apart from it, and alone". To descend (or ascend, depending upon your point of view) in this way from phenomenology to ontology or metaphysics is to exceed the proper boundaries of psychology as the study of psychic reality for philosophic speculation about the ultimate nature of reality *per se*; it is to pass beyond the study of human experience in the Imaginary and Symbolic orders (Lacan, 1977), for philosophic assertion about the ultimate nature of the Real. To epistemologically privilege either term of the binary opposition *similarity/difference* or *symbiosis/separation* and regard it as capturing the ultimate reality is itself to literalise a metaphor and to fall prey to what Burke (1939) called the "essentialising" (as opposed to a "contextualising") hermeneutic, a fall into metaphysics that Derrida (1978, 1981) regarded as characteristic of our "logocentric" Western tradition.

According to Ricoeur (1970), "'Symbols give rise to thought' [as outlined in Ricoeur (1960)], but they are also the birth of idols. That is why the critique of idols remains the condition of the conquest of symbols" (p. 543). When relative similarities are absolutised into identities—and to cite but a few examples, women literally equated with castrated men, human motives with animal instincts, human selves with ceramic artifacts, or psychological dysfunctions with medical illnesses—the consequence is a psychic regression from the differentiated experience characteristic of the secondary process and the depressive position to the undifferentiation or fusion that characterises the primary process and the paranoid-schizoid position. It is important, however, to recognise that in addition to involving fusion or undifferentiation, regressive mental functioning also entails varying degrees of defusion or splitting. It is not simply that in the primary processes metaphors are literalised such that analogies are reduced to identities, but also that contrasts based on recognition of relative differences are absolutised into antitheses, binary oppositions, or splits: the sexes, for example, being thought of literally as opposites; or psychosis and neurosis dichotomised; or the "drive-structure" and "relational-structure" models of the mind represented as simply irreconcilable (Greenberg & Mitchell, 1983, chs. 1 & 12); or human relations forced into the reductive pattern of such (phallic-Oedipal, anal, and oral) binary roles as castrator/castrated, superior/inferior and feeder/fed; or the paranoid-schizoid (PS) and depressive (D) positions of mental life (Klein, 1946) dichotomised and dualistically opposed rather than dialectically interrelated.

The one-sided conception of psychopathology as "forbidden mixture" developed by Chasseguet-Smirgel (1984) in "Perversion and the Universal Law" needs to be complemented by recognition of the pathologies of "forbidden separation". Whereas the Bible, as Chasseguet-Smirgel points out, certainly does proscribe regressive fusion, as in incest and other violations of the boundaries separating the sexes and the generations, it also prohibits regressive defusion, as in the splitting of the Godhead which is the object of the monotheistic critique of dualism: "Hear, O Israel, the Lord our God is one Lord" (*Deuteronomy* 6:4 *KJV*). Since, in my view, the true "universal law" proscribes both regressive fusion and regressive splitting, it necessarily opposes such modern forms of Manichaeism as the Freudian and Kleinian dualism of *Eros* and *Thanatos*, but only when understood as primary, biologically-given libidinal and aggressive drives. For instead of recognising the universal conflict between the forces of life and death, love and hate, intrinsic to our human nature as the consequence of an inevitable "fall" from an Edenic condition of original integrity—the Blakean (1788–94) Fall from Innocence into Experience—instinctual (biological) dualism, like Gnostic interpretations of the doctrine of "original sin" that lose sight of the "original innocence" before the Fall, reifies the resulting ambivalence and splitting and mistakes it for the biologically-given essence of the mind.

Kierkegaard (1849) interprets the *Genesis* story of the eating of the fruit of the tree of knowledge of good and evil not as history but as myth.

It is a mythical account of the loss of animal and infantile innocence with the emergence of self-awareness at some point in the second year of life—that is, of a self that as a synthesis of mind and body, possibility and necessity, is capable of relating to and realising itself as such. Though a passionate Christian (albeit an equally passionate critic of Christendom), Kierkegaard implies, *contra* Augustinian doctrine, that the preverbal infant is innocent until falling into sin with the rise of language, self-consciousness, and freedom. Unlike the Augustinian view, this is compatible with the Jewish doctrine that sin is not "original" but universally and inevitably developed at a later age owing to an inclination towards it. According to Rabbi Reuven Hammer (n.d.), "Judaism teaches that human beings are not basically sinful. We come into the world neither carrying the burden of sin committed by our ancestors nor tainted by it. Rather, sin, *het*, is the result of our human inclinations, the *yetzer*, which must be properly channelled."

In my view, regressive splitting and fusion function as defences against core anxieties of absolute incorporation or engulfment on the one hand and absolute separation or abandonment on the other. But while the fundamental anxieties motivate the various concretised associations, fixed ideas, and black and white thinking—the psychic rigidification or mental totalitarianism—that serve to defend against them, they do not merely give rise to defensive reification but are themselves manifestations *of* it. For such anxieties embody the myths of totalised identity (complete loss of boundaries or de-differentiation) and totalised difference (complete loss of connection or links) that always already reflect regressive fusion and defusion.

Although these twin anxieties are most evident in the borderline "need/fear" dilemma that represents unsuccessful resolution of the "rapprochement crisis" of separation-individuation (Mahler, Pine, & Bergman, 1975), I believe that in more primitive and global forms they also underlie psychotic, and in milder forms neurotic, pathology as well. In other words, there is a continuum of psychopathological reactions of undifferentiation and disintegration ranging from the mild (neurotic), to the moderate (borderline and narcissistic) and the severe (psychotic). Emancipation from psychic enslavement by the myths of oneness and separateness in their varying degrees and manifestations requires a therapeutic process of demythologisation or deliteralisation in which "dead" or "dying" metaphors and contrasts are "resurrected" or "revived". In coming to be recognised as merely relative the myths of absolute engulfment and abandonment lose their power to dominate our subjectivity. In returning to "life" they at the same time liberate us from the "deadly" serious, primary process world of psychotic incorporation and polarisation, fusion and defusion. In this way, therapeutic deconstruction permits a degree of transcendence of the splitting and fusion characteristic of PS and advance to the more differentiated and integrated secondary process order of reality and relatively mature (secondary) identifications characteristic of D.

But today older unilinear models of mental growth as from primary to secondary process or PS $\rightarrow$ D have been transcended owing to the overcoming of the PS splitting entailed in conceptions of primary process and PS as all-bad and secondary process and D as all-good. For there is good in primary process (vitality, order, creativity) and in PS (passion, commitment, decisiveness), and there is bad in secondary process (disaffected or devitalised abstraction, intellectual intelligence devoid of emotional intelligence) and in D (excessive dispassion, indecision, fence-sitting, paralysis). In this light modern Kleinians have revised the formula of development to describe a flexible oscillation between the two positions (PS $\leftarrow \rightarrow$ D) that attempts to combine what is creative and useful in each. Another approach to overcoming the inadequate dualism of primary/secondary process and PS/D is Winnicott's (1955, 1971) conceptualisation of the transitional area between primary and secondary process, PS and D, the area of illusion and of cultural experience. In this light we can speak of a "transitional process" in which similarities and differences are neither fully registered nor denied. It is an area of play in which there is a willing suspension of both belief and disbelief.

In contrast to both the extreme undifferentiation and unintegration characteristic of primitive incorporation and polarisation (PS), and the domain of secondary identification and differentiation (D), lies the transitional area of partial or incomplete differentiation and integration characteristic of transitional phenomena and the introjective/projective organisation (Meissner, 1981). In the latter domain a psychic space, hitherto entirely "foreclosed" (Lacan, 1977), incompletely established, collapsed, or blurred is opened or reopened permitting the subject to "live" through the "play" of signification. It seems we are only free to play and to create when we are no longer seriously threatened, that is, when we have some critical distance, not only from the twin dangers of engulfment and abandonment (PS), but also from an excessively rationalistic and dispassionate outlook (D). Only through opening up this transitional space can the subject be liberated from the primary identifications and binary oppositions (all-good/all-bad; heaven/hell; attacker/victim) characteristic of the primary process, as well as the excessively rational, mundane, and "serious" as opposed to playful attitude characteristic of secondary process thinking and of the depressive position.

The re-projection of introjected objects into the transitional space offered, for example, by art, religion, marriage, or psychoanalytic therapy sometimes represents the cracking up, as it were, of the narcissistic shell out of which the Lacanian (1977) "subject" or Winnicottian (1960b) "true self" may be born, allowing a vitalising type of play and illusion to occur in the transitional space between PS and D. In this way, transitional phenomena may come to serve the function clearly attributed to them by Winnicott (1955), namely, to facilitate the crucial *transition* to mature object relations in reality. But since, according to Eliot (1935), "Humankind cannot bear very much reality" (p. 8), transitional phenomena also provide a much-needed holiday from reality-testing, a vacation from a mundane or profane reality in which the sacred may be remembered and worshipped and passionate love rekindled.

* * *

Demythologising of "dead" metaphor and contrast has long been practised in theology (Bultmann, 1958, 1961; Macquarrie, 1955). For while religion is myth, it is not merely myth. Long before Freud (1916–17) revealed the conscious ego as "not even master in its own psychic house" (p. 285), Jesus asked that his crucifiers be forgiven "for they know not what they do" (*Luke* 23:34 *KJV*). And long before Freud (1920g) grasped the fact that his eighteen-month-old grandson was attempting to master his rapprochement crisis through his *Fort!/Da!* game with the spool, the Gospels gave us the "good news" that crucifixion is followed by resurrection, Good Friday by Easter Sunday—or, as Winnicott (1969) made the point in another context:

> A new feature thus arrives in the theory of object-relating. The subject says to the object: "I destroyed you," and the object is there to receive the communication. From now on the subject says: "Hullo object!" "I destroyed you." "I love you." "You have value for me because of your survival of my destruction of you." "While

I am loving you I am all the time destroying you in (unconscious) *fantasy.*" (p. 90; Winnicott's emphasis)

As Frye (1991) repeatedly argued in relation to the Bible as myth, while not to be taken literally, as in every sort of fundamentalism, neither must rejection of such literalism extend to the myth itself and, hence, to loss of the important wisdom it contains. What Frye called for is not the *destruction* of myth and metaphor, but rather their *deconstruction* or *demythologisation*. The application of this method to the doctrine of transubstantiation that literalises the metaphor of bread and wine as the body and blood of Christ is not necessarily to devalue the Eucharist. On the other hand, insistence upon the purely symbolic nature of the ritual, promoting what is taken to be a more mature mode of Christian communion through secondary rather than primary identification with Jesus as an idealised—but not idolised—ego ideal escapes what is essentially psychotic only to be captured by what is excessively sane. What is lost is the area of creative play in the transitional area in which both belief and disbelief are held in suspension or temporarily transcended.

Like Bonhoeffer (1953), who viewed Bultmann's project of demythologisation of the Gospels as a "typical liberal reduction process (the 'mythological' elements of Christianity are dropped, and Christianity is reduced to its 'essence')" (p. 110), Frye (1991) insisted that the attempt "to squeeze everything possible into ordinary history, with the bulges of the incredible that still stick out being smoothed away by a process called demythologising" is destined to failure for "... the Gospels are all myth and all bulge, and the operation does not work" (p. 17). Viewing demythologising as the misguided attempt to translate myth into "historically factual narratives" (Frye in Cayley, 1992, p. 178), Frye (1991) argued that "It's impossible because the Bible is a tissue of metaphors from beginning to end" (p. 177).

Likewise, Bonhoeffer (1953) wrote: "I am of the view that the full content, including the mythological concepts, must be maintained. The New Testament is not a mythological garbing of the universal truth; this mythology (resurrection and so on) is the thing itself—but the concepts must be interpreted in such a way as not to make religion a pre-condition of faith ..." (p. 110). Again, he wrote: "My view of it today would be not that he [Bultmann] went too far, as most people seem to think, but that he did not go far enough. It is not only the mythological conceptions, such as the miracles, the ascension and the like (which are not in principle separable from the conceptions of God, faith and so on) that are problematic, but the 'religious' conceptions themselves. You cannot as Bultmann imagines, separate God and miracles, but you do have to be able to interpret and proclaim both of them in a 'non-religious' sense" (p. 94). In calling for concepts to be interpreted "in such a way as not to make religion a pre-condition of faith" Bonhoeffer offers us the important distinction between religion and faith, a distinction that opens up for us the possibility of a post-religious or non-religious faith.

Whatever Bultmann may have meant by demythologising, in the sense in which I am employing the concept it refers precisely to the enterprise Bonhoeffer and Frye were themselves engaged in: the enlivening or resurrection of myth ("dead" metaphor) through its recognition *qua* metaphor, as distinct from its literalisation or misrecognition as referring to facts of the external, historical, or physical, as opposed to the internal, psychic, existential, spiritual, or metaphysical orders of reality. It is precisely such literalisation that, I believe, Bonhoeffer referred to as "religion" and such deliteralisation that he had in mind in calling for a "religionless Christianity"—a non-religious Christian faith. In a psychoanalytic context, such therapeutic deliteralisation permits transcendence, not only of our patients' concretisations, but also of the various forms of psychoanalytic fundamentalism which have at times given our profession more the appearance of a religion than a science. Bonhoeffer's point is valid with respect to both theological and psychoanalytic concepts: "You ... have to be able to interpret and proclaim ... them in a 'non-religious' sense." In other words, if we need a "religionless Christianity" we are in equal need of a "religionless psychoanalysis".

It is characteristic of an ideology, almost a defining feature of one, to fail to recognise itself as such. Hanly (1993), for example, writes of the regression of psychoanalysis into ideology on the part of the insufficiently analysed psychoanalyst who has failed to resolve his or her idealisation of the training analyst. But whether those who are at least aware of potential ideological misuses of psychoanalysis extend this awareness to include the widespread idolisation of Freud by the Freudians, Klein by the Kleinians, Kohut by the Kohutians, Lacan by the Lacanians, etc., or at least include their own denomination in this critique and not just those of the others, is an open question. One used to hear rumours, for example, of psychoanalytic institutes that refused admission to candidates or potential faculty members known to be "religious". Whether such exclusion was extended to those whose religiosity was expressed in a dogmatic adherence to psychoanalytic ideologies, classical or revisionist, is quite another matter. Of course, if it were so extended such institutes would self-destruct, for their very exclusion of the "religious" (unless their interpretation of this concept were sufficiently sophisticated to include the religions of psychoanalysis, which I doubt) is evidence of their own unrecognised (and therefore all the more dangerous) religiosity.

Although far more egregious examples of the literalisation of psychoanalytic metaphors are, regrettably, not hard to find, even the thinking of as philosophically sophisticated a psychoanalytic theorist as Roy Schafer can be shown to suffer in this regard. In asking whether internalisation is a process or a fantasy, Schafer (1976, ch. 8) would have done better to recognise that his opposition between a literal psychological process and a mere fantasy is inappropriate. While internalisation may certainly be a fantasy, it is also a metaphor and our psychology—like any other science for that matter—is essentially comprised of metaphors of this sort. I have earlier expressed this view with respect to those who are concerned about the potential reification of the concepts of id, ego, superego, conscience, and psychic structure itself. These are neither real entities, nor mere fantasies; they are metaphors. To his credit, in reviewing this issue Meissner (1981), unlike Schafer, is uncomfortable with the implication that internalisation is mere fantasy; he wants to retain the concept as part of a scientific psychology of psychic structure-formation. There is no problem with this once we recognise that psychological science, like all science, is unavoidably metaphorical.

Our concepts are metaphors. But it is important to recognise that whereas the metaphors of natural science refer to the orders of inorganic and organic substance, those of psychology, philosophy, and theology refer to what Freud called "psychic reality", the post-biological, superorganic, existential, or spiritual order of the *psyche* or soul. (I prefer *psyche* to *mind* because of the excessively rationalist and intellectualist connotations of the latter.) The soul can only "live" in the space opened up when "dead" metaphor and contrast undergo "resurrection". For this to occur "crucifixion" must first have been accomplished and the "brokenness", "fallen-ness", "abjection", and "dereliction" inflicted by the primordial "cut" (the fall [up] into language, self-awareness, separateness, and freedom) accepted rather than denied. For Lacan (1977), "The Holy Spirit is the entry of the signifier into the world" (p. 48).

No doubt recognition and "acceptance of castration", symbolised in Christianity by the stations of the Cross and the holes in the hands and feet of Jesus and the wound in his side, has always been difficult for human beings to accomplish. While they do not "foreclose" such recognition altogether, the regressive forces at work in the contemporary culture of narcissism make it difficult to maintain; while not entirely closing up the primal wound, they make it difficult to keep open.

It goes without saying that a mature religion like a healthy psychological science should be free from the idolatry that arises from the literalisation of metaphor. Although given our current cultural regression things appear to be getting worse rather than better in this regard, it is regrettably the case that human individuals and the institutions they create have always been infected by the confusion of the spirit and the letter. Jesus was impatient with his disciples' chronic tendency to take his parables literally:

> And he cautioned them, saying, "Watch out—beware of the yeast of the Pharisees and the yeast of Herod." They said to one another, "It is because we have no bread." And becoming aware of it, Jesus said to them, "Why are you talking about having no bread? Do you still not perceive or understand? Are your hearts hardened? Do you have eyes, and fail to see? Do you have ears, and fail to hear? And do you not remember?". (*Mark* 8:14–18 *NRSV*)

A good deal of biblical teaching may be understood as a critique of our perpetual "fall" into such literalism and a call to transcend it by enlivening or "resurrecting" our "dead" metaphors and contrasts.

To fundamentalist psychoanalysts, whether "classical" or "revisionist", the employment of their sacred terms as metaphors and the mixing of theoretical frameworks which they insist must remain apart—like the meat and the dairy products in orthodox Jewish practice—appears heretical, promiscuous, and perverse. However, as Frye (1991) among others has pointed out, ideas that taken literally are absolutely incompatible frequently appear complementary on the metaphorical level. For example, whereas Greenberg and Mitchell (1983, chs. 1 & 12) insisted that the "drive-structure" and "relational-structure" models of the mind are simply irreconcilable, reflecting incompatible Hobbesian individualist and Aristotelian, Rousseauian, or Marxian social conceptions of human nature, once we appreciate the metaphorical status of Freud's concept of the "drive" (*Trieb* not *Instinkt*) and, by liberating it from its alleged somatic sources, recognise it as human motivation or "desire" in the broadest sense, then the two models become fundamentally compatible, for such "drives" are already relational. Without announcing the fact, this is essentially the strategy pursued after Hartmann's (1939) introduction of the concept of an initial "undifferentiated matrix" out of which the id, like the ego and superego, develops, by Jacobson (1964) and Kernberg (1976) for whom "drive" amounts to an affective-cognitive gestalt composed of self and object representations together with linking affects developed in the context of the earliest object relations. Loewald (1980) makes it explicit: "Instincts, understood as psychic, motivational, forces, become organised as such through interactions within a psychic field consisting originally of the mother-child (psychic) unit" (pp. 127–128).

* * *

Following Winnicott (1955), Modell (1968), and Meissner (1981), we recognise the "transitional area" between fully "alive" or secondary process thinking, and completely "dead" or primary process thought. Between the subjective object and primitive incorporation and polarisation, and the objective object and mature identification and differentiation, lies the field of transitional phenomena and the introjective-projective organisation that represents its internalisation. But recognising the significance of transitional phenomena in no way requires one to devalue objectivity, as in a good deal of the postmodern discourse dominant in academia over the past few decades. In this vein, some writers in the area of psychoanalysis and religion came to regard the transitional area, the area of mystery and paradox, not as a necessary but temporary resting-place from the strain of reality-testing, a means to facilitate the difficult transition from subjective to objective, but as an end in itself, a superior place to settle in and take up residence abandoning the quest for objectivity altogether. While recognition of the essential psychological functions served by transitional phenomena provides a much-needed corrective to Freud's reductive devaluation of illusion or the virtual in religion (while valuing it in art), writers such as Meissner (1984) and J. W. Jones (1991) sought to redefine religion itself as transitional.

Although in *The Future of An Illusion*, Freud (1927c) considered religion illusion (a belief not known to be either true or false but believed because one wants it to be true), only three years later, in *Civilization and Its Discontents*, without explaining his reasoning for doing so, Freud (1930a) redefines it as delusion (a belief known to be false but believed nonetheless). It has not always been noticed that this shift from agnosticism to atheism technically meant Freud himself surrendered to illusion, believing God does not exist because he wants this to be true, when neither the existence nor the non-existence of God can be proved. But although for this reason agnosticism is the only scientifically tenable position, the fact is that most theoretical agnostics are practical atheists, not denying the existence of God but operating on the assumption he does not exist until encountering convincing evidence that he does. In the modern secular world many people find it impossible to believe in the existence of a supernatural god or gods and it is with this definition of religion in mind that, with Freud, and against Meissner and Jones, I consider religious belief delusional, consigning it not to the transitional area, which in my view is beyond both belief and disbelief, but to the paranoid-schizoid position, the field of subjective or narcissistic rather than transitional phenomena.

Of course "religion" is often defined more broadly than belief in a supernatural god or gods, to include, for example, non-theistic religions such as Buddhism, but the analysis offered here is confined to theism. In today's secular world many people find belief in the supernatural incompatible with sanity. But faith is another matter altogether. Although "faith" has often been understood as a matter of beliefs and propositions held not merely in the absence of support from reason and evidence but even against them (e.g., the *credo quia absurdum*), I am employing the term in its distinctly Hebraic rather than Hellenistic sense, not as a matter of belief as in religion, but of devotion, a matter of the heart rather than the mind or intellect. Although falling in love can sometimes lead to psychosis it need not: it can remain, while it lasts, in the transitional area, and even when the honeymoon is over and the work of mature loving in the depressive position begins, romantic, transitional passion can often be rekindled. In my view, Christian faith, distinct from Christianity as religion, is a matter of falling in love with Jesus. Certainly one can fall out of love; but sometimes one can fall back in, repeatedly. As Kee (1971) has pointed out, today belief in a supernatural God constitutes a major stumbling-block in the way of Christian faith:

It is not generally recognized by religious people that while a man may choose to have faith, he cannot choose belief. What we believe—about ourselves, our society, our world—depends on the culture in which we are raised. ... In a religious age men have religious beliefs; in a secular age they have secular beliefs, that is, they interpret and explain the world in its own terms. Ours is a secular age and that is why in our time all religious beliefs have become problematic, especially belief in God. And if belief in God is the presupposition, the prior condition of Christianity, then Christian faith will not be possible in our secular age. To demand faith is one thing, to require belief is quite another, since changing our beliefs is not something that can be brought about by an act of will. (p. ix)

In Kee's view, and in mine, the demand for belief in a supernatural God is a false stumbling-block that stands in the way of encountering the real one: "If in accepting Jesus Christ as the way, the truth and the life, men are required to accept first the ancient world-view with its patently false account of the natural world, then there can be no question of becoming Christian" (p. xv). But the end of religion confronts us once again with the real faith issue: what are we to make of Jesus Christ? Faced with this question, it is possible today for atheists to answer with Christina Rossetti (1872): "What I can I give Him, give my Heart." This is Christian faith, not religion. It lives in the transitional area, beyond belief and disbelief.

Meissner (1984) and J. W. Jones (1991) do not distinguish religion and faith in this way. They avoid the question of secular Christianity by viewing religion itself as transitional rather than, as in Freud's view and mine, delusional. Their attempt to move religion out of PS into the transitional area was an attempt to go "beyond demythologising" to the valorisation of the paradoxical and that which cannot be clearly differentiated or integrated. But this celebration of the transitional entails a misrepresentation of Winnicott's own attitude, for he did not valorise the transitional, however much he, unlike Freud, sympathised with it. For Winnicott, the transitional was literally that: its function was both to facilitate the navigation of the difficult passage to the state at which the painful and yet liberating fact of separation between subject and object could finally be borne, and also to provide a periodic resting-place from the strain of reality-testing. Winnicott remained in this sense a Freudian: he would have agreed that "In the last resort we must begin to love in order not to fall ill" (Freud, 1914c, p. 85). And Winnicott (1963) clearly believed that a mature love, characterised by a "capacity for concern", depends upon the subject having, with the indispensable help of transitional phenomena, successfully separated from and mourned the loss of the subjective object and, in this way, achieved recognition of and mature relatedness to the objective object. This view of the ultimate function of transitional phenomena is in no way to deny the crucial importance of the area of cultural experience in which both the mundane objective world and the psychotic subjective world are occasionally transcended. It is one thing to celebrate the transitional as a temporary suspension of both belief and disbelief, quite another to seek to exploit the transitional to justify moving "beyond demythologising" back to belief.

For Heidegger (1927), it is by means of a "marginal experience"—such as the shocking recognition of the reality of personal death—that an individual may be shaken out of inauthentic and awakened to authentic existence. I think there is some justification for associating the narcissism of Winnicott's relations with subjective objects with the pathology of his "false self" and with Heidegger's inauthentic existence, and Winnicott's relations with objective objects with his "true self" and with Heidegger's authentic being-in-the-world. Contrary to the psychoanalytic fundamentalism that insists upon taking theoretical concepts exclusively on the literal level I think the following equations are—no doubt at the risk of some oversimplification—nevertheless both justifiable and useful.

Freud	*pleasure principle*		*reality principle*
Freud	narcissism		object love
Klein	PS position		D position
Lacan	Imaginary		Symbolic
Lacan	specular ego (Imaginary)		subject (Symbolic)
Mahler	sep-individuation phase		self & object constancy
Winnicott	subjective object	transitional object	objective object
Winnicott	false self		true self

One of the potential benefits to be derived from lining up disparate concepts in this way is the discovery of conceptual parallels that may lead us to reconsider the usual way in which a particular concept is generally understood. For example, it may at first seem strange to associate Winnicott's (1960b) "true self" with his (1969) "objective object" and his "false self" with the "subjective object". Thinking in terms of the developmental timetable, it is tempting to associate the true self with simple somatopsychic being that, existing from the beginning would overlap chronologically with relations with subjective rather than objective objects. Similarly, it is usual to think of the false self as a later development reflecting a certain dissociation from simple somatopsychic being; it therefore seems strange to associate it with relations with subjective objects.

On further reflection, however—and especially in light of Winnicott's (1967) knowledge of and reference to Lacan's (1977, ch. 1) notion of the birth of the "ego" in a state of alienation in "the mirror phase"—it seems preferable to distinguish the true self from original somatopsychic being and from the time of relations with subjective objects and to see it, instead, as an authentic sense of self acquired precisely, like Lacan's (Symbolic) "subject" as distinct from his specular (Imaginary) "ego", through the overcoming of the narcissism inherent in relations with subjective objects. In this view, Winnicott's "false self" would correspond to Lacan's "ego" as a narcissistic structure reflecting an omnipotent denial of reality, including the reality of one's somatopsychic being as *being-toward-death*.

In "The Use of an Object and Relating through Identifications", Winnicott (1969) is concerned with "the move away from self-containment and relating to subjective objects into the realm of object-usage" (p. 88). One of the confusing things about this paper is that Winnicott has an eccentric use of the terms "relating" and "usage"—he employs them in precisely an opposite sense from that in which they are normally understood. What he is really concerned with is the shift from a narcissistic attitude towards objects as extensions or projections of the self to what most would regard as a more advanced mode of object-relating in which the object is recognised as separate and distinct from the self. Winnicott is concerned with the process whereby the subject comes to place the object "outside the area of the subject's omnipotent control; that is, the subject's perception of the object as an external phenomenon, not as a projective entity, in fact recognition of it as an entity in its own right" (p. 89).

The originality of Winnicott's contribution lies in his recognition that "This change ... means that the subject destroys the object" (p. 89), "... that after 'subject [narcissistically] relates to object' comes 'subject destroys object' (as it becomes external); and then may come *'object survives* destruction by the subject'" (p. 90; Winnicott's emphasis). He continues:

> A new feature thus arrives in the theory of object-relating. The subject says to the object: "I destroyed you." "I love you." "You have value for me because of your survival of my destruction of you." "While I am loving you I am all the time destroying you in (unconscious) *fantasy*." Here fantasy begins for the individual. The subject can now *use* [i.e., relate to] the object that has survived. (p. 90; Winnicott's emphasis)

Winnicott continues:

> It is important to note that it is not only that the subject destroys the object because the object is placed outside the area of omnipotent control. It is equally significant to state this the other way round and to say that it is the destruction of the object that places the object outside the area of the subject's omnipotent control. In these ways the object develops its own autonomy and life, and (if it survives) contributes-in to the subject, according to its own properties.
>
> In other words, because of the survival of the object, the subject may now have started to live a life in the world of objects, and so the subject stands to gain immeasurably; but the price has to be paid in acceptance of the ongoing destruction in unconscious fantasy relative to object-relating.
>
> Let me repeat. This is a position that can be arrived at by the individual in early stages of emotional growth only through the actual survival of cathected objects that are at the time in process of becoming destroyed because real, becoming real because destroyed (being destructible and expendable). (p. 90)

In other words, for Winnicott, the subject is only able to achieve mature relations with objective objects through a process of separation from the subjective object—a process entailing both the "destruction" of the latter and, at the same time, a giving up of the illusion of omnipotence and the need for omnipotent control which underlies both enmeshment with the subjective object and resistance to recognising the otherness of the objective object.

Winnicott writes: "It is generally understood that the reality principle involves the individual in anger and reactive destruction, but my thesis is that the destruction plays its part in making the reality, placing the object outside the self" (p. 91). Or again: "The assumption is always there, in orthodox theory, that aggression is reactive to the encounter with the reality principle, whereas here it is the destructive drive that creates the quality of externality. This is central in the structure of my argument" (p. 93). Finally, according to Winnicott:

> *There is no anger* in the destruction of the object to which I am referring, though there could be said to be joy at the object's survival. From this moment, or arising out of this phase, the object is *in fantasy* always being destroyed. This quality of "always being destroyed" makes the reality of the surviving object felt as such, strengthens the feeling-tone, and contributes to object-constancy. The object can now be used [i.e., related to]. (p. 93; Winnicott's emphasis)

This subtle complex of insights of Winnicott's seems not to have been completely assimilated by the psychoanalytic community. Some critics reject his insight into the necessary role of destruction in establishing the reality principle on the grounds of what they take to be his acceptance of the assumption of an innate destructiveness. Referring to this aspect of Winnicott's thought, Bacal (Bacal & Newman, 1990), for example, states that: "Winnicott's view that the object becomes usable because it survives the infant's destructiveness, and that the infant develops a capacity for concern for the object as he becomes aware of his destructive intent, would be untenable to self psychologists, as they reject the idea of a primary destructiveness" (p. 191).

But a close reading of this essay, together with additional commentary on its central themes contained in Winnicott's (1989) posthumously published *Psychoanalytic Explorations*, reveals that Winnicott himself had a somewhat ambiguous attitude towards this assumption. In the original paper he writes that:

> It appears to me that the idea of a developmental phase essentially involving survival of object does affect the theory of the roots of

aggression. It is no good saying that a baby of a few days old envies the breast. It is legitimate, however, to say that at whatever age a baby begins to allow the breast an external position (outside the area of projection), then this means that destruction of the breast has become a feature. I mean the actual impulse to destroy. (p. 92)

While it is clear that Winnicott did not see destructiveness merely as a *reaction* to the perception of the otherness of the object—for he refers repeatedly to "the actual impulse to destroy" as playing a part in the establishment of the object *qua* other—it would be a mistake to conclude that by this "actual impulse to destroy" he is simply referring to the idea of innate destructiveness. He writes (1969):

It will be seen that, although destruction is the word I am using, this actual destruction belongs to the object's failure to survive. Without this failure, destruction remains potential. The word "destruction" is needed, not because the baby's impulse is to destroy, but because of the object's liability not to survive, which also means to suffer change in quality, in attitude. (p. 93)

So not only is there "no anger in the destruction of the object to which I am referring" (p. 93), but the destruction is only potential and only becomes actualised if the object fails to survive. This idea is quite distinct from any simple notion of a primary destructiveness.

Regarding the death instinct, in his posthumously published "The Use of an Object in the Context of *Moses and Monotheism*" (1969), Winnicott (1989) writes:

To warn the reader I should say that I have never been in love with the death instinct and it would give me happiness if I could relieve Freud of the burden of carrying it forever on his Atlas shoulders. To start with, the development of the theory from a statement of the fact that organic matter tends to return to the inorganic carries very small weight in terms of logic. There is no clear relationship between the two sets of ideas. Also, biology has never been happy about this part of metapsychology while on the whole there is room for mutuality between biology and psychoanalysis all along the line, up to the point of the death instinct. (p. 242)

Even more significantly, in his "Comments on My Paper 'The Use of an Object'" (1969), Winnicott (1989) states that "In this vitally important early stage the 'destructive' (fire-air or other) aliveness of the individual is simply a symptom of being alive ..." (p. 239). He continues: "I realise that it is this idea of a destructive first impulse that is difficult to grasp. It is this that needs attention and discussion. To help I wish to point out that I am referring to such things as *eagerness*" (p. 240). Hence, the infant's eagerness—perhaps its "ruthless" love (Winnicott, 1949)—is felt by the infant to be destructive if and when the object fails to survive. However, when the object does survive (and without retaliating or changing its attitude), then such eagerness and "ruthlessness" are either not felt to be destructive or, if so, such destructiveness can be integrated without disastrous consequences for self-esteem.

While some critics have dismissed Winnicott's thinking in this area on the mistaken grounds of his adherence to the concept of the death instinct, others reject what he has to say regarding the move away from the subjective through the transitional towards the objective object on the grounds that contemporary infant research (Stern, 1985) has called into question the idea of an early phase of undifferentiation between self and object which Freud's, Winnicott's, and Mahler's thinking assumes. Of course it was Melanie Klein's rejection of the notion of an initial stage of "primary narcissism" prior to object-relating that constituted one of her major divergences from orthodox Freudian thought. Today, however, in light of infant research it is widely acknowledged, even by those who long defended the notion, that the idea of an early phase of absolute undifferentiation, merger, or symbiosis must be abandoned, although this in no way invalidates other aspects of the theory of separation-individuation. However, in a sense, all this is beside the point. For whatever Freud may have meant by "primary narcissism" and Mahler, Pine, and Bergman (1975) by "symbiosis", by "secondary narcissism" and the "subjective object", Freud and Winnicott do not mean to refer to absolute undifferentiation at all; they are referring to a state in which the cognitively differentiated object is emotionally experienced primarily through projections of the subject's own phantasies and self representations and predominantly in terms of the subject's pressing needs. And they mean to contrast this sort of narcissistic object-relation to one in which the subject is more able to get beyond such projections and egocentric demands for need-satisfaction and to recognise and make contact with the real otherness of the object.

To associate maturity with successful separation-individuation and mourning is in no way to epistemologically privilege separation over connection in psychic life; it is merely to insist that a mature connection proceeds from and maintains a sense of separateness, just as a mature autonomy assumes an underlying sense of connection. It is essential to appreciate the crucial transitional (introjective and projective) dimension of experience lying between the purely subjective and the fully objective—between "dead" and fully "alive" metaphors and contrasts, and between psychotic incorporation and polarisation and healthy identification and self-definition. But the transitional area is beyond both belief and disbelief and constitutes no justification for belief (religion) as distinct from transitional celebrations of faith (devotion and love), or for withdrawal from the ongoing need to mourn the loss of the subjective object. We must resist the perennial temptation to reduce both psychosocial maturity and the faith that calls us to it to the celebration of connection over separation:

> Do not think that I have come to bring peace to the earth; I have not come to bring peace, but a sword. For I have come to set a man against his father, and a daughter against her mother, and a daughter-in-law against her mother-in-law; and one's foes will be members of one's own household. Whoever loves father or mother more than me is not worthy of me; and whoever does not take up the cross and follow me is not worthy of me. Those who find their life will lose it, and those who lose their life for my sake will find it. (*Matthew* 10:34–39 NRSV)

I believe it is necessary to distinguish the penultimate cure by introjection or "transmuting internalisation" (Kohut, 1977) of the empathically attuned analyst as a good object or "selfobject" from the ultimate cure entailing structural change through separation from and mourning the loss of the introjected objects, thus enabling mature identification with the more fully differentiated, as distinct from the subjective or transitional, object. In my view a mature faith dialectically transcends both the paranoid-schizoid and depressive positions. Whereas in the subjective and narcissistic domain of the former (PS) one embraces (knowingly or not) either the resurrection (*Da!*) without the crucifixion (*Fort!*), or *vice versa*, in the latter (D) narcissism and splitting are overcome. To the degree that it has been able to successfully mourn the loss of Eden and relinquish hope in either a natural or supernatural Heaven, the mature subject, although situated "under the Cross", will at the same time have escaped from "death" and Hell—that is, from the "hysterical misery" that Freud (Breuer & Freud, 1893–95) felt we would agree that "much will be gained" if it can be transformed into "common unhappiness" (p. 305).

But man cannot live by D alone any more than by PS, for to be captured entirely by depressive position disbelief is as untenable as to be captured by belief. "Common unhappiness" is ultimately not good enough. Without periodic relief through transitional experience reality is unbearable and essentially psychotic regressions from it become inevitable. It is a fundamental Freudian insight that repression inevitably sets up a disguised return of the repressed. "Whoever pushes rationality forward also restores new strength to the opposite power, mysticism and folly of all kinds" (Nietzsche, *The Will to Power*, quoted in Sagan, 2001, p. 1). Frequent re-vitalising play in the transitional area saves us from soul-destroying capture by either belief or disbelief.

* * *

Although Meissner (1981) recognised the greater maturity of secondary identification as distinct from introjective or transitional modes of relating, only three years later he (1984, ch. 7) discusses religion (as distinct from faith) as transitional. But religious belief falls out of the transitional area. He writes that "Just as the transitional object of the child can degenerate into a fetish object, transitional religious experience can be distorted in less authentic, relatively fetishistic directions … [in which] … religious objects or practices begin to take on a magical quality …" (Meissner, 1984, pp. 181–182). But while this certainly applies to faith, which can at times regress from the transitional area into the magical, fetishistic, paranoid-schizoid position—that is, into religious belief—religion itself already represents such fetishism. Whereas Meissner (1981) viewed transitional phenomena as entailing the blurring of subject/object differentiation, now it is only their "less authentic", "relatively fetishistic" distortions that do so. This move is necessitated by Meissner's decision to view religion as transitional (i.e., introjective and projective) which by his own earlier definition is to see it as a regression from mature object relations. His later distinction between "authentic" and "inauthentic" transitional phenomena represents an attempt to make allowance for the possibility of "authentically" transitional types of religion which may be considered psychologically mature. If by the transitional we refer to a domain of incomplete differentiation and integration, however advanced this may be over the radical undifferentiation and disintegration characteristic of fetishism or autism, this must surely be distinguished from the domain of mature differentiation and integration that Meissner (1981) himself associated with secondary identification as distinct from introjection of transitional relations. It is one thing to argue that a temporary suspension of both belief and disbelief by resort to the transitional area of cultural experience, the area of the arts and of faith, is essential for human well-being, but quite another to claim maturity for one who seeks to take up permanent residence in this area.

In any case, religion as distinct from faith is a matter of belief and therefore always already outside the transitional area. In the spirit of the radical theologians (Altizer, 1967; Altizer & Hamilton, 1968; Bonhoeffer, 1953; Kee, 1971) we are called in this secular era to transcend religion by successfully mourning the "death of god" and, if we are Christian, moving on to a "religionless Christianity" based on a mature identification with Jesus who, in surrendering his magical omnipotence and omniscience—"*Eli, Eli, lama sabachthani?*", that is to say, "My God, my God, why hast thou forsaken me?" (*Matthew* 27:46 KJV)—calls upon us to surrender ours. In this view, however much we may at times resort to celebration of a transitional faith beyond both belief and disbelief, we must ultimately accept crucifixion (castration; abjection) as the necessary condition for resurrection from the death-in-life represented by self- rather than other-centredness, the idolatry of the narcissistic or specular ego.

Ironically, in justifiably criticising Freud's failure to apply his epigenetic understanding to religion, Meissner's own analysis suffers from a similar defect: he fails to distinguish mature from immature modalities of *unbelief*. While correctly pointing out that "Freud's rationalism and his agnostic disbelief were not free from conflict and clearly rested on powerful underlying motivations" (p. 55), Meissner fails to make sufficiently clear that just as there exist mature modalities of religious experience (that, *contra* Meissner, I regard as post-religious faith), so there exist mature expressions of unbelief. For in addition to the oral unbelief that refuses to "swallow" religious "poison", and the anal unbelief that defiantly asserts autonomy against a cosmic toilet-trainer, and the phallic-Oedipal unbelief that, rejecting Jesus as an unmanly, negative

Oedipal son who submits to castration by his father, refuses to "bend the knee" to the paternal (or maternal) law, there is the healthy unbelief that simply experiences no need for religious categories in order either to attain or to express its psychosocial maturity. Nowhere in his discussion of the developmental vicissitudes of the "God-representation", does Meissner (1984, ch. 6) acknowledge the fact that while all children inevitably form a representation of an idealised object, by no means all are exposed to a religio-cultural universe of discourse that would lead them to identify the idealised object with "God".

Unfortunately, when Freud (1907b) pointed out that one who embraces what he regarded as the collective neurosis of religion is thereby spared the necessity of creating a personal neurosis, he neglected to notice that both the psychoanalytic dyad and the psychoanalytic movement may, like religion, offer a collective neurosis, reliance upon which may obscure both the failure and the necessity to grow up. The incorporation and idolisation, and the introjection and idealisation of Sigmund Freud certainly represents little advance over the incorporation and idolisation, and the introjection and idealisation of Jesus Christ—as the history of both churches so abundantly reveals. In this light, analogous to the post-religious outlook of religionless Christianity is the post-ideological stance of a truly scientific psychoanalysis.

I suspect the differences between the psychologically mature who identify with a religious tradition (in a post-religious or secular manner) and those who do not boil down to a preference for different metaphorical languages in which to express a common experience and faith. Some may find this, like Tillich and Bultmann, in the language of existentialism and the demythologised symbols of their religious traditions; others in certain of the languages of contemporary psychoanalysis. This is not, however, to subscribe to the relativism that denies that some metaphorical languages and traditions may be better than others at symbolising the complexities and subtleties of psychologically mature human experience. Just as certain of the languages of contemporary psychoanalysis may be better than others at capturing specific aspects of psychic reality, so certain religious and philosophical traditions may succeed better than others in metaphorically representing various dimensions of the existential, moral, and spiritual reality of human existence.

Nor does it imply that psychology is the standard by which such traditions are to be judged. Since the demythologising of religious symbolism yields essential wisdom, complementing yet at times surpassing the insights so far achieved by psychosocial science, it is equally valid to judge psychology by the standard of demythologised religion. In light of the insight offered by a demythologised Christianity into cruci-fixion as a necessary precondition and constant companion of resurrec-tion, we might differentiate between those psychoanalytic traditions, such as those of Freud, Klein, Lacan, and Winnicott, that have some appreciation of this fact and have evolved a technique to accommodate it, from traditions such as those of Fairbairn, Guntrip, and Kohut that have at times come close to abandoning it altogether. Albeit with some reservations, Kohut (1977, 1984) was prepared to settle for the less exacting model of the cure through introjection or "transmuting inter-nalisation" of the analyst as a good object or "selfobject", and many of his followers have done so without reservation. But while acknowl-edging that under some circumstances the cure by introjection—the "transference cure"—is "good enough" and even the most that can rea-sonably be hoped for, many in the mainstream psychoanalytic tradi-tion continue to aspire to the higher standard of the more fully analytic cure through separation from and mourning the loss of the introjects as the necessary precursor of mature identification.

Despite Winnicott's seemingly Kleinian emphasis upon the role of "destruction" and separation in the achievement of mature object rela-tions and his embrace of what Kohut (1979, p. 12) rejected as a "health-and-maturity-morality", his entire theory operates from a premise shared with the psychology of the self. (It is part of Winnicott's strength that, owing to his deliteralised use of concepts, he is able to bring together ideas which for others seem poles apart.) Only a self with enough cohe-sion due to a "good-enough" early "holding environment" (Winnicott, 1960a) and sufficient "optimal responsiveness" (Bacal, 1985) from its past and present "selfobjects" is able to survive the narcissistic injury and ontological anxiety occasioned by the discovery of the objective object, that is, by separation, surrender of omnipotence, and advance into the depressive position, and to permit the "destruction" of the sub-jective object and, in this way, to progress from archaic to mature object relations.

The encounter with absence, "lack", "nothingness", or non-being inherent in the act of deconstructing concretised metaphor and con-trast, and in psychic differentiation and integration in general, can promote maturation in those with enough inner strength or external "selfobject" support to permit them to absorb it. But those lacking such resources, rather than being resurrected to "life" through the encounter with "death", may in fact only be further deadened or destroyed by it. Avoidance of the latter outcome requires both a preliminary introjection of sufficient goodness to enable temporary resort to the transitional area and to permit mourning to take place, as well as provision of essential holding, containment, and responsiveness during the subject's "passion". Such therapeutic provision, in my view, is not merely a preliminary to analysis proper, making interpretation possible, but an essential part of the therapeutic action of psychoanalysis. I do not believe analysis cures by interpretation alone, any more than man lives by bread alone (*Deuteronomy* 8:2–3; *Matthew* 4:4). Valid interpretation of psychodynamics is *essential* for the cure, but only when offered by an analyst who *cares* (*Caritas, Agape*) for the patient. Food delivered by the mother is not enough; it must be delivered by a loving mother. An analyst who validly interprets but does not *care* is not good enough, any more than an analyst who cares but does not offer timely and truthful interpretations.

* * *

According to Paul Tillich (1952):

> The ultimate source of the courage to be is the "God above God"; this is the result of our demand to transcend theism. Only if the God of theism is transcended can the anxiety of doubt and meaninglessness be taken into the courage to be. … But such a church which raises itself in its message and its devotion to the God above the God of theism without sacrificing its concrete symbols can mediate a courage which takes doubt and meaninglessness into itself. It is the Church under the Cross which alone can do this, the Church which preaches the Crucified who cried to God after the God of confidence had left him in the darkness of doubt and meaninglessness. To be as part of such a church is to receive a courage to be in which one cannot lose one's self and in which one receives one's world. (pp. 180–182)

But can one surrender the God of theism while retaining faith in the "God above God"? Is it not essential to carry the project of demythologising beyond the God of theism to include the "God above God" as well? Why are we engaging in "god-talk" at all? As Bonhoeffer (1953)

254 THE STILL SMALL VOICE

put it, "My view of it today would be not that he [Bultmann] went too far, as most people seem to think, but that he did not go far enough. It is not only the mythological conceptions, such as the miracles, the ascension and the like (which are not in principle separable from the conceptions of God, faith and so on) that are problematic, but the 'religious' conceptions themselves. You cannot as Bultmann imagines, separate God and miracles, but you do have to be able to interpret and proclaim both of them in a 'non-religious' sense" (p. 94). Just as you cannot separate God and miracles, so you cannot separate God and the God above God. Unless the demythologisers are willing to carry their project to its conclusion in an entirely secularised and religionless outlook, they are vulnerable to the contempt in which they were held by Freud.

In *The Future of an Illusion* Freud (1927c) addresses the "philosophy of As If" and other intellectually sophisticated (or sophistic) arguments in favour of a demythologised understanding of religion:

> In reality these are only attempts at pretending to oneself or to other people that one is still firmly attached to religion, when one has long since cut oneself loose from it. Where questions of religion are concerned, people are guilty of every possible sort of dishonesty and intellectual misdemeanour. Philosophers stretch the meaning of words until they retain scarcely anything of their original sense. They give the name of "God" to some vague abstraction which they have created for themselves; having done so they can pose before all the world as deists, as believers in God, and they can even boast that they have recognised a higher, purer concept of God, notwithstanding that their God is now nothing more than an insubstantial shadow and no longer the mighty personality of religious doctrines. (p. 31)

Is Tillich's "God above God" such a vague abstraction, "an insubstantial shadow and no longer the mighty personality of religious doctrines"?

Three years later, in *Civilization and Its Discontents*, Freud (1930a) states his critique even more vehemently: "It is ... humiliating to discover how large a number of people living to-day, who cannot but see that this religion is not tenable, nevertheless try to defend it piece by piece in a series of pitiful rearguard actions. One would like to mix among the ranks of the believers in order to meet these philosophers, who think they can rescue the God of religion by replacing him by an impersonal, shadowy and abstract principle, and to address them with the warning words: 'Thou shalt not take the name of the Lord thy God in vain!'" (p. 73). Despite having read these passages many times over the years, I am still astonished to find the great agnostic of *Future* (for whom religion was illusion), who three years later in *Civilization* embraced atheism (for now religion was delusion), resonating with the attitude of the passionate Christian, Blaise Pascal, whose *credo* was "God of Abraham. God of Isaac. God of Jacob, not of the philosophers and scholars" (Rist, 1938, p. 289), and scolding professed believers for taking the name of their Lord in vain. As young people say today: awesome!

The distinguished Princeton philosopher and Nietzsche scholar, Walter Kaufmann, shared Freud's attitude towards the demythologising philosophers, or at least those who claimed their philosophical abstractions were somehow tantamount to or congruent with the essence of traditional Christian religion. While acknowledging that Hegel had set a precedent for Bultmann, Tillich, and company, Kaufmann (1965) considered Hegel more honest, viewing Christianity as a primitive, mythological precursor of his philosophy rather than claiming his philosophy to be identical with the essence of Christianity:

> Hegel's treatment of Christianity in his last years has often been misunderstood. Among religions, he considers it supreme insofar as it seems to him to come closest to the truth comprehended ultimately in his philosophy. ... In its relation to philosophy, however, religion is as a child compared to a man: it is an anticipation in less developed form of what finds mature expression in philosophy. ... When Hegel avails himself of Christian categories, he never implies acceptance of the Christian faith in the supernatural, in miracles, or in the incarnation and resurrection; he merely finds the Christian myths more suggestive and appropriate anticipations of his philosophy than the myths of other religions. ... That he ... became a precedent for theologians like Tillich and Bultmann is undeniable. But if one should consider the procedure of all three reprehensible, there are still important differences in Hegel's favour. What he did very occasionally, *en passant*, ... they have made their full-time occupation. ... Above all, far from treating the latest philosophy as a remarkable anticipation of Christianity, provided only that the latter were radically reinterpreted on the basis of this philosophy, Hegel presented the very opposite picture: in his system Christianity

was treated as an anticipation in mythological form—on the level
of vague notions and feelings—of truths articulated in philosophy.
(section 65, pp. 271–275)

* * *

As we have seen, Lakoff and Wehling (2012) point out that, owing to its
rationalism and traditional reluctance to moralise, the Left surrenders
moral discourse to the Right which takes full advantage: where progressives argue policy, conservatives argue morality and often win—
"Because morality is central to identity and, hence, trumps policy."
What they refer to as the morality of the Right corresponds, in the terms
employed here, to the morality of the superego, while the morality of
the Left corresponds to conscience. "Progressive morality fits a nurturant family: parents are equal, the values are empathy, responsibility
for oneself and others and cooperation," while "Conservative morality
fits the family of the strict father, who is the ultimate authority" and in
which "You are responsible for yourself and not anyone else and no one
else is responsible for you." In my view the de-moralising discourse of
both traditional and contemporary psychoanalysis has, like much of the
discourse of the democratic left, had similarly destructive effects, not
least in its failure to discriminate conscience, the ethic of nurturance,
from superego, the ethic of authority, and its failure to fully recognise
and confront the destructiveness of the latter.

Essentially the same distinction applies in the case of religion. As
Fromm (1950), among others, pointed out, whereas progressive religion
represents the values of sympathy, equality, and cooperation (i.e., conscience), conservative religion is paternalistic, hierarchical, and authoritarian (superego). I prefer to reserve the term "religion" for the latter,
associating the former with the later Bonhoeffer's (1951) "religionless"
Christianity and its equivalents within other faith and secular ethical
traditions. The distinction between superego and conscience parallels
Martin Luther's differentiation between law and gospel, Moses and
Christ. For Luther, "[T]he only 'real theologian' was one who 'knows
well how to distinguish the gospel from the law'" instead of confusing
the two and teaching "'the very opposite, namely, that Moses is Christ
and Christ is Moses'" (Pelikan, 1984, p. 168). I advance a parallel claim:
the only real psychoanalyst is one who knows well how to distinguish
the conscience from the superego instead of confusing the two and
teaching the very opposite, namely, that the superego is the conscience

and the conscience the superego. Luther's distinction is an elaboration of that proclaimed in the six antitheses of the Sermon on the Mount (*Mathew* 5:21–48 *KJV*)—"Ye have heard. But I say unto you"—in which Jesus distinguishes an ethic of rules and reproach (superego) from an ethic of the heart (conscience). As Pelikan points out, "It was the special ministry of Moses to proclaim the wrath of god in the law, and the death that was the consequence of man's disobedience. Thus Luther portrayed Christ as saying to Moses: 'I will not preach as you, Moses, are obliged to preach. For you must proclaim the law. … Therefore your preaching produces only wretched people; it shows them their sins, on account of which they cannot keep the law'" (p. 168). In Victor Hugo's (1862) classic, *Les Misérables*, Jean Valjean is not redeemed by Javert (the superego), who produces only wretched people, showing them their sins, on account of which they cannot keep the law, but by the Bishop (the conscience).

But as Pelikan goes on to point out, it is a superficial reading of Luther's distinction that rejects "the authority of Moses and the Old Testament in favour of the sole authority of Christ and the New Testament" (p. 169). According to Pelikan, "[F]ar from equating the Old Testament with law and the New Testament with gospel, he [Luther] found the message of the gospel throughout the Scriptures. … Moses had predicted his own surrender of authority to Christ, as the prophet whom men were to heed. At the same time, Luther recognised that there were commands throughout the New Testament. This meant that there was gospel in the Old Testament and law in the New" (p. 169). Is it then an error to suggest that law can be displaced by gospel, superego overcome by conscience? I think the answer to this question, as for so many others, may be found in Jesus's own statement on the matter: "Think not that I am come to destroy the law, or the prophets: I am not come to destroy, but to fulfil" (*Matthew* 5:17 *KJV*).

Jesus, Terry Eagleton (2007) writes, "seems to have regarded his own life, death and resurrection as the fulfilment or consummation of Mosaic law. The idea that he stood for love against law, inner feeling against external ritual, is a piece of Christian anti-Semitism" (p. xxv). "For one thing," Eagleton writes, "Jesus is interested in what people do …" (p. xxv). In this connection, against those who sought to use the Lutheran doctrine of salvation by grace and faith alone as an evasion of the need for committed action, in *Discipleship* Bonhoeffer (1937, published in English as *The Cost of Discipleship*) emphasised that, although salvation cannot be purchased by "works", there exists no valid faith outside the faithful action to which Christians are called. Furthermore, as Eagleton points out, "[T]he Judaic law is itself the law of love. It belongs to the law, for example, to treat your enemies humanely. Being kind to your enemies is not a Christian invention." Yet in seeking not to destroy but to fulfil the law, Jesus reveals it to be the law of conscience, not the law of the superego:

> Jesus saw himself as the fulfilment of the law of the Father in the sense that his own person revealed it to be the law of love. ... He reveals the Father as friend, comrade, lover and counsel for the defence, rather than as patriarch, judge, superego or accuser. The latter is a Satanic or ideological image of God .... The Father is manifested by Jesus as a vulnerable animal, the flayed and bloody scapegoat of Calvary. Jesus' broken body is the true signifier of the law. ... It is the law which is transgressive, not the subversion of it. ... Jesus also consummates the law by demonstrating that the love it commands, pressed to a limit, will inevitably issue in death. To fulfil the law in this way, however, is also to transcend it: in place of tablets of stone is now flesh and blood, the body of a political criminal who by accepting his own death for the sake of others has somehow emerged on the other side of it. The law is abolished by being fulfilled. (Eagleton, 2007, pp. xxv-xxvi)

Kierkegaard (1843) associated the ethic of rules with conventional morality and believed the "knight of faith" was sometimes, like Abraham, called by God to engage in a "religious suspension of the ethical", to break with the law of men out of loyalty to the higher law of God— even a God who demands infanticide, though who, in this instance, relented and accepted an animal sacrifice instead. Given mankind's long history of religiously motivated violence, and our experience of terrorism of all kinds and in all traditions, this is an idea I find frightening. If I hear a voice calling Abraham to sacrifice Isaac, how am I to know the voice is God's and not Satan's, or a hallucination, and how am I to know whether this Abraham is me? According to Kierkegaard (1849), "[T]o have faith is precisely to lose one's mind so as to win God" (p. 68). He dismissed rational objections to faith as sheer disobedience: "It is therefore certain and true that the first person who thought of defending Christianity in Christendom is *de facto* a Judas No. 2; he too betrays with a kiss, except his treason is that of stupidity. To defend something is always to discredit it" (p. 119). This is an attitude one finds echoed to some degree in the emphasis upon "simple obedience" in Bonhoeffer's (1937) *Discipleship*: "The forces that wanted to get between the word of Jesus and obedience were just as great back then as they are today. Reason objected; Conscience, responsibility, piety, even the law and the principle of Scripture intervened to inhibit this most extreme, this lawless 'enthusiasm.' Jesus' call broke through all of this and mandated obedience. It was God's own word. Simple obedience was required" (p. 77). It is important to note that in his later *Letters and Papers from Prison*, Bonhoeffer (1953) distanced himself to some extent from his earlier attitude: "I thought I could acquire faith by trying to live a holy life, or something like it. It was in this phase that I wrote *The Cost of Discipleship*. Today I can see the dangers of this book, though I am prepared stand by what I wrote" (p. 125).

In my view it is crucial not to confuse conscience with either the laws of men or the laws of "God", let alone with the superego, for sometimes people are called upon by the superego, the law, and what they take to be God to act unconscionably. Whenever one feels called by "God", the superego, or the law, to act unconscionably, it is time to exchange one's love of God, or the law, for love of one's fellow human beings, and to subordinate one's superego to one's conscience. Hence, following the Bonhoeffer of the *Letters and Papers from Prison* as distinct from the Bonhoeffer of *Discipleship*, I wish to replace Kierkegaard's "religious suspension of the ethical" with what I think of as *the ethical suspension of the religious*—suspending superego in favour of conscience (that is, identification with the nurturer) whether or not one symbolises the latter as the call of Christ. As we have seen, in Hugo's (1862) novel (Volume Five, Book Fourth), the policeman/superego, Javert, is finally touched by conscience and derailed. Confronted with the "terrible rising of an unknown moral sun", he chooses suicide.

In a 1967 lecture delivered at Coventry Cathedral, Bonhoeffer's life-long friend and colleague, Eberhard Bethge complained that the "isolated use and handing down of the famous term 'religionless Christianity' has made Bonhoeffer the champion of an undialectical shallow modernism which obscures all that he wanted to tell us about the living God" (Bethge as quoted by Metaxas, 2010, p. 485). Metaxas writes that "The strange theological climate after World War II and the interest in the martyred Bonhoeffer were such that the few bone fragments in these private letters were set upon as by famished kites and less noble birds, many of whose descendants gnaw at them still. All of which has led to a tremendous misunderstanding of Bonhoeffer's theology and which lamentably washed backward over his earlier thinking and writing. Many *outré* theological fashions have subsequently tried to claim Bonhoeffer as their own and have ignored much of his *oeuvre* to do so" (p. 484). No doubt some will consider my own gnawing at and use of some of his ideas to be *outré*, however much I seek to indicate my awareness of the distance separating Bonhoeffer from some of the other trends of thought characterising radical theology and the "death of God" movement.

Certainly Bonhoeffer was profoundly influenced by Karl Barth (1938) who wrote: "In religion man bolts and bars himself against revelation by providing a substitute, by taking away in advance the very thing which has to be given by God. It is never the truth. It is a complete fiction, which has not only little but no relation to God" (p. 303). In asserting that "[R]eligion is no more than the garment of Christianity," Bonhoeffer (1951) goes on to say that "Barth, who is the only one to have started on this line of thought, has still not proceeded to its logical conclusion" (pp. 91–92). Although Metaxas (2010) appears to want to deny it, this is exactly what the later Bonhoeffer sought to accomplish. In "Metaxas's Counterfeit Bonhoeffer", Weikart (n.d.) reviews a range of theological responses to the biography that suggest its author "serves up a Bonhoeffer suited to the evangelical taste", attempting to play down the radical challenge that Bonhoeffer's late thought constitutes to any Christian orthodoxy.

As we have seen, Bonhoeffer felt that, in "a world come of age", Bultmann and the demythologisers had not gone far enough. "[I]f we reach the stage of being radically without religion—and I think this is more or less the case already," then "the lynchpin is removed from the whole structure of our Christianity to date" (p. 91). In this religionless situation, Bonhoeffer wonders whether the whole question of personal salvation has any relevance: "Are we not really under the impression that there are more important things than bothering about such a matter?" (p. 94). What Bonhoeffer feels is certainly worth bothering about is clear: "Is there any concern in the Old Testament about saving one's soul at all? Is not righteousness and the kingdom of God on earth the focus of everything …? It is not with the next world that we are concerned, but with this world as created and preserved and set subject to laws and atoned for and made new" (pp. 94–95).

While this sounds as if Bonhoeffer might be prepared to surrender not only religion but even God himself in favour of conscience, this would be mistaken, for to abandon a "religious" *concept* of God is not at all to abandon God. Certainly he called for the extension of demythologising even to the idea of God; but he seeks only to replace the "religious" idea of God by a non-religious one:

> God is teaching us that we must live as men who can get along very well without him. The God who is with us is the God who forsakes us (*Mark* 15:34). The God who makes us live in this world without using him as a working hypothesis is the God before whom we are ever standing. Before God and with him we live without God. God allows himself to be edged out of the world and on to the cross. God is weak and powerless in the world, and that is exactly the way, the only way, in which he can be with us and help us. *Matthew* 8:17 makes it crystal clear that it is not by his omnipotence that Christ helps us, but by his weakness and suffering. (p. 122)

Bonhoeffer substitutes a non-religious for a religious conception of God. For him, "[O]nly a suffering god can help" and we are "challenged to participate in the sufferings of God at the hands of a godless world" (p. 122). Some seven decades later, can we carry the project of demythologisation further, perhaps to its conclusion, surrendering not only all concepts of God, but God himself, replacing him, or at least equating him, with the universal dimension of human conscience, as distinct from superego—that is, with the ethic of nurturance, charity, and compassion? God knows, any attempt to live a conscientious life is to participate in the sufferings of conscience at the hands of a conscienceless world. Is not Christ's fourth cry from the Cross (*Matthew* 27:46 *KJV*) a call to share in his, not merely apparent or temporary, abandonment by God? And does not the image of a crucified God who could not come down amount to a call to surrender omnipotence, both God's and our own, and thus to surrender God himself?

According to Eagleton, "The modern world has witnessed what one might call a transition from the soul to the psyche. Or, if one prefers, from theology to psychoanalysis" (p. 17). In seeking to further this transition, it is useful to observe how important distinctions we are only now beginning to make in psychoanalysis, such as that between superego and conscience, have been prefigured in theology, in this case in the

Reformation differentiation between law and gospel and in the New Testament itself. But Eagleton's following statement that "In each case [in both theology and psychoanalysis], human beings are born in sickness" (p. 17) is controversial in respect to both. As we have seen, for Judaism human beings are not "born" in sickness, though they inevitably fall into it. And despite his passionate Christianity, the same holds true for Kierkegaard whose interpretation of *Genesis* as myth rather than history deviates from Augustinian doctrine, affirming a prelapsarian time of infantile innocence before the fall (up) into language, self-awareness, freedom, and sin. Whereas Freud himself, at least in his frequent periods of biological literalism, postulated an innate, unlearned, biologically-given drive towards death, many of his followers deliteralised this notion and came to associate death with the rise of the idolatry of the specular ego, itself a dead image, an image that, for Lacan at least, was not there at the beginning, arising only later as the infant comes to be captured in the mirror-phase by the Imaginary and, hence, by narcissism. As we have seen, Klein is ambiguous on this matter, at times appearing to accept Freud's notion of a literal, primary drive towards death, while at others seeing aggression and paranoia as a consequence of, albeit inevitable, frustration.

I believe these are more than pedantic academic distinctions. While agreeing with Eagleton that "[T]he root of all political wisdom is realism" (p. 155), and rejecting the "mindless progressivism" that would deny "that things are so dire with us that only a deep-seated transformation could hope to put them right" (p. 156), those interested in the emancipatory potentials of both theology and psychoanalysis must accept the reality and inevitability of the Fall, while at the same time insisting that it is in fact a fall from a state of grace and innocence that, constituting our core, may in principle and even in reality be revivified. This said we are back in agreement with Eagleton when he writes that we are "thereby not beyond redemption. Happiness is not beyond our grasp; it is just that it requires of us a traumatic breaking down and remaking, for which the Christian term is conversion" (p. 17). As psychotherapists who seek to help patients survive such breakdowns and find inner peace, we need to understand the difference between superego and conscience. While rejecting their equation of the rational ego with conscience, I believe Alexander and Ferenczi, like Victor Hugo, were justified in their radical critique of the superego, though unlike its symbolic representative, Javert, who chooses suicide, the superego can no more be eradicated than the paranoid-schizoid position in which it resides. But it can be contained, disempowered, and displaced by a liberated conscience and this is the essence of the psychoanalytic cure. For the superego "produces only wretched people; it shows them their sins, on account of which they cannot keep the law". But the law is abolished by being fulfilled and in its fulfilment revealed as the law of love. Whereas the superego (PS) had imprisoned conscience, now liberated conscience (D) overpowers the superego and redirects its aggressive energy into creative rather than destructive channels.

* * *

A final, intrinsically psychoanalytic point: I anticipate deep *resistance* to this critique of the superego and call for its disempowerment in favour of conscience. Despite Freud's own increasing demonisation of the superego, people will accuse Alexander, Ferenczi, and me of demonising it, of splitting, making conscience all-good and superego all-bad, and they will prefer to say the superego is, like all other compromise-formations, a mixture of good and bad. They will downplay their departure from Freud and Klein on this point, abandoning their view of the superego as an internal persecutor, preferring Schafer's (1960) vision of a "loving and beloved superego". They will prefer to speak of modifying an archaic harsh superego into a more reasonable and forgiving one rather than acknowledge its intrinsic cruelty and the need for its disempowerment by conscience. In all this they will be continuing the psychoanalytic whitewash of the superego, the ongoing denial of the inherent badness of the normal, not merely the abnormal superego, and the related scapegoating of the id.

And by now it should be obvious why: for the superego is unconsciously associated in our minds with the parents and hence, for some, with God, and few of us wish to look clearly at their limitations or leave them behind. The demand that we grow up, forsake parents and superego and their projections, and learn to live by our conscience seems harsh, as does Christ's statement that "I am come to set a man at variance against his father, and the daughter against her mother, and the daughter in law against her mother in law. And a man's foes shall be they of his own household" (*Matthew* 10:34–38 *KJV*)—almost as if this requirement, like the demand that we transcend religion, expresses a death-wish towards the parents. But to grow up and leave home is not to kill anyone, though it may feel like it to all parties involved.

To separate, as Winnicott understood, is not a murderous act, though when the others from whom we separate and individuate react by feeling killed we can come to feel we are killing them when, in reality, we are only becoming independent, self-responsible adults. Hans Loewald (1979) is among the few Freudian analysts who have liberated themselves sufficiently from the father complex to grasp that the healthy resolution of the Oedipus complex is not renunciation out of fear of castration but *symbolic fulfilment* of Oedipal desire—finding a sublimated way to kill the rivals and possess the desired object. As Sagan (1988, Chapter Five) points out, Freud's (1909b) case history of "Little Hans" makes this clear: Hans is freed from his phobia only after he has two dreams, one in which he marries and has many babies with his mother and another in which a plumber comes and takes away his "behind" and his "widdler" replacing them with bigger and better ones. It is high time that we too overcome fear and inhibition and find the courage to subordinate the superego to the still small voice of conscience.

CHAPTER ELEVEN

Dead end kids: projective identification and sacrifice in *Orphans*

Non vos relinquam orphanos, alleluia. Vado, et venio ad vos, alleluia.
Et gaudebit cor vestrum, alleluia.

After decades of mutual ignorance and suspicion in more recent years an increasingly interesting and sophisticated dialogue between psychoanalysis and theology has been developing (Fromm, 1950; Homans, 1968, 1970; Jacobs & Capps, 1997; J. W. Jones, 1991; Küng, 1990; Lake, 1966; Leavy, 1988; Meissner, 1968, 1984; Ostow, 2007; Rizzuto, 1979; Spezzano & Gargiulo, 2003; Symington, 1994; Wyschogrod, Crownfield & Raschke, 1989). Since Lyle Kessler's (1987) play *Orphans* lends itself to both psychoanalytic and theological interpretation, the present essay is intended both as an exercise in applied psychoanalysis in the field of literary and cinematic studies and, at the same time, as a demonstration of the complementarity that may sometimes exist between hermeneutic perspectives often considered antithetical. The play opened in Los Angeles in 1983 and has subsequently been performed in Chicago, New York, and London. Kessler himself wrote the screenplay for the 1987 film version directed by Alan J. Pakula and starring Albert Finney as Harold, Mathew Modine as Treat, and Kevin Anderson as Philip. Although faithful in most respects, the film differs from the play in a number of ways that provide significant evidence of authorial intention.

The contrasting psychoanalytic concepts of projective identification and sympathetic identification (defined below) illuminate the central action and meaning of the play and provide psychoanalytic insight into the nature of sacrifice in both its destructive and creative forms, phenomena that are of fundamental significance in various religious traditions. In the face of abandonment the elder of two orphaned brothers hardens his heart, identifies with a harsh superego or Fairbairnian (1952) "internal saboteur", splitting off his pain and dependency needs, his "libidinal ego", and projectively identifying these into his younger brother whom he induces to submit to his domination and control. In essence the adolescent brothers represent the two aspects of a single self split owing to traumatic loss and deprivation. In marked contrast to this pathological dynamic is the redemptive psychology of Harold, their saviour, whose altruistic love transcends sadomasochism in that in sacrificing himself for the "dead end kids" with whom he is sympathetically identified, he simultaneously realises and affirms the pattern of values and ideals, the conscience, at the core of his identity.

* * *

The two abandoned brothers have been living together in a ramshackle old house in Philadelphia ("The City of Brotherly Love") ever since their father deserted the family and their mother either died or disappeared. The older boy, Treat, having frustrated attempts by the child-welfare authorities to take them into custody, has been providing for his brother Philip and himself through petty crime. The film, unlike the play, opens with Treat mugging a man in the park, but apparently only after he has concluded that his victim is a former "family man" who has, like the orphans' father, abandoned his wife and children. The younger brother, Philip, convinced by Treat that he once almost died from a severe asthma attack on leaving the house, is terrified of the outside world. He spends his time watching game shows and reruns of old movies on TV, playing out fantasy adventures of the Errol Flynn variety, and secretly reading and improving his vocabulary, an activity proscribed by his older brother from whom all evidence of this interest in "the word" must be hidden. In an early scene, Treat returns home with the booty from his day's work and searches for Philip who, as the text of the play makes clear, has been hiding in a closet containing their mother's coats. Treat wants to get rid of these reminders of their mother, but Philip is attached to them, as well as to a woman's shoe which Treat throws out of the window but which Philip later retrieves, despite his terror of the outdoors. In the film, Philip is also attached to a little toy lamb which is contemptuously tossed aside by his older brother.

Into this unusual domestic scene stumbles Harold, an aging Chicago gangster "on the lam" from his former mob associates who seek to retrieve a briefcase full of "stolen securities" with which he has absconded. In both cinematic and dramatic texts (pp. 64–65) there is an interesting play on Philip's verbal confusion of "lam" and "lamb". Intending to steal the drunken Harold's briefcase, Treat lures him back to the house and, concluding from its contents that Harold is a VIP, decides to kidnap him. While Treat is at work attempting to contact Harold's associates in the hope of obtaining a "ransom", Harold, with the skill of a Houdini, "miraculously" frees himself from his bindings before the very eyes of an amazed Philip who instantly becomes his devoted disciple. Before long, Harold not only succeeds in creating order out of the chaos of the house, but also in persuad-ing Philip to open the attic window and breathe in the night air. The film depicts Philip, with Harold's encouragement, leaning out of the window, overwhelmed with joy as he becomes drenched in the falling rain. By means of a combination of loving authority, worldly wisdom, financial incentives, and the judicious use of his revolver and his fists, Harold also succeeds, against considerable resistance, in turning Treat into his "personal bodyguard and all-around man" (p. 53). At one point (p. 59), Treat even goes so far as to boast of his willingness to "sacrifice" himself for Harold's sake. But despite his mentor's best efforts to train him to control his anger and his grandi-osity and to teach him prudence and self-control, Treat's impetuosity indirectly leads to Harold's "betrayal" to "the mob" and ultimately to his death.

* * *

It is certainly possible to interpret *Orphans* as a story of deprivation of fathering and its belated provision by Harold as a kind of substitute father, healer, teacher, therapist, or saviour. A Freudian perspective might focus upon the Oedipal themes evident in Philip's idealisation of Harold, Treat's consequent resentment at his displacement as the object of Philip's dependence, his resistance to Harold's authority, and the fulfilment of his death-wish towards the father represented by the lat-ter's murder at the conclusion. A Lacanian (1977) interpretation might centre on the emancipation of the orphans from their sadomasochistic enmeshment in the pre-Oedipal, narcissistic universe of the Imaginary through the "Oedipalisation" or triangulation effected by Harold, whose entry disrupts the pre-existing dual union, turning the dyad into a triad. In this view, Harold performs the hitherto missing "paternal function" of registering *le nom-du-père*, the "name-of-the-father", homophonic with *le non-du-père*, the No (i.e., the law) of the father and, to me at least, verbally evocative of the ritual invocation of the Trinity: "In the name of the Father, the Son, and the Holy Spirit".

On the other hand, while such paternal themes are prominent in the play, *Orphans* is equally a story of the deprivation of mothering. Father deserted the family, but mother also disappeared, albeit leaving such traces as a red shoe and a fur coat. And if Harold fathers the two orphans, he certainly mothers them as well. For the purposes of the essentially object-relational analysis offered here (Fairbairn, 1943, 1944; Guntrip, 1971; Kernberg, 1975; Klein, 1935, 1940, 1946, 1948; Winnicott, 1955, 1960b, 1971), it is unnecessary to enter the vexed debate over what constitutes mothering as opposed to fathering for, in this perspective, *Orphans* is considered really to be about caring in a broad sense that includes both of these conventionally differentiated functions. It is about the terrible emotional consequences of deprivation of essential care, such as, for example, the delinquent child's hostility and conflict with authority which, as the play suggests, are rooted in deprivation rather than in any innate aggressive drive.

The play depicts a symbiotic union maintained by mutual projective identification between two emotionally wounded individuals who externalise in their relationship the split and sadomasochistic structure of the disordered self. Finally, it portrays the healing or cure of such pathological conditions, or the redemption of such states of dereliction, exemplified in the orphans, Philip and Treat, and in Harold himself. For Harold too is an orphan, albeit one who—through the intercession of the cook ("that big German son-of-a-bitch") at the Chicago orphanage in which he grew up who inexplicably took a liking to him and dispensed extra servings of food to his favourite—managed to survive his deprivation and, more, to develop a capacity not merely to empathise but to sympathetically identify with the deprived and even to love and give everything he has for the salvation of these "dead end kids".

* * *

While *Orphans* may be read as a depiction of the psychopathological consequences for the individual of deprivation of mothering and fathering, it may also be interpreted from the sociological and theological perspectives as addressing the subject of separation, loss, abandonment, and the agony of dereliction on the historical and existential levels as well. According to an extensive sociological literature on the so-called decline of paternal authority in modern society (Marcuse, 1970)—a thesis that would seem to be supported by the prevalence of the theme of the absent father in the history of American cinema—we in the West exist, like Philip and Treat, in a "society without the father" (Mitscherlich, 1970). But such a fatherless, or rather parentless society (since one can also posit a relative failure of the maternal and more generally familial functions) is likely to be experienced as a godless one as well, the sense of abandonment by any caring authority spreading beyond the horizon of the family to include the universe as a whole. While secular and religious thinkers may differ on whether the sense of existential emptiness or *anomie* is a metaphysical projection of our social condition (Berger, 1967; Durkheim, 1897), or whether the social condition itself may be a consequence of metaphysical doubt, they share a large measure of agreement that in either case the result is a widespread threat to both individual identity and social order.

I think the play suggests that, in an important sense, we all, at least at times, and especially in our culture's current "epoch of homelessness" (Buber, 1938), experience ourselves as orphans, "thrown", in Heidegger's (1927) sense, into a world we never made. In this situation, feeling abandoned by our Creator and Caregiver, we can react in either of two ways. Like Philip, we may succumb to anxiety, inhibition, arrested development, and dependence upon (and often abuse by) some apparently stronger substitute attachment figure, some leader or *Führer* like Treat. Or, like Treat himself, we can harden our hearts, split off our pain, helplessness, separation anxiety, and longing and, adopting what Ian Suttie (1935) called a "taboo on tenderness", live out a façade of tough independence and aggressive self-sufficiency that masks our repressed (and frequently projected) emotional pain, anxiety, depression, loneliness, and longing. In a seemingly parentless world, or a godless one if you prefer, abandoned children seem to sort themselves into one or the other (or both, on different levels of a single, split psychic organisation) of the two types represented here by Philip and Treat. On one hand, with Philip, we have the hysterics, depressives, and masochists, individuals who, losing any sense of themselves as effective subjects, experience themselves as objects, slaves, or victims of fate or the whims of others (a position conventionally occupied by women in patriarchal society). On the other hand, with Treat, we find the obsessive compulsives, narcissists, and sadists, those, in other words, who attempt to usurp the absent deity's position as an omnipotent subject or master (a strategy customarily adopted by the patriarchal male).

In this light, the domestic situation of Treat and Philip is a caricature of traditional marital sex roles: Treat is the phallic, sadistic, narcissistic breadwinner who, repressing his own anxiety and dependency, projects (or, more accurately, projectively identifies) these unwanted parts of the self into his insecure, depressive, masochistic partner who remains shut in at home, agoraphobic, the object, recipient, or container of Treat's projection of his nightmare images of castration and helplessness. This containment is maintained (as it is in the stereotypical patriarchal marriage) through Philip's complementary introjective identification with his brother's projections and his projective identification into Treat of his own disavowed active capability, assertiveness, and aggression. This analysis is in no way contradicted by the fact that although Treat abuses Philip in various, often playful, ways he at the same time takes care of him, saving them both from the clutches of the child-welfare department, bringing home the Hellman's mayonnaise, even putting hydrogen peroxide on Philip's cuts with a maternal tenderness (for Treat represents a binding or symbiotic mother as much as a domineering husband/father). Abusive husbands are not infrequently protective and tender towards the objects of their abuse, expressing towards them all the contradictory impulses of love and hate, tenderness and violence that a child inflicts upon its teddy bear. While fully supporting the demands of women to be treated as more than transitional objects (Winnicott, 1971) for the use of men, as the play reveals, for such positive change to take place it is not sufficient for the Treats among us to integrate their projected pain, dependence, and helplessness. Since a bipersonal, interactional, or symbiotic system is in play here, it is at the same time essential for the Philips to find the courage to overcome their masochism through the integration of their projected and retroflected aggression, to leave their prisons (which are also their nests or refuges) and acquire the capacity to stand on their own feet—but hopefully not by identifying with their erstwhile oppressors, for there are already too many muggers in the park.

* * *

The concept of projective identification (Klein, 1946; Sandler, 1987) is notorious for having many conflicting, vague, and overlapping meanings, so let me clearly define the sense in which I wish to use it here. Although Klein herself mostly employed the concept in a "one-body" sense as a subject's phantasy that parts of the self now reside in another, Bion (1962, Chapter Twelve) and others elaborated it in "two-body" terms. By interpersonal projective identification I mean the unconscious process in which split-off and/or repressed feelings, self-states, and self- and object-images are projected by a subject into an object who not only comes to be seen by the subject as containing the projected elements of the self, but that actually is unconsciously manoeuvred into having and even enacting the feelings, states, roles, and characteristics that have been projected. Having thus subtly influenced the object into actually feeling or enacting the projected part (i.e., introjectively identifying with it), the subject now seeks to control it actively or passively. In this way, the subject comes to feel a spurious sense of mastery over unacceptable, denied, or disowned parts of the self; the subject feels relief, for now the disturbing contents are no longer felt to be in the self but in the other whom he has unconsciously manoeuvred into embodying them.

I am indebted to a colleague (Rodin, 1990) for the following illustration of this process. A mother unable to contain her own distress and anger would come home and, with her baby with her in the kitchen, start loudly slamming the kitchen cupboards until the baby was screaming, at which point the mother herself relaxed and became a competent soothing adult, soothing herself vicariously through the baby who was now enacting her own split-off and projected distress.

The Freudian concept of identification with the aggressor in which, for example, the abused child later becomes an abusing adult, or to take another example, the dominated woman subsequently becomes a domineering bully, highlights the victim's repression of his or her helplessness and trauma and defensive identification with the power and mastery of the aggressor. But while it describes characterological change in the subject, it does so within a "one-body" psychology and does not address the key element in interpersonal projective identification: the intersubjective process through which another is unconsciously manoeuvred into actually feeling and playing the part either of an aggressor or a helpless and traumatised victim.

An example of identification with the aggressor would be that of the little girl who got over her fear of ghosts by pretending to be one: "'There's no need to be afraid in the hall,' she told her little brother, 'you just have to pretend that you're the ghost who might meet you'" (A. Freud, 1936, p. 111). But while this is a good illustration of identification with the aggressor, it misses the essential feature of projective identification, which in this case would be the unconscious process through which another person is actually made to feel they have seen a ghost or induced to behave like one. A subject may certainly identify with the aggressor and project the role of the victim onto someone else, but to induce the other to actually feel and act like a victim entails interpersonal projective identification. Furthermore, the concept of identification with the aggressor captures only one of the dual dimensions of projective identification, for it is equally possible to reverse roles, identify with the victim, project the role of aggressor upon another, and unconsciously manoeuvre the other into actually feeling and enacting the part. Not infrequently psychotherapists encounter patients who shift rapidly back and forth between these two forms of projective identification in ways that are, initially at least, most confusing to their therapists (Kernberg, 1975). At one moment the therapist is unconsciously made to feel like an intimidated child before the patient who seems all-powerful and frightening. But, in the next, he finds himself feeling angry and inclined to be cruel and rejecting towards the patient, who has shifted into the role of the threatened and intimidated child.

The process of projective identification is at the root of very many chronic marital, interpersonal, and intergroup conflicts. Typically, the narcissistic and sadistic subject (Treat) projects his split-off anxiety, helplessness, and dependency into an object whom he then induces, often with society's and the victim's own collusion, to play the anxious, masochistic, depressive, and dependent part (Philip). The subject (master) then begins to regard the devalued object (slave) as an albatross around his neck, so he breaks away. Once free of the subject's constant projections, the object typically, like Philip, begins to recover its disavowed subjectivity and agency. But, while the former object grows stronger and more independent, the erstwhile subject begins, like Treat, to fall apart. Without his depressed or anxious object to contain them, his projections begin to fail and the disowned parts of the self start to return and he becomes increasingly anxious and depressed. A complete reversal of roles may even occur and, like Philip towards the end of the play, the liberated slave may make her or his former master "it". Hopefully, however, the emancipated one will not merely reverse the roles but, again like Philip, declare that the old sadomasochistic game is over.

* * *

An important truth, understood by experienced analysts, and conveyed in *Orphans*, is that people like Philip (and those depressed and anxious wives) who on the surface appear so disturbed, may often turn out to be far stronger, healthier, and more intact than those who, like Treat, possess a narcissistic shell or "false self" (Winnicott, 1965) that enables them, initially at least, to appear to possess far greater ego strength. Despite his confinement to the house, his terror of the outside world, his living in a fantasy world, and his marked dependence upon Treat for basic provision, Philip's very weakness is in a sense the source of his greater strength. Philip does not have radically to split-off his dependency feelings and related elements of his emotional life, precisely because he can depend on Treat (who, of course, secretly depends on him in a different way but to an even greater degree).

Like the mothers of so many so-called borderline patients who undermine their children's efforts towards independence because of their unconscious need to maintain a symbiosis with them in order to sustain their own precarious identities, Treat is an abusive parent. Paradoxically, however, his very availability to Philip as a parent-figure, albeit in many ways a bad one, nevertheless enables the latter to remain in touch with core aspects of his true self. Under Treat's protection, however sadistic, confining, and controlling, Philip is able to retain a capacity for imaginative play: he does little else all day but play and also teach himself to read, in this way getting himself the education that Treat, like a patriarchal husband, seeks to deny him in order to keep him dependent and controlled. Not having to totally split off and deny dependency, Philip is able to remain sufficiently in touch with his attachment needs to use transitional objects—the little toy lamb (the theological significance of which we may speculate about) and the mother's shoe—objects that represent a link to his childhood attachment figures, primarily the mother.

Treat, on the other hand, having no one to depend on but himself, has had to split off his child self altogether in order to become a prematurely (pseudo) self-sufficient adult, capable of providing for himself and his younger brother. Treat's attachment needs and his separation pain have had to be massively dissociated and projectively identified into Philip and, hence, Treat has only hostility and contempt for the transitional objects that threaten to remind him of his child self and his attachment longings and separation pain. Something of the above dynamic was represented long ago in Hegel's (1807) discussion of the master/slave dialectic whereby, over time, the slave comes to occupy the stronger position through the master's very dependence upon him or her. But contemporary psychoanalysis has an important addition to make to the Hegelian analysis in its recognition that a central element of the slave's paradoxical advantage lies in the fact that his or her very domination at the same time constitutes a kind of protection, thanks to which he or she has been able to avoid the extremes of dehumanisation to which the master has been driven.

An important implication of this analysis is that any hope for mitigation of the chronic violence, exploitation, and scapegoating to which humanity is heir lies, as Suttie (1935) realised, in the revaluation and recovery of those qualities of sensitivity, tenderness, and vulnerability commonly associated with childhood and femininity. In the play, these qualities are embodied, albeit in a masochistic distortion, in the gentle personality of Philip and, in a healthier fashion, in Harold's sympathetic (rather than projective) identification with the orphans, an identification that makes possible his acts of creative self-sacrifice on their behalf. In our culture, these qualities are symbolically associated with the figure of the lamb, a frequent object of sacrifice, as in the case of the *Agnus Dei*. Hopefully, any political system which seeks to realise these values will be moved by a compassionate and forgiving awareness of the painful dilemma of the Treats of this world (among whom, after all, we are all included to some degree). Granted, they are no "treat" to live with because of their chronic insistence that their pain be experienced by those they depend on as scapegoats rather than by themselves. However, merely to scapegoat them is to become rather than to heal them.

* * *

But we must have no illusion that the healing that is necessary can be achieved short of a radical psychosocial transformation, turning or conversion. For surely today, even apart from theological doctrines of the "fall of man" and "original sin", few can doubt that our enmeshment in the sadomasochistic disease, if not a defining feature of our human nature, is to say the least profound. Our destructiveness towards one another, ourselves, and our environment appears so pervasive that, as the play suggests, without the unsolicited, unexpected, and seemingly fortuitous intervention of a powerful helper, the situation would indeed appear to be hopeless. But Harold's arrival has changed everything. At the beginning of the film, Treat displays a fleeting look of panic when he comes home and is momentarily unable to find his brother. However, at the conclusion, when he discovers that, thanks to Harold's encouragement, a newly confident Philip has actually left the house, his aggressive narcissistic shell, already weakened by Harold's loving authority, shatters completely and he is found by Philip crumpled at the top of the stairs in an almost foetal position, clinging to his mother's coat.

However, as psychoanalysts know only too well, the profound resistance to cure is never so easily overcome. Treat quickly tries to re-establish the old projective-identification system but, owing to Harold's gracious intercession, a redeemed Philip is now strong enough to refuse the projections. Having once been lost, Philip now is found. He knows where he is. Harold has given him a map. In a desperate attempt to force Philip back into his control, Treat, as if possessed, tears up the map (an allusion to Holy Scripture and its revelation of who we are?) and attacks, almost killing his brother in a final demonic attempt to turn him back into his object or creature so that Treat can sustain his illusory sense of himself as an omnipotent subject or creator. This effort is bound to fail, for if Philip were killed then, as Sartre (1943) following Hegel (1807) understood, the victory would at the same time amount to a defeat. For Treat would in that case find himself alone with no one to reflect and support his spurious grandeur by containing and thus obscuring his actual brokenness (Vanier, 1988).

The moral of the story can be stated in both psychoanalytic and theological terms. To the extent that we refuse to integrate our childhood pain, we visit it upon others through projective identification. To the extent to which we refuse to take up our own cross, we crucify others. In Philip's case matters are a little more complex, for here the failure to take up one's own cross results, if not in a sort of self-crucifixion, then at least in a masochistic sacrifice of the self to an idol as an escape from the more frightening demands of life. In the terms developed in this book, we can say that to the extent that we refuse to reconcile with conscience, we will continue to be tormented by the superego, or identify with it and torment the others upon whom we have projected our guilt. Reconciliation with conscience requires integration of our childhood pain, a crucifying experience (well symbolised in the Stations of the Cross) that is the essential condition for recovery of the true self and a capacity for sympathetic identification with others. Refusal to integrate childhood pain leaves us with a false self and a superego that inflicts torment either upon the self or, through projective identification, upon scapegoated others.

While Philip's masochistic dependency rather easily gives way to healthy self-assertion with Harold's encouragement and the instruction he provides in the art of living, Treat's sadism and omnipotent self-sufficiency yield only in the face of Harold's personal exemplification of the art of dying. In the final scenes of the play it is not only Harold who is crucified but, witnessing and in a sense identifying with this crucifixion, Treat himself undergoes the painful but liberating distintegration of his false self and the tentative emergence of his true self—a death and resurrection through which he is finally able to recognise and acknowledge his identity as one of the community of "dead end kids".

* * *

If much of the foregoing has concerned the pathological process of projective identification, in Harold's capacity for sympathetic identification (as distinct from a merely cognitive empathic identification) we see a positive alternative. For Harold too belongs to the community of orphans. Unlike his movie heroes, the Dead End Kids who had a little "top-of-the-mornin" Irish mother to cook them corned beef and cabbage, Harold and the others at the orphanage "didn't have no mommy or daddy" (p. 20). According to Harold:

> Orphans always hungry ... orphans always coughing up blood, orphans dropping dead all the time, terrible mortality rate at an orphanage! ... Motherless orphans, middle of the night Chicago, orphans on a big hill facing Lake Michigan. Wind come through there making a terrible sound ... Orphans pulling their blankets up over their heads, frightened orphans crying out. You know what they were crying? ... Mommy! Mommy! Honest to god! Motherless

orphans don't know a mommy from a daddy, don't know a mommy from a fuckin' tangerine! (pp. 23–24)

Throughout the film Harold continually sings or whistles:

> *If I had the wings of an angel*
> *Over these prison walls I would fly*
> *Straight to the arms of me mutter*
> *And there I'd be willin' to die!*[1]

In the middle of the night the hungry orphans would sneak downstairs and raid the refrigerator. "German slept there, one eye open, break your back if he caught you, break every bone in your body" (p. 23). But, "Thank god for that bloody fucking German son of a bitch," for he took a liking to Harold for some unfathomable reason and gave him "big heaping plates of meat and potatoes" that enabled him to survive. In other words, Harold, like Philip, did receive some caring, however limited. In Philip's case it came from Treat; in Harold's from the German. Hence, despite becoming a gangster, Harold never entirely identified with the aggressor. He also identified with the good aspects of the German as a carer, as well as with the positive images of family life that he glimpsed in the movies.

Like Philip, who watched old Errol Flynn movies on TV while Treat was away during the day, Harold retained a capacity for imaginative and cultural experience: "I loved that woman. Corn beef and cabbage cooking day and night. I used to work up a hearty appetite just sitting in them dark Chicago movie houses watching those Dead End Kids" (pp. 20–21). One of the words that the autodidactic Philip has underlined in a magazine is "dispensation" (p. 15), a term defined as the "ordering, management, esp. of the world by Providence" (*Concise Oxford Dictionary*, 1982, p. 276). It is his identification with the kids who are fed and with the mother who feeds them, as well as with the German cook who fed him, that leads Harold to "dispense" hearty meals of corned beef and cabbage and everything else he possesses for the benefit of the orphans. With Sagan (1988) I have argued that while the superego is grounded in early identification with the aggressor, conscience has its roots in early identification with the nurturer. I will refrain from further comment on such "oral" themes, except to point to their association with a mother's giving of her own bodily substance in the act of nursing her children and with the Holy Eucharist as the ritual re-enactment of the Last Supper, in which those who believe in Him symbolically feed on Christ's body and blood.

It has become evident to social scientists and psychoanalysts that human beings are sometimes able to make use of empirically absent or entirely abstract attachment figures, significant others, or "selfobjects" (Knoblauch, 1995) to sustain identity and self-esteem in the absence of positive response and affirmation, or in the presence of hostility and negation in their current milieu. We know something of the important supportive function performed by imaginary playmates for lonely or unloved children; of the role of fantasies of future appreciation by posterity in enabling innovative artists to keep working despite depreciation of their art by their contemporaries; of the importance of memories of previous experiences of acceptance in helping people to cope with current rejection; and of the role of faith in sometimes helping people resist the overwhelmingly dehumanising forces of their environment (Frankl, 1946). All of these are instances of the creative capacity possessed, to a greater or lesser degree, by many people to employ the symbolic function of the human psyche to generate images of consolation and affirmation with which to resist current adversity, devaluation, and negation of the self. It goes without saying that adherents of different philosophical and religious worldviews, even while agreeing on the existence and importance of such images as components of *psychic* reality, will disagree regarding the status of the extrapsychic reality to which such images are sometimes felt to correspond.

Unlike Freud (1927c, 1930a) who was prone to denigrate such phenomena as regressive or infantile illusions based upon wishful thinking, Winnicott (1971) appreciated the crucial adaptive functions of such uses of the imagination. For Winnicott, they belong with play, art, religion, and human cultural life in general to the "transitional area" of experience which mediates or transcends such binary oppositions, polarities, or dichotomies as fantasy and reality, the subjective and the objective, belief and disbelief. Such phenomena originate, according to Winnicott, in the child's use of its first "not-me" possession, its special bit of blanket, teddy bear, or other "transitional object" which, paradoxically, is at one and the same time both a "me" and a "not-me" possession, both self and other, inner and outer, created and discovered, invented and found.

For Winnicott the transitional "area of illusion" is a zone of human experience that transcends both the merely subjective and the merely objective. It is an area that lies between and in a sense "above" the antitheses of PS (paranoid-schizoid position) and D (depressive position), of narcissism and object love. Take, for example, a relatively healthy person's experience of falling in love. There are intense, bipolar swings of emotion, idolisation beyond idealisation, a sense of something magical, paranoid jealousy, intense joy, and at times equally intense despair. It is a temporary state that can occasionally collapse into frankly psychotic demonisation, often into devaluation or utter indifference ("Whatever could I have seen in him or her?"), or settle down into a more stable object love in which the magic tends famously to be lost over time as the "cosy chemicals" come to displace those mediating passionate intensity (Fisher, 1994) unless creative ways are found by the couple to intermittently recover their passion for one another. But most would agree that their lives would have been impoverished without one or more experiences of this temporary madness that is not really madness unless it falls out of the transitional area into psychosis rather than indifference or mature object love.

The same may be said of related experiences of the sacred. Fundamentalists who bring to such experience supernatural and magical ideas taken quite literally are operating on the paranoid-schizoid level and are, in this sense, essentially psychotic (if they actually take it seriously and are not just pretending). On the other hand, the "sanity" of those living in an entirely profane and objective world with no access to the transitional area of creative play and illusion are excessively fixated in the depressive position. Yet some people manage to retain a transitional sense of the sacred, succumbing neither to belief nor disbelief but, rather, maintaining that playful suspension characteristic of the transitional area that is essential for meaningful, non-psychotic experience of ritual, dance, liturgy, literature, cinema, and other arts, including the discovery phase of scientific creativity and the experience of a vital marriage in which passion is kept alive or periodically rekindled. While Freud (1927c) disparaged illusion in religion, he revered it in the arts. Even today many still equate the sacred with religion, failing to comprehend what Sagan (2001, Chapter Ten) and others recognise as "the secular sacred"—devotion to human rights, democratic ideals, the marital bond, the lives of children, human life in general, the natural environment, etc. Just as religion has attempted to hijack morality, so it has tried to monopolise the sacred. Whereas religion is "the belief in and worship of a superhuman controlling power, especially a personal God or gods" (OED), the sacred is not essentially a matter of *belief* at all, but rather of value-commitments, devotion, reverence, and love— matters more of the heart than the mind. In this light it becomes possible to grasp the basis of, for example, a thoroughly religionless, secular Christianity as a commitment to Jesus as "the way, the truth and the life" (Kee, 1971) quite apart from any religious belief in god. A secular faith of this kind is not only capable of devotion to the values it holds sacred, but also of emotionally intense transitional ritual, liturgical and sacramental expressions of such devotion akin to emotionally moving experiences in the arts, or in a marriage that retains the benefits to be derived from what we might think of as the "marital arts"—those that help to periodically return it from the merely mundane and prosaic to the poetic, the passionate, and the mysterious qualities of the transitional area.

Recognition of the PS splitting involved in the older Kleinian unidirectional notion of development (PS→D) led to the revised notion of healthy mental functioning as a kind of flexible oscillation (PS←→D). Since there is good as well as bad in both PS and D, this is a valid theoretical advance, an approach to the idea of something *between* or *beyond* or at the very least *irreducible* to these polarities. But the notion of oscillation between PS and D, the attempt to integrate what is good in both positions, the passion and intensity of PS with the realism and responsibility of D, however valuable in itself, does not seem to me to capture the essential idea of the transitional area as one in which there is a willing suspension of both belief and disbelief. This suspension is precarious: it can easily collapse into either belief or disbelief. To take but one example: transitional symbols of something sacred, such as bread and wine as signifiers of Christ, can easily succumb to literalisation or concretisation, becoming magically identified with what they are meant to symbolise, "symbolic equations" (Segal, 1957) on the paranoid-schizoid level, as in the Roman Catholic doctrine of the transubstantiation. On the other hand, to treat the Eucharistic elements as mere signifiers or "symbolic representations" on the level of the depressive position is to leave the transitional area in the opposite direction of excessive objectivity, in which case the liturgical play breaks down, as when a film breaks and the house lights come up accompanied by the groans of annoyance and disappointment on the part of a frustrated and disillusioned audience.

As Winnicott (1971) understood, transitional uses of the imagination frequently lead human beings to a heightened, rather than a diminished sense of reality, promote biological and psychological survival, and lead, at least in the case of creative genius, to the significant transformation of what passes for consensual reality itself. But it is important to recognise that the notion of the transitional area of illusion can be exploited to justify belief as against disbelief; when properly understood it refers to the willing suspension of *both*. It must be remembered that Winnicott referred to these phenomena as "transitional" because he viewed them as necessary to help human beings achieve a *transition* that he, like Freud, regarded as essential: the transition from relating only to subjective or narcissistic objects to relating to objective objects as in both science and true object love. But Winnicott at the same time understood that just as "Man shall not live by bread alone" (*Deuteronomy* 8:3; *Matthew* 4:4), so he shall not live, at least in health, by science and objectivity alone, or even by object love as distinct from the "ec-static" love characteristic of the transitional area.

* * *

But not all children and adults are equally able to employ transitional phenomena, just as they vary in their capacity for what Erikson (1950) called "basic trust", a phenomenon clearly related to "faith" understood in its Hebraic and existential sense as distinct from Hellenistic notions of faith as assent to propositions and catechisms. The absence of transitional objects in a child's early experience or his inability to engage in imaginative play is a significant indicator of pathology. It seems that a capacity for imaginative play is both a sign of healthy development and a protection against pathology. The capacity to utilise images of supportive significant others and to have confidence in their love and concern ("Jesus loves me, this I know ...") would appear to depend upon at least a minimal experience of positive response from actual as opposed to transitional carers. However, this is not to deny that particularly gifted children are sometimes able to extract or create at least some of the support they need even in very unfavourable circumstances.

But to return to the characters in the film: both Harold and Philip, having received some degree of care, are able to utilise the transitional phenomena of their cultural milieu to sustain themselves. Unlike

Treat, whose experience may either have been more impoverished and traumatic or who may have lacked sufficient innate creative capacity to make use of transitional phenomena to ease his pain to the point at which it could be borne rather than having to be denied, Harold and Philip are not forced to split-off their childhood experience. Hence, it remains available to them as the basis for sympathetic identification and compassion, as in Harold's Christlike devotion to his "dead end kids":

HAROLD: You're not a Dead End Kid, are you?
  TREAT: A Dead End Kid?
HAROLD: 'cause if you were a Dead End Kid I'd give you everything
          I had ... I swear to God ... I'd give you the very shirt off my
          back.
  TREAT: You don't have to go that far.
HAROLD: There are no limits as far as the Dead End Kids and me are
          concerned.
  TREAT: No kidding.
HAROLD: I love those fucking Dead End Kids! (p. 19)

Through their identification with the nurturer, having received love from their carers, healthy parents wish in turn to pass this gift on to their own offspring, thus also making "reparation" (Klein, 1964) for destructive wishes and acts towards both preceding and succeeding generations. Similarly, Harold desires to give to the orphans as he had been given to.

It would be incorrect to call Harold's sympathetic identification with the orphans a projective identification. For although he sees his orphan self in them, this self is not split-off or repressed. Rather, it is an integrated aspect of his overall personality, an integration made possible by the care he, like Philip, received. Not having been split-off, Harold's child self is available to him as a more or less conscious resource for sympathetic identification rather than for denial, projection, and control. Hence, through sympathetic rather than projective identification, Harold can vicariously receive what he seeks to give to the deprived boys. And he seeks to give them everything he has.

HAROLD: This is a real tragic situation I've wandered into, one boy's a
          delinquent ... the other boy's shoulders are just dying for a
          gentle encouraging squeeze.

PHILIP: They are?

HAROLD: Anybody ever give your shoulders an encouraging squeeze?

PHILIP: I don't think so.

HAROLD: That's a tragedy. Every young man's shoulders need an encouraging squeeze now and then.

PHILIP: Treat never did that.

HAROLD: I imagine not. What about your father?

PHILIP: I don't know. He ran away from home when I was small.

HAROLD: He deserted the family?

PHILIP: Yes.

HAROLD: Well, I know shoulders, Philip. If I know anything, I know about shoulders. ... You want me to give them a squeeze, try it out, see how it feels?

PHILIP: (hesitantly) I don't know.

HAROLD: You don't have to touch me. I'll touch you ...

There follows a moving scene that, for me at least, calls to mind the central image on the ceiling of the Sistine Chapel in which Michelangelo depicts God reaching out to bring Adam to life through his touch.

PHILIP: Well, maybe that would be all right.

HAROLD: That would be fine. Come on over here. Come on. ... How's that feel?

PHILIP: (lets out a deep breath) Feels okay.

HAROLD: Feels good?

PHILIP: Yes.

HAROLD: Feels real good?

PHILIP: Yes, feels real good.

HAROLD: Feels encouraging, huh?

PHILIP: Uh huh.

HAROLD: Makes you feel there's hope.

PHILIP: Yes.

HAROLD: (squeezing shoulder) This is what you missed.

PHILIP: Yes.

HAROLD: That feeling.

PHILIP: I missed that.

HAROLD: You got it now.

PHILIP: I do?

HAROLD: Forever and ever, Philip. I would never leave you.
(pp. 37–38)

* * *

In the light of this allusion to Christ's promise that "I am with you always, even unto the end of the world" (*Matthew* 28:20 *KJV*), it becomes evident that, in addition to its various psychoanalytic meanings, Kessler's play may at the same time be viewed as an allegory of the arrival of the guest who heals and redeems and who, although betrayed and crucified, nevertheless triumphs over death by living on in the hearts of those who believe in him. The allegorical betrayal is fulfilled when Harold is delivered over to "the mob" (whose "securities" he has stolen) by a combination of circumstances arising from Treat's initial attempts to obtain a "ransom" and later by his envy of Harold's power and his inability to master his aggression.

Having performed his miracles (the Houdini escape, the transformation of the house, the provision of food, clothing, money, and a map), communicated most of his teaching, and even administered a baptism (in the scene in which he exposes Philip to the rain), Harold had nearly completed his ministry. But not quite since, as he himself says, "We're talking about life and death, Treat, mortality! The human condition!" (p. 45) and, hence, his final lesson to his "dead end kids" must take the form of an encounter with death itself. Whereas the film leaves us wondering why Harold apparently chooses to leave the boys, in the play the events leading up to the final scene are more satisfactorily explained. Harold takes Philip for a walk in the course of which he is spotted by his enemies. Telling Philip to keep on walking, Harold heads off in a different direction drawing his enemies after him (in this way "sacrificing" himself). Later he returns to the house with a wound in his side to die on the sofa in a cruciform position. But only after having provided Philip with his map and having told him, "Don't worry ... I'll always be with you ... Forever and ever. You can count on me" (p. 96).

And this Redeemer's healing mission seems really to have been fulfilled: like the orphans who once enjoyed a brief escape from the orphanage and who, although beaten on their return, had nevertheless seen what they had to see (p. 96), so Philip and Treat had encountered what they needed to encounter in Harold. Philip's healing was well advanced by the time of Harold's death. Treat, on the other hand, had consistently resisted his saviour, even causing Harold momentarily to despair and, echoing Christ's words in the Garden of Gethsemane, to mutter to himself: "I wish to god I could get out of this lousy business. I wish to god I could go back to Chicago" (p. 62). Prior to Harold's death, Treat had consistently rejected his many offers of an encouraging squeeze. Now, finally, he reaches out to touch him. And this touch has a devastating effect in breaking down his final defences against the pain of his early losses. As in the case of a previous doubting Thomas (*John* 20:27-29), it leads to the collapse of all resistance and to a final confession of faith. Just as Philip previously accepted with gratitude Harold's location of him in time and space—"We're tucked away safe and sound at the very edge of the Milky Way which is swimming in the great ocean of space ... circling the sun ... in the Western Hemisphere, North American Continent, State of Pennsylvania, City of Philadelphia ... The sixty-forty block ..." (pp. 71–72)—now, at last, Treat can accept the identity Harold had freely offered him from the beginning: "Harold! Harold!" he cries, "I am a Dead End Kid, Harold! I am a fucking Dead End Kid!" (p. 98).

Note

1. From "The Prisoner's Song," written by Guy Massey (1924), Shapiro Bernstein & Co., Inc. In *Orphans* the lyrics are modified from the original "Straight to the arms of my darling" to "... the arms of me mutter".

SUMMARY

Indeed, it is almost a kind of cunning to come in the guise of compassion in order to talk about sin.

—Søren Kierkegaard (1850)

Whereas Freud himself viewed conscience as one of the functions of the superego, in *The Still Small Voice: Psychoanalytic Reflections on Guilt and Conscience*, following the lead provided by Eli Sagan's *Freud, Women and Morality: The Psychology of Good and Evil* (1988) and elaborating on certain of the ideas of Melanie Klein, I argue that superego and conscience are distinct mental functions and that, therefore, a fourth mental structure, the conscience, needs to be added to the psychoanalytic structural theory of the mind. I claim that while both conscience and superego originate in the so-called pre-Oedipal phase of infant and child development they are comprised of contrasting and often conflicting identifications. The primary object, still most often the mother, is inevitably experienced as, on the one hand, nurturing and soothing and, on the other, frustrating and persecuting. Conscience is formed in identification with the nurturer; the superego in identification with the aggressor. There is a principle of reciprocity at

287

work in the human psyche: for love received one seeks to return love; for hate, hate (the talion law).

While frustration leading to a sense of persecution and to hatred is inevitable, for even the best carer imaginable is unable to entirely prevent frustration and pain (the "basic" or existential pain to which humanity is heir and that is nobody's fault), encounters with the "surplus" frustration above and beyond this minimum (that *is* the fault of particular carers and of the society that is responsible for caring for the carers) adds to the mental pain that generates hatred and the desire for revenge. Conscience, grounded in love, inevitably opposes the hatred that fuels the sadistic superego that directs it at others who serve as scapegoats or back against the self in the form of the persecutory guilt and shame that underlie most psychopathology. Anyone who is at all psychologically functional has been loved, however poorly, and on some level knows this. Feeling identified with the nurturers to whom we owe our physical and psychological life, we feel an inclination, an obligation, to love. However repressed, this inclination to love, grounded in identification with the nurturer, is opposed to the hatred grounded in identification with the aggressor. Conscience fuelled by love is opposed to the superego fuelled by hate. It is to better grasp this internal conflict between superego and conscience that I call for recognition of the conscience as the fourth structure of the mind in addition to id, ego, and superego. Out of the conflict among these four mental agencies come the various compromise-formations of which our experience and behaviour are comprised.

Just as, for Freud, *Eros* and *Thanatos* are not themselves viewed as compromise-formations but rather as the clashing forces that, when fused rather than defused, issue in the range of compromise-formations that we see, so I do not view id, ego, superego, and conscience as compromise-formations but as the conflicting forces generating them. As Freud (1930a, p. 144) hoped that eternal *Eros* would assert itself in its immortal struggle with *Thanatos*, so I hope that conscience may be strengthened in its immortal struggle with the superego. In fact, for me, *Eros* and conscience, *Thanatos* and superego, are synonymous terms. What some consider the "loving and beloved" superego is what I call conscience. Like Franz Alexander, Sandor Ferenczi, and Melanie Klein, I recognise the superego as a bad, internal, persecutory object that not infrequently takes the form of what Freud (1923b) himself called "a pure culture of the death instinct" (p. 52). I believe the tendency of many psychoanalysts to defend the superego, to resist calls for its disempowerment in favour of conscience, to insist it is a compromise-formation and to seek to compromise with it instead, is grounded in fear of and deference towards the parental authority that, for some, is unconsciously equated with "God" despite most often being experienced as more demonic than divine.

Unlike my forebears, Alexander and Ferenczi, I do not propose the superego's replacement by the rational ego for, in my view, rationality cannot serve as the source of values. Following Jean-Jacques Rousseau, I find the roots of morality not in reason but in feeling, in sympathetic identification or "pity". With Pascal, I hold "the heart has reasons reason cannot know". Such "reasons of the heart" form the core of conscience. Unlike the torments inflicted by the demonic superego that merely uses transgression as an excuse to do what it wants—punish and torment the ego—the conscience, what Winnicott called "the capacity for concern", is genuinely troubled by failures to love. We either face our bad conscience, acknowledge and bear genuine (depressive) guilt, and through contrition, repentance, and reparation learn to accept forgiveness, or we are forced to suffer the torments of the damned—persecutory guilt inflicted by the sadistic internal persecutor and saboteur, the superego.

While psychoanalysis has focused upon the destructiveness of id-driven wrongdoers, it has had little to say about the damage done by those driven by the superego. Freud and subsequent psychoanalysis has largely whitewashed the superego while demonising the id, the alleged "beast" in man, when in reality animals are seldom beastly, at least not in the ways humans often are. While aware of its destructiveness in the clinical realm, psychoanalysts have largely ignored the ideologies of domination—the sexism, racism, heterosexism, childism, classism, possessive individualism, consumerism, and commodity fetishism—that are internalised from unconscionable societies into the unconscionable superego. Because the superego is unconsciously equated with the parents (and therefore with both God and the Devil), we have as a discipline sought to honour and protect our parents by looking away from their sins and projecting them onto a scapegoat—the animals and the alleged animal in man—in this way to protect ourselves from imagined parental (divine and demonic) wrath and retribution.

Psychoanalytic therapy has always been grounded in a moral ethic that it practises while refusing to preach. From Freud on, psychoanalysts have sought to "de-moralise" what is an intrinsically moral enterprise.

Like the "scientific socialists", the scientific psychoanalysts have sought to disguise their humanistic morality behind a façade of positivism. But the dictum "where id was, there shall ego be", far from representing a value-free, scientific/medical perspective, entails a moral ethic valuing not merely the conscious over the unconscious, but prudence and self-control over impulsive acting-out, sublimation over primitive drive, the binding of *Thanatos* by *Eros* and, most significant, the transcendence of narcissism in favour of object love. In practical terms, psychoanalysis has always subscribed to the Judaeo-Christian ethic of love while trying its best to disguise the fact. In the political domain humanistic liberalism and socialism have sometimes suffered disadvantage in relation to their loudly moralising reactionary opponents owing to their need to focus upon issues in an apparently pragmatic, "de-moralised" way instead of openly avowing their moral vision. In the same way, psychoanalysis has been hampered by its need to find self-deceptive euphemisms such as promoting "mental health" or the overcoming of "pathological narcissism" to describe a pilgrim's progress towards becoming a more responsible and loving rather than irresponsible and hating human being.

Paralleling the psychoanalytic ethic of evolution from the paranoid to the depressive or reparative position is the psychoanalytically informed evolutionary social theory advanced by Talcott Parsons, Robert Bellah, and Eli Sagan. I review this perspective and outline Sagan's theory of "modernity psychosis" that describes the bizarre forms of "backlash" we are witnessing today and that constitute the resistance to the moral demand to carry to its conclusion the modernisation project of universal emancipation from all forms of tyranny and domination in favour of universal mutual recognition (itself, for some, a less embarrassing euphemism for love). Sagan reminds us that while the democratic project represents one of the two faces of modernity, totalitarianism represents the other.

Since radical cultural relativism has now been relativised and there is widespread recognition in philosophy and social science as well as all major world religions of the existence of a universal moral ethic, the ethic of charity or reciprocity (don't do to others what you don't want them doing to you), I argue there is no need for psychoanalysis to be embarrassed by its adherence to this ethic. Whereas for Freud the superego is the only judge with no other judge to judge it, today the universal ethic of charity is capable of judging both the superego and the societies that shape it. In my view the universal ethic requires no religious foundation. Taking literally the statement that God is love (*I John* 4:8 *KJV*), I claim the obverse holds as well: love (conscience) is "god- and good-enough" for me.

Drawing on the work of Hannah Arendt, Terry Eagleton, and others, I critically review the concepts of psychopathy, evil, and the death drive. I dispute the existence of an entirely conscience-less primary psychopath in favour of the idea of a continuum of degrees of "the psychopathy of everyday life". With Eagleton I hold that evil acts are often committed by people who cannot themselves be considered evil as this term applies only in the case of sadistic psychopaths who, having thoroughly repressed conscience, derive perverse enjoyment by ridding themselves of their own unbearable nothingness through inflicting pain, humiliation, and death upon others and who, in this sense, are far from "banal". While the utterly un-Darwinian notion of a biologically based drive towards death is disputed, some of the many other meanings given to this term are discussed, such as: aggression; destructiveness; the fear of annihilation; the wish to separate or disconnect; the death-wish as a reaction to unbearable frustration and pain; a superego-driven masochism; the transcendence of the biological through accession to the Symbolic; or the lure of the infinite on the part of Faustian man. In the psychoanalytic literature it is only in context that one is sometimes able to decode what a particular author means by the use of this term.

In the penultimate chapter, I advocate a demythologising, deliteralising, or deconstructive approach to the Bible as metaphor, but one that escapes Freud's derogation of this approach by acknowledging, with Hegel at his most honest, that its result is no longer to be equated with religion. Although there is an important distinction to be made between Dietrich Bonhoeffer's early "religious" work on discipleship and the later "religionless Christianity" of the *Letters and Papers from Prison*, in my view the latter is as capable as the former of generating discipleship, but of a non-religious type. As Eagleton points out, the Reformation distinction between law and gospel, Moses and Christ, prefigures that between superego and conscience—a distinction that is not to be conflated with that between the so-called "Old" and "New" Testaments, for law and gospel, superego and conscience, are to be found in both. "Think not that I am come to destroy the law or the prophets: I am not come to destroy but to fulfil" (*Matthew* 5:17 *KJV*). Whereas the superego utilises the law in order to condemn and punish, the conscience, grounded in identification with the nurturer, mediates the love that assists fallen and broken human beings in their never entirely successful struggles to keep the law, and forgiveness in the face of inevitable failures.

The final chapter focuses upon the play and film, *Orphans*, that offers through the transitional experience of artistic illusion an emotional understanding of several of the key themes of this book. On one hand, the play illustrates the pathological use of interpersonal projective identification to sacrifice the other by splitting-off one's unbearable childhood pain and inducing it in the scapegoat. On the other hand, it illustrates the process in which through grace—that is, through receiving nurturance—people are sometimes enabled to bear and integrate rather than split-off their childhood pain and, as a result, are able to sustain sympathetic identification with suffering others and to offer them in turn the healing nurturance and containment they themselves have received. If one has received sufficient nurturance to be able to make use of transitional phenomena, one can sometimes receive further nurturance through illusion and cultural experience that can help one contain childhood pain rather than splitting it off and projecting it.

It has often been pointed out that just as, according to Winnicott, one must not ask whether the child's transitional object is imaginary or real, so the appreciation of vital illusion and cultural experience of every form depends upon a "willing suspension of disbelief". But this phrase does not fully capture the attitude that is essential to maintain in the case of transitional phenomena, towards which there must be a willing suspension of *both* belief *and* disbelief. It has not always been appreciated that belief is as much a failure of transitional illusion as is disbelief. In the case of discipleship, devotion to and worship of what one holds sacred, one is vulnerable to falling out of the transitional area into either belief (religion) or disbelief (pseudo-rational indifference to the sacred), the paranoid-schizoid position or the depressive position. In addition to a totalising literalistic, supernatural faith and an equally totalising rationalist loss of faith is a vital transitional faith that creatively transcends both belief and unbelief and is capable of emotionally meaningful participation in ritual and sacramental celebration as in related experiences of the arts. Such a faith and practice is beyond belief and disbelief.

Paralleling Freud's statement that "He who has neither science nor art, let him have religion," one might be tempted to say "He who has no conscience, let him have a superego," if it were not for the fact that neither a superego nor religion will help those in whom conscience is repressed, for neither religion nor the superego are up to the job. Apart from conscience the superego knows only how to hate and punish. And without conscience religion inevitably takes an authoritarian and "superegoic" form. But one need not fear the psychic revolution entailed in displacing and disempowering the superego in favour of conscience. Although such transformation must entail "a traumatic breaking down and remaking for which the Christian term is conversion" (Eagleton, 2010, p. 17), it results in the emergence, like a rose e'er blooming, of a conscience, the yoke of which is easy and the burden of which is light (*Matthew* 11:30). The psychoanalytic conditions for such a conversion are the formation, suffering, working through, and final resolution of a transference neurosis that can sometimes liberate one to love and to work, and to play and to fight for what one holds sacred.

The following chart attempts to summarise many of the concepts deployed throughout this book:

Chart

PS	PS ←→ D	D
part-objects (all + or all -)		whole-objects (both + and -)
part-selves (all + or all -)		whole-selves (both + and -)
pre-ambivalence		ambivalence
splitting		integration
narcissism		object love
persecutory anxiety		depressive anxiety (capacity for concern)
persecutory guilt (self-punishment and shame)		depressive (reparative) guilt
SUPEREGO		**CONSCIENCE**
self-flagellation		bandaging
projective identification		sympathetic identification
subjectivity		objectivity
depression		sadness and mourning
manic elation	play	sober stoicism
falling in love	transitional area of illusion essential for passion to be retained or rekindled	mature loving
idolisation	idealisation	realism
erotised transference	erotic transference	resolution of transference
primitive defences		higher level defences
belief	willing suspension	disbelief
RELIGION	**FAITH**	**SCIENCE**

Web resources

Shared Belief in the "Golden Rule" (a.k.a. Ethics of Reciprocity). http://old.reonline.org.uk/ks5/tt_nframe.php?tt_alinks.php&17_342&http%3A%2F%2Fwww.teachingvalues.com%2Fgoldenrule.html (retrieved from the internet March 11, 2013).

REFERENCES

Abraham, K. (1911). Geovanni Segantini: A psycho-analytic study. *Psychoanalytic Quarterly, 6*: 453–512.

Abraham, K. (1919). A particular form of neurotic resistance against the psychoanalytic method. *International Journal of Psychoanalysis, 56*: 179–185.

Adorno, T. (1966). *Negative Dialectics*. New York: Continuum, 1983.

Alexander, F. (1925). A metapsychological description of the process of cure. *International Journal of Psychoanalysis, 6*: 13–34.

Alford, F. (1989). *Melanie Klein and Critical Social Theory: An Account of Politics, Art and Reason Based on Her Psychoanalytic Theory*. New Haven, CT: Yale University Press.

Altizer, T. (1967). *The Gospel of Christian Atheism*. London: Collins.

Altizer, T. & Hamilton, W. (1968). *Radical Theology and the Death of God*. London: Penguin.

Alvarez, A. (1971). *The Savage God: A Study of Suicide*. New York: W. W. Norton, 1990.

American Psychiatric Association (1980). *Diagnostic and Statistical Manual of Mental Disorders-III*.

Arendt, H. (1963). *Eichmann in Jerusalem: A Report on the Banality of Evil* (*revised edition*). New York: Viking, 1968.

Arlow, J. (1979). Metaphor and the psychoanalytic situation. *Psychoanalytic Quarterly, 48*: 363–385.

Arlow, J. (1982). Problems of the superego concept. *Psychoanalytic Study of the Child, 37*: 229–244.

Babiak, P. & Hare, R. D. (2006). *Snakes in Suits: When Psychopaths Go to Work.* New York: Harper Collins.

Bacal, H. A. (1985). Optimal responsiveness and the therapeutic process. In: A. Goldberg (Ed.), *Progress in Self Psychology* (pp. 202–226). New York: Guilford.

Bacal, H. A. & Newman, K. (1990). *Theories of Object Relations: Bridges to Self Psychology.* New York: Columbia University Press.

Bach, J. S. (1734–35). *Christmas Oratorio.* Eugen Jochum, Conductor, 1972–73. C. Vitali (Libretto trans.). Germany: Philips Classics CD #422 2522.

Balint, M. (1959). *Thrills and Regressions.* New York: International Universities Press.

Barnett, B. (2007). *You Ought To! A Psychoanalytic Study of the Superego and Conscience.* Psychoanalytic Ideas Series, Wise, I. and Williams, P. (Eds.), Parsons, M. (Foreword). London: The Institute of Psychoanalysis and Karnac.

Barrett, W. (1958). *Irrational Man: A Study in Existential Philosophy.* New York: Random House, 1990.

Barth, K. (1938). *Church Dogmatics, Vol. 1.* G. Bromiley & T. Torrance (Eds.). Edinburgh: T. & T. Clark, 1956.

Bellah, R. N. (1964). Religious evolution. *American Sociological Review, 29*: 358–374.

Bellah, R. N. (2011). *Religion in Human Evolution: From the Paleolithic to the Axial Age.* Cambridge, MA: Harvard University Press.

Berger, P. (1967). *The Sacred Canopy: Elements of a Sociological Theory of Religion.* New York: Doubleday.

Berger, P. (1977). *Facing up to Modernity: Excursions in Society, Politics, and Religion.* New York: Basic.

Berman, M. (1975). Review of Erik Erikson (1974), *Life History and the Historical Moment* (New York: W. W. Norton). *New York Review of Books* (March 30): pp. 1–2.

Bion, W. R. (1959). Attacks on linking. *International Journal of Psychoanalysis, 40*: 308–315.

Bion, W. R. (1962). *Learning from Experience.* London: Heinemann.

Bion, W. R. (1965). *Transformations.* London: Heinemann.

Bion, W. R. (1970). *Attention and Interpretation: A Scientific Approach to Insight in Psycho-Analysis and Groups.* London: Tavistock.

Blake, W. (1788–94). *Songs of Innocence and of Experience.* In: *The Portable Blake.* New York: Viking, 1968.

Bloom, P. (2010). The moral life of babies. *New York Times Magazine,* May 3.

Bollas, C. (2000). *Hysteria.* London: Routledge.

Bonhoeffer, D. (1937). *Discipleship. Dietrich Bonhoeffer Works, Vol. 4.* M. Kuske & I. Tödt, I. (Trans.); G. Kelly & J. Godsey (Eds.); B. Green & R. Krauss (Trans.), *The Cost of Discipleship.* Minneapolis, MN: Fortress Press, 2003.

Bonhoeffer, D. (1951). *Letters and Papers from Prison.* London: Fontana, 1959.

Bowlby, J. (1958). The nature of the child's tie to his mother. *International Journal of Psychoanalysis, 39*: 350–373.

Bowlby, J. (1969–80). *Attachment and Loss, Vols. 1–3.* London: Penguin.

Bowlby, J., Figlio, K. & Young, R. M. (1986). An interview with John Bowlby on the origins and reception of his work. *Free Associations, 1*: 36–64.

Brenner, C. (1982). *The Mind in Conflict.* New York: International Universities Press.

Brenner, C. (1994). The mind as conflict and compromise formation. *Journal of Clinical Psychoanalysis, 3*: 473–488.

Brenner, C. (1998). Beyond the ego and the id revisited. *Journal of Clinical Psychoanalysis, 7*: 165–180.

Brenner, C. (2002). Conflict, compromise formation, and structural theory. *Psychoanalytic Quarterly, 71*: 397–417.

Breuer, J. & Freud, S. (1893–95). *Studies on Hysteria. S. E., 2*: 1–305. London: Hogarth.

Britton, R. (2003). *Sex, Death, and the Superego: Experiences in Psychoanalysis.* London: Karnac.

Bruyn, S. T. (1966). *The Humanistic Perspective in Sociology: The Methodology of Participant Observation.* Englewood Cliffs, NJ: Prentice-Hall.

Buber, M. (1938). *Between Man and Man.* R. G. Smith (Trans.). London: Collins, 1961.

Buber, M. (1957). *Psychiatry.* William Alanson White Memorial Lectures, Fourth Series. Vol. XX, No. 2 (May). [Reprinted in Buber, M. (1998). *The Knowledge of Man: Selected Essays.* Amherst, NY: Humanity.]

Bultmann, R. (1958). *Jesus Christ and Mythology.* New York: Charles Scribner's Sons.

Bultmann, R. (1961). *Kerygma and Myth.* W. Bartsch (Ed.). New York: Harper & Row.

Burke, K. (1939). Freud and the analysis of poetry. In: P. Meisel (Ed.), *Freud: A Collection of Critical Essays* (pp. 73–94). Englewood Cliffs, NJ: Prentice-Hall, 1981.

Burke, K. (1968). Definition of man. In: *Language as Symbolic Action: Essays on Life, Literature, and Method* (pp. 3–24). Berkeley, CA: University of California Press.

Burston, D. (2007). *Erik Erikson and the American Psyche: Ego, Ethics, and Evolution.* Lanham, MD: Jason Aronson.

Canadian Broadcasting Corporation (2005). *Lord Black of Crossharbour: The Life and Times of Conrad Black.* [Documentary (originally aired March 24).]

Carroll, J. (1985). *Guilt: The Grey Eminence behind Character, History and Culture.* London: Routledge & Kegan Paul.

Carveth, D. L. (1977). Sociologism and psychoanalysis: a study of implicit theories of human nature in "symbolic interactionism," "reality constructionism," and psychoanalysis. [A thesis submitted in conformity with the requirements for the degree of doctor of philosophy in the University of Toronto.]

Carveth, D. L. (1984a). Psychoanalysis and social theory. *Psychoanalysis and Contemporary Thought, 7*: 43–98.

Carveth, D. L. (1984b). The analyst's metaphors: a deconstructionist perspective. *Psychoanalysis and Contemporary Thought, 7*: 491–560. Translated into German and reprinted as *Die Metaphern des Analytikers. Eine dekonstructionistische Perspektive.* In: M. B. Buchholz MB (Ed.), *Metaphernanalyse.* Gottingen, Germany: Vandenhoeck & Ruprecht. Reprinted in an E-book issue of *PSYART: A Hyperlink Journal for the Psychological Study of the Arts, 5* (2001), B. Melnick & N. Holland (Eds.). http://www.psyartjournal.com/article/show/1_carveth-metaphor_and_psychoanalysis_the_analysts (retrieved from the internet: March 11, 2013).

Carveth, D. L. (1992). Dead end kids: Projective identification and sacrifice in *Orphans. International Review of Psycho-Analysis, 19*: 217–228.

Carveth, D. L. (1994). Dark epiphany: the encounter with finitude or the discovery of the object in *The Body. Psychoanalysis and Contemporary Thought, 17*: 215–250.

Carveth, D. L. (1996). Psychoanalytic conceptions of the passions. In: J. O'Neill (Ed.), *Freud and the Passions* (pp. 25–51). University Park, PA: Penn State University Press.

Carveth, D. L. (1998). Is there a future in disillusion? Constructionist and deconstructionist approaches in psychoanalysis. *Journal of the American Academy of Psychoanalysis and Dynamic Psychiatry, 27*: 325–358.

Carveth, D. L. (2001). The unconscious need for punishment: expression or evasion of the sense of guilt? *Psychoanalytic Studies, 3*: 9–21.

Carveth, D. L. (2006a). Self-punishment as guilt evasion: theoretical issues. *Canadian Journal of Psychoanalysis, 14*: 172–196.

Carveth, D. L. (2007a). Degrees of psychopathy vs. "the psychopath." Comments on J. Reid Meloy's "A psychoanalytic view of the psychopath." [Presented at the 18th Annual Day in Psychoanalysis, Toronto, April 28, 2007. Filmed and broadcast by TVOntario; video and audio podcast here: http://www.tvo.org/TVOsites/WebObjects/TvoMicrosite.

woa?video10149. Summarised as part of a conference report by Watson, W. (2008).]

Carveth, D. L. (2007b). Self-punishment as guilt evasion: the case of Harry Guntrip. *Canadian Journal of Psychoanalysis, 15*: 56–76.

Carveth, D. L. (2010). Superego, conscience, and the nature and types of guilt. *Modern Psychoanalysis, 35*: 106–130.

Carveth, D. L. (2011a). On the psychoanalytic sociology of Eli Sagan. *Clio's Psyche, 18*: 357–361.

Carveth, D. L. (2011b). Four contributions to the theory of the superego, guilt and conscience. Review of Sagan, E. (1988), *Freud, Women, and Morality: The Psychology of Good and Evil*; Westerink, H. (2009), *A Dark Trace: Sigmund Freud on the Sense of Guilt*; Barnett, B. (2007), *You Ought To! A Psychoanalytic Study of the Superego and Conscience*; Reiner, A. (2009), *The Quest for Conscience and the Birth of the Mind. Canadian Journal of Psychoanalysis, 19*: 349–360.

Carveth, D. L. (2012a). Freud's and our paranoid myth of the "the beast." *Canadian Journal of Psychoanalysis, 20*: 153–157.

Carveth, D. L. (2012b). Freud: more Hellenistic than Hebraic. Contribution to a symposium on James Anderson's "The Influence of Sigmund Freud's Jewishness on His Creation of Psychoanalysis." *Clio's Psyche, 19*: 220–223.

Carveth, D. L. (2013). Guilt. *Vocabulary for the Study of Religion* (VSR), in press.

Carveth, D. L. & Carveth, J. H. (2003). Fugitives from guilt: postmodern demoralization and the new hysterias. *American Imago, 60*: 445–480.

Carveth, D. L., Cavell, M., Eigen, M., Greenberg, J. & Lewis, M. (2007). *Roundtable: What is Guilt?* Philoctetes Center for the Multidisciplinary Study of Imagination, New York (February 22, 2007). Video: http://philoctetes.org/event/what_is_guilt

Carveth, D. L. & Gold, N. E. (1999). The pre-oedipalizing of Klein in (North) America: Ridley Scott's *Alien* re-analyzed. *PSYART: A Hypertext Journal for the Psychological Study of the Arts.* http://www.psyartjournal.com/article/show/1_carveth-the_pre_oedipalizing_of_klein_in_north_a (retrieved from the internet March 11, 2013).

Cassirer, E. (1944). *An Essay on Man.* New Haven, CT: Yale University Press.

Cayley, D. (1992). *Northrop Frye in Conversation.* Concord, Ontario, Canada: Anansi.

Chasseguet-Smirgel, J. (1984). *Creativity and Perversion.* New York: W. W. Norton.

Chesterton, G. K. (1927). *The Secret of Father Brown.* In: *The Complete Father Brown.* London: Penguin, 1981.

Chomsky, N. (2007). The responsibility of intellectuals. Interview by Gabriel Mathew Schivone. *Arts & Opinion*, 6(6). http://www.artsandopinion. com/2007_v6_n6/chomsky-4.htm (retrieved from the internet March 11, 2013).

Cleckley, H. M. (1976). *The Mask of Sanity (fifth edition)*. St. Louis, MO: Mosby.

Connolly, J. (2001). *The Killing Kind*. New York: Pocket.

Derrida, J. (1978). Freud and the scene of writing. In: P. Meisel (Ed.), *Freud: A Collection of Critical Essays* (pp. 145–182). Englewood Cliffs, NJ: Prentice-Hall, 1981.

Derrida, J. (1981). *Dissemination*. B. Johnson (Trans.). Chicago: University of Chicago Press.

Derrida, J. (2001). *The Work of Mourning*. P.-A. Brault & M. Naas (Trans. & Eds.). Chicago: University of Chicago Press.

Deutscher, I. (1949). *Stalin: a Political Biography (revised edition)*. London: Pelican, 1972.

Deutscher, I. (1954, 1959, 1963). *The Prophet Armed: Trotsky, 1879–1921; The Prophet Unarmed: Trotsky, 1921–1929; The Prophet Outcast: Trotsky, 1929–1940*. New York: Verso.

Dinnerstein, D. (1976). *The Mermaid and the Minotaur: Sexual Arrangements and Human Malaise*. V. Gornick & A. Snitow (Introduction); A. Harris (Afterword). New York: Other Press, 1999.

Dodds, E. R. (1951). *The Greeks and the Irrational*. Berkeley, CA: University of California Press, 1997.

Durkheim, E. (1987). *Suicide: A Study in Sociology*. New York: Free Press, 1997.

Eagleton, T. (2007). *Terry Eagleton Presents Jesus Christ: The Gospels*. T. Eagleton (Introduction); G. Fraser (Texts selected & annotated). London: Verso.

Eagleton, T. (2009). *Reason, Faith and Revolution: Reflections on the God Debate*. New Haven, CT: Yale University Press.

Eagleton, T. (2010). *On Evil*. New Haven, CT: Yale University Press.

Edens, J. F., Lilienfeld, S. O., Marcus, D. K. & Poythress, N. G., Jr. (2006). Psychopathic, not psychopath: Taxometric evidence for the dimensional structure of psychopathy. *Journal of Abnormal Psychology, 115*: 131–144.

Eigen, M. (1991). Guntrip's analysis with Winnicott: A critique of Glatzer and Evans. *Contemporary Psychoanalysis, 17*: 103–112.

Eliot, T. S. (1935). Burnt Norton. In: *Four Quartets*. London: Faber & Faber.

Erdelyi, M. H. (1985). *Psychoanalysis: Freud's Cognitive Psychology*. New York: Freeman.

Erikson, E. (1950). *Childhood and Society*. New York: W. W. Norton.

Erikson, E. (1958). *Young Man Luther: A Study in Psychoanalysis and History.* New York: W. W. Norton, 1962.

Erikson, E. (1968). *Identity: Youth and Crisis.* New York: W. W. Norton.

Eskelinen De Folch, T. (1988). Guilt bearable or unbearable: A problem for the child in analysis. *International Review of Psycho-Analysis, 15*: 13–24.

Fairbairn, W. R. D. (1941). A revised psychopathology of the psychoses and psychoneuroses. In: *Psychoanalytic Studies of the Personality* (pp. 28–58). London: Routledge & Kegan Paul, 1952.

Fairbairn, W. R. D. (1943). The repression and return of bad objects (with special reference to the "war neuroses". In: *Psychoanalytic Studies of the Personality* (pp. 59–81). London: Routledge & Kegan Paul, 1952.

Fairbairn, W. R. D. (1944). Endopsychic structure considered in terms of object-relationships. In: *Psychoanalytic Studies of the Personality* (pp. 82–136). London: Routledge & Kegan Paul, 1952.

Fairbairn, W. R. D. (1952). *Psychoanalytic Studies of the Personality.* London: Routledge & Kegan Paul.

Fenichel, o. (1945). *The Psychoanalytic Theory of Neurosis.* New York: W. W. Norton.

Ferenczi, S. (1928). The elasticity of psycho-analytic technique. In: M. Balint (Ed.), E. Mosbacher and others (Trans.), C. Thompson (Intro.), *Final Contributions to the Problems and Methods of Psychoanalysis* (pp. 87–101). New York: Basic, 1955.

Fernando, J. (2000). The borrowed sense of guilt. *International Journal of Psychoanalysis, 81*: 499–512.

Filkins, D. (2012). Atonement: a troubled Iraq veteran seeks out the family he harmed. *New Yorker*, October 29.

Fisher, H. (1994). *The Anatomy of Love.* New York: Random House.

Foner, P. (Ed.) (1973). *When Karl Marx Died: Comments in 1883.* New York: International Publishers.

Frankl, V. E. (1946). *The Doctor and the Soul: From Psychotherapy to Logotherapy.* New York: Knopf, 1955.

Frattaroli, E. (2001). *Healing the Soul in the Age of the Brain: Why Medication Isn't Enough.* New York: Penguin.

Frattaroli, E. (2013). Reflections on the absence of morality in psychoanalytic theory and practice. In: S. Akhtar (Ed.), *Guilt: Origins, Manifestations, and Management.* New York: Jason Aronson.

Freud, A. (1936). *The Ego and the Mechanisms of Defence.* New York: International Universities Press, 1966.

Freud. E.L. (Ed.) (1961). *Letters of Sigmund Freud 1873–1939, 1–478.* London: The Hogarth Press.

Freud, S. (1900a). *The Interpretation of Dreams. S. E.,* 4–5: 1–627. London: Hogarth.

Freud, S. (1905d). Three essays on the theory of sexuality. *S. E., 7*: 123–246. London: Hogarth.

Freud, S. (1905e). Fragment of an analysis of a case of hysteria. *S. E., 7*: 1–122. London: Hogarth.

Freud, S. (1907b). Obsessive actions and religious practices. *S. E., 9*: 115–128. London: Hogarth.

Freud, S. (1909b). Analysis of a phobia in a five-year-old boy. *S. E., 10*: 1–150. London: Hogarth.

Freud, S. (1912b). The dynamics of transference. *S. E., 12*: 97–108. London: Hogarth.

Freud, S. (1912e). Recommendations to physicians practising psycho-analysis, I. *S. E., 12*: 109–120. London: Hogarth.

Freud, S. (1912–13). *Totem and Taboo. S. E., 13*: vii–162. London: Hogarth.

Freud, S. (1914c). On narcissism: an introduction. *S. E., 14*: 67–102. London: Hogarth.

Freud, S. (1915a). Observations on transference-love (further recommendations on the technique of psycho-analysis III). *S. E., 12*: 157–171. London: Hogarth.

Freud, S. (1915c). Instincts and their vicissitudes. *S. E., 14*: 109–140. London: Hogarth.

Freud, S. (1916d). Some character-types met with in psycho-analytic work. *S. E., 14*: 311–333. London: Hogarth.

Freud, S. (1916–17). Introductory lectures on psycho-analysis (Part III). *S. E., 16*: 241–463. London: Hogarth.

Freud, S. (1917e). Mourning and Melancholia. *S. E., 14*: 237–258. London: Hogarth.

Freud, S. (1920g). Beyond the Pleasure Principle. *S. E., 18*: 1–64. London: Hogarth.

Freud, S. (1921c). Group psychology and the analysis of the ego. *S. E., 18*: 65–143. London: Hogarth.

Freud, S. (1923b). The Ego and the Id. *S. E., 19*: 3–66. London: Hogarth.

Freud, S. (1924c). The economic problem of masochism. *S. E., 19*: 157–173. London: Hogarth.

Freud, S. (1925d). An autobiographical study. *S. E., 20*: 1–74. London: Hogarth.

Freud, S. (1925j). Some psychical consequences of the anatomical distinction between the sexes. *S. E., 19*: 248–258. London: Hogarth.

Freud, S. (1926d). *Inhibitions, Symptoms and Anxiety. S. E., 20*: 75–176. London: Hogarth.

Freud, S. (1927a). Concluding remarks on the question of lay analysis. *Int. Journal of Psychoanalysis, 8*: 392–401.

Freud, S. (1927c). *The Future of an Illusion. S. E., 21*: 1–56. London: Hogarth.

Freud, S. (1930a). *Civilization and Its Discontents. S. E.*, 21: 57–146. London: Hogarth.

Freud, S. (1931b). Female sexuality. *S. E.*, 21: 225–243. London: Hogarth.

Freud, S. (1933a). *New Introductory Lectures on Psychoanalysis. S. E.*, 22: 3–182. London: Hogarth.

Freud, S. (1940a). *An Outline of Psycho-analysis. S. E.*, 23: 139–208. London: Hogarth.

Fromm, E. (1941). *Escape From Freedom.* London: Routledge, 1942.

Fromm, E. (1950). *Psychoanalysis and Religion.* New Haven, CT: Yale University Press.

Frye, N. (1963). *The Educated Imagination.* Toronto: CBC Publications.

Frye, N. (1991). *The Double Vision: Language and Meaning in Religion.* Toronto: University of Toronto Press.

Furer, M. (1967). Some developmental aspects of the superego. *International Journal of Psychoanalysis, 48*: 277–280.

Gabbard, K. & Gabbard, G. (1987). *Alien* and Melanie Klein's night music. In: K. Gabbard & G. Gabbard (Eds.), *Psychiatry and the Cinema (second edition)* (pp. 277–291). London: American Psychiatric Press, 1999.

Giddens, A. (1982). *Sociology: A Brief but Critical Introduction.* New York: Harcourt Brace Jovanovich.

Gilligan, C. (1982). *In a Different Voice: Psychological Theory and Women's Experience.* Cambridge, MA: Harvard University Press.

Giroux, H. A. (2012). The "Suicidal State" and the war on youth. *Truthout,* April 10. http://truth-out.org/opinion/item/8421-the-suicidal-state-and-the-war-on-youth (retrieved from the internet March 11, 2013).

Glatzer, H. & Evans, W. (1997). On Guntrip's analysis with Fairbairn and Winnicott. *International Journal of Psychoanalytic Psychotherapy, 6*: 81–98.

Gray, M. (n.d.). Waylon's Buddy: Jennings never forgot his mentor. http://m.mtv.com/news/article.rbml?id=1452295&artist=holly_buddy (retrieved from the internet March 11, 2013).

Gray, P. (1994). *The Ego and Analysis of Defense (second edition).* New York: Jason Aronson, 2005.

Greenberg, J. & Mitchell, S. (1983). *Object Relations in Psychoanalytic Theory.* Cambridge, MA: Harvard University Press.

Greenson, R. (1968). Disidentifying from mother: Its special importance for the boy. *International Journal of Psychoanalysis, 49*: 370–374.

Grinberg, L. (1964). Two kinds of guilt: their relations with normal and pathological aspects of mourning. *International Journal of Psychoanalysis, 45*: 366–371.

Groopman, J. (2000). Hurting all over: With so many people in so much pain, how could fibromyalgia not be a disease? *The New Yorker,* November 13: pp. 78–92.

Grunberger, B. (1979). *Narcissism: Psychoanalytic Essays*. J. S. Diamanti, (Trans.). New York: International Universities Press.

Guntrip, H. (1949). *Psychology for Ministers and Social Workers*. London: Independent, 1951.

Guntrip, H. (1956). *Mental Pain and the Cure of Souls*. London: Independent.

Guntrip, H. (1969). *Schizoid Phenomena, Object Relations and the Self*. New York: International Universities Press.

Guntrip, H. (1971). *Psychoanalytic Theory, Therapy, and the Self*. New York: Basic.

Guntrip, H. (1975). My experience of analysis with Fairbairn and Winnicott— (how complete a result does psycho-analytic therapy achieve?). *International Review of Psycho-Analysis*, 2: 145–156; reprinted *International Journal of Psychoanalysis*, 77 (1996): 739–754.

Habermas, J. (1971). *Knowledge and Human Interests*. J. J. Shapiro (Trans.). Boston: Beacon Press.

Hammer, Rabbi R. (n.d.). *The Jewish View of Sin*. http://www.myjewish learning.com/holidays/Jewish_Holidays/Yom_Kippur/Themes_and_Theology/Jewish_View_of_Sin.shtml (retrieved from the internet March 11, 2013).

Hanly, C. (1993). Ideology and psychoanalysis. *Canadian Journal of Psychoanalysis*, 1: 1–17.

Hantman, J. (2004). The techno-schizoid: technology in film as bridge or resistance to intimacy. *Canadian Journal of Psychoanalysis*, 12: 85–101.

Hantman, J. (2006). Review of Mitchell, J. (2003), *Siblings: Sex and Violence*. *Free Associations* online: http://www.psychoanalysis-and-therapy.com/human_nature/free-associations/hantman.html (retrieved from the internet March 11, 2013).

Hantman, J. (2008). The normopath. [Unpublished paper.] http://www.inthebreakdown.com/normopathy.html (retrieved from the internet March 11, 2013).

Hare, R. D. (1993). *Without Conscience: The Disturbing World of the Psychopaths among Us*. New York: Pocket.

Hare, R. D. (2003). *Hare Psychopathy Checklist-Revised (second edition)*. [Technical Manual.] Toronto: Multihealth Systems.

Harris, G. T., Rice, M. E. & Quinsey, V. L. (1994). Psychopathy as a taxon: Evidence that psychopaths are a discrete class. *Journal of Consulting and Clinical Psychology*, 62: 387–397.

Hartmann, H. (1939). *Ego Psychology and the Problem of Adaptation*. New York: International Universities Press, 1958.

Hazell, J. (1991). Reflections on my experience of psychoanalysis with Guntrip. *Contemporary Psychoanalysis*, 27: 148–166.

Hazell, J. (1996). *H. J. S. Guntrip: A Psychoanalytical Biography*. London: Free Association.

Hedges, C. (2011). Occupiers have to convince the other 99 percent. *Truthdig*, op. ed. October 24. http://www.truthdig.com/report/item/occupiers_have_to_convince_the_other_99_percent_20111024/ (retrieved from the internet March 11, 2013).

Hedges, C. (2012a). Ralph Nader: Occupy the minimum wage and impact the election. *Truthdig*, op. ed. February 27. http://www.truthdig.com/report/item/nader_to_occupy_help_raise_the_minimum_wage_20120227/ (retrieved from the internet March 11, 2013).

Hedges, C. (2012b). Handmaidens to barbarity. *Truthdig*, op. ed. August 6. http://www.truthdig.com/report/item/the_science_of_genocide_20120806/ (retrieved from the internet March 11, 2013).

Hegel, G. W. F. (1807). *The Phenomenology of Mind*, 2 Vols. J. Baillie (Trans.). New York: Macmillan, 1910.

Heidegger, M. (1927). *Being and Time*. J. Macquarrie & E. S. Robinson (Trans.). New York: Harper, 1962. Hemingway, E. (1934). *Death in the Afternoon*. New York: Charles Scribner's Sons.

Hillman, J. (1972). *The Myth of Analysis: Three Essays in Archetypal Psychology*. New York: Harper & Row.

Hofstadter, R. (1944). *Social Darwinism in American Thought*. Boston, MA: Beacon, 1992.

Holy Bible. The New Revised Standard Version with Apocrypha. Nashville, TN: Nelson, 1989. [NRSV]

Holy Bible. King James Version. Cleveland, OH: World Publishing. [KJV]

Homans, P. (Ed.) (1968). *The Dialogue between Theology and Psychology*. Chicago: University of Chicago Press.

Homans, P. (1970). *Theology after Freud: An Interpretive Inquiry*. Indianapolis, IN: Bobbs-Merrill.

Horowitz, M. H. (2005). On revenge. [Paper presented to the Toronto Psychoanalytic Society, April 1.]

Hugo, V. (1862). *Les Misérables*. I. F. Hapgood (Trans.), *The Complete Works of Victor Hugo (1802- 1885)*. Delphi Classics, 2012: www.delphiclassics.com

Huxley, J. (1947). The uniqueness of man. In: *Man in the Modern World* (ch. 1, pp. 1–23). New York: Mentor.

Jacobs, J. & Capps, D. (Eds.) (1997). *Religion, Society, and Psychoanalysis: Readings in Contemporary Theory*. Boulder, CO: Westview Press.

Jacobson, E. (1964). *The Self and the Object World*. New York: International Universities Press.

Jacoby, R. (1975). *Social Amnesia: A Critique of Contemporary Psychology from Adler to Laing*. Boston: Beacon.

Jaspers, K. (1947). *The Question of German Guilt*. E. B. Ashton (Trans.). New York: Capricorn.

Jones, E. (1961). *The Life and Work of Sigmund Freud*. L. Trilling & S. Marcus (Eds.). London: Penguin.

Jones, J. W. (1991). *Contemporary Psychoanalysis and Religion: Transference and Transcendence*. New Haven, CT: Yale University Press.

Jones, R. A. (1986). *Emile Durkheim: An Introduction to Four Major Works*. Beverly Hills, CA: Sage.

Kant, I. (1785). *Grounding for the Metaphysics of Morals (third edition)*. J. W. Ellington (Trans.). Indianapolis, IN: Hackett, 1993.

Kardiner, A. (1977). *My Analysis with Freud; Reminiscences*. New York: W. W. Norton.

Karen, R. (1992). Shame: The rediscovery of what some psychologists regard as the primary cause of emotional distress. *Atlantic, 269*: 40–70.

Kaufmann, W. (1965). *Hegel: A Reinterpretation*. New York: Doubleday.

Keats, J. (1819). *The Poetical Works of John Keats*. New York: Thomas Y. Crowell, 1895.

Kee, A. (1971). *The Way of Transcendence: Christian Faith Without Belief in God*. London: Penguin.

Kelly, M. (1995). The road to paranoia. *The New Yorker*, June 19: pp. 62–64.

Kernberg, O. (1975). *Borderline Conditions and Pathological Narcissism*. New York: Jason Aronson.

Kernberg, O. (1976). *Object Relations Theory and Clinical Psychoanalysis*. New York: Jason Aronson.

Kernberg, O. (1991a). Sadomasochism, sexual excitement, and perversion. *Journal of the American Psychoanalytic Association, 39*: 333–362.

Kernberg, O. (1991b). Aggression and love in the relationship of the couple. *Journal of the American Psychoanalytic Association, 39*: 45–70.

Kernberg, O. (1993). The couple's constructive and destructive superego functions. *Journal of the American Psychoanalytic Association, 41*: 653–677.

Kessler, L. (1987). *Orphans*. New York: Grove Press.

Kierkegaard, S. (1843). *Fear and Trembling*. A. Hannay (Trans. & Intro.). London: Penguin, 1985.

Kierkegaard, S. (1844). *The Concept of Anxiety: A Simple Psychologically Orienting Deliberation on the Dogmatic Issue of Hereditary Sin*. R. Thomte & A. B. Anderson (Ed. & Trans.). Princeton, NJ: Princeton University Press, 1980.

Kierkegaard, S. (1849). *The Sickness unto Death*. A. Hannay (Trans.). London: Penguin, 1989.

Kierkegaard, S. (1850). *Practice in Christianity. Kierkegaard's Writings, XX*. H. V. Hong & E. H. Hong (Eds. & Trans.). Princeton, NJ: Princeton University Press, 1991.

Klein, M. (1934). On criminality. In: *Love, Guilt and Reparation and Other Works* (pp. 258–261). London: Hogarth, 1975.

Klein, M. (1935). A contribution to the psychogenesis of manic-depressive states. *International Journal of Psychoanalysis, 16*: 145–174.

Klein, M. (1940). Mourning and its relation to manic-depressive states. *International Journal of Psychoanalysis, 21*: 125–153.

Klein, M. (1946). Notes on some schizoid mechanisms. *International Journal of Psychoanalysis, 27*: 99–110.

Klein, M. (1948). A contribution to the theory of anxiety and guilt. *International Journal of Psychoanalysis, 29*: 114–123.

Klein, M. (1957). Envy and gratitude. In: M. Khan (Ed.), *Envy and Gratitude and Other Works, 1946–1963* (pp. 176–235). London: Hogarth, 1975.

Klein, M. (1964). Love, guilt and reparation. In: Klein, M. & Riviere, J. *Love, Hate and Reparation* (pp. 57–119). New York: W. W. Norton.

Klein, M., Heimann, P., Isaacs, S. & Riviere, J. (1952). *Developments in Psycho-Analysis*. London: Hogarth.

Knoblauch, S. H. (1995). The selfobject function of religious experience. *Progress in Self Psychology, 11*: 207–217.

Kohut, H. (1959). Introspection, empathy and psychoanalysis: An examination of the relationship between mode of observation and theory. *Journal of the American Psychoanalytic Association, 7*: 459–483.

Kohut, H. (1971). *The Analysis of the Self*. New York: International Universities Press.

Kohut, H. (1977). *The Restoration of the Self*. New York: International Universities Press.

Kohut, H. (1979). The two analyses of Mr. Z. *International Journal of Psychoanalysis, 60*: 3–27.

Kohut, H. (1984). *How Does Analysis Cure?* A. Goldberg (Ed.). Chicago: University of Chicago Press.

Kris, E. (1938). Review of Anna Freud's *The Ego and the Mechanisms of Defence*. *International Journal of Psychoanalysis, 19*: 115–146.

Kristeva, J. (1982). *Powers of Horror: An Essay on Abjection*. New York: Columbia University Press.

Krohn, A. (1978). *Hysteria: The Elusive Neurosis*. (Psychological Issues Monograph 45/46.) New York: International Universities Press.

Küng, H. (1990). *Freud and the Problem of God*. E. Quinn (Trans.). New Haven, CT: Yale University Press.

Lacan, J. (1977). *Écrits: A Selection*. A. Sheridan (Trans.). New York: W. W. Norton.

Lacan, J. (1982). *Feminine Sexuality: Jacques Lacan and the Ecole Freudienne*. J. Mitchell & J. Rose (Eds.), J. Rose (Trans.). New York: W. W. Norton.

Lacan, J. (1994). *Le séminaire, livre IV: La relation d'objet*. Paris: Editions du Seuil.

Lake, F. (1966). *Clinical Theology: A Theological and Psychological Basis to Clinical Pastoral Care*. Abridged by M. H. Yeomans. New York: Crossroad, 1987.

Lakoff, G. & Johnson, M. (1980). *Metaphors We Live By*. Chicago: University of Chicago Press.

Lakoff, G. & Wehling, E. (2012). Why did Walker win Wisconsin? *Truthout*, June 13. http://truth-out.org/opinion/item/9751-the-wisconsin-blues (retrieved from the internet March 11, 2013).

Langs, R. (1978). *Technique in Transition*. New York: Jason Aronson.

Lasch, C. (1979). *The Culture of Narcissism: American Life in an Age of Diminishing Expectations*. New York: Warner.

Leavy, S. A. (1983). Speaking in tongues: some linguistic approaches to psychoanalysis. *Psychoanalytic Quarterly, 52*: 34–55.

Leavy, S. A. (1988). *In the Image of God: A Psychoanalyst's View*. New Haven, CT: Yale University Press.

Lemaire, A. (1970). *Jacques Lacan*. D. Mace (Trans.). London: Routledge & Kegan Paul, 1977.

Lifton, R. J. (1986). *The Nazi Doctors: Medical Killing and the Psychology of Genocide*. New York: Basic.

Loewald, H. W. (1971). Some considerations on repetition and repetition compulsion. In: *Papers on Psychoanalysis* (pp. 87–101). New Haven, CT: Yale University Press, 1980.

Loewald, H. W. (1979). The waning of the Oedipus complex. *Journal of the American Psychoanalytic Association, 27*: 751–775.

Loewald, H. W. (1980). On motivation and instinct theory. *Papers on Psychoanalysis* (pp. 102–137). New Haven, CT: Yale University Press, 1980.

Loewald, H. W. (1981). Regression: Some general considerations. *Psychoanalytic Quarterly, 50*: 22–43.

Lykken, D. (1957). A study of anxiety in the sociopathic personality. *Journal of Abnormal and Social Psychology, 55*: 6–10.

Macquarrie, J. (1955). *An Existentialist Theology*. London: SCM Press.

Mahler, M., Pine, F. & Bergman, A. (1975). *The Psychological Birth of the Human Infant: Symbiosis and Individuation*. New York: Basic.

March, W. (1954). *The Bad Seed*. New York: Rinehart.

Marcuse, H. (1970). *Five Lectures: Psychoanalysis, Politics and Utopia*. J. J. Shapiro & S. M. Weber (Trans.). Boston: Beacon Press.

Margolis, D. (1996). *Freud and His Mother*. Northvale, NJ: Jason Aronson.

Markillie, R. (1996). Some personal recollections and impressions of Harry Guntrip. *International Journal of Psychoanalysis, 77*: 763–771.

Marx, K. (1867). *Capital: Critique of Political Economy, Vol. I.* Chicago: Charles H. Kerr.

Massey, G. (1924). *The Prisoner's Song.* New York: Shapiro Bernstein.

Matt, C. (1999). God, science, and delusion: a chat with Arthur C. Clarke. *Free Inquiry, 19.* Amherst, NY: Council for Secular Humanism. http://www.secularhumanism.org/library/fi/clarke_19_2.html (retrieved from the internet March 11, 2013).

May, R. (1950). *The Meaning of Anxiety.* New York: W. W. Norton, 1977.

May, U. (2001). Abraham's discovery of the "bad mother": a contribution to the history of the theory of depression. *International Journal of Psychoanalysis, 82:* 283–305.

McDougall, J. (1989). *Theatres of the Body: A Psychoanalytic Approach to Psychosomatic Illness.* New York: W. W. Norton.

Mead, G. H. (1934). *Mind, Self and Society.* Chicago: University of Chicago Press.

Meisel, P. (Ed.) (1981). *Freud: A Collection of Critical Essays.* Englewood Cliffs, NJ: Prentice-Hall.

Meissner, W. W. (1968). *Foundations for a Psychology of Grace.* New York: Paulist Press.

Meissner, W. W. (1978). *The Paranoid Process.* New York: Jason Aronson.

Meissner, W. W. (1981). *Internalization in Psychoanalysis.* New York: International Universities Press.

Meissner, W. W. (1984). *Psychoanalysis and Religious Experience.* New Haven, CT: Yale University Press.

Meloy, J. R. (1988). *The Psychopathic Mind: Origins, Dynamics, and Treatment.* Northvale, NJ: Jason Aronson.

Meloy, J. R. (Ed.) (2001). *The Mark of Cain: Psychoanalytic Insight and the Psychopath.* Hillsdale, NJ: The Analytic Press.

Meloy, J. R. (2007a). Antisocial personality disorder. In: G. Gabbard (Ed.), *Gabbard's Treatments of Psychiatric Disorders (fourth edition)* (pp. 775–789). Arlington, VA: American Psychiatric Press.

Meloy, J. R. (2007b). A psychoanalytic view of the psychopath. [Paper presented at the Toronto Psychoanalytic Society's 18th Annual Day in Psychoanalysis, Ignatieff Theatre, Trinity College, University of Toronto, April 28, 2007. Filmed and broadcast by TVOntario; video and audio podcast here: http://www.tvo.org/TVOsites/WebObjects/TvoMicrosite.woa?video10149. Summarised as part of a conference report prepared by Watson, W. (2008).]

Meloy, J. R. & Shiva, A. (2008). A psychoanalytic view of the psychopath. In: A. Felthous & H. Saß (Eds.), *The International Handbook of Psychopathic Disorders and the Law: Laws and Policies,* chapter 20. Chichester, UK: John Wiley & Sons. Published online (February 15): http://onlinelibrary.

wiley.com/doi/10.1002/9780470516157.ch20/summary (retrieved from the internet March 11, 2013).

Menninger, K. (1973). *Whatever Became of Sin?* New York: Bantam.

Metaxas, E. (2010). *Bonhoeffer: Pastor, Martyr, Prophet, Spy: A Righteous Gentile Vs. the Third Reich.* Nashville, TN: Nelson.

Micale, M. S. (1994). *Approaching Hysteria.* Princeton, NJ: Princeton University Press.

Milgram, S. (1963). Behavioral study of obedience. *Journal of Abnormal and Social Psychology, 67*: 371–378.

Mills, C. W. (1959). *The Sociological Imagination.* New York: Grove.

Mitchell, J. (2000). *Mad Men and Medusas: Reclaiming Hysteria.* New York: Basic.

Mitchell, J. (2003). *Siblings: Sex and Violence.* Malden, MA: Blackwell.

Mitscherlich, A. (1970). *Society Without the Father: A Contribution to Social Psychology.* E. Mosbacher (Trans.). New York: Schocken.

Modell, A. (1968). *Object Love and Reality.* New York: International Universities Press.

Modell, A. (1971). The origin of certain forms of pre-Oedipal guilt and the implications for a psychoanalytic theory of affects. *International Journal of Psychoanalysis, 52*: 337–346.

Mulhern, S. (1994). Satanism, ritual abuse, and multiple personality disorder. *International Journal of Clinical and Experimental Hypnosis, 42*: 266.

Nash, W. (2012). Moral injury in the context of war (research). [Workshop session 508 at the National Zarrow Mental Health Symposium & Mental Health America Annual Conference, September 20, Tulsa, OK.]

Nathanson, D. (1997). From empathy to community. *Annals of Psychoanalysis, 25*: 125–143.

Nielsen, J. K. (1991). The political orientation of Talcott Parsons: the Second World War and its aftermath. In: Robertson, R. & Turner, B. S. (1991), *Talcott Parsons: Theorist of Modernity* (pp. 217–233). London: Sage.

Nietzsche, F. (1887). *On the Genealogy of Morals: A Polemic.* W. Kaufman & R. J. Hollingdale (Trans.). New York: Vintage, 1969.

Ogden, T. (1986). *The Matrix of the Mind: Object Relations and the Psychoanalytic Dialogue.* Northvale, NJ: Jason Aronson, 1993.

Ostow, M. (2007). *Spirit, Mind, & Brain: A Psychoanalytic Examination of Spirituality & Religion.* New York: Columbia University Press.

Padel, J. (1996). The case of Harry Guntrip. *International Journal of Psychoanalysis, 77*: 755–761.

Parsons, A. (1964). Is the Oedipus Complex universal? In: W. Muensterberger & A. Axelrad (Eds.), *The Psychoanalytic Study of Society, III* (pp. 278–328). New York: International Universities Press.

Parsons, T. (1964). Evolutionary universals in society. In: *Sociological Theory and Modern Society* (pp. 490–520). New York: Free Press, 1967.

Parsons, T. (1977). *The Evolution of Societies*. J. Toby (Ed.). Englewood Cliffs, NJ: Prentice-Hall.

Pascal, B. (1669). *Pensées*. A. J. Krailsheimer (Trans.). London: Penguin, 1966.

Pelikan, J. (1984). *The Christian Tradition: A History of the Development of Doctrine, Vol. 4: Reformation of Church and Dogma, 1300–1700*. Chicago: University of Chicago Press.

Racker, H. (1957). The meanings and uses of countertransference. *Psychoanalytic Quarterly, 26*: 303–357.

Rand, A. (1962). *The Virtue of Selfishness*. New York: Signet.

Rangell, L. (1974). A psychoanalytic perspective leading currently to the syndrome of the compromise of integrity. *International Journal of Psychoanalysis, 55*: 3–12.

Rangell, L. (1976). Lessons from Watergate: A derivative for psychoanalysis. *Psychoanalytic Quarterly, 45*: 37–61.

Rangell, L. (1980). *The Mind of Watergate: An Exploration of the Compromise of Integrity*. New York: W. W. Norton.

Rangell, L. (1997). Interview with Leo Rangell. *IPA Newsletter, 6*: 1.

Rangell, L. (2000). A psychoanalytic view of the impeachment process. *Psychoanalytic Dialogues, 10*: 309–313.

Reich, R. (2012). As Santorum and Romney battle for the loony right, the rest of us should not gloat. *Truthout*, March 17. http://www.truth-out.org/santorum-and-romney-battle-loony-right-rest-us-should-not-gloat/1330451380 (retrieved from the internet March 11, 2013).

Reik, T. (1948). *Listening with the Third Ear*. New York: Arena, 1972.

Reiner, A. (2009). *The Quest for Conscience and the Birth of the Mind*. J. Grotstein (Foreword). London: Karnac.

Ricoeur, P. (1960). *The Symbolism of Evil*. New York: Harper & Row, 1967.

Ricoeur, P. (1970). *Freud and Philosophy: An Essay on Interpretation*. D. Savage (Trans.). New Haven, CT: Yale University Press.

Rieff, P. (1959). *Freud: The Mind of the Moralist*. New York: Doubleday.

Riesenberg-Malcolm, R. (1980). Self-punishment as defence. In: P. Roth (Ed.), *On Bearing Unbearable States of Mind* (pp. 93–112). London: Routledge.

Rist, M. (1938). The God of Abraham, Isaac, and Jacob: A liturgical and magical formula. *Journal of Biblical Literature, 57*: 289–303.

Rizzuto, A. M. (1979). *The Birth of the Living God*. Chicago: University of Chicago Press.

Roazen, P. (1976). *Erik H. Erikson: The Power and Limits of a Vision*. New York: Free Press.

Roazen, P. (2005). *Edoardo Weiss: The House that Freud Built*. London: Transaction.

Robinson, P. (1969). *The Freudian Left: Wilhelm Reich, Geza Roheim, Herbert Marcuse*. New York: Harper & Row.

Rodin, G. (1990). Personal communication.

Rogers, R. (1978). *Metaphor: A Psychoanalytic View*. Berkeley, CA: University of California Press.

Rosetti, C. R. (1872). "In the Bleak Midwinter." *The Poetical Works of Christina Georgina Rossetti (1830–1894)*. Poem #426. London: Macmillan, 1904.

Rousseau, J.-J. (1754). *Discourse on Inequality*. Whitefish, MT: Kessinger Legacy Reprints, 2010.

Rycroft, C. (1968). *A Critical Dictionary of Psycho-Analysis*. Totawa, NJ: Littlefield, Adams, 1973.

Safán-Gerard, D. (1998). Bearable and unbearable guilt: a Kleinian perspective. *Psychoanalytic Quarterly, 67*: 351–378.

Sagan, E. (1974). *Cannibalism: Human Aggression and Cultural Form*. New York: Harper.

Sagan, E. (1979). *The Lust to Annihilate: A Psychoanalytic Study of Violence in Ancient Greek Culture*. New York: Psychohistory Press.

Sagan, E. (1985). *At the Dawn of Tyranny: The Origins of Individualism, Political Oppression, and the State*. New York: Knopf.

Sagan, E. (1988). *Freud, Women, and Morality: The Psychology of Good and Evil*. New York: Basic.

Sagan, E. (1991). *The Honey and the Hemlock: Democracy and Paranoia in Ancient Athens and Modern America*. Princeton, NJ: Princeton University Press.

Sagan, E. (2001). *Citizens and Cannibals: The French Revolution, the Struggle for Modernity, and the Origins of Ideological Terror*. Lanham, MD: Rowman & Littlefield.

Sandler, J. (Ed.) (1987). *Projection, Identification, Projective Identification*. London: Karnac.

Sandler, J. (1960). On the concept of the superego. *Psychoanalytic Study of the Child, 15*: 128–162.

Sartre, J.-P. (1943). *Being and Nothingness: A Study in Phenomenological Ontology*. H. Barnes (Trans.). New York: Philosophical Library, 1953.

Sartre, J.-P. (1946). *Existentialism and Humanism*. P. Mairet (Trans.). London: Eyre Methuen, 1973.

Sartre, J.-P. (1960). *The Critique of Dialectical Reason*. A. Sheridan-Smith (Trans.). London: New Left, 1976.

Sartre, J.-P. (1969). Itinerary of a thought. *New Left Review, 58*: 43–64.

Schafer, R. (1960). The loving and beloved superego in Freud's structural theory. *Psychoanalytic Study of the Child, 15*: 163–188.

Schafer, R. (1976). *A New Language for Psychoanalysis*. New Haven, CT: Yale University Press.

Schafer, R. (Ed.). (1997). *The Contemporary Kleinians of London*. Madison, CT: International Universities Press.

Schopenhauer, A. (1818). *The World as Will and Idea*. New York: Dover, 1966.

Searles, H. (1962). The differentiation between concrete and metaphorical thinking in the recovering schizophrenic patient. In: *Collected Papers on Schizophrenia and Related Subjects* (pp. 560–583). New York: International Universities Press, 1965.

Searles, H. (1975). The patient as therapist to his analyst. In: Searles, H. (1979), *Countertransference and Related Subjects: Selected Papers* (pp. 380–459). Madison, CT: International Universities Press.

Segal, H. (1957). Notes on symbol formation. *International Journal of Psychoanalysis, 38*: 391–397.

Segal, H. (1964). *An Introduction to the Work of Melanie Klein*. London: Hogarth, 1975.

Shengold, L. (1989). *Soul Murder: The Effects of Childhood Abuse and Deprivation*. New Haven, CT: Yale University Press.

Sheppard, A. (2006). Countering the hazards of psychoanalytic work. *Canadian Journal of Psychoanalysis, 14*: 254–268.

Shorter, E. (1992). *From Paralysis to Fatigue: A History of Psychosomatic Illness in the Modern Era*. New York: Free Press.

Showalter, E. (1997). *Hystories: Hysterical Epidemics and Modern Media*. New York: Columbia University Press.

Sifneos, P. (1996). Alexithymia: past and present. *American Journal of Psychiatry, 153*(7S): 137–142.

Spezzano, C. & Gargiulo, G. (2003). *Soul on the Couch: Spirituality, Religion, and Morality in Contemporary Psychoanalysis*. New York: Routledge.

Spitz, R. (1958). On the genesis of the superego components. *Psychoanalytic Study of the Child, 13*: 375–404.

Spotnitz, H. (1969). *Modern Psychoanalysis of the Schizophrenic Patient: Theory of the Technique (second edition)*. New York: Human Sciences Press, 1985.

Spotnitz, H. (1976). *Psychotherapy of Preoedipal Conditions: Schizophrenia and Severe Character Disorders*. Northvale, NJ: Jason Aronson, 1995.

Spotnitz, H. & Meadow, P. (1976). *Treatment of the Narcissistic Neuroses (revised edition)*. Northvale, NJ: Aronson, 1995.

Steiner, G. (1969). The language animal. *Encounter*, August: 7–23. Reprinted in *Extra-Territorial: Papers on Literature and the Language Revolution*. New York: Atheneum, 1971.

Stern, D. (1985). *The Interpersonal World of the Infant: A View from Psychoanalysis and Developmental Psychology*. New York: Basic.

Stoller, R. (1974). Hostility and mystery in perversion. *International Journal of Psychoanalysis, 55*: 426–434.

Stoller, R. (1979). *Sexual Excitement*. New York: Pantheon.

Stoller, R. (1985). *Observing the Erotic Imagination*. New Haven, CT: Yale University Press.

Stout, M. (2005). *The Sociopath Next Door: The Ruthless versus the Rest of Us*. New York: Broadway.

Strachey, J. (1934). The nature of the therapeutic action of psycho-analysis. *International Journal of Psychoanalysis, 15*: 127–159.

Sturrock, J. (Ed.). (1979). *Structuralism and Since: from Levi-Strauss to Derrida*. Oxford: Oxford University Press.

Sullivan, H. S. (1953). *The Interpersonal Theory of Psychiatry*. New York: W. W. Norton.

Suttie, I. D. (1935). *The Origins of Love and Hate*. London: Free Association, 1988.

Sykes, J. (Ed.). (1982). *The Concise Oxford Dictionary (seventh edition)*. Oxford: Oxford University Press.

Symington, N. (1980). The response aroused by the psychopath. In: J. R. Meloy (Ed.), *The Mark of Cain* (pp. 283–296). Hillsdale, NJ: The Analytic Press, 2001.

Symington, N. (1994). *Emotion and Spirit*. London: Karnac.

Symington, J. & Symington, N. (1996). *The Clinical Thinking of Wilfred Bion*. New York: Routledge.

Szasz, T. (1961). *The Myth of Mental Illness: Foundations of a Theory of Personal Conduct*. New York: Harper & Row.

Szasz, T. (1976). *Karl Kraus and the Soul-Doctors: A Pioneer Critic and His Criticisms of Psychiatry and Psychoanalysis*. Baton Rouge, LA: Louisiana State University Press.

Taylor, C. (1991). *The Malaise of Modernity*. Toronto: Anansi.

Taylor, G. J., Bagby, R. M. & Parker, J. (1997). *Disorders of Affect Regulation: Alexithymia in Medical and Psychiatric Illness*. Cambridge: Cambridge University Press.

Tillich, P. (1952). *The Courage to Be*. London: Collins.

Toby, J. (1977). Parsons' theory of societal evolution. In: Parsons, T. (1977). *The Evolution of Societies* (pp. 1–23). J. Toby (Ed. & Intro.). Englewood Cliffs, NJ: Prentice-Hall.

Turbayne, C. (1962). *The Myth of Metaphor*. New Haven, CT: Yale University Press.

Tustin, F. (1986). *Autistic Barriers in Neurotic Patients*. New Haven, CT: Yale University Press.

Twain, M. (1885). *The Adventures of Huckleberry Finn*. Raleigh, NC: Hayes Barton Press, 2005.

Ury, C. (1998). The Nietzschean monster: Reconsidering guilt in developmental theory. *Canadian Journal of Psychoanalysis, 6*: 51–74.

Vanier, J. (1988). *The Broken Body*. London: Darton, Longman & Todd.

Waelder, R. (1930). The principle of multiple function: Observations on overdetermination. In: *Psychoanalysis: Observation, Theory, Application*. New York: International Universities Press, 1976.

Watson, W. (2008). Conference report: A psychoanalytic view of the psychopath. *Canadian Journal of Psychoanalysis, 16*: 275–287.

Westen, D. (1999). The scientific status of unconscious processes. *Journal of the American Psychoanalytic Association, 47*: 1061–1106.

Whitehead, A. N. (1925). *Science and the Modern World*. New York: Free Press, 1997.

Wiekart, R. (n.d.). Metaxas's counterfeit Bonhoeffer: An evangelical critique. Review of Metaxas, E. (2012). http://www.csustan.edu/history/faculty/weikart/metaxas.htm (retrieved from the internet March 11, 2013).

Wilson, E. O. (1998). *Consilience: The Unity of Knowledge*. New York: Knopf.

Winnicott, D. W. (1949). Hate in the counter-transference. *International Journal of Psychoanalysis, 30*: 69–74.

Winnicott, D. W. (1955). Transitional objects and transitional phenomena—a study of the first not-me possession. *International Journal of Psychoanalysis, 34*: 89–97. [Reprinted in *Playing and Reality*. London: Tavistock, 1971.]

Winnicott, D. W. (1960a). The theory of the parent-infant relationship. In: *The Maturational Processes and the Facilitating Environment* (pp. 37–55). London: Hogarth, 1965.

Winnicott, D. W. (1960b). Ego distortion in terms of true and false self. In: *The Maturational Processes and the Facilitating Environment* (pp. 139–152). London: Hogarth, 1965.

Winnicott, D. W. (1962). Ego integration in child development. In: *The Maturational Processes and the Facilitating Environment* (pp. 56–63). London: Hogarth, 1965.

Winnicott, D. W. (1963). The development of the capacity for concern. In: *The Maturational Processes and the Facilitating Environment* (pp. 73–82). London: Hogarth, 1965.

Winnicott, D. W. (1967). Mirror-role of mother and family in child development. In: *Playing and Reality* (pp. 111–118). London: Tavistock, 1971.

Winnicott, D. W. (1969). The use of an object and relating through identifications. *International Journal of Psychoanalysis, 50*: 711–716. [Reprinted in Winnicott, D. W. (1971), *Playing and Reality* (pp. 86–94). London: Tavistock.]

Winnicott, D. W. (1971). *Playing and Reality*. London: Tavistock.

Winnicott, D. W. (1974). Fear of breakdown. *International Review of Psycho-Analysis, 1*: 103–107.

Winnicott, D. W. (1989). *Psycho-Analytic Explorations*. C. Winnicott, R. Shepherd & M. Davis, (Eds.). London: Karnac.

Wittgenstein, L. (1958). *Philosophical Investigations*. London: Blackwell.

Wolin, S. (2003). Inverted totalitarianism. *The Nation*, May 19. http://www.thenation.com/article/inverted-totalitarianism?page=full (retrieved from the internet March 11, 2013).

Wolin, S. (2008). *Democracy Incorporated: Managed Democracy and the Spectre of Inverted Totalitarianism*. Princeton, NJ: Princeton University Press.

Wrong, D. H. (1961). The oversocialized conception of man in modern sociology. *American Sociological Review, 26*: 183–193. [Reprinted together with a "Postscript 1975" in Wrong, D. H. (1976). *Skeptical Sociology* (pp. 31–54). New York: Columbia University Press.]

Wurmser, L. (1981). *The Mask of Shame*. Baltimore, MD: Johns Hopkins University Press.

Wurmser, L. (1987). *Flucht vor dem Gewissen: Analyse von Uber-Ich und Abwehr bei schweren Neurosen (Flight from Conscience: Analysis of Superego and Defence in the Severe Neuroses)*. Heidelberg, Germany: Springer.

Wurmser, L. (1998). "The sleeping giant": A dissenting comment about "borderline pathology." *Psychoanalytic Inquiry, 8*: 373–397.

Wurmser, L. (2000). *The Power of the Inner Judge: Psychodynamic Treatment of the Severe Neuroses*. Northvale, NJ: Jason Aronson.

Wyschogrod, E., Crownfield, D. & Raschke, C. (1989). *Lacan & Theological Discourse*. Albany, NY: State University of New York Press.

Young-Bruehl, E. (2012). *Childism: Confronting Prejudice against Children*. New Haven, CT: Yale University Press.

Žižek, S. (2000). *The Fragile Absolute or, Why is the Christian Legacy Worth Fighting for?* London: Verso.

Žižek, S. (2003). *The Puppet and the Dwarf: The Perverse Core of Christianity*. Cambridge, MA: MIT Press.

Films

The Bad Seed (1956). Mervyn LeRoy, dir. Warner Bros.

Orphans (1987). Alan J. Pakula, dir. Lyle Kessler (play); Lyle Kessler (screenplay). Lorimar Motion Pictures.

INDEX

317